*The International Library of Sociology*

# SOVIET LEGAL THEORY

*Founded by KARL MANNHEIM*

*The International Library of Sociology*

# THE SOCIOLOGY OF THE SOVIET UNION
In 8 Volumes

| | | |
|---|---|---|
| I | Chekhov and His Russia | *Bruford* |
| II | Educational Psychology in the USSR | *Simon and Simon* |
| III | Family in the USSR | *Schlesinger* |
| IV | History of a Soviet Collective Farm<br>(The above title is not available through Routledge in North America) | *Belov* |
| V | The Nationalities Problem and Soviet Administration | *Schlesinger* |
| VI | Psychology in the Soviet Union | *Simon* |
| VII | Soviet Legal Theory | *Schlesinger* |
| VIII | Soviet Youth | *Meek* |

# SOVIET LEGAL THEORY

## Its Social Background and Development

by

RUDOLF SCHLESINGER

LONDON AND NEW YORK

First published in 1945 by
Routledge

Reprinted in 1998 by
Routledge
2 Park Square, Milton Park, Abingdon, Oxon, OX14 4RN

Simultaneously published in the USA and Canada by Routledge

711 Third Avenue, New York, NY 10017

Transferred to Digital Printing 2007

*Routledge is an imprint of the Taylor & Francis Group, an informa business*
First issued in paperback 2013



*British Library Cataloguing in Publication Data*
A CIP catalogue record for this book
is available from the British Library

Soviet Legal Theory

ISBN 978-0-415-17815-0 (hbk)
ISBN 978-0-415-86423-7 (pbk)

**Publisher's Note**
The publisher has gone to great lengths to ensure the quality of this reprint but points out that some imperfections in the original may be apparent

# CONTENTS

## BIBLIOGRAPHY

# PREFACE

This book deals with Soviet conceptions of Law. As is natural in a country where Law is regarded as an expression of social conditions and social needs, those conceptions are sociological rather than legal, i.e. they deal with Law not as an isolated system of values and norms but as an agent in social life. Some of the concepts that we are to discuss in this book are in fact what are commonly called "legal theories", that is to say, theories evolved by lawyers for the purposes of the Law. The greater part have been elaborated not by lawyers but by politicians, sociologists and economists; some have even been evolved with the intention of demonstrating the alleged obsolescence of Law in a society of the Soviet type. Some—perhaps the most important—have not been elaborated explicitly at all, but are implied in the actual working of Soviet legislation.

Under such circumstances the title of the book may be regarded only as an approximately accurate indication of its contents. But it was the best available. "Soviet conceptions of Law" would have been open to even more serious misunderstanding because of the widespread confusion between Law on the one hand, and Justice and Morals on the other. It might also have raised expectations of a detailed treatment of the concrete contents of the Soviet legal system which cannot be satisfied in this book. I have tried to deal with the evolution of the fundamental concepts of Soviet Law within the framework of the general evolution of Soviet society. Thus I have written a sociological and economic rather than a legal book. Such an approach may be right or wrong, according to the philosophy of Law that may be accepted; but it is an approach which would seem natural to the people about whom I write. The study of revolutionary Russia can make the maximum contribution to science and social reconstruction in other countries only if it starts from Russian rather than from imported, Procrustean standards.

I am not sufficiently a philologist to aspire to make a contribution to highly controversial subjects like the correct transcription of Russian words, or even the translation of the technical terms of one legal system into those of another, completely different in its structure. My aim has been to make the meaning intelligible with as little effort on the part of the reader as possible. I have added a footnote only in those cases where there was danger of misunderstanding, not in all those where my choice of terms is controversial.

Dr. Mannheim, the editor of this Library, not only encouraged me to write this book, but also made some most valuable suggestions in discussing the typescript. Mr. Andrew Pears revised the style.

I thank those organisations, British and of refugee scholars, the support of which made it materially possible for me to write this book. I am also deeply obliged to the librarians of Chatham House and of the Society for Cultural Relations with the U.S.S.R. who gave me every assistance in collecting the materials needed.

LODE, CAMBRIDGE,
*December 1944.*

## PREFACE TO THE SECOND EDITION

When this book was first published, twenty-eight years after the Russian Revolution, the study of Soviet institutions in the Western World was in a state where every effort at tackling new problems, however limited the resources of material, had, at least, the merit of demonstrating the applicability of ordinary scientific methods to as controversial a field as the Soviet Union. Whatever else may be said about the development of Western relations to the U.S.S.R. during the last five years, it is a fact that, together with a mushroom-like growth of propagandist publications of the worst kind, the study of the U.S.S.R. as a definite branch of sociology has won its place in academic life. There is a number of books and periodicals aiming at the treatment of the subject according to the normal standards of scholarship. Workers in this field are still having to fight against those who defend the propagandist's monopoly in a sincere interest in social progress and those who claim a monopoly in patriotism for the journalist ; but this may be regarded as a healthy symptom of the potential influence of quiet and sober work upon the formation of public opinion. From the point of view of the author of one of the earlier books representing this trend, it is clear that the mere demonstration of the possibility of working even with very restricted documentation is no longer sufficient: the use of the broader (though still insufficient) material which has since become available should be explored.

My attempt to satisfy that need will have to wait until a completely revised edition of this book is possible; as far as the development of our subject is concerned, a suitable opportunity for improved analysis will be given after the enactment of the new Codes, the discussion of which forms an important opportunity for the development of theoretical legal thought in the U.S.S.R.[1] At present we are still restricted to an assessment of the respective strength of conflicting trends. I think, however, that the attitudes to the main problems were fairly elaborated at the period with which the first edition of this book closed. In a postscript, I have tried to summarise the most important of the new facts; but I feel no need to correct the main line of interpretation. Because of the fundamental change in the international position of the U.S.S.R., the changes in the interpretation and application of International Law are more important than those made in any other field; and I am greatly obliged to my publishers for having given me the opportunity of using this new edition of *Soviet Legal Theory* as an occasion for bringing the ninth and tenth chapters of this book up to date. So far as the historical parts of the book, and the most general issues of Soviet political theory are concerned, I shall restrict myself to a few observations in this Preface.

There has been a number of recent Soviet publications on the first stages of the growth of Soviet Law.[2] They show a tendency to emphasise the continuity between the trend now prevailing and that which dominated the enactments of the first revolutionary period; the correspondence of these latter with the original intentions of the Bolshevik leaders is emphasised. The later criticisms by Soviet historians of Law against the allegedly insufficient break with pre-revolutionary law carried out in the First Decree (not to mention the interpretation of the later decrees as a complete breach with firm legality) are resolutely rejected, together with any suggestion that the Social Revolutionaries, including the then People's Commissar for Justice, played any major part in the actual development of

[1] A summary of the 1947 stage of that discussion has been given by Prof. John N. Hazard in *The American Slavic and East European Review*, vol. VII, February, 1948.

[2] Cp. P. Mishunin, "On the History of the First Decree on the Courts" (of Nov. 24, 1917, see below, p. 60), in *Voporisy Istorii*, 1949, No. 4, and the works of Arsenyev, Durmanov, and Kozhevnikov, quoted in the additions to the Bibliography.

early Soviet legal policy. Such an appreciation of the past by present Soviet authors seems to support my view that, whatever the terminology applied by them for the description of the present, the latter is, to a large extent, a continuation of originally *bourgeois*-democratic elements in the Russian revolution which were embodied in early Bolshevik policy, and that there has been no sharing of actual power at any stage of the Bolshevik revolution.

My interpretation of the N.E.P. has been criticised from two opposite points of view. Dr. H. A. F., reviewing my book in the *Sidney Morning Herald*, December 8, 1945, felt that I interpreted the N.E.P. too much *ex evento*, as a transitional step towards the establishment of fully-fledged socialism, and reproached me for " reducing the guarantee character of the N.E.P. to a minimum ", with the implication that its abolition was possible without a complete breach in the continuity of Soviet legality.[3] On the other side, Mr. Andrew Rothstein, writing in *The Modern Quarterly*, Autumn 1948, reproached me for having overemphasised the spontaneous element in Soviet developments rather than the leaders' foresight, from the very start in 1918, and for having ignored Lenin's repeated explanations of the purposes of free trade. On this latter point I can leave my readers to check the justification of Mr. Rothstein's criticism themselves. While my Australian critic was right in interpreting my standpoint as implying that *some* limitation of the N.E.P. was intended from the very start, Mr. Rothstein has not and could in no way prove that precisely *that* type of transformation, as eventually accomplished in the " second revolu-

[3] But I use the opportunity to thank my critic for having drawn my attention to an error of fact, by far the most serious one which I have discovered in the book. On p. 88 I state that the maximum duration, of six years, for a leasehold of a nationalised enterprise was established by the Civil Code. It was, in fact, established by an Instruction of the Supreme Council of National Economy (V.S.N.Kh.) of April 25, 1922 (i.e. before the enactment of the Civil Code), which remained in force during the N.E.P.-period (cp. Kantorovich, op. cit., pp. 169–70). Provision was made, in that Instruction, for exceptional cases in which leases of more than six years' duration could be permitted by a special decision of the central government; and in that hypothetical case, the upper limit of art. 154 of the Civil Code, which is twelve years, would have come into force. My mistake as to the source of the six years' limit is obviously unimportant for my argument. In so far as the difference between Dr. H. A. F. and me is caused by different interpretation of facts, it is based upon my assessment of the leaseholder of nationalised enterprises and the *kulak* (whose legal position on the nationalised land was similar) as the central figure of the N.E.P., while Dr. H. A. F. emphasises the importance of the trader, owner of his stock. The fact that I regard the N.E.P. mainly from the point of view of the existence of a private-enterprise sector *in production* is reflected also in my argument with Mr. Rothstein (see note 25 on p. 272 below).

tion ", was envisaged by Lenin. I would be the last to deny the importance of the element of planning and its increase during the last two decades, but I also feel that any scholar in the subject should reject the myth which always describes the past in terms of the present (with appropriate modifications to fit the changes in present needs). Like everything else, Bolshevik policy is the result of development : even if it were true that the solutions chosen in a process of trial and error were the only possible ones, and that the present leaders from the very start envisaged a course roughly corresponding to the actual course of events, it would still be necessary to analyse the conditions of the 'twenties in the light of the conditions then prevailing. The analysis of those conditions may of course help to make it clear why one of the various competing groups of leaders was successful, and why their policies developed in a certain way. Any other approach is mythological, not historical.

The general concepts of the ultimate prospects of Soviet society, current in the U.S.S.R., have developed further in the direction envisaged in the first edition of this book. The realisation of " the higher stage of a communist society " is described as the actual task of the present generation, realisable in a few Five Year Plans as soon as production per head will have overtaken that of U.S.A. ; but the definitions now current in the U.S.S.R. of that stage reduce its distinction from socialism, now realised in the U.S.S.R., to (1) an assimilation of the labour conditions of the peasants (as distinct from the present kollkhoz) to those of the State enterprises, and the resoluting abolition of the contrast between town and countryside ; (2) an abolition of the social contrast between physical and intellectual labour by raising the intellectual level of manual workers (though the division of labour and professional specialisation will survive, and perhaps even increase) ; (3) distribution of the social product according to needs, i.e. a situation in which the State can dispense with the inequality of incomes as an incentive to work. The differences between this conception of the higher stage of a communist society, and that developed by Marx in the *Critique of the Gotha Programme*, concern the following points : (1) the possibility that full Communism may triumph even in a single country, and that therefore the State must be preserved as a protection against the capitalist environment ; (2) the impossibility of an abolition of the division of labour (including that between physical and intellectual labour) ; (3) the retention of an obligation (as distinct from a mere moral urge) for citizens to work in the communist as well as in the socialist society.[4] The first,[5] and especially the third point (which is not bound to any hypotheses about the future international constellation) are of decisive importance for the prospects of Law ; Vishinsky, indeed, has recently gone to the length of stating that theoretical speculations about its eventual withering away are not in the interest of the Soviet State.[6] We are interested not so much in the doctrinal aspects of such developments as in the fact that they reflect real shifts of emphasis in the interpretation of the present tasks of Soviet Law. The theory of the eventual withering away of State and Law was relevant not because of its (clearly Utopian) verbal meaning, nor even because of its historical importance as a link between Marxism and the liberal tradition ; in its effects, as part of the State ideology, it denoted an aversion against legal regulation the practical outcome of which might vary between serious attempts to mitigate the hardships caused by a strict law, and excuses for administrative or managerial arbitrariness. The recession of the theory into the background implies a recognition of the need for an increased, and even severer, legal enforcement of civic discipline, a tendency which the reader will find illustrated in the postscript to this book. On the other hand, he will also find evidence supporting the view that planned economics, though they obviously do not cause a mitigation of the Law, need not deprive the citizen of the advantages of the security provided by the Law and of well-established guarantees against unjust conviction (unjust, of course, in terms of the social system defended by the Law).

No undue generalisations should be drawn from the experiences of Soviet socialism, acquired in a country so different from the Western World, and in conditions the repetition of which is excluded by the very fact that this first large-scale experiment in national planning had to be carried out in opposition to a hostile world. If lessons can be drawn from the experiences of one society as to the possibilities of another, they presuppose a very sober historical analysis of the actual background of such

[4] Cp. e.g. A. Stepanyan's paper *On the Conditions and Ways of the Transition from Socialism to Communism*, in the collection *O Sovietskom Sotsialisticheskom Obshchestve* (on Soviet Socialist Society), published by the Institute of Philosophy of the Academy of Sciences of the U.S.S.R., Moscow, 1948, especially pp. 484–9.

[5] See below, p. 244.

[6] In *Sovietskoye Gossudarstvo i Pravo*, 1948, No. 6, p. 10.

experiences. Neither a legal ideology developed as an answer to the challenge of social change, nor the State ideology of any of the national societies resulting from it, forms a suitable starting point for such analysis.

RUDOLF SCHLESINGER.

INVEREOCH, KILMUN, ARGYLLSHIRE,
*February 1950.*

# SOVIET LEGAL THEORY

## CHAPTER I

## INTRODUCTION

### The Dispute on the Essence of Law and the Special Conditions of Soviet Law

It is the intention of this book to deal with the growth of the theoretical conceptions which have accompanied and influenced the evolution of Soviet Law. The main interest in this Law is that it is the first modern [1] Law of a society which is not based upon private ownership of the means of production; and the central point of the discussions which follow is the extent to which Law is possible in such a society. Foreign critics of the U.S.S.R. and of socialism in general have denied this possibility and have described socialism as a state of lawlessness and arbitrary rule. Discussions within the U.S.S.R. have inquired whether socialism would demand new means of regulating human behaviour which would be superior to traditional Law. In some cases it has not been possible to dissociate the first form of the argument from the second.[2] Such issues are largely a matter of definition. But in order to take up a stance from which to approach the opinions of the Soviet lawyers we have to start from a working definition of Law, and from a survey of the various forms in which it appears in the U.S.S.R.

A preliminary definition which reduced our problem to a series of truisms would be inadequate. If we content ourselves with the statement that "wherever there is a society, there is also Law",[3] then there is no problem in the existence of Soviet or any other Law. Even if a more concrete approach is taken and Law is identified with the existence of fixed regulations for

[1] In this book, we are not concerned with the question of whether the most primitive forms of regulating human behaviour, in a society prior to any form of private property in means of production, could be described as Law. Marxism would deny it. The question of Law in a pre-capitalist (feudal or slave-holding) society with pre-capitalist forms of property (see below, p. 27) is quite a different matter.

[2] See below, p. 156.

[3] Korovin, op. cit., 1924, p. 6. It ought to be remembered that this is an utterance by an international lawyer, and that the vagueness of their subject induces his kind of lawyers everywhere to be satisfied with rather vague definitions of Law.

human behaviour, duly published and enforced, there can be no doubt that such regulations exist in the U.S.S.R., that the everyday behaviour of the individual citizen as well as the daily transactions of the bodies administering Soviet economy are governed by them. And no Soviet theorist has been so utopian as to dream of a state of society where something of this kind would not be needed. On the other hand we cannot accept those definitions that identify Law with the rule exercised by lawyers, or with the existence of a power vested in the courts superior to that of the other organs of the State. Such theories play a highly contested rôle in the U.S.A. and have also been accepted by certain schools of legal thought in this country (although they were strictly rejected by the Austinian school). In other countries their rôle is rather insignificant. The U.S.S.R., especially, would answer such a definition simply by the statement that, whatever its interest in Law, it has never aimed at establishing the ruling power of lawyers, and that, however desirable it may be to safeguard the independent working of the specific law-administering organs of the State from other State organs, these organs and the law administered by them are certainly part and effluence of the State.

A working definition of Law, sufficient to meet its problems in general and under the special conditions of the U.S.S.R., can be found if we follow the classical approach of the positivist school, since Ihering on the Continent and Austin in this country.[4] We may define Law as the sum of the general rules of behaviour enforced by the State. By emphasising the general character of these rules, as opposed to a sum of individual cases decided by the organs of the State according to their individual merits, we emphasise a fundamental characteristic of Law and of the principle of legality as distinct from arbitrariness, namely its predictability and its formally equal approach to all cases that equally satisfy the conditions established in the law for certain reactions of the State machinery. By emphasising compulsion by the State as the characteristic sanction of all legal rules we distinguish Law clearly from other agencies intended to regulate social behaviour that work either through the individual conscience (like religion and ethics) or through social pressure outside the State machinery, such as moral conceptions in general. The positivist definition of Law gives full scope to meet and to

[4] See P. Ihering, *Law as a Means to an End*, English ed., Boston, 1913, pp. 239–40, and Austin, *Jurisprudence*, 4th ed., vol. I, p. 98.

discuss the fundamental problems of Soviet Law : whether the generality and formal equality of Law is compatible with the needs of a period of revolutionary transition, and whether compulsion by the State is needed for regulating the behaviour of the members of a Communist society. Amongst the Soviet lawyers themselves, the positivist approach to Law has always held undisputed sway.[5]

Positivism clearly accepts any given legal system as such, but no less clearly refrains from judging the " meta-legal ", especially moral, validity of any legal system.[6] But the efficiency of the State requires that its command should be accepted as binding. Since that command has lost its former religious authority it is a primary purpose of legal ideology [7] to provide arguments for the alleged morally binding force of these commands, or, if the ideology opposes the existing legal order, to describe the standards to which a legal system ought to comply in order to be accepted as binding. The lawyers applying the legal system are bound to regard the norms composing it not as mere norms of compulsion but as corresponding to general principles of Justice or Morality realised in Law.[8] Hence the tendency, which is opposed to Positivism, to construct a " Natural Law ", i.e. a system of supposedly legal norms, the validity of which is not derived from the existing legal order but, conversely, ought to condition the latter's validity. This tendency has held sway as long as the young national state was confronted by a generally accepted religious and moral ideology, and also when the decreasing force of the religious ideology demanded its replacement by some other, more suitable to seventeenth-nineteenth-century needs. Natural Law was accepted as the basis from which the liberal revolutionaries argued against the validity of the existing feudal laws, and was dropped by them once they had succeeded in shaping a legal system corresponding to the needs of the middle-classes. More recently the threat to the latter's rule has resulted in some renaissance of the theories of

[5] See below, pp. 18, 74, and 243–4. For the specific problems of International Law see below, pp. 285–87.

[6] See Kelsen, " The Pure Theory of Law," in *Law Quarterly Review*, vol. LI, p. 535.

[7] In this book, unless stated to the contrary, we use the term " ideology " in the general sense, i.e. to denote theoretical conceptions as conditioned by social facts. Some only of these ideologies (as very evident from the example given in the text) are ideologies in the narrower sense used by Mannheim (*Ideology and Utopia*, London 1934), i.e. denote such conceptions the social function of which is the defence of the existing social order.

[8] Kelsen, op. cit., vol. L, p. 481.

Natural Law, especially in the U.S.A.[9] Characteristic of Natural Law, especially in its modern conceptions, is the juxtaposition of Law and Power, as distinct from the positivist position according to which Law is the order according to which the compulsory machinery of the State works. For the adherent of Natural Law, Law connotes equality and not subjection, and is a relation between equals, not between a superior and an inferior.[10]

From the sociological point of view it is not difficult to recognise in such an approach an idealisation of the relations supposed to exist between the members of a society based on independent private entrepreneurs in competition with each other, whose mutual relations are to be ordered by the Law. From the point of view of juridical analysis the supposed equality of the partners to the Law is but an idealisation of the formal equalitd involved in the principle of generality which we have recognisey as an essential characteristic of any legal order: If the reactions of State machinery to the doings of the individual members of the society are deemed predictable (and this is a fundamental condition of the efficiency of a legal order) all citizens are " equal before the Law ", i.e. their actions, if equally corresponding to certain conditions established in the general rule, are followed by equal reactions on the part of the State machinery. This criterion is purely formal: in a state denying certain property rights to women the equality of all citizens before the Law may still be realised in the sense that everyone answering the formal demands of the Law, whether man or woman, is equally granted the rights corresponding to his or her respective status. But even if distinctions in rights are restricted to those which, by the general consent of public opinion in a given period, are recognised as justified,[11] there remains actual inequality in the possibility of making use of " equally granted " rights. The ideology of " equality before the Law " does not demand that, say, anyone who inflicts certain damages upon another ought to pay a certain compensation, but only demands that everyone's claims, *if* brought before the courts and defended by all means

[9] See Ch. G. Haines, *The Revival of Natural Law Conceptions*, Harvard University Press, 1930. A characteristic expression of the trend described is Bodenheimer, *Jurisprudence*, New York, 1940.

[10] Ibid., p. 21, and see Chapter V of this book, pp. 155–6. Bodenheimer (loc. cit., p. 26) recognises the relation of his views to those of Pashukanis.

[11] As is done now in regard to minors or the mentally deficient, not to mention those cases where women, and even the Negroes may be " naturally " included amongst the minors for certain purposes. 100 years ago this was " natural " in all Western countries.

provided for by the law, including costly appeals to the higher courts, should be equally dealt with. The modern adherent of the Natural Law school will not deny that virtual inequality, say between capital and labour, may allow the rule of formal equality before the Law to result in a condition of subjection, and will satisfy himself with the remark that relations of subjection and domination are alien to the idea of Law.[12] We shall see [13] that his theoretical juxtaposition of the conceptions of Law and Power may result in a defence of actual inequality.

The failure of any representative of the Natural Law school to find the self-invented principles of "Natural Law" in process of being realised in existing Law, would itself prove no more than the need to invent new patterns of "Natural Law"—as, indeed, successive representatives of this trend have been doing now for 700 years, not to mention their predecessors in antiquity. But quite apart from individual explanations of "Natural Law", its very foundations, the juxtaposition of Law and Power (*alias* the compulsion as exercised by the existing states) is bound to obliterate the characteristics of Law as distinct from Morality. It is quite impossible, even for representatives of the Natural Law school,[14] to draw this distinction otherwise than by the fact that the first group of rules for social behaviour are enforced by the State, and the latter by the unofficial pressure of public opinion. On the other hand, the main argument of the modern representatives of Natural Law against positivism is the latter's failure to distinguish between states ruled by Law, and states ruled by Power,[15] and to erect insurmountable barriers between Law and Administration.[16] It is impossible to prevent the use of any kind of definition: a man may describe as Law those

[12] Bodenheimer, op. cit., pp. 26–7. [13] See below, pp. 7–8.

[14] See Bodenheimer, op. cit., p. 80. "Political means of enforcement" is, of course, merely another term for what elsewhere is labelled "Power" by the same author. Compare Duguit, "The Law and the State," *Harvard Law Review*, November 1917, p. 4.

[15] Ibid., *passim*, e.g., p. 57. B. is completely wrong in describing Kelsen's statement according to which "every state is a government of Law" as obliterating the limits between Law and arbitrariness, unless his basic assumption that only a certain type of society is capable of legality is presupposed. According to Kelsen (op. cit., vol. LI, p. 534) "every expression of the life of the State is a legal act", but "a human act (for example an act of the persons holding supreme power in a State) is only designated as an act of State by virtue of a legal norm which qualifies it as such". Every state is, for Kelsen, a government of Law for the simple reason that systems of compulsion not working according to established systems of norms could not be described as states, within the Kelsenian system.

[16] Bodenheimer, op. cit., p. 91. Kelsen (op. cit., pp. 521 ff.) makes a gradual distinction between the more general rules described as laws and their more specified application by administration and judicial decisions. It is true he puts these two on the same level, to the disapproval of most lawyers.

types of social relations which he likes, and as Power those which he dislikes, and conclude with strict logic from such definitions that there can be no Law outside the type of Society which he favours. The question is whether such definitions are fruitful for social investigation or only for propaganda. For investigating the legal system of the U.S.S.R. they are certainly not fruitful, since amongst their fundamental assumptions they exclude the very notion that there could be any kind of Law in a state of the type represented by the U.S.S.R.

Traditional jurisprudence bases Law—at least in its most important parts—on a system of Rights, i.e. individual claims which are enforced by the State if they conform to certain conditions established by the Law. A positivist approach which is neutral to the respective merits of various social systems will describe the conferring of rights upon individuals by the legal order merely as a special technique of which the Law may, but need not, avail itself. It is the specific technique of the capitalist legal order, in so far as this is built upon the institutions of private property and therefore directed specially towards individual interests.[17] As we shall see below, it may be an overstatement to regard this technique as restricted to a capitalist system. But certainly Kelsen is accurate when he describes the conception of independent subjective right, which is even more "just" than the objective law, as a device to protect the institutions of private property from damage at the hands of the legal order.[18]

Now the application of this device is an essential of the Natural Law theories. "Power, in the world of social life, represents the element of struggle, war, and subjection. Law, on the other hand, represents the element of compromise, peace, and agreement. Power represents the dynamic element in the social order . . . Law, on the whole, is a static force".[19] Such a statement contains ideological elements, in the narrowest sense of the word, and especially the assertion that Power is needed only in order to carry through changes of the existing order as

[17] Kelsen, op. cit., vol. L, pp. 495–6.

[18] Ibid., p. 493. This description might be regarded as an unjustified generalisation if applied even to approaches (e.g. Laski, in *A Grammar of Politics*) which submit the *moral* validity of existing law to the test of whether it conforms to certain conceptions of social Justice. But Kelsen is dealing with authors who speak of "just" in the sense of supreme legality, as for example the Supreme Court of the U.S.A., when deciding whether legislative acts are compatible with its interpretation of the Fundamental Rights as established in the Constitution.

[19] Bodenheimer, op. cit., p. 10.

distinct from preserving it, and that on the other hand compromise and agreement must necessarily work through the means of Law as long as this order is preserved.[20] But, in fact, a statement like the foregoing is the simple consequence of the attitude of the Natural Law school which explains Law by certain individual rights as established within the existing social order. For similar reasons in the conservative trend in American jurisprudence changes in the existing legal order, even when carried through by completely constitutional means, are regarded as illegal.[21] From such a point of view there can be no Soviet legality, and no socialist legality at all.

According to the modern Natural Law school, Law (as opposed to Power) presupposes an equilibrium of power between the participants in the legal relations, as also between Individual and State. If a state like the U.S.S.R. grants to its citizens "social rights", i.e. rights to the provision of certain conditions for their well-being by the operation of the public services, it will not be able to ensure the full satisfaction of these rights unless it controls most of the economic resources of the country. But if it does so, it will of necessity combine political with economic power and be in a position to make the fulfilment of its obligations dependent upon the complete obedience and loyalty of its citizens. From the point of view of the Law, increasing recognition of social rights might be considered as partial retrogression to the rule of Power, unless the recognition of social rights is coupled with a recognition of individual rights.[22] It is clear that such individual rights as regards property in private means of consumption, matrimonial relations, etc., would not be sufficient to counterbalance the economic power of the State. For this, individual rights to property in the essential means of production would be needed. But these would involve the likelihood of private monopolies which, as our author recognises,[23] may tend to be supplemented by political power and thus to exclude the supposed rule of Law from the other side. It is very difficult, when confronted with such explanations, to disagree with Kelsen's opinion that "the individual engaged in an apparently insoluble conflict with society is nothing else than an ideology fighting for certain

[20] An interesting instance was the appeasement in December, 1928, by the German Government of the steel-mill owners, who had refused to submit to a binding decision of the statutory Arbitration Tribunal, by virtually recognising the law-breaking attitude of the employers as legal. It only just preceded the establishment of the dictatorship of Big Business.

[21] See also Haines, op. cit., pp. 337–42.

[22] Bodenheimer, op. cit., pp. 22–4.

[23] Ibid., p. 21.

interests against their limitation by a collective system ".[24] The problem of our book is to investigate how far that collective system may apply Law as a means of regulation. A theory which describes this system as *a priori* illegal is, obviously, unsuitable as our starting point.

In their criticism the Natural Law school insist upon the difficulty of explaining, by means of the positivist interpretation, two particular characteristics of Law as opposed to arbitrariness: namely, the due competence of the State organ issuing the commands, as distinct from usurpation and from acts *ultra vires*, and the principle of generality as regards the rules and the consequent formal equality of all subjects to the Law. The first difficulty is, indeed, nearly insurmountable if the sovereign is to be regarded naturalistically as a certain physical person in the Austinian sense. But within the purely juristic conception of positivism this difficulty can be solved by the simple proviso that only those acts of the State organs which conform to their competences within the legal norm on which the State works can be attributed to the State.[15] Permanent and successful action by the supreme State organs " *ultra vires* " would have to be interpreted as an extra-legal phenomenon, a " revolution from above ", producing a change in the legal order and the further acts of such a state would have to be interpreted within the altered framework. As regards the principle of generality the inherent difficulty is not restricted to the positivist interpretation of Law: for while there may be cases where individuals themselves form a group from the point of view of the purposes of the law under discussion, so that special legislation for these cases would not cease to be general,[25] yet there will hardly be agreement as to the point where the desired formal generality begins to result in actual inequality, in view of the completely different conditions to which formally equal standards are applied. Mine-owners may resent any special legislation dealing with coal-mines, and employers in general any rule concerning the contract for labour as distinct from other kinds of contract. They may complain of " arbitrary " discrimination against them, of " privileges " accorded to miners or to workers in general. The workers concerned—and probably also the legislators who

[24] Op. cit., vol. L, p. 497, cp. also Bodenheimer, op. cit., p. 28.

[25] See, for example, McIver, *The Modern State*, London, 1926, pp. 256–7. Apart from Sovereigns who, by law, are a class in themselves, there are cases where one powerful enterprise monopolises one important industry the conditions of which differ from those of others.

have enacted such laws—will hold the opposite view. There is no conception of Natural Law that could help us to decide whether conditions in coal-mines differ from those of other industrial enterprises enough to render special legislation for them necessary lest formally equal rulings (such as equal hours) should result in completely different conditions of life for the workers concerned. In fact, there is nothing in a positivist or any other conception of Law that would enable such a decision to be made. Questions like these cannot be answered by legal theory. But the desirability of generality from the point of view of the efficiency of the legal order can be expressed in positivist terms at least as well as in those of Natural Law.

Unless one assumes an inherent superiority of general formal equality over a method of attempting to meet concrete conditions as equally as possible, and an inherent superiority of the Judge over the Administrator, it is impossible to make a hard-and-fast distinction between legislation and administration. But within a positivist approach it is fully possible [16] to distinguish between legal orders which contain a well-elaborated hierarchy of more general and more specified norms and which solve the maximum number of issues as generally as possible, and those systems where the onus of the decision rests upon the judge or administrator, and the impression which the merits of each individual case make upon him personally. It is quite true that Kelsen's Pure Theory of Law (the most coherent elaboration of positivist principles) contains no standard against which the merits or demerits of various legal orders can be judged. In my opinion, however, this is no argument against a positivist approach, or the Pure Theory of Law specifically, but simply a proof of the limitations of a purely juristic approach in general. It can but provide formal results : it is the task of the sociology of Law to investigate the origins and probable results of any system of Law.[26] But whatever the shortcomings of the purely formal positivist approach, at least it prevents the exclusion from sociological analysis of phenomena which may be interesting in that they are new, and furthermore it is not limited by the ideological standards of past law which have been elevated into the "*a priori*" requirements of "Natural Law".

Soviet Law manifests fundamentally new features both in

[26] Kelsen, op. cit., vol. L, pp. 486–7, and in his book *Der soziologische und der juristische Staatsbegriff*, Vienna, 1920, recognises the need for such investigation. So Laski's criticism (op. cit., p. VI) expresses the naturally diverse emphasis which the sociologist and the lawyer respectively are likely to lay upon their subjects.

the state from which it emanates and in the economic structure of the society which it has to serve, but as regards general formal structure it provides little essentially new material. Since its authors [27] had to start out from existing codes and systems, they simply reproduced " Criminal Law ", " Matrimonial Law ", " Civil Law ", and " Administrative Law ", etc., without giving much thought to the question of their specific reality under the new conditions.

In general, Law (apart from International Law) is divided into two categories : Civil Law [28] deals with the individual claims of citizens who are in principle regarded as equal. In so far as the State may be, say, the owner of a railway, it has the status of a private citizen and is subject to Civil Law. In Public Law the subject is supposed to be confronted by the authority of the State. Civil Law has, for practical purposes, such subdivisions as Commercial Law, Land Law, Matrimonial Law, etc., while Public Law may be subdivided relatively easily [29] into three categories : Constitutional Law deals with the general structure of State organs and the formation of State decisions. Administrative Law regulates the relation between the citizen and the administrative machinery, and between the various links of the latter. Criminal Law institutes sanctions against certain actions that are described as crimes. The division, like so many survivals from totally different conditions, is artificial enough even in the normal capitalist state ; quite a lot of legal fiction is needed to describe, say, the begetting of a child as a legal transaction comparable with contract, or tort if out of wedlock. Further, the more emphasis that is laid upon individual rights as the basis of Law proper, the more difficult it is to make a fundamental difference between the lawsuit of a mother who, under Civil Law, sues her divorced husband, father of her child, for the right to meet this child on certain days a week, and that of another mother whose child has been transferred to an educational institution and who

[27] See below, Chapter III, section (*c*), and Chapter IV, section (*b*).

[28] We use, in this book, the current Continental terminology from which Soviet jurisprudence (and Russian jurisprudence in general) has started, verbally translating its terms. In English jurisprudence, Private Law would be the nearest approach.

[29] Going into detail, one would have to stress the word " relatively ". Administrative penalties, say for violating the rules of the road, are only slightly different from the smaller penalties of the Penal Code. And the amount of general administrative rulings on economic and similar matters included in a Continental Constitution, depends mainly on the political conditions at the time of the constitutional compromise.

complains, under Administrative Law, that the headmaster of that institution does not allow her such access to her child as she feels entitled to. But in the liberal conception of society the traditional division of Law has the big advantage that it corresponds to the division between the sphere of everyday life as where members of the community are left free in their transactions with one another, and those disturbances or transformations of everyday life where the State has to interfere. Within the framework of the traditional liberal ideology a prosperous society might be described as one which showed a maximum number of Civil Law transactions amongst its members, whether commercial or matrimonial, and a minimum of administrative interference, constitutional amendments, and, of course, criminal prosecutions. As is well known this conception has already been virtually undermined in recent decades—but still it survives, at least in the minds of the lawyers, as is shown for example in their abhorrence of *Droit Administratif*, etc.

Although for the greater part of the period under discussion [30] Soviet lawyers did little to replace the traditional divisions by new ones, their difficulty is that the traditional divisions clearly contradict the real problems of the society within which they live. The major part of the economic life of the country is administered by the State according to a central plan, i.e. according to principles of subordination rather than of co-ordination. Within this centralised system, the decision whether to apply Civil or Administrative Law is regarded simply as a question of efficiency in management. Although the claim of a mother for alimony would be decided under Civil Law, a Soviet lawyer would be even more emphatic than his progressive colleagues in other countries that the decision ought to be dominated by the public interest in creating the best conditions for the education of the child, and he could base this explanation on the text of the Law.[31] Yet he will readily admit that his private position as a tenant of a municipal flat is affected more by administrative rulings regarding priority claims, contributions to current repairs, etc., than by the truly Civil Law suit that would follow if he were to be divorced and his own and his wife's respective claims to the flat would have to be decided. He is well aware of the extent to which Civil Law and Administrative Law are intermingled in regulating the everyday life of the Soviet citizen as well as the

[30] This has changed only since 1938. See below, Chapter VIII, pp. 252 ff.
[31] See below, p. 104.

working of Soviet economics, and he would not for a moment doubt that the latter as much as the former is Law proper.

Our friend knows, from his professional experience, that, say, an appeal against a third conviction for theft does not merely apply to the direct sentence of one year's imprisonment or so, but to the right of the N.K.V.D.[32] to banish the man for five years, after his sentence has been served, as a dangerous recidivist to some place where forestry-work, or canal building is the only available employment, and where he would live under strict police-supervision, with the possibility of having to stay another five years if he behaved badly. In any case, the N.K.V.D. acts according to certain fixed rules, and they may ask our friend and the other judges concerned in the case whether the prisoner is a genuine recidivist. Our friend knows that his fellow-judges in capitalist countries, when passing judgment in similar cases, inflict certain social sanctions to be executed by "public opinion" which are in addition to and more important than the term of imprisonment. These sanctions may be more harmful to the future of the prisoner than some years of regular work under a strict discipline but under normal conditions and for regular wages. And apart from the private benevolence of some judges who attempt with uncertain success to assist those whom they have convicted after sentence has been served, these social sanctions are much less open to judicial influence than the N.K.V.D. methods, though here too there are strong extra-judicial influences at work in deciding the prisoner's fate. For instance, shortage of labour in the construction of water-communications may influence not only the decision to banish the prisoner after his term of imprisonment has been served, but it may also determine whether good behaviour at the place of internment should be rewarded by an early return to his former domicile or, on the other hand, by the granting of facilities for building a new permanent existence as a skilled worker in the new place.

Our friend, the Soviet judge, knows that there are other branches of the N.K.V.D.'s activities which are handled according to rules different from those he feels himself bound by when deciding a case. He knows that he may often have to sign a warrant for arrest on no other grounds than the declaration of the N.K.V.D. that they have serious suspicions of a man and

[32] The People's Commissariat for Internal Affairs, which has taken over the functions of the former O.G.P.U.

that the public interest prohibits their divulging all the details even to the local Judge—and he knows, too, that only in the few cases which are brought to trial before the ordinary court will he ever learn the details. Some will be released because the N.K.V.D. themselves have no case—but others will be banished because the N.K.V.D. are convinced that the prisoner is politically dangerous, though the case, however strong, may not be suitable for normal judicial procedure. As a Communist and Soviet patriot our friend regards these things as necessary for the defence of his fatherland. But he is judge enough and lawyer enough not to include them in his theoretical analysis of Law.

In spite of all consideration of the public interest, and all the intermingling of legal and other elements in the working of the State machinery which the U.S.S.R. shares with other countries, our friend is quite well aware that Law is an agency for regulating human behaviour, a specific agency distinct from other methods of promoting the welfare of the community. He remembers the case of a barrister [33] who demanded a private honorarium from his clients in addition to the fee they had paid to the barristers' collective (from which a barrister is normally paid, according to the number of cases dealt with by him). The lawyer's behaviour certainly offended the professional honour, and endangered the authority of the legal profession by raising the suspicion that a barrister, if given a special inducement to excel himself, could improve the chances of his client in Court. And indeed a lawyer could hardly demand his private honoraria without raising expectations among his clients which he was unable to satisfy. But after the Leningrad Court had sentenced the barrister for deceit (art. 169 of the Criminal Code), the sentence was quashed by the Supreme Court, and, in addition, some enlightenment was given to the Court about the difference between professional misbehaviour (for which the barristers may take disciplinary measures including expulsion from their body), and a criminal offence which they were not allowed to construct unless the action committed corresponded to the clear description in the Code. Our friend knows very well that such strict conceptions of Law are not always applied and that there are legitimate as well as illegitimate attempts "to fill the *lacunæ* of the Criminal Code".[34] But, in his country, there do exist

[33] See Strogovich, op. cit., pp. 126–7.
[34] See below, p. 226.

distinct conceptions of Law, as distinct from Morals and public interest.

Our friend the Soviet lawyer and his fellow-judicial practitioners in the U.S.S.R. will feel themselves divorced from what are elsewhere regarded as the most interesting issues of Law. Being interested in the theoretical aspects of his profession, and a regular reader of his *Sovietskoe Gossudarstwo*,[35] our friend knows enough about the contested theoretical issues of Soviet Civil Law. But, in spite of the fact that Civil and Criminal cases are dealt with, in the U.S.S.R., by various benches of the same court, he is not likely to hear very much from his fellows who sit on Civil Law benches, beyond the constant trouble with dwelling-flat claims, alimony, inheritance (of course, of very modest dimensions and of little theoretical interest in a country where the law [36] prescribes the persons in favour of whom you are allowed to make a will)—and claims for damages for personal injury that come before his own bench along with the appeals from the lower People's Courts. Those issues that concern the foundations of economic life are dealt with by a special State organ, the State Arbitrage.[37] This organ when giving its decisions is bound to pay attention not only to the letter of the Law, but also to the economic interests of the State in the name of which one of its agents sues another. From our friend's standpoint, an important economic contract between State enterprises becomes interesting when non-fulfilment raises the suspicion of criminal negligence, or worse. So he—and anyone else investigating actual cases dealt with by the periodicals which serve the Soviet legal profession—will be confronted with a large mass of theory, but only a restricted number of specially interesting cases in the most fundamental fields of Civil Law. In every country the very existence of legal theory is due to the specific functions of the legal profession. In a country where the central figures in this profession, the Judge and the Public Attorney,[38] have less to do with complicated issues of Civil Law than any-

[35] The theoretical organ of Soviet Jurisprudence. *Sovietskaja Justicija* would be rather elementary for a higher Judge, and *Socialisticheskaja Sakonnost* will be read mainly for reasons of interest in the arguments likely to be used by the Public Prosecutor in the next session.

[36] See below, p. 82.

[37] See below, pp. 192 and 216.

[38] The rôle of the barrister is much less important. Besides, in view of the restricted rôle he plays, his outlook would be even more dominated by issues of Criminal Law than that of Judge and Attorney (also the latter plays an important rôle in Civil Procedure, see below, p. 95).

where else, this fact is bound to be reflected in the distinctness with which legal theories are elaborated.

The federal structure of the U.S.S.R. is responsible for another special feature of Soviet law which must be noted at the beginning of our investigation. As we have to deal with fundamental theoretical problems rather than with the substance of the Law, we can omit most of the details left to the codes of the various Union Republics for solution, and restrict ourselves to the practical material supplied by the legislation of the largest of them, the R.S.F.S.R. (the Russian federation). But in some cases [39] the differences caused by varying economic and cultural levels of development are of theoretical interest. The reader must not conclude that where such differences are omitted on the score of unimportance the law mentioned is necessarily valid for the whole of the U.S.S.R. Similarly it must be borne in mind that some of the laws quoted as interesting illustrations have since been amended. We have not tried to describe the legal system of the U.S.S.R., we have merely attempted to present the fundamental social facts and theoretical conceptions dominating its development. The individual law, like the court case, serves simply as an illustration of those conceptions put into practice.

Most Soviet theories have been elaborated in an atmosphere of factional struggle, in which various schools have reproached one another for failing to interpret Marxist sociology, or for being blind to the real needs of the Soviet State. While the latter kind of criticism sheds light upon the evolution of our subject itself, the former can have but little interest for most readers of this book, who are not likely to be familiar with those Marxist theories, the interpretation of which is questioned. For the Western public, a description of these theoretical developments must consist of an outline of the clearly differentiated stages in the growth of the U.S.S.R., and the transitions from one to another, without wasting time in purely scholastic argument. Much of that argument and of the extremist theories that caused it, have always been restricted to the people who had to lecture on Law and to write on its problems rather than to those who had to legislate and to apply the Law. Any attempt of ours to keep close to the latter's point of view should make our study more interesting for the non-theorist and at the same time tend to avoid exaggerated attitudes towards the theories. The theory

[39] See below, p. 234, and the quoted article by D-ov.

of Law is never the Law itself in its working, and it is with the former that this book has to deal. But a theory apart from its intended working would not be a relevant theory from the sociologist's point of view.

## CHAPTER II

# THE THEORETICAL FOUNDATIONS OF THE SOVIET CONCEPTIONS OF LAW

### (a) Classical Marxism and Law

To understand the Marxist attitude towards Law, we must start by distinguishing between Society and State after the manner inherited from Hegel and the classical liberal theorists. " Bourgeois society " (to use the definition of Marx and Hegel) is the entity of those social relations which men enter unconsciously and in the delusion that they are acting on their own free individual decisions, though the latter are objectively determined by the laws of political economy. State, on the other hand, implies compulsion exercised consciously for the sake of enforcing certain rules. Of these two fundamental fields of human life, Hegel insists that the State is " the realisation of morality " and, indeed, the supreme aim of human civilisation, in strongest contrast to the liberal theorists, for whom the State is at best a necessary evil, or rather an unreasonable police force interfering with the normal interplay of the laws of free competition. But both of them agree in assuming that there is a fundamental distinction between Society and State. In this, Marx was at one with them, but he rejected their belief that the relations between these two fields were, for good or for evil respectively, dominated by the interference of the State in Society.

The original contribution of Marxism to the dispute, apart from its rejection of the moral evaluation of such historical relationships, may be stated as follows : *Firstly*, the basis of Society is precisely described in terms of the mutual relations into which men enter in producing their material means of subsistence, and these relations are conditioned by the existing forces of production, i.e. by the extent to which mankind has learned to master Nature. *Secondly*, these social relations are described in terms of the prevailing economic structure of a given society. Thus, the attitude of the individual members of this society is typified according to their relative position in the socio-economic relationship, that is to say, their class-position. *Thirdly*, the general attitude of men towards social problems of any kind is tentatively explained in terms of class as the fundamental division in social life. Thus the history of mankind, since the rise of class-divisions, is explained as a history of class-struggles. It follows that State is to be regarded as dependent on Society and the latter's fundamental class-division.

> The State is by no means a power imposed on society from without, just as little as it is " the reality of the moral idea ", " the image and the reality of reason," as Hegel maintains. Rather, it is a product of society at a particular stage of development ; it is the admission that this society has involved itself in insoluble self-contradictions and is cleft into irreconcilable antagonisms which it is powerless to exorcise. But in order that these antagonisms, classes with conflicting economic interests, shall not consume themselves and society in fruitless struggles a power, *apparently* standing above society, has become necessary to moderate the conflict and keep it within the bounds of " order " ; and this power, arisen out of Society, but placing itself above it and increasingly alienating itself from it, is the State. . . . As the State arose from the need to keep class antagonisms in check, but also arose in the thick of the fight between the classes, it is normally the state of the most powerful, economically ruling class, which by its means becomes also the politically ruling class and so acquires new means of holding down and exploiting the oppressed class.[1]

Marxism regards Law, under modern conditions, as an emanation of the State. Thus it acquires its general characteristics from those of the State. On the questions which most Western legal theorists regard as the fundamentals of their science, Marx and Engels have left only occasional utterances, but these leave no doubt that the founders of Marxism were positivists in that they did not recognise any kind of Natural Law.[2] Law as well as State, they say, is a historical phenomenon. It is a superstructure upon the economic basis of society, i.e. upon those relations which men enter in carrying on the social process of production. Whilst the State may attempt to create the illusion of " standing above class ", Law (at least Civil Law) cannot do so : for it has to express, within its framework, the basic social relations themselves. Property relations, for example, are mere legal expressions for existing relations of production, and social classes may be described as owning (or not owning) certain kinds of property. But legal and political forms of social

[1] Engels, *The Origin of Family*, etc., English ed. of 1943, pp. 193–4 and 196.
[2] See Engels' letter to Marx, No. 756 in vol. III of the edition by the Marx-Engels Institute, and also the polemique against " natural laws " in his *Anti-Duehring*.

consciousness must be distinguished from the underlying economic basis. While dependent on the latter, they have also an independent life of their own. Thus the relations of production in one period may influence subsequent periods. Law can never be "higher" than the particular economic structure of society and the resultant cultural development. But it certainly can be backward in relation to the actual stage of economic development. Unless the old forms can be used for changing social purposes, or re-interpreted to serve new needs, they may prove serious obstacles for the development of society, and actual political struggle may be needed to solve the contradiction. Thus it is certainly wrong to interpret Marxism by stating that the "superstructures", amongst which is Law, reflect economic conditions automatically. Law not only reacts upon economics, but is also influenced by various forms of social consciousness even more remote from economic life than Law itself—for example by religious and philosophical conceptions. In this interaction of the various forms of social life, economics are only dominant because men must eat before they can theorise, and because the evolution of the productive forces (i.e. of the relations between Man and Nature which underlie the relations of production) forms that independent variable which makes possible a dynamic interpretation of Society.[3]

The State, from which Law emanates, is a product of the struggle of classes and is dominated by those classes responsible for social production. Therefore, Law is bound to serve, and to develop with, the economic interests of those classes.[4] The society to be protected by Law is always the existing one, and what serves the prosperity of the class responsible for social production serves the general prosperity of that society. This holds true even when Law interferes with the interests of individual members of the ruling class in the interest of the functioning of the social order as a whole, as, for instance, legislation

[3] This exposition is mainly based on Marx's preface to the *Critique of Political Economy* (1859), his *Critique of the Gotha Programme of German Social Democracy* (1875), Engels' *Ludwig Feuerbach and the Outcome of classical German Philosophy*, and his letter to Conrad Schmidt, October 27, 1890. For the interpretation of Property relations as mere expressions of existing economic relations see, apart from the preface to the *Critique of Political Economy*, also *Capital* (English ed. of 1887), vol. I, p. 56. Much confusion has been caused by failure to distinguish between the actual legal forms which all economic relations are bound to take, and, on the other hand, general conceptions of Law (whether enacted in Codes or merely in textbooks) which, like any other ideology, may or may not correspond to the reality which they try to influence.

[4] Cp. *Communist Manifesto*, ed. Ryazanoff, London, 1930, p. 44 and (annex) p. 160.

interfering with the right of mine-owners to employ children. And it holds true even if, within the ruling class, there are no groups which are both willing and able to enforce the general interests of a capitalist society against individual capitalists, so that the pressure necessary to have the law enacted must be exercised by the miners themselves. By safeguarding the health of the younger generation of workers, and by preventing unsound methods of competition between capitalists, the miners, in such a case, would serve the interests of the existing capitalist society : in other words, their sectional interest would form part of the interest of the existing society, although, during a struggle for reforms in themselves compatible with capitalist society, the political consciousness and organisation of the miners might grow to a point incompatible with its survival.

Thus the question of the extent to which interests other than those of the individual members and sections of the ruling class can influence legislation, does not affect the primary issue of the dependence of Law on the material interest of the ruling class, except during periods of immediate transition from one economic system to another. It is the inherent needs of the economic system itself that shape the framework within which legislation has to work, and the needs it must satisfy. Should legislation—say in the hands of a socialist majority—cease to meet the elementary needs of the society which it desires to transform, it could form but a transitional stage to a new order of society. Once this was achieved, the new economic foundations would limit the possibilities of legislation. In this sense, as long as there is a class-society there will be class-justice : for, apart from any individual or group bias due to the social origin, education and method of appointment, the judges are simply doing their duty in preserving the existing order of society and its functioning, and by interpreting all ambiguous formulations of laws in conformity with their conception of the ultimate purpose of Law. The use of the term " class-justice ", in Marxist theory, is simply a way of describing the existing state and its Law in terms of class, although the most frequent users of the term do so because they themselves are still bound by the ideologies upon which that Law rests, and themselves believe in the possibility of maintaining a class-less legal system.[5]

The Marxist interpretation describes a general framework within which Law evolves and has to work, and the way by

[5] See E. Fraenkel, *Zur Soziologie der Klassenjustiz*, Berlin, 1927, pp. 40 ff.

which the coercive power of the State will secure the purposes of the society's class-structure. But not all rules of behaviour enforced by the State are necessary elements of that structure.[6] And further, once a certain fundamental approach is taken for granted, there is some variety of choice in legislation as well as in judicial interpretation of the Law. Amongst the various factors influencing this choice Marxism recognises also the inherent working of the legal ideology, whatever the latter's social origins. In his letter to Conrad Schmidt, of October 27, 1890, Engels describes how the division of labour shapes various social bodies, which are distinct from the bulk of society engaged in carrying on social production, and how the ideologies cultivated by those bodies influence economics. Law is one of them. Once the division of labour makes a body of professional lawyers necessary, a new and independent sphere is opened up which, for all its general dependence on production and trade, still has its own capacity for influencing these spheres as well. Engels, of course, does not refer to the commonplace that laws are generally enacted with the intention of influencing economics. Speaking of the origins of that intention he does not explain it completely by the mere economic facts :

> In a modern state, law must not only correspond to the general economic position and be its expression, but must also be an expression which is *consistent in itself* . . . And in order to achieve this, the faithful reflection of economic conditions is more and more infringed upon. All the more so the more rarely it happens that a code of law is the blunt, unmitigated, unaltered expression of the domination of a class—this in itself would already offend the " conception of Justice ". . . . Thus to a great extent the course of the " development of Law " [7] only consists : first in the attempt to do away with the contradictions arising from the direct translation of economic relations into legal principles, and to establish a harmonious system of law, and then in the repeated breaches made in this system by the influence and pressure of further economic development, which involves it in further contradictions.
>
> The reflection of economic relations as legal principles . . . happens without the person who is acting being conscious of it ; the jurist imagines he is operating with *a priori* principles whereas they are really only economic reflexes. . . . And it seems to me that the inversion, which, as long as it remains unrecognised, forms what we call *ideological conception*, reacts in its turn upon the economic basis and may, within certain limits, modify it.

[6] Cp. the definition given by H. Laski in *A Grammar of Politics*, ed. 1937, p. x.
[7] Engels stresses that he is speaking mainly of Civil Law.

Thus, classical Marxism regards ideological conceptions of Justice, Natural Law, etc., as realities in so far as men are not conscious of the social origins of their ideologies. It regards positive Law as the outcome of the continuous interaction between these ideologies and changing social conditions, which create new needs.[8] The basic difference between Marxism and any idealist conception of Law is not that Marxism denies the importance of non-economic factors in determining the content of this or that law or code of laws, but that it tries to investigate the historical, and ultimately the socio-economic[9] origins of the human conceptions influencing law, and that it denies an ultimate validity to any of these conceptions.

For our purposes the most important application of these principles is the discussion of the problems of Law in the transition from a capitalist to a communist society, to be found in Marx's *Critique of the Gotha Programme of German Social Democracy* (1875). To understand the emphasis laid in that document on certain aspects of the problem, and also the direction in which it has influenced Soviet thought, it is necessary to recall the actual polemic out of which the *Critique of the Gotha Programme* arose. Like Lenin's *State and Revolution*, forty years later, Marx's critique was directed against the reformist idealisation of the existing state (particularly if the latter should become a democratic republic) and against the refusal to use revolutionary power once the working-classes were confronted with bourgeois democracy. In opposition to such an attitude he stressed the essentially coercive character of every state, and the ultimate rejection of both coercion and the State, by Communism:

> As the State is only a transitional institution which is used in the struggle, in the revolution, in order to hold down one's own adversaries by force, it is pure nonsense to talk of a "free people's state";[10] as long as the proletariat still *uses* the State it does not use it in the interests of freedom but in order to hold down its adversaries, and as soon as it becomes possible to speak of freedom the State as such ceases to exist.[11]

[8] The strong emphasis laid on this interaction is evidently to be explained by the fact that Engels lived in this country, with its largely judge-made Law. On the Continent direct description of the connection between social trends and parliamentary enactments would have been much easier.

[9] We use this term in view of the fact that "economic" might be misunderstood by orthodox academic economists. "Economics" in the Marxian sense deal exclusively with relations between *men*, the underlying relations between Man and Nature being described as "productive forces".

[10] The formula used in the Draft of the *Gotha Programme*. It was accepted in spite of Marx's and Engels' criticism.

[11] Engels' letter to Bebel (accompanying Marx's critique), March 18–28, 1875.

Obviously, Engels could not ignore the fact that the State, as an institution, does not only function in periods of revolutionary crisis, when its main purpose is to decide the struggle for the future structure of society. But Marx and Engels found this fact irrelevant in discussing whether their party, when the moment of revolution actually arrived, could realise freedom. They dealt with that problem as revolutionary realists. Besides, to emphasise the purely compulsive side of the State was very natural for nineteenth-century thinkers accustomed to regard the organisation of the real life of Bourgeois Society, to use the Hegelian term [12], as if it were automatically regulated by economic laws, with the State playing the rôle of the policeman. It was especially natural in a polemic against those Prussian Socialists who idealised the State yet could not idealise the Prussian police. More than any others Marx and Engels have emphasised the need for replacing the automatism of economic laws by a state playing a positive, organisational, rôle. But they wanted to draw a sharp line between its functions as a future form of social life, and its hitherto compulsive functions which they regarded as a necessary evil, to be applied ruthlessly by a future socialist regime merely in order to dispense with them altogether. They felt such clear distinctions especially necessary because they were apprehensive of the assumption of positive organisational functions by the Prussian police state, and because, on the other hand, they found compulsion most evident where it was immediately connected with the existing class-structure of society. Therefore, they defined the State as an organisation of coercion distinct from society. It would be finally applied when the victorious working-classes used it as an instrument to expropriate the former ruling class and to break their resistance to the establishment of the new, classless, society.

> As soon as there is no longer any class of society to be held in subjection, as soon as, along with class-domination, and the struggle for individual existence, based on the former anarchy of production, the collisions and excesses arising from them have also been abolished, there is nothing more to be repressed which would make a special repressive force, a State, necessary. . . . The interference of State power in social relations becomes super-

[12] "Civil Society", may be preferable as a translation of "*buergerliche Gesellschaft*", to the current "bourgeois society" in all those cases where no criticism of the *bourgeoisie* from the proletarian point of view, but a juxtaposition of State and Society, is intended. In his letter to Bebel Engels says that he uses the word "State" for denoting "the government machinery . . . or the State in so far as it forms a special organism separated from society through division of labour". See below p. 206.

fluous in one sphere after another . . . the government of persons is replaced by the administration of things and the direction of the processes of production. The State is not " abolished " ; it *withers away* ".[13]

Clearly, what is expected to wither away is not political organisation as such, which, on the contrary, is expected to exercise the most important functions in social life and to administer the social process of production. If Marx and Engels had not been handicapped by the polemic on the subject with the anarchists [14] and by the need to prove to the latter that theirs was the better way to get rid of the State, they could have spoken, more correctly, of the oppressive *functions* of State withering away—provided that with the need to oppress classes the need of compelling individuals would also cease in due course. In any case, Marx and Engels never became conscious of the fact that real dissociation between economic organisation and political compulsion is much too complicated a problem to be solved by a mere logical distinction, and by the proposal to replace the word " State " in the Socialist programme by the word " Community ".[11] Marx wrote that " freedom consists in converting the State from an organ standing above society into one completely subordinated to it ".[15] But he never discussed how this could be realised once Society [12] in its organised form was identical with the new state.

In this connection Marx answered many of the most important problems of Soviet society and Soviet law fifty years in advance. A " Communist society " in its first stage, having evolved out of its capitalist predecessors, can secure general participation in social production and maximal output only by using those incitements to which capitalism has accustomed the workers, namely payment according to the work done. Having abolished class distinctions such a society will give equal recompense for equal work. Unequal work will be recompensed unequally. Marx would regard the Law of this society as " still in principle bourgeois Law ",[16] to use a phrase afterwards much quoted in Soviet legal discussions,[17] " although principle and practice are

[13] Engels, *Anti-Duehring*, English ed. of 1942, pp. 308–9.

[14] Engels to Bebel, in *Critique of the Gotha Programme* (English ed. of the Marxist-Leninist Library, p. 41).

[15] Ibid., p. 27.

[16] Ibid., p. 12. The English translation of the German word " *Recht* " (which may mean right as well as Law, with a capital), by " right " distorts much of the sense in the edition quoted. We have corrected it, according to the actual meaning.

[17] See below, p. 204.

no longer in conflict ", i.e. although formal equality before the Law is no more a mere ideology covering actual inequality according to social position. Natural inequality still remains in the physical ability of various men and women to work as well as in the needs to be satisfied out of the recompense received from Society for work done. The right of each worker to equal payment for equal work done

> is a right of inequality in its content, like every right. Law by its very nature can only consist in the application of an equal standard. But unequal individuals (and they would not be different individuals if they were not unequal) are only measurable by an equal standard in so far as they are brought under an equal point of view, are taken from one *definite* side only, . . . everything else being ignored.[18]

Only at a higher stage of its evolution would the Communist society be able to drop " the narrow legal point of view ", and expect everyone to participate in social work according to his or her abilities while, irrespective of his contribution, he would be allowed to participate in social consumption according to his needs.

From such a description of the problem—it is hardly more—two essential features of the classical Marxian approach become evident. Firstly, the actual socialist revolution and the State emerging from it are conceived as the ultimate consummation of the original ideals of the bourgeois democratic revolutions. Such a conception, although never clearly expressed, corresponds to the revolutionary tactics of Marx and Lenin, who regarded the establishment of a working-class dictatorship as the culminating point of a social movement, setting out, in 1848 Germany or 1917 Russia, from aims corresponding to those of the French revolution in 1793. The " First stage of the Communist society " (to-day the term " Socialism " has become usual for describing this stage) is a normal state which safeguards Law. This Law secures the actual as well as the formal equality of all citizens independent of their social origin by generally enforcing its rules, without regard to the actual inequality of the individual citizens as regards personal abilities and individual needs.

Secondly, for this very reason, Law, even that of the socialist state, is not regarded as a desirable method for the ultimate organisation of social life. For the higher stage, Communism proper, another form of social regulation is intended. This

[18] *Critique of the Gotha Programme*, pp. 12–13.

would differ from Law in content as well as in the manner of carrying out its rules, which, instead of being general, would take account of individual abilities and needs. They would be enforced not by " a special organism separated from society through division of labour " [12] but by Public Opinion. According to taste, very different descriptions of this " higher stage of Communist society " are imaginable, ranging from a full realisation of the ultimate ideals of Liberalism and Anarchism to an iron discipline in which none would dare oppose a majority decision.[19] So special compulsory machinery would prove superfluous and decisions could be taken according to the merits of the case. Marx and Lenin certainly cherished the first conception. But for this very reason Marx, political realist that he was, deemed " the higher stage of the Communist society " to be a mere ultimate aim (a *utopia* in Mannheim's sense of the word).[20] Within his system it served as a limitation of the functions of Law in general and as a basis for criticising reformist glorifications of the existing law. Unhappily, for many revolutionary Marxists it also became an obstacle to investigating the concrete legal problems which might confront a revolutionary state once it was established, and attempted to shape its Law.

### (*b*) The Problem of Law in the Reformist Interpretation of Marxism

Many misunderstandings of the Marxist attitude have arisen from the fact that continental Social Democracy, especially the German variety, described itself as Marxist without at any time really absorbing the tenets of Marxism. Investigations of the attitude of active right-wing trade-unionists in Republican Germany [21] clearly show that, in spite of all the criticism of Lassalle by Marx and Engels, conceptions of Natural Law prevailed and were accepted. In addition, the cult of the existing republican state, together with distrust of the use which conservative

[19] This is a possible interpretation of the attitude taken by Lenin in *State and Revolution*, op. cit., vol. VII, pp. 93–4).

[20] I.e., independently of the question whether the utopia of to-day may not become a possibility in centuries to come. Lenin's attitude to the problem changed, even within *State and Revolution*. In so far as he tried to regard Communism as a more actual perspective, this was done at the expense of the liberal side of Marxism. See the preceding note and below, Chapter VIII, pp. 244–5.

[21] See Fraenkel, op. cit., pp. 32–7. Functionaries of the German Metal Workers' Union, sent to its Central School, were likely to be rather right-wing Social Democrats. A few Communist exceptions seem to be indicated by Fraenkel's remark (p. 36) on " intermingling of socialist and anarchist conceptions "—evidently a hint at the Marxist theory of State.

Judges might make of greater freedom of decision, resulted in a very formalist approach to the interpretation of the existing laws. The leading legal theorist of post-1918 German Social Democracy was Radbruch. He represented the idealist interpretation of Law, and even of Politics, as the realisation of certain fundamental systems of values, and belonged to the modern revival of conceptions based on Natural Law.[22]

It is not mere chance that the one remarkable contribution of reformist Socialism to our problem was made by the Austrian Renner.[23] Austrian Social Democracy combined a very moderate approach to issues of practical politics with a systematic defence of some of the foundations of Marxist ideology. For the latter was the only form in which Social Democracy might hope to withstand the threatening splits, between national groups before 1918, and between the radical and the reformist wing in post-1918 Austria. Renner rejected the reformist delusion that an automatic transition to socialism could take place by the mere working of processes of economic concentration within capitalist society.[24] So his opposition to the political approach of Marx and the Bolshevists might be regarded as irrelevant for the appreciation of the theoretician Renner, had it not influenced his general approach to the problem. His criticism of capitalist society is based upon the contradiction between the legal ideology and the actual working of the existing institutions. He is conscious [25] of the fact that, with a changing social content, the social functions of the modern legal institutions of property have been exercised, in earlier social systems, by very different institutions, such as slavery and serfdom. But in the period investigated by Renner, the period of transition from a society of independent small producers of commodities to modern capitalist industry, it is not the legal institutions that have changed, but their actual social function. Although he is conscious that there is no classless " general will " in a class-divided society,[26] and although his approach to Law in general is clearly positivist,[27] he tends to appeal to the general interests of " Society " to adapt its laws to changing social needs. In consequence, it never

[22] *Grundzuege der Rechtsphilosophie*, Leipzig, 1914.

[23] *Die Rechtsinstitute die Privatrechts und ihre soziale Funktion*, Tuebingen, 1929. The first edition has been published, 1904, in the Vienna Marx-studies, under the pseudonym Josef Karner. An English translation of it under the title *The Institutions of Civil Law and their Social Functions* will appear in the International Library of Sociology and Social Reconstruction.

[24] Op. cit., p. 170.

[25] Ibid., p. 24.

[26] Ibid., p. 4.

[27] Ibid., pp. 7 and 55–6.

becomes clear whether Renner is speaking about a capitalism which is merely reformed, with institutions adapted to the new conditions, or a fundamentally different social system. This very failure to see the revolutionary element in social change enabled him to see the continuity that links every new society with its predecessors.

Renner sees the evolution of judicial institutions, under capitalism, manifesting itself in the changes of the subject-matter with which the formally stable institutions have to deal. Property, though in theory remaining what it was, means very different things according to whether it is possessed by a majority or only by a small minority of those subject to the Law.[28] As the Law can bind only individuals the social relations between those individuals arise largely *praeter legem*, so changing the actual content of the rights and duties of the individuals subject to the Law.[29] With the development of capitalism Property, formally concerned with mere things, evolves into an unofficial state, subjecting thousands of people dependent on the property-owner to a discipline only indirectly regulated by the Law.[30] Institutions which originally were merely complementary to the primary institution of property, like the contract of employment, began to dominate the lives of the majority of the people, while the central institution of property was reduced to no more than a distributive function as regards the profits.[31] But still the legal content of the right of property—total legal control over a thing by a person—has remained unchanged. Renner on one occasion remarks that a change in the content of the legal norm might have been effected by the restriction of the possible subjects of certain kinds of property, and by declaring a number of goods to be *res extra commercium.*[32] He misses such a development in modern capitalism but he does not seem to have noticed that, in fact, just such a modification of the right of property had taken place in the Soviet Civil Code.[33] So he restricts himself to some general remarks on the transition to socialism: Property, but not the supplementary institutions connected with it by modern legal development, was essential for capitalism, and there was no reason to abolish property in means of consumption or even in some means of production (for example, those of the scientist or artist). The contract of sale and the

[28] Op. cit, p. 152, and *passim*.
[29] Ibid., p. 162.
[30] Ibid., pp. 45 ff.
[31] Ibid., pp. 60 ff.
[32] Ibid., p. 37.
[33] See below, Chapter IV, pp. 96–7.

contract of employment would remain primary institutions in a socialist as well as in a capitalist society, though with changed social content.[34] It is remarkable how nearly these observations approached the realities of the U.S.S.R., which, in fact, Renner preferred to ignore. His dislike of the way in which Soviet institutions were established, prevented him from sharing the delusions of the Bolsheviks who, while establishing these institutions, still declined to accept their work as definitive. Renner's conceptions of evolutionary socialism in Central Europe were delusions, but they helped him to see socialism as an outcome of its capitalist predecessors, and he was able to restrict his expectations of the new order to a goal, which others, more hopeful and energetic, were able to achieve.

### (*c*) Lenin's Interpretation of the Marxist Theory of State

Classical Marxism has influenced Soviet conceptions of Law mainly through Lenin's *State and Revolution*, written in the late autumn, 1917, on the eve of the bolshevist conquest of power.[35] Lenin believed that his own contribution was mainly a revival of classical Marxist theories, which were obscured by the reformist evolution of Western Social Democracy. To-day, now that most of the writings of Marx and Engels have been published, there can be no doubt that Lenin's interpretation was in essentials correct.[36] This was largely because the concrete conditions of the Russian revolution were very similar to those out of which classical Marxism had emerged,[37] and because both *State and Revolution* and the *Critique of the Gotha Programme* had the same general aim : that of combating reformist delusions that the existing bourgeois state was a fitting instrument for the establish-

[34] Ibid., pp. 98 and 76–7.

[35] Reprinted in *Selected Works*, vol. VII. The English edition has serious shortcomings, especially in using the words " right " and " Law " which in English are distinct. We did not refrain from correcting quotations, where necessary.

[36] It is an interesting fact that the problem of the attitude of socialism towards State and Law arose in the form of a philological discussion on the meaning of the classical Marxist writings, and was fought out in German Social Democracy, in the late 'nineties, by careful selection from classical writings, to use a mild expression. This shows that one of the most worrying features of Soviet writings, the habit of " proving " ideas by quotations, has roots much deeper than the working of the One-party-system in the U.S.S.R. It is certainly connected with the existence of Party and the need for a generally accepted party creed. But conditions of factional struggle (in Germany as well as later in Russia) were most favourable for nourishing the habit.

[37] See A. Rosenberg, *A History of Bolshevism*, German ed., 1930, English ed., 1934. Rosenberg's case, strong in so far as the difference between conditions of 1848 Germany and 1917 Russia on the one hand, and Western (especially Anglo-Saxon) on the other, is concerned, seems much weaker as regards the allocation of modern imperialist Germany.

ment of a socialist society. So Lenin had the same reasons as Marx for emphasising the utopian element in the critique of the existing state, that is, the ultimate hope for a stateless society. But, confronted with the immediate task of organising a socialist revolution, he had to refute the reproach of utopianism, in the usual sense of the word, by dissociating the tasks of the revolution to be achieved from the ultimate aims of the revolutionary Labour movement. The task of the movement was, according to Lenin, " the expropriation of the capitalists, the conversion of *all* citizens into workers and employees of *one* ' syndicate '—the whole state—and the complete subordination of the work of this syndicate to the . . . state of the Soviets ". Until the higher phase of Communism is reached, " the Socialists demand the *strictest* control, by Society *and by the State*, of the amount of labour and the amount of consumption ; but this control must . . . be carried out not by a state of bureaucrats, but by a state of armed workers ".[38] So far the conception is quite clear, as is the intention of all the polemics against State in general ; Lenin demanded a strong state for carrying out the necessary reorganisation desired, but, very reasonably, he did not trust the Tsarist bureaucracy and army as suitable instruments for executing those tasks. The logical conclusion is the need to build a new State machinery, based on the real, that is armed power of that class which might alone be trusted to carry through the revolution—namely the workers.

The explanation of the rôle of Law in the society to be established would be completely consistent had not the desire for utopian criticism of State and Law in general seduced Marx[39] and Lenin into describing also the law of the state which they desired to establish as " bourgeois ".

> In the first phase of Communist society (generally called Socialism) " bourgeois Law "[16] is *not* abolished in its entirety, but only in part, only in proportion to the economic transformation so far attained, i.e. only in respect of the means of production. " Bourgeois Law " recognises them as the private property of separate individuals. Socialism converts them into *common* property. To *that extent*, and to that extent alone, " bourgeois Law " disappears. However it continues to exist so far as the other part is concerned, it remains in the capacity of regulator in the distribution of products and allotment of labour among the members of society.
>
> If we are not to fall into utopianism, we cannot imagine

[38] Op. cit., p. 89.

[39] See above, p. 24.

that, having overcome capitalism, people will at once learn to work for society *without any standard of Law* ; indeed, the abolition of capitalism *does not immediately* create the needed prerequisites for such a change. There is yet no other standard than that of " bourgeois Law ". To this extent, therefore, there is still a need for a state which, while safeguarding the public ownership of the means of production, would safeguard the equality of labour and equality in the distribution of products. The State withers away in so far as there are no longer any capitalists, any class, and consequently no *class* can be suppressed. But . . . there still remains the protection of " bourgeois Law " which sanctifies actual inequality. For the complete withering of the State complete Communism is necessary ".[40]

This explanation seems to beg the question by simply doing away with all oppressive functions of the State other than those needed to enforce the smooth working of economics. But Lenin expressly rejects as utopian the assumption that excesses of *individuals* would automatically cease with the abolition of class-divisions. He merely asserts, first, that to suppress such excesses, being mere excesses of individuals, no special State machinery would be needed beyond the unorganised forces of society, and, secondly, that " *after* the removal of the economic causes of Crime, excesses of individuals will inevitably begin to wither away. With their withering away, the State will also wither away ".[41]

Socialists usually uphold the economic interpretation of the causes of crime, and this is partly justified by the experiences of the U.S.S.R. However, this interpretation is hardly defensible beyond a certain point ; for it is impossible to demonstrate that *all* kinds of crime will automatically wither away once material want is overcome. But after accepting this, there are in *State and Revolution* two different explanations of the withering away of the State and the time when it may be expected : one, when a stage of economic and social organisation is reached where Society could afford to feed its small number of idlers without compelling them to work, and another, when the society has eliminated *all* kinds of crime (not only those, like theft, which would be senseless in a Communist society). In any case, Lenin's analysis means some advance on Engels' identification of the " withering away of the State " with the withering away of *class*-oppression.[42]

Apart from the problem of protecting its internal system

[40] Op. cit., pp. 89–90. [41] Ibid., p. 83.
[42] See above, pp. 23–4.

against external dangers, a problem which Lenin evidently avoids,[43] the state of the transitional period, in his conception, no longer has any need to oppress one class in the interests of another, i.e. it is no more " state " in the original Marxist sense. But it is still needed to enforce labour discipline upon its citizens, to safeguard and regulate the inequality in the distribution of the social product which results from the unequal contributions which each individual makes to production, and to prevent individual excesses, such as crimes. So it remains an instrument of oppression—although oppression of single individuals and not of social classes as a whole. Lenin has stated clearly that the higher phase of Communism cannot be " introduced ". Thus, the whole assumption of the eventual coming of that phase might be regarded as a mere theoretical reservation in the sense that human progress will not come to a standstill once socialism is achieved, and that further advance towards real individual freedom depends on achieving such material prosperity of the socialist society that inequality of income, based upon unequal contributions to production, is no more needed. But now, unhappily, the double meaning of the word " bourgeois " becomes apparent. Marx and Lenin used it to denote the fact that even in a socialist society Law protects separate individual interests, a function which is opposed to the highest standards of social Justice. But " bourgeois " means, primarily, a certain class within a capitalist society. When Marxists speak of " bourgeois " in connection with the State (which is, according to Marxist theory, a class-bound organisation) they are bound to regard it as a characterisation of the class-character of the state under discussion. Thus it is simply confusing when Lenin concludes, that " bourgeois Law in regard to distribution of articles of *consumption* inevitably presupposes the existence of the *bourgeois State*, for Law is nothing without an apparatus capable of *enforcing* the observance of the standards of Law. Consequently, for a certain time not only bourgeois Law, but even the bourgeois State remains under Communism, without the bourgeoisie.[44] And herein lies much of the responsibility

[43] But which to-day is regarded in the U.S.S.R. as the main justification for the survival of State even in a Communist society as long as it is surrounded by a capitalist environment (see below, Chapter VIII, p. 244). Lenin's attitude may be explained in two alternative ways : either he regarded world-revolution as so imminent that the need for external defence would cease long before the conditions for basing social life on purely voluntary discipline had been created—or he might have had a very long-term view as regards the time needed for the latter process.

[44] Op. cit., p. 90.

for later confusion in Soviet discussions on State and Law. Marx, to whom Lenin here refers, is completely free from responsibility for this sample of Dialectics—and Lenin himself has only occasionally used it. He was far too able a politician to describe the state which he built as the product of the defeated class, merely because this state and its Law clearly showed the traces of its predecessors. The logical mistake is evident: certainly Law needs a state to enforce it, and, within the Marxist system, the class-nature of a state can be described in terms of the class-nature of the rules which it enforces. For example, a state with a Social Democrat government which protects a capitalist order of production is, in the eyes of Marxists, a bourgeois state, ruled, indirectly, in the interests of the bourgeoisie. But for this very reason a state *without* a bourgeoisie, i.e. without the capitalist system of production, can never be a bourgeois state, whatever terms are used to denote the fact that it is not a state of angels, and that Law in general does not denote an angelic state of affairs.

The utopian aroma in Lenin's thinking did little harm to the legislation of the state which he built—apart from providing some of its less realistic legal theorists with material for abstract discussions under a regime where the art of quotations played a large rôle in discussions.[36, 45]. But there were other more important points where Lenin appears to have relinquished his clear conception of Socialist Law in the interests of the actual political struggle. It is at these points that the conception of a "dictatorship" emerges.

Lenin has used the term "dictatorship" in two different senses. It applies primarily, as Marx and Engels used it, to a monopoly of power exercised, at a certain stage in any revolution, by the most consistent of the revolutionary parties for the purpose of carrying through the struggle and defeating the counter-revolution at all costs, without regard for legal formalities. This happened in 1648 in England and in 1793 in France. Marx hoped for it in vain in 1848, but it happened, in consequence of Lenin's policies, in Russia in 1917. For a Marxist the dictatorship of his party is the dictatorship of the proletariat, in the sense that it is exercised in the interests of and with the support of that class which can carry through the transition to a socialist society against all obstacles. But there is nothing in Marxist sociology to insist that "proletarian" rule (i.e. the socialist state

[45] See below, p. 204.

until the hypothetical period of its " withering away "—maybe some centuries) must function according to the demands of such revolutionary crises as 1648, 1793, 1917 throughout the whole of its existence. The French Radical Socialists are similar in their political platform and social backing to the Jacobins of 1793, but, when in power, they do not exercise their rule according to the Jacobin principles of 1793.

Secondly Lenin has used the term " dictatorship " for emphasising the general statement of Marxist sociology that any state is ruled by a certain class, in opposition to the Social Democrat theory that the democratic republic, especially if ruled by a coalition government, is a classless state. In this sense Lenin's statement is irreproachable, even for a period (like the U.S.S.R. to-day) when certainly no social classes in the Marxist sense can be subject to oppression. Any political regime protects some kind of socio-economic structure against its potential opponents, and can be described as the rule of the classes primarily interested in the maintenance of that structure. If the social interest of certain classes is identified with the preservation, or the achievement of a certain socio-economic structure, the simple fact that no state can protect more than one socio-economic structure may be described as the " dictatorship " of the social class interested in that structure. But it is incorrect to conclude that in all cases where one of those meanings of the term dictatorship holds true all implications of the second prove right : in short, that class-rule contradicts legality. Marxism regards any kind of legality as a distinct form of class-rule. It supposes that class-rule can be exercised (and, as the rule, *is* exercised) in the form of laws corresponding to the needs of the particular society, i.e. of its leading classes. Lenin was the last to deny this. But, in the struggle for power, he used terms which later could be used as weapons by people who did not wish to see the revolutionary state functioning according to its own laws.

In attacking Russian Cadets in 1905, and Western Social Democrats in 1920,[46] Lenin defined dictatorship as " unrestricted power, beyond the law, resting on force in the strictest sense of the word ", in order to make clear that revolutionaries, if they desire success, must not observe the laws of the state they want to overthrow. In addition, he praised revolutionary organs acting during the 1905 revolution for " exercising authority

[46] *Works*, Russian ed., vol. IX, p. 116, and English ed., vol. VII, p. 251.

and creating a new *revolutionary* law." [47] It is quite evident that the law beyond which dictatorship ought to act, according to Lenin, is that of the system it desires to overthrow—whilst the self-consciousness of the new system is measured by its ability and readiness to establish new rules of its own. During the whole post-1917 period Lenin never ceased to demand "revolutionary legality," which meant the observation of the laws of the new order by the individual organs created by it. Local initiative in applying the laws of the new state to the varying local conditions was highly desirable, but local arbitrariness which, in the name of "revolutionary initiative", violated that uniformity which the revolutionary state wanted to secure by its laws, was not.[48] The fundamental position of Lenin is completely clear, especially considering his long-term view of the State as discussed above. But this did not prevent enemies as well as supporters of the new system from describing it as essentially lawless, whether this be meant as reproach or as praise.

[47] Ibid., p. 254.
[48] *Works,* Russian ed., vol. XXVII, pp. 298 ff.

## CHAPTER III

# THE BASIC CONCEPTIONS OF THE FIRST REVOLUTIONARY PERIOD

### (a) The Principles of Soviet Economic Legislation during the Establishment of the New Regime

The first period of the Soviet regime is generally described as that of War-Communism. While generally useful this description is insufficient for our investigation : although from a very early stage (virtually since the end of 1917) conditions of civil war dominated Soviet policies, it is, however, possible, and relevant from the theoretical point of view, to make some distinction between those decrees that realised policies already envisaged by the leading party when taking power (or immediately resulting from those first steps), and other measures the enactment of which was at least hastened by external conditions.

Bolshevism's approach to the economic problems arising out of the conquest of power was described on the eve of the Revolution in Lenin's " Can the Bolsheviks retain State Power ? "[1] the outstanding contribution of revolutionary Marxism to the problem of social transition. Its very purpose, a polemic against those sympathisers and members of the Bolshevist party who doubted whether a socialist regime could be established in a backward and predominantly peasant country, demanded an emphasis on the positive elements in the situation, and on the possibility of using certain parts of the social organisation already in existence under the capitalist regime. " Can the Bolsheviks retain State Power ? " differs in emphasis from *State and Revolution*, which was written at the same time, against those who desired to accept the bourgeois state. But there can be not the slightest doubt that in " Can the Bolsheviks retain State Power ? " Lenin explained the fundamental ideas moving him and his party on the eve of conquest.

In much more elaborate terms than in *State and Revolution*, which was intended to explain classical Marxist theory, the Soviets are described as the new, somewhat centralising, State apparatus, called upon to replace the old one. Within the framework of the new state, Workers' control of capitalist enterprises,

[1] *Works*, English ed., vol. VI, pp. 250 ff.

exercised by Shop Stewards and *ad hoc* organisations, would not involve syndicalist anarchy, but would form the necessary transitional step to enable the hitherto oppressed class to administer economics themselves; it would establish "a national all-embracing accounting of the production and distribution of goods." Where economic as distinct from political administration is involved, the idea of simply smashing the old bureaucratic machinery of the bourgeoisie and establishing a completely new proletarian machinery is out of the question. Lenin clearly distinguished between a rejection of any coalition or political co-operation with the organisation of the defeated classes, and a nihilistic approach to the economic organisation created by them.

> Beside the pre-eminently "coercive" machinery . . . there is in the modern state an apparatus closely connected with the banks and syndicates, an apparatus that performs a vast amount of work of an accounting and statistical nature. . . . This apparatus must not be broken up. . . . The big banks are the "state apparatus" we *need* for the realisation of socialism, and which *we shall take* from capitalism ready-made. Our problem here is only to *lop away* those capitalist growths which disfigure this otherwise excellent apparatus and to make it *still bigger*, still more democratic, still more comprehensive.[2]

Lenin's use of the phrase "still more democratic" in discussing a type of organisation developed by capitalist monopoly refers to the general Marxist thesis that modern capitalist enterprise is already a truly social undertaking involving the whole totality of the people. It only needs to be made directly responsible to society in order to render it both socialist and democratic, and at the same time free from the "disfigurations" caused by capitalist competition. Evidently Lenin thought that the first stage of the transition was passed as soon as the employees of banks, syndicates, commercial concerns, etc., while continuing their former work, were transformed into State employees.[3] Though he knew he must break the resistance of most of the former capitalists, managers, etc., Lenin was ready "to pay good money" to those economists who, under the guidance of the new state, would help in elaborating its economic plans.[4] He had in mind a State syndicate with an elaborate hierarchy of employees, in which democratic self-government would take effect mainly through the participation of trade-unions and shop stewards in the management of the individual factory where they would keep a constant check on corruption and

[2] Op. cit., pp. 265–6. [3] Ibid., p. 267. [4] Ibid., p. 278.

bureaucratic methods, as indeed was the case in the U.S.S.R. in the late 'twenties and earlier 'thirties. A man able to describe such a system as "still more democratic" than monopoly capitalism would have been indifferent towards the acrimonious discussions as to whether it was "state-capitalist" or not. State capitalism in a state controlled by the working-classes and planning consistently in the interest of Society as a whole involved, to Lenin at least, Socialism, once private capitalist interests had ceased to dominate life of Society.

The problem of expropriation is particularly interesting both to those who regard capitalist property as sacrosanct, and to those who believe that inequality of income is the main defect of a capitalist society. Lenin treated it as a secondary question, as indeed it is for any Marxist in comparison with the planlessness, the economic crises and the waste of potentially productive resources in a capitalist system, including using them for unproductive purposes. Like Engels, Lenin seeks to solve that problem by compromise : if capitalists are willing to collaborate in building the new society, they may purchase a respite and find for themselves and for their children an honourable place in it.

> The vital point will be not so much the confiscation of capitalist property as the establishment of universal, all-embracing Workers' Control over the capitalists and their possible supporters. Confiscation will lead us nowhere, for it lacks the element of organisation, accountancy, or correct distribution. Confiscation may easily be replaced by a fair tax . . . provided only that we make it impossible to escape rendering returns, to conceal the truth, or to evade the Law.[5]

(The existence and importance of the latter, in the new state of affairs, was self-evident to Lenin.)

The policies of the later "New Economic Policy", at its best, and of the period of respite after the Second Five Year Plan, follow in a direct line from the attitude described above. And this, in the present writer's opinion, represents the essential line in the development of Soviet Russia, though, of course, any such line can only be an abstraction. In "Can the Bolsheviks retain State Power ?" and still more in the *Drafts on the Socialisation of National Economy* written by Lenin one month after the conquest of power [6] some proposals may be found which, because of the order in which their realisation was attempted, seem rather to belong to "War-Communism" although they had been

[5] Op. cit, pp. 267–8. [6] English ed., vol. VI, pp. 442 ff.

envisaged by Lenin long before the emergencies that later enforced their enactment. Apart from those measures actually taken by the Soviet state during the first months of its existence, we find, among these proposals of Lenin, a " Duty to Work ", to be applied particularly to former *bourgeois* failing to participate in useful work, and enforced not by the mechanism of a society in which there is no place for unearned income, but by administrative pressure and by withholding ration books. According to Lenin's proposals [7] " Consumers' Communes " were to be established by nationalising the existing Consumers' Co-operatives (a step which was not actually taken before 1919).[8] All Joint Stock Companies were immediately to be nationalised, not merely those which failed to comply with the regulations on Workers' Control, as actual Soviet legislation at the time stipulated. Certainly all of these proposals can be explained by Lenin's realisation of the degree of resistance which would have to be met and answered by emergency-measures, without necessarily assuming that he gave way to utopian conceptions of the society immediately to be achieved. In times of civil war it might be necessary to force the former *bourgeois*, who could not be safely armed, at least to dig trenches and to keep the roads in order. So also it might be necessary to make food-distribution independent of the whims of right-wing Social Democrat leaders of the Co-operatives, who were avowed antagonists of the new regime. But in these proposals, Lenin never hints at the mere emergency-character of the measures proposed, and utopian idealisations of emergency measures into " true Communism " were not discouraged, to say the least of it. In fact, the realisation of any socialist demands was dominated by the need to defend a revolution whose first decisive steps had not been socialist.

Satisfaction of the peasants' demands was the key to the realisation of any revolutionary programme in Russia. While taking power, on the night of November 7, 1917, the Soviet Congress enacted the Decree on the Land.[9] The basic political compromise of the Bolshevists was that, whilst they avoided any sharing of actual power, they accepted the land programme of the Social Revolutionaries, who, with their strong peasant

[7] Ibid., p. 445. [8] See below, p. 50.

[9] S.U. 1917/3, October 26, 1917. The publication days of the Soviet laws, up to March 1, 1918, correspond to the old Julian calendary—according to the new Western calendary the decree was published November 8, 1917. We quote the Soviet laws always according to the calendary in force at the time of their enactment, and with the date of the latter (not that of the publication).

backing, were their only serious competitors. Therefore the decree simply enacted the expropriation of all the big estates and their stocks, leaving the average (*rjadovoj*) peasants' and Cossacks' land as before (art. 5). The District Soviets were to dispose of the land. Until the decision of the Constituent Assembly was made, they had to follow the directions given in the "Peasants' *Nakas*" (Instruction) of August 19, 1917, which was a summary of the peasants' demands set out by the Social Revolutionaries and published, as an annex to the Land Decree, with the authority of the Soviet congress. It was here, and not in the Land Decree itself, that the fundamental principles were proclaimed: *all* land (not only that of the big estates) was to be nationalised. Estates suitable for large-scale cultivation were to be taken over, where expediency permitted, by the State or by "communities."[10] All the stock of the big farms, but not that of the smaller, was to be expropriated. Article 5 of the *Nakas* stated that it was to be done without compensation, whilst the corresponding article of the Decree had in theory left the decision to the Constituent Assembly. Thus the Soviet Congress, whilst itself refraining from immediately abolishing private property in the land cultivated by peasants, encouraged the District Soviets, i.e. the immediate representatives of the peasants, to do so. Article 6 of the *Nakas* established the general right of all citizens to use the land, provided that, and only as long as, they could cultivate it with the help of their families, or in co-operative partnership. The employment of hired labour was prohibited. But article 7 ordered the distribution of the land to be carried through "on an equality basis, conforming with either the labour standard or the consumption standard, as local conditions shall warrant." If "local conditions" should warrant distribution according to the labour standard, the well-to-do peasant, with a higher labour capacity on his farm, would reap the benefit. If they should warrant distribution according to consumption standards, by "mouths" or "souls", to use the old Russian term, as was the case in most Russian *Gubernia*,[11] then the poor peasants with many children and few implements of production would have to let the "superfluous" land and the labour of the "superfluous" children to

[10] The applied term "*obchina*" denotes the traditional village-community and, in this sense, was popular with the peasants. But it was intentionally ambiguous, to include modern co-operative organisation as well. Only in the latter sense could it fit the Socialist programme.

[11] See Lenin, vol. VIII, p. 8.

their *kulak* neighbours, in contradiction to the preceding article which prohibited the employment of hired labour, and to the definition of " abolition of private property in land ", given in article 1 of the *Nakas*, which included also the abolition of the right to purchase, to sell, to mortgage and otherwise to alienate land. Article 8 ordered that organs of democratic self-government should periodically re-distribute the land.[12] But the " original nucleus " (that is, the share of the land held by each family prior to the acquisition of new land from the expropriated large estates) was declared inviolable. The peasant, when leaving the village, was even granted the right to influence the future apportioning of the land hitherto cultivated by himself (article 8, 4). This probably involved his accepting from the successor, in whose favour he disposed, a certain reward, whatever article 1 might say about the abolition of the right to sell the land.

The Peasants' *Nakas* contained in itself the fundamental contradiction between the fact that the peasants demanded nationalisation of the land in order to get a title to the landlords' land and to rid themselves of exploitation by mortgages and usurers, whilst the main use they desired to make of the land was to establish flourishing private enterprises. Lenin, no doubt, was glad that the contradiction was expressed within a document formulated by the peasants themselves, and not as a conflict between their demands and the decrees of a Bolshevist-controlled authority. But the contradiction had to be solved in some way, and many questions that would be regarded in normal times as fundamental issues of legislation were answered less formally by the revolutionary organs. A by-law on the activities of the local Land Committees issued by the Central Land Committee [13] defined the average peasant or Cossack not to be expropriated (according to art. 5 of the Land Decree) as one who did not employ hired labour, so that the small agricultural capitalist was brought within the scope of expropriation. The local Land Committees were also granted (arts. 33–35) a competence which the " Peasants *Nakas* " had not thought of, namely " to supervise and to organise agricultural production."

[12] Previously this had been done only with the land held in communal ownership of the village, as distinct from the land belonging to the landlords and to the peasant entrepreneurs (*kulaks*) who made use of the Stolypin reforms. These very lands—as distinct from those hitherto distributed amongst the peasants, which passed under permanent usufruct by their holders—now became subject to periodical redistribution.

[13] S.U.R. 1917/8, No. 105, Dec. 4, 1917.

After the dissolution of the Constituent Assembly, the Land Law of February 19, 1918 [14] systematically enacted the principles of the new order. It clearly distinguishes between landed property, which is abolished unconditionally and without compensation, and "the Right to Use the Land" (art. 3 ff.) which appertains to those who cultivate the land. Only State farms are allowed to employ hired labour (art. 13). The prospect of transition to more rational and collective forms of cultivation is emphasised (art. 11, *d*, *e*), and agricultural Communes, co-operatives and societies are mentioned before individual families and citizens as legitimate claimants to the public land fund (arts. 20, 13; and 21/22). Under the prevailing conditions such precedence might be regarded as rather theoretical. In distributing the land amongst the individual peasant families egalitarian principles, with regard to the number of family members able to participate in agricultural work,[15] were to be applied (art. 12).

The Right to Use the Land is derived from various principles (art. 37): the use of land for agricultural purposes is justified by personal labour, and for all other purposes (educational, mining, building, etc.) by social needs. In the case of building, personal needs are added as an additional legitimation. Thus private ownership in small houses is implicitly recognised. The right is realised by using the land. It cannot be automatically transferred by inheritance, and the children of a deceased peasant are expected, while continuing to use the land, to make a new application to the village Soviet to attest their right (arts. 39, 3; 45; 46).

The State still remains in the background: it is granted a monopoly of trade in agricultural machinery and seeds (art. 18), and in grains (art. 19). Practical exercise of these rights was handicapped at that time by the lack of sufficient material resources, which since then has been made good. But another right granted to the State by the 1918 Land Law (art. 17), the right to appropriate the differential rents on better soils, has remained merely theoretical up to the present day, unless the profits made by the State in dealing in grains and the graduation of the deliveries asked from the *kollkhoses* in different regions, are taken as its realisation.

While based upon individual peasant enterprise, with the prospect of future co-operative development under the State's

[14] S.U. 1918/346.

[15] See above, pp. 40–1.

guidance as a merely theoretical aim, the Land Law, although enacted with full participation of the Social Revolutionaries, was much stricter than the Peasants' *Nakas* in limiting the possibilities of capitalist evolution in the enlarged and strengthened peasant enterprise. It enacted those achievements which the majority of the Russian people defended in defending the Revolution—but it did not enact the aims pursued by the class and party leading the Revolution. Steps towards socialism were possible only in industry, that is in the field of large-scale enterprise, most of which was hitherto owned by Joint Stock Companies, many of them in foreign hands.

The principles laid down in " Can the Bolsheviks retain State Power ? " were enacted by the Statute on Workers' Control.[16] The entrepreneur is still regarded as responsible for management and, jointly with the shop stewards, for preserving working discipline and the equipment belonging to the factory. In administering the factory he is bound to carry through the orders of the local organs of Workers' Control (virtually the shop stewards) though he is allowed three days' delay[17] if he wants to appeal to the higher organs of Workers' Control (that is, to the economic departments of the Soviets). Very few entrepreneurs were found ready to continue working under such conditions. Therefore from December onwards many decrees [18] enacted the expropriation of this or that enterprise for failure to comply with the decree on the Workers' Control, or for " mismanagement." [19] From January, 1918, onwards decrees on the establishment of State monopolies are to be found for certain key trades which were, if necessary, combined with the expropriation of the enterprises needed for running the monopoly,[20] even in absence of reproaches against the former management. Assets and obligations of such enterprises were taken over by the State, to be administered by the Supreme Economic Council. All employees, including the managers, were taken over into the Public Service. There was no compensation—the very existence of the former share-holders was ignored.

The key-position of Russian economics, the banks, had

[16] S.U.R. 1917/8, Nov. 16, 1917.

[17] This point had been lacking in Lenin's Draft (*Works*, vol. VI, p. 400).

[18] S.U.R. 1917/8, Nos. 69, 95, 130, 190, 192 and many others, the first dealing with big mining undertakings.

[19] Ibid., No. 140 (a large electric power station), 191 (the Petrograd Putilov Works), and others.

[20] S.U.R., No. 282, dealing with the nationalisation of two leading iron trade enterprises for regulating the distribution of pig-iron.

been nationalised and declared a State monopoly as early as December 14, 1917,[21] and six weeks later it was found necessary to confiscate their shares : [22] a flourishing trade in such shares amongst people who doubted the stability of the new regime forced the latter to declare its views *expressis verbis*. Two days later,[23] evidently as a result of the international situation, the National Debt was repudiated, the Foreign Debt without any compensation, and the Internal Debt with provision for smaller holders (those with less than 10,000 roubles, the equivalent of about £1,000 pre-war value) to be compensated by new bonds. The latter were eventually annulled by the inflation of the currency—as happened to State creditors in some other countries with less revolutionary views on finance.

Apart from this point, where the international connections of Finance enforced a quick decision on the property-issue, the general attack against unearned income opened only in the period after the Brest Litovsk Peace, i.e. in a period of open civil war. On April 27, 1918, the Right of Inheritance was restricted to a maximum of 10,000 roubles.[24] The same limit was set to the rights of former owners as well as mortgagees when on August 20, 1918,[25] private property in urban buildings was abolished. In cities with more than 10,000 inhabitants not only the land, as had already been implied by the Land Law, but also the buildings erected on it (industrial buildings apart) were municipalised if their value, or revenue, surpassed a certain minimum fixed by the local Soviet (art. 2), which also enjoyed a monopoly of future building (art. 5). In smaller towns and villages private building on the municipalised land was allowed. But houses in smaller Russian towns are hardly suitable to be let to tenants. So the law may be interpreted as the abolition of ground-rent as a source of private income, applied now to the towns in addition to the country.

In those days of extreme indigence, the prospects for town-planning, which might eventually result from the municipalisation of urban lands, belonged only to a remote future. Even now, it is generally the State that finances house-building. With inflation in full swing, the right of the local Soviet to dispose of the revenue from rent (arts. 12–13) was hardly an asset for municipal finance. So, up to the present day, this one important

[21] S.U. 1917/150.
[22] Ibid., No. 295, January 26, 1918.
[23] Ibid., No. 353.
[24] See below, pp. 81–2.
[25] S.U. 1918/674. Article 9 of the decree, concerning mortgages, explicitly refers to the Decree on the Annulation of the National Debt.

form of municipal property in Soviet Russia has hardly achieved any economic importance. But decentralisation in the administration of the existing housing accommodation as well as in town-planning has shaped the conditions for one of the most important fields of local self-government in the U.S.S.R.

In spite of the frequent use of the term "equality" in the decrees of that time (especially in those that show the influence of the left-wing Social Revolutionaries, the junior partners of the Bolsheviks in the government coalition) the society to be established after the abolition of unearned income was not conceived on completely egalitarian lines.[26] The regulations of January 19, 1918 [27] for wages in the Petrograd metallurgical and engineering factories, certainly a key-position from the point of view of the regime, established, quite apart from the apprentices, differentiations in the wages to be paid for various occupations up to the ratio of 2 : 3. The scale of wages for the employees of the Post and Telegraph Service [28] provided for monthly salaries of between 215 and 600 roubles for skilled workers, and the Post Director could earn 800 roubles. Article 1 of the regulations for the Petrograd Metal Workers announced the considerations which ought to decide the remuneration due to each occupational group as follows : (1) the necessary subsistence minimum, (2) professional qualification, complexity of the work and precision demanded in its execution, (3) difficulties, hard and dangerous conditions of work, (4) the position of the industry within the whole economic system. Should a similar document be enacted to-day in the U.S.S.R., the same considerations would probably be enumerated—although the order of points (1) and (4) would be reversed. The fundamental difference between conditions then and now, quite apart from the increased differentiation of to-day, is the fact that the 1918 documents provided for regular and permanent differentiation in earnings only between the distinct occupational groups, but not between individual workers belonging to the same group : piecework was provided for, but only as a means to secure the regular fulfilling of the fixed norm of output. Occasional non-fulfilment of the norm might be penalised by a reduction of the normal wages up to two-thirds (art. 22), whilst evident unfitness for the job might result in transfer to a lower-paid group or even dismissal (art. 23).

[26] See above, p. 38. [27] S.U. 1918/242.
[28] Ibid., No. 262, January 21, 1918.

The fundamentals of Soviet policy, on the eve of War-Communism proper, were summarised in the "Declaration of the Rights of the Toiling and Exploited People." [29] The title suggests an elaborate declaration of principles, but the document merely enumerates measures submitted as an ultimatum to the Constituent Assembly by the Soviet Congress. After its rejection by the majority of the Constituent Assembly it was enacted by the Soviet Congress itself as the platform of the new regime. So it contains all the measures which were "provisionally" enacted by the Soviet in expectation of their ratification by the Constituent Assembly, although it is not restricted to these measures. Of the economic measures of the Soviet government, land reform, the establishment of Workers' Control, and the nationalisation of the banks is ratified in the Declaration, but no general nationalisation even of big industries is mentioned, although a large number of Nationalisation Decrees concerning individual enterprises, amongst which were some of the most important in the country, had already been enacted at the time. The only fundamental economic measure not previously enacted but enumerated in the Declaration, is the general Duty to Work (art. II, 4)—but it corresponds to the one new political measure provided for, the establishment of a Red Army (art. II, 5), and thus might be interpreted as an emergency measure. The basic new principle in the Declaration is the exclusion of the exploiting classes from participation in political power, with special reference to the actual conditions of the decisive struggle, i.e. the formal enactment of the Dictatorship (part IV of the Declaration). But there is no hint that its programme would, in the subsequent period, go beyond the measures hitherto discussed.

### (*b*) The Main Trends of Economic Legislation under War-Communism

Three years later, when attempts at wholesale nationalisation of industry had proved a failure, Lenin referred [30] to certain enactments oft he first revolutionary period, such as the nationalisation of advertising, as evidence that the original intention had been to nationalise merely the "commanding heights" in the economic sphere, while leasing smaller and less essential undertakings to private entrepreneurs. Those decrees of July,

[29] S.U., No. 205, Lenin's Draft in *Works*, vol. VI, p. 452.
[30] Vol. IX, pp. 282 ff.

1918, which were aimed at preventing the evasion of future nationalisation acts,[31] were still restricted to industrial enterprises with more than four employees, and commercial enterprises with more than one. As regards agriculture there was no wavering of official policy at the centre : yet when very thorough measures to encourage collective farming were taken,[32] the resolution of the VIIIth Congress of the C.P. rejected any forcible collectivisation, and supported the middle peasant's husbandry whenever he preferred to continue on individual lines.[33] The authorities very reasonably avoided the slightest opportunity for misunderstandings on this point,[34] for the bugbear of the enforced " Commune " was the main weapon of counter-revolutionary propaganda in the countryside. On the other hand, it is indisputable that during the War-Communist period theories were evolved that made a virtue of necessity,[35] and that, after some time, decrees were issued nationalising enterprises which the State had not the means to take over in actual practice.[36]

Whatever the original intentions of the Bolsheviks as regards industry during the first stage of the Revolution [37]—the needs of civil war very soon enforced wholesale nationalisation. On March 7, 1918 [38] nationalisation of whole industries (apart from the banks) was enacted for the first time—it concerned the production of matches, candles, rice, coffee and pepper. On May 2 a more important industry, the production of sugar, followed.[39] No socialist would have dreamed of such an order of nationalisation : and it is quite evident that the empty shops, and the refusal of private entrepreneurs to refill them, demanded such steps of a government that had somehow to honour its ration-books. Foreign trade—a branch of national economy much nearer to nationalisation from a theoretical point of view—was nationalised on April 23.[40] The wholesale nationalisation of all the largest concerns in the most important industries was enacted on June 25.[41] In general, any factory owned by a Joint Stock Company was regarded as large enough for nationalisation. But in leading industries like metallurgy, engineering and production of electricity, a minimum capital of one million roubles (£100,000) was required to bring a factory (if owned

[31] On the order of transactions in private enterprises, S.U. 1918/666.
[32] See below, p. 51.
[33] Lenin, vol. VIII, pp. 184 ff.
[34] See below, note 49.
[35] Characteristic is Bukharin's *Economics of the Transformation Period*, 1920.
[36] See below, p. 87.
[37] See above, p. 38.
[38] S.U.R. 1917/8, No. 385.
[39] Ibid., No. 457.
[40] Ibid., No. 432.
[41] Ibid., No. 559.

by a Joint Stock Company), under the general rule of nationalisation. All employees of the nationalised enterprises, including the managers and the members of the Boards of Administration, were accepted, with their previous salaries, into the public service, and forbidden to leave their posts. The large-scale enterprises of the oil-producing industries followed on July 20 [42]—more than four months after small shops producing candles had been taken over by the State! It must not be forgotten that those of the big enterprises which had resisted the introduction of Workers' Control had been taken over long before, and the manager of a big metallurgical enterprise who, as a *rara avis*, had not resisted, was certainly more trustworthy from the State's point of view than the average master candle-maker, with his strong connections with the black market. The step which Lenin had regarded as fundamental in socialist reorganisation of national economy [43] was taken on January 24, 1919, when a Budgetary Department of the State Bank was established as a Finance centre for the whole nationalised industry. At this time it proved merely transitional, for the monetary inflation frustrated all attempts at establishing "control by the rouble." [44] On January 10, 1920, the Budgetary Department of the State Bank was replaced by a general "Budgetary and Accounting Administration." To make a virtue of necessity the preamble said that—evidently in view of the approaching transition to full Communism—monetary operations had lost their importance.

The need to honour the ration-books necessitated another step of fundamental importance: April 16, 1918, the future activities of the Consumers' Co-operatives were regulated by a special decree.[45] It was a compromise with the Menshevist leaders of the Co-operatives, and Lenin, who had proposed a more thorough solution,[46] protested against its moderation. But apart from this special political issue [47] there was a more general problem which, in more moderate forms and without open divergencies, was to reappear when such trustworthy Communist organisations as the Trade Unions were called upon to undertake public functions [48]: once the organisations built

[42] S.U.R., No. 546. [43] See above, p. 37. [44] See below, pp. 191–3.

[45] S.U.R. 1917/8, No. 418. [46] See above, p. 39.

[47] For a severe criticism of the Soviet policies from a right-wing co-operator's point of view, see E. Fuckner, *Die russische Genossenschaftsbewegung 1865–1921*, Osteuropa-Institut, Breslau, I. Abt. H, 6, pp. 102 ff.

[48] The functions transferred to the Trade Unions during War-Communism caused a very sharp discussion within the Party, in 1920, when one wing of the Party, under Trotsky's leadership, tried to adapt the trade unions by militarisation to their

for representing working-class sectional interests within a capitalist society are summoned to function as organs of a socialist state (and it is, in general, non-Communist socialists who are most inclined to such solutions, which they deem more compatible with democratic self-government) the State will demand a certain control on what, now, are most important elements of its own organisation.

In the case of the Consumers' Co-operatives in 1918, the demands of the State were moderate : The Co-operatives were obliged to serve the whole public. So the special appeal they could make to increase their membership was restricted to the dividend of 5 per cent. at least which they had to pay on all purchases by members, while shopping in non-co-operative stores was burdened with an *ad hoc* introduction of a purchase tax of 5 per cent. (art. 1). Old co-operators, with a political bias against the less well-paid, and more radical, strata of the working-classes, might regret the ruling that the co-operatives had to admit everyone who paid the purely nominal fee of 50 kopeks—the rest of the membership fee being covered by the new member's future dividends (art. 2). Apart from the implications as regards the political structure of the Co-operatives' meetings this was bad business in view of the inflation. Article 3 of the law prohibited the Co-operatives from competing with one another, and in no place were more than two co-operatives allowed : one open to all citizens and one open only to the working classes (art. 4). One might suppose that the latter concession was caused less out of regard for the traditional divisions within the co-operative camp than by the desire of the State to have suitable channels available for giving extra rations to the workers. Representatives of the co-operatives had to participate in the work of the State organs, including those entitled to confiscate private enterprise competing with the co-operatives (art. 6) but no co-operative was allowed to admit private capitalists to its leading positions (art. 7).

All this might be interpreted, by those in sympathy with the new state, as the ultimate victory of all that working-class co-operation had stood for, the narrowness of the traditional organisation being necessarily abolished once co-operative principles were realised with public support for the whole population.

public function, whilst such perspectives caused the majority to begin doubting the correctness of War-Communism in general. See Trotsky, *My Life*, London, 1930, and Lenin, vol. IX, part I. For later developments see below, chapter VII, p. 217.

Those who opposed the Soviet regime [47] would feel themselves deprived of the organisations they had helped to build, the conception of peaceful growth towards what they deemed socialism being transformed into thinly veiled service of a state dominated by their political adversaries. They might also regret article 12 of the law which obliged the co-operatives to place their liquid assets with the State Bank, and to further by propaganda similar investments by all citizens. From the point of view of the new state this meant fulfilling an elementary patriotic duty—but from the point of view of its antagonists it meant totalitarian control of the co-operative funds, and the plundering of the latter by monetary inflation. In fact, it was a fundamental issue, whether sectional organisation was to be regarded as a private interest which had to look after its own business, or—to apply the most accommodating interpretation—as a democratically self-governing concern fulfilling tasks allotted to it by the State. The needs of the War did not for long permit even this lenient interpretation ; before a year had passed the State-supervised Co-operatives were replaced by obligatory " Consumers Communes," [49] which had already been suggested by Lenin in December, 1917. According to the preamble it was an emergency-measure " to prevent starvation ", with the special intention of abolishing the overlapping between public food stores and general and special working-class co-operatives. Whatever ideologies were to be built round the Consumers' Communes, the reality behind them was that food was too scarce to allow premiums for initiative in self-organisation.

The scarcity of food, and the unreadiness of the individual peasants to deliver their surplus products to a state paying in rapidly depreciating money, caused agricultural organisation to go beyond that radical redistribution of land achieved by the 1917–18 reforms. The decree of the V.C.I.K.[50] " On Socialist Organisation of Agriculture ", February 14, 1919,[51] marked an attempt to return to purely socialist conceptions of land reform [52] as distinct from the 1917–18 reforms which had

[49] S.U. 1919/191, January 4, 1919. By another decree of June 30, 1919 (S.U. 342) the name " Consumers Co-operatives " was restored, to avoid misunderstandings by the peasantry who might have believed that obligatory collectivisation of agriculture—associated with the term " Commune "—was intended.

[50] *Vserossijsky* (since 1922 *Vsesojusny*) *Centralny Ispolnitelny Komitet*, All-Russian (resp. All-union) Central Executive Committee, the Supreme State organ, corresponding to Parliament.

[51] S.U. 43.

[52] For the original Bolshevist point of view cp. Lenin, vol. III, part II.

been realised with the support of the Social Revolutionaries. Article 1 clearly expressed the hitherto vague conception of the whole national territory as one land fund, to be disposed of in the interests of the Community. Article 3 developed the perspective of transition from individual to collective agriculture. Agricultural State enterprises (*Sovkhoses*), Agricultural *Communes*, and Communal Cultivation of the land were recommended as progressive in comparison with the merely transitional stage of individual peasant husbandry. According to article 8 the available land had to be allotted (1) to *Sovkhoses* and *Communes*, (2) to co-operative enterprises and for Communal Cultivation by the peasants, (3) for the maintenance of the individual peasants. In this order also State subsidies in money, seed, fodder, and implements of agricultural production were to be distributed —provided that the State had anything to distribute. But the existing agricultural collectives (mainly *Communes*) received, in fact, a subsidy of one billion roubles. The division of expropriated large estates amongst individual peasants was, in future, prohibited (art. 9). Elaborate chapters of the law dealt with the organisation of the various kinds of communal enterprise to be encouraged. Whilst the *Commune* (Chapter VII) was conceived as being run without any consideration for individual interests,[53] Communal Cultivation of the Land, in its theoretical conception (Chapter VIII), very nearly corresponded to the later typical *kollkhos*, the agricultural *Artel*.[54] In practice, as matters then stood, it was unlikely to differ from the traditional village community, revived for the satisfaction of the public demand for food deliveries. It was granted special powers, including the right to expel members who neglected their duties and to confiscate their stock in favour of the community (art. 131). But membership in all these forms of agricultural organisation remained purely voluntary. A special decree[55] established elaborate rules on the legal issues to be decided by the articles of agricultural societies and co-operatives. These articles had to be registered, and compliance with them had to be supervised by the People's Commissariat for Agriculture.

It is clear that the war-emergency forced progress in collectivist legislation beyond the point where it was compatible

[53] So, for example, article 90 ruled that all profits of the Communal economy were reserved for reinvestment.

[54] See, especially, articles 123–126 on the distribution of the proceeds in money and kind, with due regard for the interests of the individual members

[55] S.U. 1919/30, March 3, 1919.

with the economic conditions at the time. In the State enterprises normal banking functions, recognised by Lenin himself as essential conditions for the prosperity of a socialist economy,[2] were replaced by the indiscriminate distribution of paper money straight from the printing press. All citizens were compelled to enrol in State-supervised Consumers' *Communes*. Agricultural co-operation was promoted not by improved implements of production and better delivery of industrial products, for the State could provide neither, but by the pressure of food requisitions and the offer of money prizes. All these may be described as measures of war-economy. But in spite of the term War Communism, they were certainly not socialist in that they did not denote progress to a higher, collectivist form of production. But in certain fields the need to defend public property against the reaction of individual citizens to the general shortage involved a fuller elaboration of truly collectivist principles. Most interesting, in this field, is the Code on Forests, May 27, 1918.[56]

All forests were to be administered by the public authorities. The central authorities reserved for themselves the right to establish general principles directing the use of the forests (art. 66), whilst the local Soviet authorities took over the immediate administration, including the right to fix the prices for the products of the forests according to local conditions (art. 48). Some forests were declared by the central government to be "protected forests" (art. 83 ff.) and were administered exclusively in the interest of climatic advantages, public health, recreation for the citizens and general cultural value. The rest were administered with a view to satisfying public needs, and of receiving revenue from the sale of their products (art. 91). Only the latter category might be reclaimed for agricultural cultivation, but even in this case the central authorities had to give their assent according to their interpretation of the public interest. Protection of the forests against anarchic clearing by the peasants and depredation by town dwellers in search of fuel was the obvious purpose of the law which, however, had broader implications.

The general right of all citizens to use the products of the forests for necessary fuel, building materials, litter and other by-products, was established, and all were allowed to walk freely in forests, and make proposals for the latter's protection

[56] S.U. 1918/522.

(arts. 11, 12). The ultimate intention was to deliver litter, food for animals and similar products needed for peasant husbandry gratis, but " provisionally " these were to be paid for at the prices fixed by the local authorities (art. 18). As regards fuel and building materials, the sale of the products of the forests to citizens needing them was regarded as the normal and permanent procedure (arts. 19–20). Article 36 ff. laid down a general duty to work for the preservation of forests, or alternatively the payment of a special tax (art. 38). In practice, such rules simply meant a regulation of the traditional rights and duties of the peasants as regards the woods, under the new conditions created by the agrarian revolution, and, for the urban population, a new tax which the inflation prevented from becoming burdensome. During those years of extreme fuel shortage, elaborate restrictions could hardly prevent the forests near the industrial centres from being devastated. Even if the local Soviets had succeeded in exacting payment from those who took wood for fuel, inflation kept the official fuel price so low that this provision could hardly have checked consumption. But, for our purposes, the basic conception assumed by the legislator of the respective rights of the community and the individual citizen is more important than the immediate success of the act. As in other countries, the specific needs of forestry confronted the long-term with the short-term interest more clearly than in other economic spheres.[57]

The enactments of War-Communism discussed above established either principles for the administration of nationalised property by the State, or patterns of co-operative organisation laid down as suggestions, for instance, to further agricultural production. The individual citizen is involved only in so far as certain of his interests are recognised as principles directing public administration, for instance that of the forests, and, on the other hand, in so far as he is encouraged to make use of certain forms of co-operative organisation. In this sense, the legislation of War-Communism very clearly anticipated the conception of " social rights " which dominates the present constitution of the U.S.S.R. The individual citizen's right to make proposals for the improvement of forest cultivation, and a guarantee that he would not be discriminated against in the purchase of forest products from the State, the monopolist administrator of all forests, is certainly much nearer to a col-

[57] See below, Chapter IV, p. 103.

lectivist than to an individualist interpretation of Rights in general. The individual as such is granted rights to participate in various kinds of organisation and in so far as these organisations have not been shaped, or promoted, by the Soviet State itself, such rights may have to be enforced by law against the organisations themselves. This might happen not only to Consumers' Co-operatives, where the free access of every citizen might be deemed politically and economically desirable by the Soviet State, but even to organisations so little in favour with the new state as the Churches.[58] In the latter case, of course, the reason was not any interest of the State in the organisation as such, but simply the assumption that parochial self-government might prove less dangerous for the regime than the unrestricted power of the hierarchy. But it remains true that any rights granted to the individual were realised collectively.

### (c) The First Codifications of Soviet Law

The land laws and the Forest Act of 1918–19 may be regarded as type codifications of the whole Law concerning important aspects of national life. During the later codification period they were, indeed, replaced by enactments described as special Codes.[59] But, by their very genesis, they were individual enactments, called forth by the desire of the legislator to answer certain topical questions, although the answer was given in a comprehensive form. Only in two fields was codification of the Law in the more narrow, systematic sense desired: much later Stuchka [60] repeated the opinion that Matrimonial Law and Labour Law were bound to form the main elements of socialist Law. Criminal Law was regarded as bound "to wither away" with the need for political oppression, and Civil Law would go the same way once private enterprise was completely abolished. But as long as legal regulation of human relations was needed at all, it would be necessary in the relations of the citizen to his

[58] See the regulations of the People's Commissariat for Justice, of August 24, 1918 (S.U. 1918/685) on carrying through the Disestablishment Law. Articles 5 ff. provide for transferring all Church property destined by its very character for purposes of worship to the gratuitous use of those persons who actually were in possession. This virtually meant the Clergy and the established Parish Elders. But article 10 grants all inhabitants of the given locality belonging to the same denomination the right to countersign the protocol on the transfer of Churches, etc., to a given ecclesiastical community, and so to participate in the administration of that State property alongside those persons to whom it had originally been transferred. The regulation has been carried over in all subsequent Soviet legislation, including that of 1929.

[59] See below, Chapter IV, pp. 99 ff.

[60] Op. cit., 1931, pp. 37–8.

employer, the socialist State, as well as in those private relations which formed the material foundation of family life. One might give a much simpler explanation for the preference given to just these two fields of codification of Law : A government formed by a working-class party was bound to explain the principles according to which Labour must be organised. As regards Matrimonial Law that government found itself confronted with a very backward code, established according to ecclesiastical principles. Therefore, the Soviet simply as a progressive government, had to replace that code by new legislation according to general liberal and democratic principles. Lacking any parts of the former legislation applicable under the new conditions, this legislation had to be virtually complete. In Matrimonial Law, as distinct from that of Labour and Economics, the Soviet found itself in a field well prepared by progressive thought and experiment at home and abroad, and so it was not too difficult to achieve virtual completeness. The later history of the two codes of the War-Communism period was very different. Once War-Communism was dropped, the Labour Code was regarded as obsolete, or at best as an interesting theoretical experiment. But the Matrimonial Code was re-enacted at the time of the general codification in 1921–2, and in the 1926 Code it was developed consistently with its original line.[61] The difference in the fates of the two 1918 codes merely reflects the dual character of the Russian revolution. Whilst it was a complete and immediate success as a consummation of the democratic, anti-feudal revolution, it had to pass through a long period of trial and error before its own specific socialist features could achieve their realisation.

The Labour Code, of November 28, 1918,[62] in addition to its practical shortcomings, was burdened with some ideological prejudices, as was only to be expected in any first attempt. The central institution of this code was the " Duty to Work ", and this, apart from its general moral appeal, was realised in Soviet Russia only in connection with the actual needs of the war-emergency.[63] In consequence of such a tendency to generalise, the exception of groups forming the majority of the citizens, namely of agricultural and other Communes, of peasants and independent craftsmen, from the regulations of the Code had to be explained separately (Introductory art. VI).

[61] See below, Chapter IV, pp. 103–5.

[62] S.U. 1918/905.

[63] See above, p. 46.

In fact, the Code dealt merely with the contract of employment. Additional confusion was caused by article 6 which enumerated under the *Duty to Work* (i.e. the general civic duty) the various forms which the contract *for hired labour* might assume : organised and permanent collaboration in an enterprise, the offering of individual personal services (e.g. domestic ones), and the accomplishment of certain defined works (in the majority of cases this would correspond not to the contract of employment, but, say, to the hiring of certain services of a craftsman-entrepreneur). In fact, the Code dealt merely with the two first groups, i.e. the typical cases of the contract of employment : In all public as well as private enterprises the conditions of Labour were to be regulated by collective agreement between employer and trade union, subject to the confirmation by the People's Commissariat for Labour. If there was no agreement between employer and trade union, the latter might directly apply to the P.C. for Labour with the demand that its Draft Agreement (art. 8) be " confirmed ". The latter was the normal procedure for workers offering individual personal services (art. 9). For want of efficient trade union organisation for domestic workers, and since the P.C. for Labour could be interpreted as the representative of the public interest in domestic services, such regulations seemed reasonable from the trade union point of view and were in any case more favourable than those under the 1922 Code.[64] In the typical case of industrial employment, a regulation which rendered the participation of one of the parties to the agreement merely permissive and which demanded government consent in any case, meant that collective agreements were, in fact, established by the government. In spite of the fact that the authors of the Code reckoned with the continued existence of private entrepreneurs as employers of hired labour, there was no reference to a trade union right to strike—unless the " Duty to Work " should be interpreted as its negation. The individual worker was allowed to leave his employment only if the trade union recognised his reasons as weighty (art. 52), but there was no sanction against violating this obligation beyond the loss of unemployment benefit for one week (art. 53). Article 113 laid down the obligation of the worker to work conscientiously and to fulfil the established norms, in private as well as in nationalised

[64] That code itself left the matter open. But a decree of the C.I.K. of the R.S.F.S.R., of February 8, 1926 (S.U. 1926/57), referred (in point 12) the domestic workers to individual agreements with their individual employers (Danilova, op. cit., p. 63).

enterprises. Evidently, the continued existence of the former was regarded as a mere short-term transitional step towards full nationalisation, so that work in either was regarded as being equally in the public interest.

Corresponding to the Duty to Work was the right (art. 10) of "all citizens able to work . . . that their labour should be employed according to its special qualifications and that they should earn the remuneration established for this kind of work." In article 118 of the 1936 Constitution, the Right to Work is based upon the socialist organisation of all the national resources and systematic planning established since 1918, when the "Right to Work" was promised under conditions very similar to those under which non-socialist states might try to grant it. A rider to article 10 restricted the right of all citizens to employment according to their special qualifications by the provision that, if no work of this kind were available, the worker, with the assent of his trade union, might be sent to other kinds of work. The unemployed worker was obliged to accept any job within his special qualifications provided that the general conditions of the collective agreement were fulfilled (art. 24). If no such job was available, he was obliged to accept work outside his qualification until a more suitable job was found (art. 29). The 1922 Code did not mention the issue, but in 1927 it was solved in a very similar way [65] by the administration of unemployment benefit. In any case, the 1922 Code did not claim to establish a "Right to Work".

Apart from its rather confused general conceptions, the 1918 Code tried to solve the questions of the Contract for Labour, current in all countries, by giving maximum consideration to trade-unionist principles as regards hours, holidays, minimum wages, fines and other disciplinary matters. The wages were differentiated according to the qualifications of various groups of labour (art. 60), and there was also provision for remuneration of piecework and overtime (art. 62). But there was a definite tendency to keep the earnings within certain limits: no more than 150 per cent. of the normal wages might be paid for overtime (art. 64) and all other kinds of extra earnings were prohibited (art. 65). Persons who worked in two jobs (as many highly qualified specialists did at that time) were allowed to accept a salary only in one of them (arts. 66–7). This "egalitarian" tendency was contrary to the current needs of the Soviet State:

[65] See Danilova, op. cit., vol. II, p. 1508.

shortly after the enactment of the Code the People's Commissariat for Labour overruled its norms by a decree [66] "for making better use of the knowledge of specialists". They were allowed to draw remuneration for work done during their spare time in institutions other than their normal place of employment as well, though their total earnings were restricted to one and a half of the 5,000 roubles per month which was the maximum salary then in force. With doctors, teachers, research workers, etc., double employment became quite a normal way of compensating insufficient earnings, and remained so up to the middle 'thirties. Apart from cases of doctors whose advice might be useful in hospitals, such quibbling lip-service to egalitarian principles was certainly not the most rational way of using specialist knowledge.

Whilst the Labour Code failed by attempting to apply ideological principles quite beyond the economic reality, the Family Code, of October 17, 1918 [67] succeeded in facing very real tasks and became the basis for further developments. In 1918, the chief need was to make a break with the past, with the inequality of the rights of men and women, and the ecclesiastical regulation of Matrimony. The code contains elaborate rulings (arts. 71 ff.) on the conditions under which existing marriages might be declared null and void—evidently to counteract the tendency of the People's Judges to choose invalidation as the most thorough solution in all cases where existing wedlock seemed to be based upon violation of the elementary rights of women recognised by the Revolution. In the 1918 Code, as distinct from that of 1926, divorce was a simple and rather automatic procedure only if demanded by both partners (arts. 91–2). If demanded only by one side, it was granted by judicial decision (art. 98) though not bound by any formal conditions. Under the social conditions of 1918, the cause of the emancipation of women might have suffered if any husband had been free to divorce his wife when he liked, and thus to escape from his material obligations.

According to article 105 of the 1918 Code and to strict feminist conceptions, wedlock does not result in any property-relations,[68] although they may be agreed upon by the partners if so desired in accordance with the Law (art. 106 of the 1918, art. 13 of the 1926 Code). According to article 100 of the 1918 Code [68]

[66] Of March 20, 1919, S.U. 1919/174. [67] S.U. 1918/818.
[68] For the position under the 1926 Code, see below, p. 104.

the married couple were obliged to use a common name, whether it were the husband's or the wife's, or a combination of both.[69] There is, of course, complete equality of rights between legitimate and " illegitimate " children (art. 133 of the 1918, art. 25 of the 1926 Code). Parents are obliged to take care of the education of their children and especially for their training for socially useful work. All measures for the education of the children are to be jointly agreed upon by the parents (art. 151, 1918, art. 38, 1926). If they could not agree, then according to article 152 of the 1918 Code, the Court had to decide.

The legislation discussed in the last section centred round the administration of socialised productive resources. But the Law enacted in the two codes now under discussion dealt with rights and duties of individuals—although, as in any advanced Labour legislation, some of the rights of the individual citizen in this special field can only be realised through the trade union to which he belongs. In spite of the ideology surrounding the " Right to Work ", those individual rights enacted in the Labour Code cannot even be described as " social rights " in the sense of claims upon the organisation of public policy in the interests of the general welfare of all the citizens : just as in the Weimar Republic, the real right enjoyed by the Soviet worker under the 1918 Code was the right to be dealt with impartially at the Labour Exchange (called, for ideological reasons, " Department for the Distribution of Labour ") and, if unemployed, the right to unemployment benefit so long as no job offered was refused without due reason. In the Matrimonial Code, ideological reasons (in particular, the feminist ideal of complete material independence for the wife) were carried to the length of virtually thwarting the realisation of this ideal for the housewives not working outside the household, who were still in a majority. Strict separation of property acquired during wedlock would, in the case of divorce, involve depriving the housewife of all the fruits of her toils during the marriage. But the authors of the 1918 Matrimonial Code did not expect the typical Russian woman to remain a housewife. They hoped that the abolition of not only formal [70] but actual inequality in the earnings of men and women would proceed sufficiently swiftly to make the

[69] The latter was prohibited by the corresponding article 7 of the 1926 Code which allowed the partners to keep different family names while they were married.

[70] In this regard the Soviet legislation secured equal earnings for equal work done, and free access of women to any job. But it is another question how many women even to-day actually achieve the highest possible qualification.

complete division of income between husband and wife a mere realisation of individual freedom, and to render marriage " a union of the bodies and the souls, but not of the fortunes ", as a competent foreign observer [71] remarked. This was certainly not an anti-individualist tendency.

### (*d*) Legislative and Judicial Procedure during the First Revolutionary Period

Prior to the 1936 Constitution, the legislative functions of the Soviet government were very loosely circumscribed, and even to-day it is more difficult in the U.S.S.R. than elsewhere to establish a clear-cut distinction between administrative and legislative acts. Lenin [72] rejected any division of the administrative from the legislative powers of government as threatening the homogeneity and efficiency of the revolutionary regime, and this principle has been followed, although the principal objections to the liberal principle of the " balance of powers " should have ceased to carry weight once all the branches of government were controlled by one party. The decree of November 12, 1917 (new style) [73] ruled that laws could be enacted by the organ corresponding to Parliament, the V.C.I.K.,[50] as well as by the government, the Soviet of People's Commissars. The former's precedence was safeguarded by its unrestricted right to veto laws emanating from the government, but no provision was made to secure its previous assent. In fact, the first Decree on the Courts was enacted by the government for the reason that the latter was dissatisfied with the slow proceedings of the V.C.I.K. Commission,[74] where the influence of the Social Revolutionaries seems to have been stronger. In general, measures of fundamental importance, like the nationalisation of the banks, or the basic rules of Justice,[75] and all acts of codification of the Law were carried by the V.C.I.K. Other decrees concerning typical issues of legislation, like the introduction of Divorce [76] were published with the double signature of the presidents of the V.C.I.K. (Sverdlov) and of the government (Lenin)—without any notice in the official publication expressing that they acted

[71] Lambert, op. cit., vol. I, Introduction, p. 38.

[72] Vol. VII, pp. 43 ff.

[73] S.U.R. 1917/12, October 30, 1917 (old style).

[74] See Greengaus, op. cit., II, and Malkevich, op. cit. The tendency of these writers, as opposed to the attitude formerly prevailing, is to emphasise the conformity of the decree with Bolshevist principles. See below, note 82.

[75] For example the Statute on the Courts, see below, pp. 64 ff.

[76] S.U.R. 1917/8, No. 152, December 19, 1917.

with express consent of the bodies presided over by them. Soon [77] it was found necessary to enact a certain procedure for editing and publishing draft laws, to make sure that the legislative department of the Commissariat for Justice should have had an opportunity to look for formulations satisfactory from the juridical point of view. In spite of the haste over certain fundamental enactments the technique applied was quite effective, if measured by the standards of a revolutionary period. A decree like that on the introduction of the Western European calendar [78] provided thoroughly for all consequences of the transition in the various fields of civil life, leaving hardly any issues open to decision by the courts. The most serious defect of the method applied was that, lacking a clear distinction between the competences of legislation and administration, not only the government as a whole, but even individual members of the government might be tempted to exercise powers belonging rather to the legislative field. During the short period of coalition-government with the left-wing Social Revolutionaries some real discord in legislation arose from the vagueness of the delimitation of powers, and certain decrees of the Social Revolutionary Steinberg, the Commissar for Justice, are, indeed, the only documents of that period that fail completely to fall into line with the general policy of the Soviet at that time.

In discussing the general conceptions of Law prevailing during this period, we must above all bear in mind the actual position of the revolutionary government. Its basic attitude to the whole of the existing legislation was that the latter was the product of the defeated regime and should in no way be allowed to interfere with the realisation of what the new ruling classes regarded as Justice. On the other hand, it was technically impossible to enact more than a few fundamental laws, especially during the civil war. Very naturally, these laws dealt with those special features of the existing law which had long been opposed by all progressive elements in the country, and in their destruction or transformation the regime gave a clear indication of its general direction. Thus it might win that general support which the Revolution needed so much in that grave time. And should the worst come to the worst and the new regime be overthrown again, it might be difficult for a nominally Liberal government to repeal such laws as the Land Law,[14] the Divorce legislation,[76] the

[77] Ibid., No. 309, January 30, 1918.
[78] Ibid., No. 289, January 26, 1918.

introduction of Civil Registration of Marriages [79] and the disestablishment of the Church.[80] Such enactments might well remain as permanent achievements and memories even of a regime which would go down in history merely as another Paris Commune, or at best a Jacobin dictatorship, on a gigantic scale. The more new principles of this kind enacted, the better. Certainly there would have been no point in wasting valuable time and energy on the less spectacular and less topical issues concerning the detailed amendment of the existing Civil and Criminal Law which would only become necessary should a permanent Soviet order evolve.

But the everyday life of the people went on. This demanded the preservation of public order, and the settlement of the usual issues according to standards of Justice. In various centres new courts were formed on the initiative of the local revolutionary authorities,[81] with an evident tendency to get rid of the existing reactionary judiciary and of the extreme complexity and sloth of the old judicial procedure, involving, as it did, actual inequality of the citizens before the Law. In many cases the local Justice of the Peace (often a liberal intellectual) functioned as chairman of the new court, with elected assessors representing the various sections of the people. The new courts were not bound by the existing laws. But in some places the terms of a new codification of Criminal Law evolved, in the shape of lists of the offences to be prosecuted by the new courts, including disturbances of public order, theft, and black marketing. Some of the local courts thus spontaneously formed corresponded with the plans made by central Soviet legislation so closely that they were able to continue functioning after the enactment of the First Decree on the Courts.[82]

Being consciously based on the experiences of local initiative,[81] that decree provided for local courts, with a president and two assessors, provisionally nominated by the local Soviets, with the

[79] S.U.R, No. 160. [80] Ibid., No. 263, January, 23, 1918.

[81] See Greengaus, I, and Malkevich, op. cit.

[82] S.U.R. 1917/50, November 27, 1917. It has been traditional with Soviet historians of the earliest period to regard this decree as a compromise with the Social Revolutionaries and their tendency to preserve as much as possible of the existing laws and judges. This tradition is supported not only by Stuchka—whom present Soviet writers [74] may reject as " deviating " from true Leninism, but also by Kursky, (op. cit., 1919, p. 4), People's Commissar for Justice after the exclusion of the Social Revolutionaries from the government, and the most competent source imaginable. But it ought also to be kept in mind that there is, in Kursky's writing, not the slightest reference to leftist opinions of the Bolsheviks as regards abolition of the old codified Law for any other purpose than for new codification in accordance with their principles.

prospect of eventual democratic elections (art. 2). Special Revolutionary Tribunals were established in order to fight counter-revolution and profiteering (art. 8). According to article 5, laws enacted by the overthrown governments (the Tsarist and the provisional of Kerensky) should be regarded as valid only in so far as they had not been abolished by the Revolution and did not contradict the revolutionary conscience and consciousness of Justice. Laws actually abolished by the Revolution, it was explained, were those which contradicted the decrees of the new government (rather a truism) and also those contradicting the programme minimums of the Social Democrat and the Social Revolutionary parties. Thus these latter were elevated to the status of general sources of Law. They were, in fact, rather precise and might be regarded as a clear programme for legislation, or even for interpreting existing laws. It was not difficult for the judge to interpret, for example, any labour contract as if it contained a limitation of the working time to 8 hours daily, or to dismiss suits by the Church for obligatory contributions because they contradicted the programme minimums of both revolutionary parties which demanded Disestablishment. In any case, the Soviet government preferred itself to enact positive legislation demanded by these programmes rather than to let the revolutionary conscience of the local judge decide, say, which parts of former Church property ought to be confiscated like the property of any other landlord, and which, although nationalised, should be left at the disposal of the local believers, being by their very nature designated for the purposes of the cult.[80] Insurmountable difficulties would obviously have arisen from the quotation of two programme minimums as sources of Law, had not the coalition government come to a speedy end.

Much variety in local jurisdiction was bound to arise from the fact that the decree mentioned as additional sources of Law the "revolutionary conscience and consciousness of Justice". Evidently the men who drafted such decrees supposed, not unreasonably, that the judges would be inclined to apply the existing law wherever possible, and needed merely permission to deviate from it where its application might be regarded as contrary to the spirit of the new regime. Very soon an instruction by the People's Commissariat of Justice[83] introduced new principles of procedure. In criminal cases, the judges had

[83] S.U.R. 1917/8, No. 170.

to apply such punishment as was demanded " by the circumstances of the case and by revolutionary consciousness ", which had to replace the catalogue of punishment for various crimes formulated in the Tsarist Code. Parts of this Code were certainly obsolete from any progressive point of view, and many of the *lacunæ* thus arising were certainly better decided by commonsense than by long abstract explanations. But, under such circumstances, the Law inevitably lost the element of certainty and predictability.

Special legislation of the period dealt with individual reforms; some were desired on humanitarian grounds, such as the abolition of the normal jurisdiction for Juveniles under 18 years of age;[84] others were demanded by the revolutionary emergency, such as the restriction of the freedom of the Press by the establishment of a special Tribunal, with the participation of the journalists themselves.[85] Steinberg, the People's Commissar for Justice, established within the framework of his Commissariat a special Department of Cassation.[86] It had to examine appeals against judgments by the Revolutionary Tribunals and either to reject them, or to forward them to the V.C.I.K. Whether the latter, in quashing such a conviction, was exercising its right of amnesty or was acting in a supervisory judicial capacity was regarded as irrelevant—although not quite so irrelevant for the citizen concerned. Such an attitude illustrates how problematic the position of Law as a specific agency for regulating human behaviour was in those days even in the eyes of the man who was then regarded as the main advocate of the established position of lawyers.

In order to stabilise the new jurisdiction by a more competent authority than departmental decrees, the V.C.I.K., with Lenin's counter-signature, enacted the Statute on the Courts,[87] which is frequently described as the " second decree ". Jurisdiction was to proceed according to the existing laws on procedure, unless they contradicted " the sense of Justice of the toiling classes " (art. 8). There are no formal rules as regards admissible evidence: any evidence is admitted which, according to the circumstances of the case, may prove helpful in clearing it up

[84] S.U.R., No. 227, January 14, 1918.

[85] Ibid., No. 156, December 18, 1917, and No. 362, January 28, 1918 (the first being a departmental decree, the latter an enactment by the whole government, issued in consequence of Lenin's protest against the former).

[86] Ibid., No. 314, January 25, 1918.

[87] Ibid., No. 420, February 22, 1918.

(art. 14)—a principle preserved by Soviet Law up to the present day. As regards the Law to be applied, the existing Civil and Criminal Codes had to be followed unless they contradicted "socialist conceptions of Justice". And "considerations of Justice, not of formal law, have to guide the decisions in satisfying evidently just claims, independently of prescription and other formal considerations" (art. 36).

It is clear that the typical case which the authors of the statute had in mind was that of, say, the poor peasant who, under pressure from his rich *kulak* neighbour, and the State machinery friendly to the latter, had failed to pursue a claim which was regarded as just by public opinion of the village, in the forms prescribed by the Law. Now, after the victory of the Revolution, Justice had to be done. The local magistrate who might be from the ranks of the bourgeois intelligentsia, and so likely to sympathise with the "economically efficient" peasant, had to be prevented from using the existing law in the interests of those classes which it had hitherto served. The framers of the statute were not thinking of highly technical cases in Civil Law, contested between partners equally sympathetic—or otherwise—from the proletarian point of view, in which no moral conceptions of Justice could intervene. The former capitalist agents of production would be expropriated in any case—and the new public administration of economics, it was hoped, would function according to very simple principles which any intelligent worker participating in government might easily understand.[88] The conception that the fundamental problems of social administration were very simple, and could dispense with the elaborate legal machinery accessible only to specialists, was certainly helpful for those who had to build a new State machinery in face of the sabotage of the old specialists and especially the old jurists.[89] For even if the Bolshevists had seen all the implications of the tasks to be solved, such insight would have been of little value as long as there were no specialists able to handle complicated legal machinery whom the new regime could trust.

Distrust of the existing judges caused the introduction of one of the most characteristic institutions of Soviet Justice, the "People's Assessors" (*narodnje sassedatelji*). They were mentioned, by the way, in article 2 of the November Decree of 1917, for the institution had originated earlier from the various local

[88] See Lenin, vol. VI, pp. 266 ff. and *passim*.
[89] See Malkevich, op. cit.

attempts at building new revolutionary courts.[90] In article 29 of the February Statute the People's Assessors were regarded as organs for checking the President of the Court. They were allowed to remove him from his post at any stage of the proceedings and to reduce the sentence [91] as much as they desired, even to acquittal. There was no description of the procedure by which they were nominated—for, in theory, the President of the Court himself was a mere nominee of the Soviet and not bound to be a lawyer by profession. But the framers of the statute assumed that, in fact, he *would* be a lawyer, highly suspicious, if not for sympathies with the *ancien régime*, then for his inability to do Justice independently of formal considerations. So they reduced his influence as much as they could, even prohibiting him from explaining to the assessors in his *résumé* more than the rulings of the law as regards the punishment deserved. As the local Soviet could hardly avoid nominating a learned lawyer President of the Court, the term " People's Assessors " shows the intention of taking the other members of the Court from the ranks of non-professional people, with experience in social life and social organisation, but not in the Law.

On the other hand, there were guarantees against " revolutionary " arbitrariness of the individual court. According to article 8 the Judge, if deviating from existing law on procedure as " obsolete and bourgeois ", had to state the reasons for such procedure in his judgment, so that the higher judicial organs could check his interpretation of the new sense of Justice. Articles 4–5 of the Statute provided for the appeal for cassation of a judgment, article 6 for the establishment of a Supreme Judicial Control, composed of delegates from the lower courts elected for no more than one year, unless they were recalled previously by their electors or by their local Soviet.

[90] See above, p. 62. On attempts to establish the institution which, evidently, was regarded even by non-socialists as a desirable check to the Tsarist Judiciary, under the Kerensky regime, see Zelitch, op. cit., p. 260.

[91] Unification of Civil and Criminal Courts was regarded as a necessary element of the desired simplification of the legal machinery (see above, p. 62). The permanent emphasis on aspects of Criminal Procedure shows the main interest of the revolutionary legislator concentrated on those sides of the Law which the simple man of the people might most easily be concerned with. The emphasis on the special rights of the People's Assessors is a characteristic proof of the revolutionary nature of the institution: in later Soviet legislation all these rights are implied in the simple statement that the Assessors have equal rights with the President. Forming, thus, a majority of at least two to one, they can, if agreeing, overrule him in any decision. But in 1918 it was regarded as necessary explicitly to tell them that they were allowed to do so.

> If observing distortions of the Law or contradictions in the interpretation of the Law by various Courts of Appeal, the Supreme Judicial Control has to carry a principal decision which serves the Courts as a rule. . . . If the Supreme Judicial Control should be confronted by an insurmountable contradiction between the existing law [92] and the revolutionary sense of Justice, it will suggest to the legislative organ the necessity of amending the law. Only the legislative organ is allowed to overrule decisions of the Supreme Judicial Control.

Before it came into service, the Supreme Judicial Control was replaced by a normal Court of Cassation.[93] But the underlying conception of supervising the lower courts through some kind of self-government of the Judiciary was preserved in the codification of the Law of Procedure of War Communism, the Statute on the People's Courts, November 30, 1918.[94] According to article 1, the People's Courts hold three kinds of sessions: the President alone, for giving non-controversial decisions, granting divorce, ordering arrests, etc.; the President together with two People's Assessors, for the bulk of the civil and criminal cases; and the President jointly with six assessors, for judging crimes against life, grave bodily injury, rape, forgery of money or documents, bribery, or speculation in goods subject to State monopoly (it should be borne in mind that the more serious cases of the three last-mentioned types were not likely to come under the jurisdiction of the People's Court which, in contrast to the Revolutionary Tribunal, was not allowed to inflict capital punishment). The judges (Presidents of the Courts) had to be enfranchised (i.e. not members of the capitalist or landlord class) and were expected to have experience either as organisers in the labour movement, or in judicial work, preferably both (art. 12). In actual fact, when electing judges (art. 13) the local Soviet had to choose between professional revolutionaries and trade-union organisers on the one hand, and learned lawyers on the other. Normally it would select a bench made up of both types. The list of the candidates eligible for the office of People's

[92] The meaning of this sentence seems somewhat obscure, unless it is interpreted as a veiled rejection of the principle that pre-revolutionary law could be applied only if it did not contradict the " revolutionary consciousness of Justice ", established in article 36 even as regards the lowest courts. An interpretation of the sentence as referring to revolutionary Soviet legislation implies the assumption that the V.C.I.K. was ready to accept the judiciary not only as collaborators in legislation, but even as critics of its ability to express the fundamental demands of the Revolution. Such an assumption seems to any student of Bolshevist ideology much stranger than the possibility of Steinberg having succeeded in indirectly restricting the freedom granted to the lower judiciary, a freedom which he certainly disliked.

[93] By decree of July 18, 1918, S.U. 1918/589.

[94] S.U. 1918/889.

Assessors had to be made out by the labour organisations and the local Soviet (art. 15). The actual People's Assessors, called to participate in six consecutive sessions of the Court (art. 18), were chosen by lot (art. 17). Like juries in other countries, they were obliged to fulfil this civic duty.

A special Investigating Commission of six judges had to carry through a preliminary investigation before deciding whether there was sufficient ground for opening a public trial (art. 28). Defence was organised by a College of Advocates (art. 40), chosen by the Executive Committee of the local Soviet (as a rule, of course, from the ranks of existing barristers). The admission of counsel for the defence was obligatory in all cases of the serious crimes to be dealt with by a bench of seven judges, and in all those other cases where counsel for the prosecution was admitted (art. 43). In all other cases it depended on the decision of the Court. In Civil Law cases the President of the College of Advocates (against whose decision the parties might appeal to the Court) had to decide whether the participation of learned counsel was necessary (art. 46). It depended on the decision of the Court what evidence was deemed helpful to elucidate the case (art. 70).

The only written Law to be applied were the decrees of the Soviet government. If there was no Soviet law ruling the issue, " the Socialist consciousness of Justice " had to decide (art. 22). A footnote to this article prohibited reference, in giving judgment, to laws or judicial decisions of the *ancien régime*. Of course, no judge was prevented from letting his or her " Socialist consciousness of Justice " start out from the traditional, pre-revolutionary treatment of similar cases.[95] As distinct from the position under the former Statute on the Courts,[96] the judge

[95] See Stuchka, op. cit., 1931, p. 71. The assumption that " Law ", or at least codified law, has been abolished by the mentioned footnote is very widespread, not only outside the U.S.S.R., where it may be regarded as the ruling theory, but temporarily even within the U.S.S.R. (see below, p. 79). In view of the clear subordination of existing law to " Socialist consciousness to Justice " found in the previous decrees, it is very difficult for me to find any theoretical justification for that assumption. Certainly, since November 30, 1918, the application of such consciousness in direct contradiction to the laws of the *ancien régime* was further encouraged, but only with the perspective to a new codification which was envisaged by Kursky, already in a speech made in July, 1918. See Greengaus, op. cit., II, pp. 93 ff.

[96] See above, p. 66, Zelitch (op. cit., pp. 16–17 and 24) seems right when stating, contrary to Krylenko, that the change from the first to the last decree was due at least as much to a changed attitude of the Bolshevists themselves as to the fact that the Social Revolutionary People's Commissar for Justice, Steinberg, had drafted the first ones. Lenin was sufficiently educated as a lawyer to be able to criticise the decrees he had to countersign, especially if drafted by a political opponent, and Steinberg could do little against a direct opposition of his Bolshevik deputees.

was no longer obliged to explain what adaptations of the former law to the new circumstances he had deemed necessary, and for what reasons the former law was regarded as contrary to the socialist consciousness of Justice. This encouraged judicial freedom, and made the People's Assessor (or the President whose experience had been only that of an organiser in the Labour Movement) independent of his learned colleagues. But judicial freedom was encouraged still further: there were no limits to the right of a judge to mitigate punishment provided by the (Soviet) law even below the statutory minimum, provided that he stated explicitly his reasons for such a step (art. 23).

While there was a desire to encourage judicial freedom, there was certainly no intention of regarding the temporary absence of a complete code of laws as more than an inevitable transitional stage. On the contrary, official contemporary Soviet opinion [97] explained the possibility of abolishing the old laws by the growth of the new Soviet Law, and the resolution of the VIth Extraordinary Soviet Congress, November 1918 [98] declared, that "during the year of revolutionary struggle the Russian working-class has evolved the fundamental laws of the R.S.F.S.R., strict observance of which forms a necessary condition for the development and strengthening of the power of the workers and peasants." It is more questionable whether this was a complete system of Law—in spite of the enactment, up to September 1918, of 40 laws devoted to problems of Criminal Law, and 69 other decrees containing criminal sanctions. But though the Judge was granted plenty of freedom in order to fill the numerous *lacunæ* in the Law of the transitional period, there was an evident desire to evolve a homogeneous spirit in the new jurisdiction.

The popular desire to simplify judicial procedure had resulted in the abolition of formal appeal as well as of the thorough division between Criminal and Civil Law Courts. But any party to the proceedings, the local Soviet included, was entitled to demand cassation of any judgment by the "Soviet of People's Judges" (art. 81). The latter corresponded to the Judicial Control of the February Statute, but within the more modest framework of a regional Court of Appeal based upon self-government of the Judiciary. The Congress of People's Judges of the *Gubernium* (i.e. only the permanent judges, and not the People's Assessors) chose the President and a number of permanent

[97] Kursky, op. cit., 1919, p. 9. [98] S.U. 1918/908.

Assessors for this higher court, whilst the other People's Judges took turns in fulfilling assessoral duties. The "Soviet of People's Judges" might quash judgments of the People's Courts on the grounds of wrong application of the material law or the Law of Procedure, or incomplete investigation, but also on the ground of "evident injustice" (art. 89). Thus the distinction between this type of "cassation" and ordinary appeal seems somewhat artificial. A case, in which the first judgment was annulled, had to be referred for renewed trial to another bench of the People's Court, which was bound by the decision of the Soviet of People's Judges (art. 92). Further, the bench that had rendered the first judgment was sent a copy of the decision "as a directive" (art. 93).

The most characteristic differences between present-day Soviet Criminal procedure and that of other continental countries [99] are to be found in the enactments of the first revolutionary period which we have just discussed. The dependence of the Judiciary on the same State organs as those responsible for the enactment and execution of the laws is inherent in the Soviet rejection of the dogma of the division of power. On the other hand, ever since the inception of the Soviet regime, it has been attempted to render this dependence sufficiently indirect to enable the Judiciary, whilst administering the Law strictly in the general interests of public policy, to protect legality against the whims of individual public authorities. In the first period of Soviet jurisdiction this purpose was pursued by creating a self-governing judiciary, and by subjecting the lower courts, dependent as they might be on the local Soviets which elected them, to the rulings of regional "Soviets of People's Judges", and of higher judicial organs beyond the influence of a local Soviet.

The institution of People's Assessors, instead of the juries of Western countries and pre-revolutionary Russia, had already reached a stage of full development during the period under consideration. An analogy might be found in the German "*Schoeffen*", as a (right-wing) reaction against the juries in 1924. But the Soviet People's Assessors have been introduced to weaken the position of the traditional Judiciary, not to strengthen it, as in Germany. In both cases the powers of the popular assessor were larger than those of the former juries. In the

[99] The characteristics noticed by Zelitch, op. cit., pp. 11–13, are seen from the Anglo-American point of view, and some of them are common to most continental legal systems, including orthodox capitalist ones.

Soviet court their rights were equal to those of the learned President of the Court, without any distinction between questions of fact and questions of Law. Such a distinction would have been inconsistent for the Soviet which then regarded Socialist consciousness of Justice as the supreme source of Law, apart from the rather restricted field already covered by Soviet legislation which any intelligent working-class organiser could master. However, the functions attributed to the popular assessors, or co-judges, demanded a qualification superior to that of the man-in-the-street, merely chosen by the lot. Such qualification in social service, although not narrowly judicial, might involve a certain political bias not undesirable from the point of view of the regime.

Two further characteristics of present Soviet procedure, already fully developed in the Statute of November, 1918, are the strict division between investigation, preliminary inquiry, and decision in public trial ; and the supervision of the lower tribunals by the mechanism of cassation. Only one of the distinct characteristics of modern Soviet procedure, the specific function of the Public Attorneys, was left to be developed in a later period.[100]

From its very beginnings Soviet justice rejected a formalist approach to questions of Procedure. Acquittal of a guilty defendant in consequence of his dexterity in evading the law, or in making use of shortcomings of the Law of Evidence, was regarded as a feature of bourgeois justice which ought to be avoided by the new judicial organs. After the former law had lost its authority and before Soviet legislation had become sufficiently broad, there were plenty of *lacunæ* in the Law to be covered by the " Socialist consciousness of Justice ". So the principle " *nulla pœna sine lege* " could not compete with the much more popular " *nullum crimen sine pœna* ". Even in later periods, when the " Socialist consciousness of Justice " was replaced by comprehensive and codified Soviet Law, and the principle " *nulla pœna sine lege* " accepted, the Law, by the institution of analogy, was safeguarded against any attempts at evasion.[101] The temporary tribute paid by the Bolshevists to the supposed superiority of the common sense of the man in the street over any codified law may be regarded as one of the many ephemeral ideologies that accompanied the period of War-Communism. But the juxtaposition of Soviet justice to

[100] See below, p. 122.

[101] See below, pp. 107–9.

legal formalism was not ephemeral. In no stage of the development of Soviet justice has learned counsel been regarded as more than an expedient to prevent the defendant feeling that his fate might be decided by a machinery incomprehensible to him, and the institution of People's Assessors worked much more efficiently in this direction. Not in elaborate legal machinery, but in thorough investigation of all relevant circumstances of the case is Justice sought.

In discussing how far the Soviet courts of the revolutionary period succeeded in doing Justice to the personal circumstances of the individual offender, procedure taken against the avowed enemies of the regime under conditions of civil war must be omitted. On both sides many thousands died for their political convictions, either on the battlefields or before the execution squads, and neither side differentiated between these two aspects of war, although the latter was carried through by a special procedure intended to identify the irreconcilable enemies of the regime. During the first period, the Soviet court dealt rather leniently with non-political crime. Amongst 61,128 judgments available for Kursky's analysis,[102] 35 per cent. were sentences to imprisonment (four-fifths of them under conditions of probation), 8 per cent. to socially necessary work without imprisonment, 4 per cent. to fines and 10 per cent. to other punishments (chiefly admonitions)—the rest acquittals. Nearly three-quarters of the sentences to imprisonment were for offences against property; even for speculation (i.e. dealings on the black market) only 17 per cent. of the convicted were imprisoned, and 76 per cent. merely fined (the most serious cases of speculation went to the Revolutionary Tribunals). Even the Supreme Revolutionary Tribunal, whose only function was dealing with treason, or with former leading agents of the Tsarist Ochrana, passed less sentences of death than of imprisonment, and further commuted the majority of the former by the application of amnesty.[103]

In order to appreciate the general Soviet conceptions of Justice during this period it must be realised that the opposition to the principle of division of powers prevented any conception of a rule of Law as opposed to Administration. The revolutionary dictatorship was strict and its measures interfered with many of the rights of individual citizens. But a check was kept on local organs of Administration to prevent them from exercising

[102] Op. cit., p. 10. [103] Ibid., pp. 13–14.

emergency justice according to their own estimation of the needs of the revolutionary state. Although the conditions of " War-Communism " made such a check exceptionally difficult to exercise, the intentions which underlay the legislation of the first period of the Revolution were certainly not lawless.

Since the new regime distrusted the old codes without being able immediately to replace them by new statutes, the judges had little codified law at their disposal. In many cases the Soviet judge had to decide, in the terms of article 1 of the Swiss Civil Code, " according to the rule he would establish if called upon to legislate." Instead of " well-experienced teaching and tradition " he had to follow the minimum programme of the Socialist party and the " Socialist consciousness of Justice " of the people by whom he had been elected. But he had to decide according to the needs of a period of revolutionary transition. The programme minimum of the Russian Social Democrat Party was certainly less vague than the long enumerations and explanations of " fundamental rights " in, for instance, the Weimar constitution, which was intended to guide the interpretation of the Law. Doubtless, there was extreme elasticity, and locally even arbitrariness in the application of Soviet Law of the first revolutionary period. Doubtless, too, its certainty did not satisfy criteria justified in normal times. But undoubtedly it followed certain common standards. And there could be no codification before experience, under the new conditions, had been collected.

### (*e*) Theoretical Conceptions of Law during the Period of War-Communism

The first systematic exposition of the Soviet conceptions of Law is given in the *Leading Principles of the Criminal Law of the R.S.F.S.R.*, published December 12, 1919, by the People's Commissariat for Justice, as a general directive in the guiding principles for local courts.[104] The document deals only with general principles, for there had not yet been time to elaborate a Special Part, on the definition of different crimes, based on judicial

[104] S.U. 1919/590. The document has been published in the official collection of laws, but with no other signature than that of the People's Commissar for Justice. So it formed, formally, a mere departmental instruction, not a law. But, in spite of recent tendencies among Soviet theorists to disparage its importance, there can be no doubt that, at the time, it was regarded as an official expression of the principles jurisdiction ought to be guided by. So it was also received by a special departmental decree of the Ukrainian Soviet Republic, of August 4, 1920.

experience.[105] These principles clearly expressed the authors' assumption that stabilised and codified Law is a normal condition in a socialist society. In a revolution, says the preamble, the old Law breaks down together with the old state. In the course of the revolution, the armed working-classes exercise compulsion, at first according to expediency in the individual case, " but the success of their struggle results in general measures, brings them into a system, and creates new Law " in the interest of the rational working of the new state. Law is defined as " a system (regulation) of social relations corresponding to the interests of the ruling classes and secured by the latter's organised power." [106] It is remarkable, that even at the peak of the revolutionary struggle the Bolsheviks avoided giving a definition of Law that would cover *only* the relations between ruling and ruled classes, although their main interest focused round the changes which the revolution wrought in these relations. Besides, these " Leading Principles " were intended as guidance for the ordinary courts, from which most political crimes had been removed to the Revolutionary Tribunals.

Criminal Law is defined as that branch of Law which defends the social structure of the existing society against violations, called crimes,[107] by repressive measures, called " penalties ". Crime is defined as a violation of the order of social relations which is protected by Criminal Law (art. 5). At that time, there was no codified enumeration of all those social relations protected by the Law. So it was the Judge who had to decide whether or not a certain action was dangerous to society, and to convict when he decided that it was. This principle of Soviet law has not been abolished by the later codifications.[108] Penalties are compulsory measures by which the government protects a certain order of social relations against future infractions by the criminal himself or by others (art. 7). Apart from their deterrent

[105] There is not the slightest justification, in the document and in the general line of Soviet thought at the time (see above, pp. 68–9), for the interpretation, current in most foreign critics, that a Special Part was regarded as " superfluous " (see Freund, op. cit., p. 9, and Maurach, op. cit., 1933, p. 161). It was simply not yet available.

[106] For a recent Soviet definition of Law, see below, pp. 243–4.

[107] In using the term " crime ", it ought to be kept in mind that Soviet Law knows no principial graduation of offences. " Delinquencies " or " offences " would be a more fitting translation of the Russian term " crime " (*prestuplenje*). In a study specially dealing with problems of Criminal Law I should prefer such a translation. But in our general survey it is more important to make quite clear that we are dealing with offences under Criminal Law, including the most serious ones. Therefore we use " Crime ".

[108] See below, p. 107.

effect, they achieve this purpose by re-education as well as by the isolation and, in extreme cases, by the extermination, of the criminal.[109] Crime, in a class-divided society, originates from the latter's social structure, not from the personal "guilt" of the criminal. Thus, punishment ought not to "redeem the guilt". It ought to be restricted to the demands of expediency without inflicting upon the criminal injurious and needless sufferings.[110] In this rejection of a specific "penal" character of what is called "penalty", the Leading Principles of 1919 [111] went to the length of including in the catalogue of suggested "penalties" (art. 25) compulsory acts which involved no sufferings of any kind, and which were in no way deterrent to reasonable beings, such as compulsory attendance at evening classes. Of the alternatives of re-education and complete isolation (of which extermination is the extreme form), the Leading Principles, being destined for the ordinary courts, emphasise the former.

Soviet Law [112] decides the degree of protection to be applied according to the extent to which the personality of the criminal as well as his offence endanger society. The 1919 principles took into account the class position of the offender as important in assessing that danger. But, in contrast to a later phase in the development of Soviet Criminal Law,[113] they avoided going to the length of regarding class situation in itself as an aggravating or extenuating circumstance. It merely helped to bring the offence committed into its proper perspective. In deciding the necessary penalty for an offence the judge should make certain whether the offence was committed by a person belonging to the property-owning class with the intention of creating or preserving social privileges, or by a destitute person in need or starving.[114] Such distinctions serve to underline the Soviet point of view [115]

[109] Articles 8–9 of the Leading Principles of 1919. The U.S.S.R. principles of 1924 (see below, pp. 112 ff), in article 4, and the present, 1926, Code (art. 9), take exactly the same line—in spite of the change of terminology from "penalty" to "measure of social defence".

[110] Article 10 of the 1919 principles, repeated in article 26 of the 1922 Code.

[111] The distinction between "penalties" and other measures of social protection, as temporarily attempted by the 1922 principles (see below, pp. 111–12) evidently lay outside the consideration of the authors of the 1919 principles, although the latter did not go to the length of enumerating non-judicial (e.g. medical) protective measures. What they had in mind when speaking of "penalties" was evidently what the authors of the 1924 U.S.S.R. principles were to call "measures of social protection".[109]

[112] Article 11 of the 1919 principles, article 24 of the 1922 Code, and article 30 of the 1924 U.S.S.R. principles.

[113] See below, p. 113.

[114] Article 12 of the 1919 principles.

[115] For its elaboration in later codification, see below, pp. 114–18.

that severer oppression is needed against the enemy of the political and social regime than against the citizen who infringes his fellows' interests from personal motives. And this is the general trend of all Soviet Justice. It is assumed that it is much easier to re-educate a person who has violated social standards generally recognised in his own milieu than to induce a person to drop activities which his situation has accustomed him to regard as legitimate.

In spite of a theoretical distinction between preparation (art. 19), attempt (art. 18), and accomplished crime (art. 17), the necessary measures of repression are determined not by the stage which the realisation of the crime has reached, but by the degree of the danger to society. Attempt, in article 18, is defined as that stage in which the criminal has taken all possible steps to secure the criminal result, the realisation of which is prevented by factors independent of his will. So it corresponds to " accomplished attempt " as understood in the 1922 Criminal Code which might be punished on a level with the accomplished crime (art. 14). Mere preparation, or unaccomplished attempt from which the defendant desisted while his action could still influence the event, according to the Leading Principles of 1919 would have been regarded as a proof of his less dangerous character. The conception of an objective " guilt ", embodied in the objective injury done to society and to be " redeemed " by punishment, is, in the 1919 Principles, even more consistently eliminated than in the 1922 Code which (art. 19) regarded non-achievement of the criminal result at least as an attentuating circumstance. The view that the subjective criminal intention is the actual object of legal repression clearly emanates from the 1919 principles as well as from the commentators of the 1922 Code, who found the justification for punishment particularly in its influence upon the subjective chains of causation leading eventually to similar crimes.[116] Thus, subjective guilt as a basis of punishment has been recognised by original Soviet criminology.

The system of punishment established in article 25 of the Leading Principles is essentially identical with that later established in article 20 of the Criminal Code of 1922. Already it includes such characteristic penal measures of Soviet law as forced labour at the normal place of employment, i.e. temporary loss of the right to leave the employment together with the duty to pay part of the earnings as a fine ; loss of a certain office, or of the

[116] Piontkovsky, op. cit., 1924, pp. 176 ff.

right to hold public office in general; and exclusion from exercising a profession. It also includes measures that suggest a lack of distinction between penal jurisdiction and the general action of public opinion, such as boycott. Conditional sentence is provided for in article 26 (arts. 53–4 of the 1922 Code). The death penalty, then regarded as a mere emergency measure reserved for application by the Revolutionary Tribunals, lay outside the scope of the Leading Principles which were intended as a guide for the ordinary courts. Article 1 of the Statute on Revolutionary Tribunals [117] says: "The Tribunal is established for the special purpose of dealing with counter-revolutionary and all other actions threatening the achievements of the October Revolution. Correspondingly the tribunals are not limited in their competence to decide the measures of repression". It seems correct to infer from this ruling that the measures of repression applicable in the case of ordinary crimes were regarded as limited, and that the lack of fixed norms for the punishment of counter-revolutionary crimes was regarded as an emergency measure. Also in the case of the latter crimes, only the measure of repression, and not the establishment of the guilt, was left to free judicial decision. There were clear rulings on the definition of those crimes reserved for the Revolutionary Tribunals [118] and also on the procedure to be applied by the latter, including the establishment of special Courts of Cassation.[119] No judgment of the local Revolutionary Tribunal might be carried out without the defendant or any other interested citizen having the opportunity to appeal to that Court.[120] Yet the decision of the Revolutionary Tribunal "ought to be guided exclusively by the circumstances of the case and the demands of revolutionary consciousness." [121] Judicial decision, in these cases, was intended to be unhampered by any written law, and

[117] Of April 12, 1919, S.U. 1919/132.

[118] According to the law of May 4, 1918 (S.U.R. 471), counter-revolution, pogroms, corruption, use of falsified documents and espionage. All other crimes were to be transferred to the ordinary courts (arts. 2–3).

[119] The decree of June 11, 1918 (S.U.R. 545) established a Department of Cassation, at the V.C.I.K., to deal with appeals from the judgments of the Revolutionary Tribunals. In spite of the tribute paid, in its designation, to the principle of non-division of powers, the Department acted in a way very similar to that of a normal court of cassation, referring cases where the appeal was allowed to another bench of the Tribunal or (if the latter had wrongly assumed jurisdiction) to the ordinary courts. The right of the Department to mitigate the penalty made the delimitation of cassation from appeal even more problematic. The statute of April, 1919, established a Court of Cassation at the V.C.I.K.

[120] Articles 27, 28, 30 of the Statute of April, 1919.

[121] Ibid., article 25.

the principle of generality and predictability of the working of the Law appears to have been dropped, at least for the procedure of emergency jurisdiction.

Whether the results of dealing with the individual offender according to his potential danger to the regime could be said to correspond to generally accepted moral standards depended on the circumstances of the case. Most people would regard it as morally unjust when, for instance, amongst a number of White officers taken prisoner together, those who were ready to compromise with the regime were reprieved, whilst those who continued in the political principles in which they had been educated were shot. Such situations were visualised by Stuchka when he pointed out that there was no question of personal "guilt", but merely of the defence of society. In other cases the same principle might result in a degree of consideration for the conscientious objector [122] then unattained in any other country: not only was he allowed to have his military obligation transformed into some alternative service by judicial decision,[123] but the court had to consult the Joint Council of Religious Communities and Groups on the sincerity of the individual objector as well as on the compatibility of any suggested alternative form of civic service with his religious belief, having due regard for his past as well as for the teachings of sectarian literature. And this was done by a regime that officially regarded religion as "dope for the people"! In enacting such legislation the State consulted its own interests, since most of the extreme Christian sects had a distinct anti-Tsarist record, while the main alternative form of social service offered to the conscientious objector was nursing in hospitals for epidemics, a job which the conscientious objectors would do much better than others who were ready to let themselves be conscripted. In any case, the Soviet State could take such general and individual interests into account because it accepted the danger to society of the individual law-breaker as the standard according to which he should be treated, instead of some assumed sanctity of the Law.

It is not difficult to understand why the distinctly oppressive

[122] See the special decree, signed by Lenin and Stuchka, of Jan. 4, 1919 (S.U.R. No. 70).

[123] As distinct from the procedure at present established in this country, no special tribunal, but the Moscow People's Court, with competence for all the country, had to decide such cases. This may have formed a main reason for the participation of religious experts in the procedure.

side of the Law should provide the most necessary starting point for theoretical systematisation. Revolutionary conditions themselves demanded it, for they had made any traditionalist approach to Law impossible. By force of habit people might continue to respect each other's property rights, or even to punish murderers without special comment. But a new fundamental conception was needed to legitimise shooting, as an enemy of the State, the man who defended all the hitherto "sacred foundations of society", or to explain why, in spite of all theoretical criticism of property in general, theft was still harmful to society, and to demonstrate the need for organised Justice in general to people who had been accustomed to regard the existing courts as strongholds of their oppressors, and who held revolutionary initiative was the best means of getting rid of them. So Criminal Justice had to be explained theoretically—whilst the same government, in enacting its Codes on Labour, on Family, on Forests and on Agriculture, took little trouble to establish foundations of Law. In those cases the need for it was self-evident. But on the other hand, the large degree of freedom originally left to judicial decision in the criminal field made the theoretical instruction of the judge the more urgent, if some common approach to crime was to be preserved.

But in general, and not only in times of revolutionary emergency, Criminal Law is one of the most problematic fields of Law, since some consideration for the merits of the individual case has been accepted everywhere as a paramount duty of the Judge. More important from the theoretical point of view is the interpretation of Civil Law, especially for Marxists who regard the regulation of economic relations as the basic regulation of social life. From Stuchka's *Leading Principles on Criminal Law* hardly any inferences can be drawn as regards the alleged lawless character of Proletarian Dictatorship.[124] But ten years later, under the influence of theoretical fashions to be discussed,[125] the same author came to the conclusion that "from November, 1917 to 1922, Law was formally lacking", apart from its underground domination of the continued commodity exchange on the black market.[126] Unless the commodity exchange conception of Law [125] is taken for granted, "underground law" lacked certainty and generality to a much greater degree than the

[124] See above, p. 68. Stuchka's definition of Criminal Law supposes the existence of other branches of Law, working by other expedients than reprisals.

[125] See below, Chapter V.

[126] In his article "Civil Law", *Great Soviet Encyclopedy*, vol. XVIII, p. 741.

attempts of the People's Judges to conform to a "Socialist consciousness of Justice" embodied in the regime they stood for.

In order to answer the question whether or not, in 1917–22, there was Civil Law in Soviet Russia, it is relevant to know whether general conceptions of the "Socialist consciousness of Justice" can be derived from the legislative activity of the Soviet Government at the time. There can be not the slightest doubt that such conceptions existed. During the period of War-Communism were enacted not merely some hundreds of decrees, but the very elements of a new legal order. How otherwise can it be understood that, when the need arose, it proved possible hurriedly to enact a Civil Code [127] and a complete system of codification of nearly all the branches of Law which has served the needs of a large state for more than two decades. This argument becomes all the more convincing when it is realised that during the period of War-Communism no one worried about attempting a systematic elaboration of the principles which the new legislation was to follow: the principles enforced themselves, by the very logic of the position of the new government, in some hundreds of decrees each conceived "purely according to the needs of the case", and this is the best proof that the principles corresponded to the actual situation, not to some ephemeral ideology.

The principles emerging from Soviet legislation, in the sphere of Civil Law, appear at the very beginning in the fundamental decrees embodying the original conception of Soviet economics, and were comparatively little influenced by the actual emergency of civil and external war.[128] In the original land legislation and in the Decree on Workers' Control (if we assume for a moment that it had been realised and immediate wholesale nationalisation might thus have been avoided),[129] we can clearly discern a dissociation of the traditional elements of the institution of Private Property [130] into those which, as regards certain means of production, remain, although in restricted form, and those that are abolished. The right to dispose of property is abolished explicitly in the case of landed property, of shares and all titles to rent, and implicitly as regards the larger industrial enterprises

[127] See section (*b*) of the next chapter.

[128] See above, section (*b*) of the present chapter.

[129] Of course, it is possible to reject such a possibility as completely unreal and to regard Workers' Control, as present Soviet opinion does, as a mere transitional step towards full nationalisation. But for Lenin's original intentions, see above, p. 38.

[130] See, for example, article 58 of the Soviet Civil Code of 1922.

subjected to Workers' Control and to the joint responsibility of entrepreneurs and Shop Stewards for the preservation of the equipment of the factory.[131] The right of possession continues, as regards agricultural land, with the restriction that no hired labour can be used and that the amount of land in the possession of any individual family is subject to corresponding limitations. As regards factories under the regime of Workers' Control, the right of possession—and the corresponding participation in the management of the factory—is reduced to that share granted to the individual entrepreneur, including the right to appeal against decisions of the local Workers' Control to the latter's superior organs. The right of usufruct was originally limited only by taxation, as in many other countries. In the further course of nationalisation the remaining rudiments of private property in large industrial enterprises were converted into a duty to exercise managerial functions, rewarded by a normal managerial salary, in the factory previously controlled under the title of ownership.[132] Usufruct of those kinds of private property that by the very nature of rent are deprived of the productive attribute of possession, was confined to those cases demanding consideration for avoiding special hardships.[133]

A fundamental reform in the Civil Law of the period was the Abolition of the Right of Inheritance.[134] The Abolition Act of 1918 differs from the corresponding articles of the Civil Code of 1922 [135] mainly in its emphasis: In the revolutionary atmosphere the general term "abolish" was used for what, in 1922, became mere restriction of the Right of Inheritance, recognised in principle. The 1918 exemptions from the general rule of abolition became a restricted right, but there is little actual difference in the Law—apart from that shift in propagandist emphasis. Article 2 of the law of 1918 granted to the nearest relatives of the deceased (direct ascendants or descendants, brothers and sisters, wife or husband) the right to be supported out of the estate, with priority before all other creditors of the deceased (art. 8), if they were unable to work and did not possess the subsistence minimum. Independently of their ability to work and of their private means they were allowed to take

[131] See above, p. 43. [132] See above, p. 48. [133] See above, p. 44.

[134] S.U.R. 1917/8, No. 456, April 27, 1918.

[135] Articles 416 ff. The differences, apart from those mentioned in the text, concern occasional exemptions (in the case of Concessions) from the 10,000 roubles limit, and in the explicit statement (art. 421) of the principle only hinted at in article 9 of the law of 1918, namely that the implements of a non-exploiting husbandry were not affected by that limit.

G

immediate possession of the estate, especially if it consisted merely of the implements of private husbandry, or of the tools and husbandry of a small craftsman or peasant who did not employ hired labour, or if its value did not exceed 10,000 roubles. In these cases the estate immediately passed into the possession of the surviving spouse or other relatives, cases of dispute being settled by the courts. When, in 1922, the Right of Inheritance was "recognised" instead of being "abolished", brothers and sisters were excluded from the circle of those relatives automatically admitted to inheritance (art. 418), and wills were admitted, provided that they distributed the estate only amongst those next relatives admitted by the law of 1918 to intestate inheritance. All persons who during the last year had been maintained by the deceased were admitted to inheritance, testate or intestate, provided they were unable to work, or needed support. Such changes are indeed small amendments to new legislation, resulting naturally from experience.

The example described illustrates a main function of the period of War-Communism: the growth of new conceptions of Law hardly veiled in a phraseology conditioned by the feelings aroused by the recent upheaval, and the need to stress the alteration rather than the preservation of elements of the past. From the point of view of the Law, and of those who have to live under its rule, an "exemption from the abolition of the Right of Inheritance" does not differ from a "restricted recognition of the Right of Inheritance"—provided the actual content of the norms is identical.

In earlier sections of this chapter we have learned that those rights enacted by systematic codification of Law during the period under discussion can be classed as rights of the individual citizens although, as in any modern society, sectional organisation was a chief means of their realisation. Those approaches to the conception of "social rights" (i.e. guiding principles for the administration of public property in the interest of the citizens), that were enforced by the needs as well as by the ideologies of War-Communism, lacked the necessary backing of material prosperity. The one "social right" virtually realised, though not without interruptions, was the right to get something on ration-books. But the very process of consumption and of bureaucratic distribution of most of the accumulated riches of the country, without which the War could not be won and the ration-books honoured, prevented any development of the productive resources of the country which would have been necessary to make " social rights " to the products of socialist economics a reality. When the State could not supply fuel, people threatened by frost would not respect the integrity of the nationalised forests. Nor would the more diligent of the peasants readily enter *kollkhoses* without further enticements than State-subventions in consideration of the stricter supervision of food-deliveries to the State. The socialist elements of the new Law remained on paper. They were so discredited that even later, when most of them were resumed, people were afraid to refer to this period during which most of the new ideas had been born. What, with amendments, has remained of the fundamental enactments of the first period of the Revolution were the enactments of individual rights. Had the Russian Revolution ended in 1921–2, by failing to introduce the N.E.P. at the right moment, it would have gone into history as another of the great bourgeois democratic revolutions, with the principles of 1793 adapted to the conditions of the twentieth century.

## CHAPTER IV

# SOCIETY AND LAW UNDER THE NEW ECONOMIC POLICY

## (a) The Origins and the Legislative Progress of the N.E.P.

During the period of War-Communism, the limitations of all attempts at social reconstruction, beyond the needs of the war emergency, had been veiled by an ideology that described the necessities of that emergency as fundamental socialist achievements. From the point of view of this ideology, the end of War-economics meant a retreat [1]—although, from the point of view of the development to come, it meant the starting-point of real social reconstruction. From the point of view of the outside observer it means the beginning of that stage of economic development from which non-Russian attempts at social reconstruction may learn.[2] The Bolshevists themselves did not see this at first : [1] for them it was a necessary retreat, made in order to satisfy the demands of the people and to preserve the regime.

All the sufferings connected with the regime of War Communism had been willingly borne as a means to winning a war which the majority of the people deemed necessary : for the workers it meant defence of their political power, which opened for them the way to social progress, whereas for the peasant majority it meant defence of the land which the Revolution had taken from the landlords. But once the War and its emergencies were passed, War Communism lost its inherent justification, and the ideologies that had been developed to prove that it was a due consummation of socialist ideals failed to justify its inefficient expedients. For the peasants the question was now how to enjoy the land they had won. Unless they were allowed to do it in their own way, they would drop the Bolsheviks, just as the French *bourgeois* had dropped the Jacobins when, after the victory of Fleurus, the latter had ceased to be the indispensable organisers of victory, and had become a mere obstacle to the enjoyment of the fruits of victory. Lenin succeeded in 1921 where Robespierre had failed in 1794 : the

[1] Cp. Lenin, vol. IX, pp. 254 ff. [2] See below, pp. 266–7.

revolutionary party proved able to withdraw from measures it had taken partly to meet a passing emergency, partly in pursuit of utopian ideologies born out of that emergency.[3] So the country was spared the horrors of a counter-revolution—and the revolutionary party was able to advance again, as soon as the objective conditions of reconstruction would allow it. Russian independence was saved. This could not have happened if a *kulak* democracy had had the opportunity to turn the country into a raw-material market for foreign investors, instead of building an industry of her own. The Bolshevist party was given its great chance to attempt, and later to succeed in the realisation of a part of its economic programme greater than anyone in 1917 could have imagined as possible in an isolated revolutionary Russia.

For such achievements a heavy price was to be paid: If economics were temporarily allowed to evolve in a direction bound to undermine the position of the ruling party, that party had to strengthen its own internal homogeneity, and its grip on the whole life of the country. Otherwise it would not have been able to retain power in a country where for some years the urban and the rural bourgeoisie revived, nor would it have ultimately been able to overthrow them by a second revolutionary offensive, this time a " revolution from above ". Political dictatorship (in a sense narrower than that of a sociological description of the revolutionary state),[4] which originally had been an emergency regime born out of the needs of the War, evolved into a more permanent form of Soviet life. To understand the legal development during the N.E.P. it is necessary to understand both sides of that general evolution: the establishment of an economic regime that gave ampler space to private capitalism, and the strengthening of the dictatorial features of the political regime to check the growing capitalist forces.

Agriculture, and the organisation of the food-supply for the towns, had been the great failures of War Communism. The attempt to entice the peasants into collective enterprise by means of subsidies had merely resulted in the few existing collectives[5] failing to fulfil that function which might eventually be entrusted to them: to show the peasant what progress might be achieved by co-operation. " The experience of these collective farms

[3] Cp. Lenin, vol. IX, p. 113.

[4] See above, pp. 33–4.

[5] According to Lenin (vol. VIII, p. 5) there were in autumn 1919, 3,536 state farms (*Sovkhoses*), 1,961 agricultural *Communes*, 3,696 agricultural *Artels*. At present, with full collectivisation, there are about 300,000 of them all.

merely shows how *not* to organise. The surrounding peasantry jeer at or gloat over them." [6]

Where there was no collective agriculture, and no prospect of attaining it very soon, there remained private peasant enterprise. The Soviet consistently tried to encourage its productive efforts, and did so even at the height of its attempts at collectivisation.[7] But it would not concede to the peasant what he demanded, free trade in the products of the land. For a return to capitalism might have resulted from such a concession in a peasant country. Therefore, the Soviet was determined to fight "to the bitter end".[8] On the very eve of the N.E.P. the 8th Soviet Congress made yet another attempt to satisfy the individual peasant: he was offered prizes for fulfilling production plans, in the shape of a larger amount of grain to be left for his personal consumption and also preference in the supply of implements of production, under the sole condition that such prizes should not render a peasant's husbandry *kulak*.[9] This in any case would have been the difficulty in subsidising successful individual peasant enterprises: how could the subvention, if really granted in a form helpful to agricultural production, be prevented from raising the status of a small farmer to that of a small capitalist, from an actual ally to a potential enemy of the regime? At first this was a theoretical question —for the State had little to offer the peasant in the way of a subsidy. It could not even dispose of the consumers' goods needed if the peasant was to be able to use the money he got from the State for his food-deliveries. In consequence, the peasant delivered as little as he could, and the urban workers were starved to such a degree that it proved quite impossible to tackle the task of reconstruction from the industrial end.[10]

Instead of increasing industrial production and with the proceeds of that production making food-deliveries a more attractive business for the peasants, the peasant had to be induced somehow to sell his food.[10] However abhorrent it would have appeared two years before,[8] free trade in grain had to be restored, after the most urgent needs of the towns had been secured by a tax in kind (March 21, 1921). But even on the free market the peasant would hardly sell anything unless he could find

[6] Lenin, vol. IX, p. 110.

[7] See above, p. 51.

[8] Lenin, vol. VIII, p. 196.

[9] For example, by supplying him with machinery he could not use without employing poorer neighbours as labourers.

[10] Lenin, vol. IX, pp. 118 and 155–6.

commodities to purchase. The State industries could not produce these goods. Therefore, on May 22, 1921, private industry and commerce had to be admitted. As the State did not envisage transferring the most essential means of production to private enterprise, the freedom granted to the latter consisted partly in encouraging small craftsmanship (especially domestic crafts) and trade in various goods stocked by the consumers, and partly in allowing private entrepreneurs to re-establish production in shops which had been nationalised in theory, although the State had never been able to use them. According to decrees of May 17, and December 10, 1921, nationalisation of such enterprises was declared invalid, and they were to be restored to the former possessors. Article 5 of the latter decree allowed the Supreme Council for National Economics to restore to private enterprise shops with less than twenty employees, if they had actually been taken over by the State without the latter being able to make full use of them. The very possibility of such measures proved, indeed, that the former wave of theoretical nationalisation had gone far beyond the needs and even beyond the possibilities of the State. Now the latter was ready to drop all economic activities deemed unnecessary for controlling the "commanding heights" of national economy: by decree of July 5, 1921, the leasing of State enterprises to private entrepreneurs was allowed. Lenin's opinion on the situation was that in order to become economically efficient, Russia had to cover certain ground common both to State capitalism and to socialism, the latter being defined as national accounting and control. Capitalism was evil compared with socialism, but it meant progress in comparison with mediævalism and small-scale production.[11] Therefore it had to be encouraged, whatever plans for later progress towards socialism the party might have in mind.

But the would-be capitalists had their scruples too. Would the new economic policy prove stable, or was it merely a clever expedient to get those stocks out of the merchant's pocket which he might be ready to invest? "To end doubts as regards the sincerity of the new course of economic policies" a decree of the V.C.I.K. of August 25, 1921, established that only the courts were allowed to annul contracts and that, in future, nationalisation of any enterprise was allowed only by special enactment by the supreme State organs. So the entrepreneur got reason-

[11] Ibid., pp. 171 and 186.

able security against possible infringements by some new war-communist penchants on the part of his local or Gubernial Soviet. But unless the Soviet had been ready to abdicate politically, he could not get any guarantee that the way across the ground common to State-supervised capitalism and to socialism would be long enough for him to satisfy all his ambitions as a business man, before the Central Committee of the Communist Party should cause the ways to divide. The Soviet did nothing to encourage any hopes beyond the expectation that anyone who did business with the State would have some years of it—the Civil Code of 1922 fixed the limit at six years, provided he played his part in increasing the national output. We shall see below [12] that the conception of the " private entrepreneur " developed by Soviet law in this period is that of a trustee, with a share in the fruits of his endeavours rather than that of the " master of his business " as capitalist ideology imagines him—even if, in fact, the " master " is rather the trustee of some big bank. If all that happened in 1921–2 Russia should happen to-day in some other country, it is possible that people would be found ready to undertake the function of such a trustee " entrepreneur ", even at the risk that, after some years of honest work, their post should turn into that of an ordinary manager with a good salary. But, in 1922, capitalists, and especially Russian capitalists were not yet accustomed to regard State supervision as a normal and permanent phenomenon. They regarded the end of War-Communism as a proof of the bankruptcy of socialism in general, which they had always foretold, and as the eve of a new heyday for capitalist enterprise. Probably the Soviet regime would collapse, too. The Soviet, of course, did not intend to do so and was bound to look with suspicion at people who stood waiting for its downfall. It kept them politically disfranchised and regarded with some suspicion the economic activities which it had encouraged.

It is true that serious dangers to the socialist nature of Russian economics could hardly arise from these activities themselves. In September, 1922, about 4,000 industrial enterprises—about the same number as were then in public hands—were leased to private entrepreneurs, with an average of 18 employees. The proximity of this average to the legal maximum of 20 employees suggests that, without legal restrictions, private enterprise might have played a larger rôle. Under the given circumstances some

[12] Pp. 142–3.

70,000 employees in leased undertakings, with 5 per cent. of the total industrial production in their hands, were hardly a threat to the socialised sector of industry with its 1·3 million workers. But the private entrepreneurs played a larger part in wholesale commerce, whilst the retail trade was dominated by the private shopkeeper.[13] Even without any legal restrictions on private enterprise in industry it was to be expected that under Russian conditions private capitalism, once released, would concentrate on commerce. There it achieved some of the results aimed at by the instigators of the N.E.P. : it set free considerable stocks of goods and some productive resources which had been driven from the market by War Communism. Thus it gave Soviet economics that " initial ignition " which was needed to set the mechanism of commodity exchange revolving again. By its competition it forced upon the nationalised enterprises more economical methods of production and the application of business-like ways of calculation and trade,[14] without being able to threaten them seriously. On the other hand, private capitalism, let loose upon an Eastern European country with its millions of small peasant husbandries, after a period of extreme bureaucratic supervision and under the pressure of the expectation that its freedom would only endure for a few years, showed all the worst features of speculation. Disproportionately high profits were looked for as a compensation for the presumable shortness of the period during which they were to be enjoyed, and the merchant tried to make the best of the duress under which people were likely to sell and to purchase goods after a long period of starvation. Although the State did not attempt to enforce percentages of profit and interest corresponding to contemporary Western standards and showed consideration for the peculiarities of the situation,[15] the inclusion of an article (193) on usury in the Criminal Code was deemed necessary.

In view of the short-term character of an " initial ignition ", the opportunity for speculative profits during the transition to peace-economics might appear a merely ephemeral shortcoming of the N.E.P. But it was bound to appear more serious when seen against the background of an overwhelmingly peasant country, in the agricultural economics for which private enterprise was the rule, in an even higher degree than it

[13] See below, p. 131–2. [14] See below, pp. 137 ff.
[15] See below, this chapter, note 164.

was the exception in industry. Urban capitalism, in itself hardly dangerous for the new regime, might threaten its very foundations, if it were allowed to set up the pattern according to which the individual peasant's husbandry should develop.

Large-scale agricultural enterprise then existent being a conspicuous failure,[16] voluntary co-operation of the individual peasants was the obvious alternative from the point of view of a State which still pursued socialist aims. Even in industry co-operative enterprise might prove a valuable alternative to the N.E.P.-man in developing all the productive resources concentrated in the hands of small craftsmen and the traditional domestic crafts (*Kustarij*). So it was offered terms of competition more favourable than those granted to the individual entrepreneur, not only as regards taxation, but also by not limiting the size of the enterprise. Inevitably the danger arose that the freedom granted to co-operatives might be used by cunning capitalists to evade restrictions. The decree of July 7, 1921, on industrial co-operatives established their complete autonomy without government supervision, under a mere regime of compulsory registration (arts. 8 and 11). But it also demanded (art. 1) that the whole undertaking be based on the personal labour of its members. Only for certain auxiliary work, that the members themselves could not do, were wage-earners who were not members of the co-operative admitted, up to a limit of 20 per cent. of all those participating in the work. All of the latter, including the members themselves, were subject to the rulings of the Labour Code.

With scant regard for juridical niceties, this enactment by the supreme legislative authorities (the V.C.I.K. and the Soviet of People's Commissars) was "interpreted" by a directive of the People's Commissariats for Labour and for Justice, jointly with the T.U.C., of February 27, 1923, according to which the statutory hours did not apply to the members of industrial co-operatives (but, of course, to the auxiliary workers employed by them). Apart from the 20 per cent. of "auxiliary workers", apprentices, and also "candidates for membership in the co-operative" were admitted. Such rulings were intended to render the co-operative able to compete with the individual craftsman. But they also opened the doors to various evasions of the restrictions put upon private capitalist enterprise, and had to be

[16] See above, pp. 85–6.

stopped, by a decree of December 5, 1924.[17] As early as September 26, 1922, a decree had ordered the liquidation of all pseudo-co-operatives using wage labour in disguised forms. Article 129*a* of the Criminal Code established serious sanctions against " organisations that, although being in fact capitalist enterprises, cover themselves by co-operative forms for the sake of enjoying the advantages and privileges accorded by the Law to co-operatives ".

Much wider scope was granted to co-operation in agriculture than in industry. Being co-operation of individual peasants' husbandries (*dvors*) as such, not of all the individual persons participating in the work, the agricultural co-operative might easily command wage labour employed by its individual members. In fact, it did so, although special rulings prevented the rich peasants (*kulaks*) from becoming members of the managerial Board of the co-operative. But their mere membership in the co-operative was not to impair the privileges granted to agricultural co-operatives by the decree of August 16, 1921 : legal personality, autonomy and claim to registration once the formal conditions of the law were fulfilled,[18] precedence in getting orders, raw materials and credits from the State. From the point of view of the general policy of the ruling party [19] there were evident loopholes in the Law. Only administration could close them once further encouragement of capitalist elements in agriculture was felt undesirable, and this was one of the reasons for the important rôle which administrative measures were later to play in the process of collectivisation. But it ought to be kept in mind that the laws on industrial as well as on agricultural co-operatives formed reactions against the complete absorption of all co-operative activities by a centralised bureaucracy, during War-Communism.[20]

[17] Danilova, op. cit., p. 108. The maximal number of such candidates was fixed with 20 per cent. of the existing membership and the duration of their candidateship subjected to the rulings of the Labour Code which (art. 38) restricts the allowed test period for manual workers to one week, and (art. 122) apprenticeship to terms allowed by the People's Commissariat for Labour.

[18] Consent of the V.C.I.K. was demanded only for co-operative organisation on a scale larger than *gubernial*—evidently for avoiding unofficial re-establishment of a political peasants' party.

[19] As opposed to its right wing, who, like Bukharin, believed in the possibility of the small rural capitalists " growing into socialism ".

[20] For the " industrial " and " agricultural " departments for " producers co-operatives " in the Central Organisation of Consumers Co-operatives were in fact mere departments of the war-economic bureaucracy. Therefore their liquidation, in article 12, respectively 6 of the respective decrees on industrial and agricultural co-operatives, formed a preliminary condition of the latter's establishment.

## (b) The Codification of Soviet Law

To understand the later theoretical disputes about the compatibility of Law and Socialism, quite apart from all statements of classical Marxism on this issue, it must be remembered that one historical fact stood out before the controversialists: the codification of Soviet Law had been the outcome of the N.E.P., i.e. of a series of concessions made, if not to capitalism, then to certain principles of capitalist economics. And, like most of their colleagues in continental European countries, Soviet legal theorists regarded only codified Law as Law proper. Thus the contemporaneity of the codification of Soviet Law and the N.E.P. was bound to have a strong influence on the sociological interpretation of that Law.

As we have seen in the last chapter, quite apart from the general importance of uncodified Law (a point on which English legal theory will differ from continental opinion), most of the essential elements of the Soviet legal system had developed during the period of War-Communism. That period was not quite so "Communist" as it appeared in some of its own ideologies. Its Law was certainly not a distinctly socialist Law, and contained the most important elements upon which legislation of the N.E.P. period could build. N.E.P. Law, on the other hand, was not at all designed to serve the needs of the N.E.P.-men and to express the concessions made to capitalism. It had to limit them. Above its cradle were inscribed the words of Lenin: "It is time to stop the retreat!"[21]

On October 31, 1922, when introducing the Civil Code in the session of the V.C.I.K., Lenin[22] explained it as an expression of

> our policy [the N.E.P.] which we have firmly established and as regards which there cannot be any vacillations. . . . We have endeavoured to establish a clear limit between what ought to be regarded as the legitimate private sphere of any citizen, and what ought to be regarded as a misuse of the N.E.P., as an attitude which we are not ready to legalise, however legal it may be in all other states. The event will prove whether the amendments which you [the V.C.I.K. in the second reading] have carried for this very purpose . . . are efficient enough. . . . If actual life should produce misuses not provided for by us, we shall immediately carry out the necessary amendments. Our legislative machinery is sufficiently elastic for this purpose. . . .

[21] Lenin, vol. IX, p. 314. See also below, pp. 106 and 150.
[22] Lenin, *Works*, Russian ed., vol. XXVII, p. 319.

The evident aim of the codification of Soviet Civil Law was to give private enterprise, as admitted by the decree of May 22, 1921, the necessary legal security whilst preventing the use of these rights for other purposes than those intended by the legislator. "Civil rights are protected by the Law unless they are exercised in a sense contrary to the economic and social purposes for the sake of which they have been established" (art. 1 of the Civil Code). Thus, as opposed to a mere formal description of the conditions needed for the validity of a legal transaction, the latter's economic consequences are introduced into the judicial perspective. The validity of the legal transaction is decided by the degree to which the economic consequences intended by the partners to the transaction conform to those intended by the legislator who introduced that specific legal institution. This legislator is always the Soviet legislator, even if a corresponding institution existed in pre-revolutionary law: article 6 of the introductory law to the Civil Code of November 11, 1922, prohibits any interpretation of this code on the basis of pre-revolutionary legislation and judicial practice. There was no revival of the former legality, only partial reception of Western laws.[23]

So it is correct to interpret the Civil Code, in the sphere of mutual relations between private enterprise and the State, as prohibiting the former from exercising any function which is not explicitly permitted.[24] In contrast with capitalist states, State enterprise is regarded as the normal state of affairs. Private enterprise exists not by any original right of its own, but because and in so far as it is permitted in the public interest. There are no rights but those created by the State, and the legislator can in no case be supposed to have intended to thwart its own legal and political system. An explanation of the general economic purposes pursued by the Soviet is given in article 4 of the Civil Code, according to which the capacity of all citizens (including the capitalists who were then politically disfranchised) as subjects of Law is recognised "in order to develop the pro-

[23] Stuchka, op. cit., 1931, pp. 109 ff.

[24] Amfiteatrov-Ginsberg, op. cit., p. 360. It would be incorrect to generalise this thesis into a general statement that in the U.S.S.R. all things that are not explicitly allowed, are prohibited. There is in Soviet ideology no fundamental bias against personal freedom in general corresponding to that against private enterprise. On the contrary, realisation of maximal personal freedom is always regarded as the ultimate purpose of State interference (see above, Chapter II, pp. 23–4). So also in Criminal Law the illegality of an action has to be proved by the prosecution, at least (if the principle of analogy is applied, see below, pp. 107–8) in the general sense that it has threatened the common weal.

ductive resources of the country ". It might be concluded, for example, that the property of the *kulak* in fodder for his livestock was recognised, but that property in stocks of grain artificially withheld for cornering the market was not protected by the law. Elaborate economic analysis might be needed to decide whether a certain grain stock had been retained merely to secure a favourable price for the product, i.e. to enjoy profits the granting of which had been regarded by the State as a suitable stimulus of production, or in order to thwart the grain-purchasing policy of the State and thus to endanger socialist economics. Economic analysis of the actual social backgrounds of a legal transaction was needed to check its conformity to the purposes of the law, for example to distinguish between a real and a mere pseudo-co-operative, i.e. an enterprise which was " capitalist in fact ".[25] Such inclusion of economic analysis in the conditions necessary to confirm any legal transition certainly goes beyond mere consideration for " public order " as current in many other countries.[26] It gives, *a priori*, any institution of Soviet Civil Law a meaning at least potentially different from that of analogous institutions in the Civil Law of other states, even if the respective Soviet institution has been copied from the Law of those states.[27] Thus, private property, in Soviet Law, is always to be regarded as an institution secondary to public property, and admitted only in the latter's interest. In doubtful cases the assumption, in the U.S.S.R., is always in favour of public property.[28]

Article 33 of the Civil Code provides for the annulment, by the Court, of any legal transaction concluded by a person under duress to his evident detriment. Not only the injured person (for example, the poor peasant who has entered into an obviously crooked deal with a *kulak* under the latter's pressure) but also the organs of the State and the competent social organisations are entitled to demand such annulment. The rule may be interpreted as a strengthening of the principle of freedom of consent to a contract, by means of guarantees which are more

[25] See above, p. 91.

[26] This analogy is correct when drawn, as by Lambert-Patrouillet, Introduction, pp. 35 ff., to art. 30 of the Soviet Civil Code which invalidates any transaction performed for illegal purposes, or in order to evade the Law, or to injure the State. But it would certainly prove political bias in the capitalist sense if a French or American judge should interpret a contract according to whether it furthers private as against public enterprise. The opposite argument, by a Soviet judge, means simply doing his duty in interpreting the Law according to its avowed intentions.

[27] As has been done in a very large degree. See Stuchka, op. cit., 1931, pp. 108–9.

[28] Ibid., pp. 250–1

efficient than those accepted in other countries, and which work even if continued pressure should prevent the injured person from looking after his own interests. But the analysis, especially from the point of view of formal procedure, may proceed one step further and assume that so-called private rights in Soviet Law are not *actual rights of private persons*, but *rights established by the State in favour of private persons*, in order to secure the public interest in the latter's welfare. Article 2 of the Code of Civil Procedure orders the public Attorney to initiate, to continue, and to participate in Civil Law suits independently of the will of the parties immediately interested, if the public interest so demands.

A combination of the public interest and that of the individual workers and peasants is found in article 5 of the Introductory Law to the Civil Code, according to which legal relations existing prior to its enactment and remaining still undecided under the existing laws ought to be ruled by the new norms only if this should be " demanded by the interests of the Workers' and Peasants' State and of the toiling masses ". But the latter's interests are evidently to be interpreted collectively, i.e. according to whether or not their group interests may be furthered by creating a certain precedence—independently of whether the individual claimant was, say, a poor peasant or a *kulak*. Without that article the Civil Code would not only have allowed certain private capitalist activities which fitted into the system of the N.E.P., but would also have involved the reinterpretation of all the legal relations of the preceding period to the point of a restoration of capitalism. To describe these rulings of Soviet Civil Law as its " class-clausulæ ", as is frequently done within the U.S.S.R. and abroad (although, of course, in a very different spirit), has little meaning beyond the general Marxist explanation of politics in terms of class-interests. Such rulings clearly distinguish the working of Soviet Law, even of the N.E.P. period, from some functions generally ascribed, in a positive or critical sense, to ordinary Civil Law, namely from the indiscriminate protection of any kind of property and contract. But the rulings do not establish group privileges within the framework of those institutions as recognised by Soviet Law. Thus, they do not impair its generality.

The widespread assumption that Civil Law, by its very nature, is bourgeois,[29] together with the functionalist approach

[29] See above, pp. 30–1.

of the authors of the Soviet Civil Code [30] resulted in a peculiar combination of the general clausulæ hitherto discussed with the concrete institutions which they were intended to limit. Although giving full scope for such specific Soviet institutions as the limitation of the Right of Inheritance,[31] the general content of the Civil Code was much more traditional than was necessary under the circumstances and considering its hurried enactment. Where a new and specific legal institution, with its own right and duties, say that of the leaseholder of nationalised enterprises is established,[32] the Soviet Civil Code, instead of devoting some special articles to this institution, prefers to make clear its *specifica* in notes contained in articles dealing with the " normal " case of lease between private partners, although under actual Soviet urban conditions the " exception " was much more frequent. In a very orthodox legal way, the institution of property is described as the sum of the rights of possession, usufruct, and disposition (art. 58). No attempt is made to modify the traditional institution any further by general theory of Law, although actual modification, begun by the first revolutionary legislation,[33] was continued by the Civil Code itself.[34] As envisaged by Renner [35] the transformation of property relations proceeds not by changing the theoretical content of the right of property, but by restricting the number of potential holders of certain kinds of property and by declaring an increasing number of objects *res extra commercium.* The latter is done fundamentally in the articles 21 (the soil) and 22 (means of production of nationalised enterprises, so that the latter could never be purchased, but only rented by private entrepreneurs). In consideration of public order, in article 23, arms, ammunition and securities of the pre-revolutionary governments (which, though they had been annulled, were still potential objects of speculations on a downfall of the regime) are excluded from private ownership. These restrictions of legal transactions are followed by a catalogue of the potential holders of certain kinds of property (arts. 52 ff). The land, forests and railways *must* be publicly owned—private persons cannot enjoy more than leasehold. As

[30] After the first draft, by a commission of specialists, had been rejected, for not giving due consideration to the specific functions of Soviet Law, another one was produced, by Prof. Hoichbarg and one assistant, and enacted within three months. Prof. Hoichbarg was an adherent of Duguit's theories. See Stuchka, op. cit., 1931, pp. 108 ff.

[31] See above, pp. 81–2.

[32] See below, 142.

[33] See above, pp. 80–1.

[34] See below, pp. 142 and 247 ff.

[35] See above, p. 28.

a rule (with the exception of special concessions by private law) all undertakings employing more than the legal maximum of workers allowed for private enterprise [36] *must* be under public or co-operative ownership. Private persons *may* own non-municipalised buildings, industrial and commercial [37] undertakings employing no more than the legal maximum (apart from special concessions), means of production, all objects of legal internal commerce,[38] money and securities, and all objects of private consumption. Of course, also, these goods *may* be owned by the State or by co-operatives. Soviet Law of the N.E.P. period allowed far wider scope to private enterprise than was actually intended by its authors: the Law secured a certain essential minimum of State property whilst all further progress in socialist enterprise was to be realised by economic competition with private enterprise in a field legally open to both of them. For this reason Soviet Civil Law appeared much more *bourgeois* than it actually was. Later, bourgeois critics complained of "Soviet lawlessness" when, in accordance with the original intentions of the legislator,[39] in the actual working of the Law, private enterprise proved unable to hold those positions theoretically allowed to it. But later Soviet theory [40] regarded Civil Law as a compromise to be dropped as soon as possible.

Correspondingly the Labour Code of November 9, 1922, looked like a mere reform legislation satisfying trade-unionist demands to the maximum of progressive standards. Certainly it was enacted at a time when no one could predict the achievements of private capitalist enterprise and the application of capitalist methods in public enterprise [41] under the N.E.P., and it was intended to grant Labour the minimum guarantees it needed under the new conditions.[42] On the other hand, the private entrepreneur, also, was given guarantees against a War-Communist interpretation of his civic duties. The general Duty to Work (the central institution of the 1918 Labour Code [43]) was restricted to emergency cases, with due exceptions for young and elderly people (art. 11). The normal law of Labour under the 1922 code is a law of contract, as a rule, a collective con-

[36] By the law of December 10, 1921 (see above, p. 87), which was not amended during the N.E.P., this maximum was fixed at 20.

[37] There is no mention of agricultural enterprise—it comes in only as the sum ot the implements of production owned by the peasant *dvor*. See below, pp. 101–2.

[38] The State monopoly of foreign trade was secured by article 17 of the Code.

[39] See above, pp. 93–4.

[40] See below, pp. 149 ff.

[41] See below, pp. 140–1 on State factories closing down if working with a loss.

[42] Stuchka, op. cit., p. 79.

[43] See above, pp. 55–6.

tract binding all employees, whether members of the trade union which has participated in the contract, or not (art. 16). The collective contract establishes minimum conditions for labour which cannot be impaired by any individual contract less favourable for the employee. Similarly, no contract is valid if it establishes conditions of labour less favourable than those demanded by the Code (art. 4). Freedom of contract is further restricted by special rules to juvenile workers (art. 31): any contract for labour, the continuation of which may prove harmful to young persons may be annulled if this be demanded by parents, tutors, or by any institutions or officials charged with the care of the young.[44] With the exception of some jobs demanding special personal scientific qualification, or political confidence, all employment has to go through the Employment Exchanges (arts. 5 ff.).

Trade unions are recognised as the only legitimate representatives of the employees' interests (art. 157), and all possible consideration is given to furthering their activities, especially those of the trade-unionist Factory Committees elected according to the by-laws of the trade union concerned (art. 156).[45] Amongst their functions is " supporting the normal working of *State* industries and collaboration, through the competent organs of the trade union, in planning and directing national economics " (art. 158 e.). This collaboration, within the socialised sector, and, according to the general spirit of the Code, restricted to defending the special interests of labour, is all that has remained of the 1917 conceptions of " Workers' Control ".[46] As regards *private* undertakings the trade union has no right to interfere with the management, but it maintains the right to strike. According to article 49 any contract of labour may be annulled by the demand of the trade union concerned. If there is no agreement on a new contract, the conflict will be submitted to those organs of conciliation that have no powers beyond those of non-compulsory suggestion.[47] In theory, the trade union could strike also in a nationalised enterprise—but Communist-controlled trade unions would hardly do so, except in cases of extreme individual mismanagement. The private entre-

[44] See above, pp. 94–5.

[45] The Soviet trade unions have always been organised on industrial lines. So always only one union is concerned.

[46] See above, p. 43.

[47] See the remark to article 172, Labour Code. Compulsory arbitration was established only for the interpretation of the meaning of existing agreements and in the case of conflicts, if both parties had agreed to submit to arbitration (art. 171).

preneur [48] would interpret the fact that a trade union controlled by the party ruling the State called a strike against him, as an unfriendly act of the State, intended to hamper him in relation to his competitors, the nationalised enterprises. But this would not help him : apart from formalities the State might point out that private enterprise had been encouraged, not for its own merits, but in order to improve the general standard of living. Sacrifices made by socialist-minded workers in the interest of future socialist reconstruction did not justify similar sacrifices in the interest of private profit at the expense of those in whose interest this private profit was tolerated. In due course,[49] when private enterprise was restricted to a minimum, the distinctly trade-unionist conception of Soviet Law of Labour, as embodied in the 1922 Code, would become chimerical just as the conceptions of the 1918 Code based on civic Duty had faded with the admission of capitalist methods of management.

For Russia's social structure, the development of agriculture was decisive ; that branch of the national economy then occupied more than 80 per cent. of the total population. The Land Code of October 30, 1922, retained the principle of Land Nationalisation (art. 1) and of a centralised Land Fund (art. 3), as enacted by the revolutionary legislation. But in explaining these principles it increased the scope left to private enterprise in comparison not only with the 1919 Land Law, which emphasised socialised agriculture, but even with the legislation of 1917–18.[50] Amongst the persons and organisations entitled to use agricultural land (all other land remained in direct possession of the State) article 4 of the Land Code enumerates (a) the cultivators of the soil and their communities, (b) urban settlements, (c) State farms. The use of the land is subjected to general supervision by the public organs, and is restricted by the rules of the Law as well as by the statutes and decisions of agricultural communities to which the peasant happens to belong (arts. 7–8 and 10). But there is complete freedom of secession from such communities and provision is made for the dissenters being granted their share in the land fund of the village (arts. 91 and 114). There is no temporary limit to the Right to Use the Land, and it can be lost only according to the rules of the Law (art. 11). If the peasant desires individual, as distinct from collective, exercise of his Right to Use the Land

[48] Especially the foreign concessionaire.

[49] See below, pp, 217–9.

[50] See above, pp. 40–3.

(art. 10), this right comes nearer than in any previous Soviet enactment to private ownership in the ordinary bourgeois sense: article 27 merely prohibits the buying and selling and testamentary disposition of the land. Lease of land, which had been prohibited as early as by the 1917 Land Decree, was allowed in 1922, although ideology demanded that it be described as a mere emergency measure conditioned by the temporary inability of the lessor to use his share in the Land Fund himself (for example, in consequence of lack of cattle-stock); but the duration of leasehold was restricted to one rotation period of the crops (usually three years). The regional Soviet Executive Committee was allowed to grant special extensions up to a lease-term of two rotation-periods (arts. 28 ff.). The Third Union Soviet Congress, May 20, 1925, made further concessions to small capitalist enterprise in agriculture "according to the temporary economic conditions of the village"—the emphasis on "temporary" becoming clear when the anti-*kulak* campaign started three years later. Amongst these concessions were the permission to lease land for the duration of three rotation periods and further facilities for employing wage labour in agriculture. Employment of labourers, which had been completely prohibited by the "*Peasants' Nakas*" of 1917, was allowed by the 1922 Code "as an auxiliary and temporary measure" (art. 39), and on condition that the employer's husbandry "retained its toiling character", i.e. that all members of the *kulak* family capable of working participated in physical labour (art. 40). Already in the 1922 Code there were provisions for the protection of labour (art. 41) which would have had no place if its employment had been conceded merely as an occasional form of neighbourly help. In the regulations of 1925 [51] the existence of farms with three and more permanently employed wage-earners, i.e. of the small capitalist (*kulak*) enterprise, was regarded as a normal phenomenon. Thus, large estates were the only form of rural capitalism the development of which was prevented by law. For they could not be formed without purchase, or at least long-term leasehold of land, which remained impossible. And even with the most favourable interpretation, it would have been impossible to describe them as "toiling", in the sense that the *kulak's* family participated in physical work and that the work of the hired labourers might be described as merely "auxiliary". From 1922 to 1925 there was, indeed, a certain ideological change

[51] Decree of April 18, 1925. See Danilova, op. cit., pp. 37 ff.

in the description of the *kulak*. In 1922 he was sanctioned by the fact that he toiled. In 1925 he got greater freedom, but he was described more properly as a capitalist temporarily necessary for the development of the country. The second ideology made it easier to get rid of him, if this should be desired.

Just as in the industrial field, we have here to distinguish between the amount of scope given to capitalist enterprise by N.E.P.-legislation and the further development which it encouraged.[52] The traditional village community, hitherto the main obstacle to the growth of village capitalism, did not enjoy special privileges as against peasants who desired to secede from it. But its dispersal was not encouraged, as it had been by Stolypin's legislation. It enjoyed, for all important purposes, the status of a legal entity (art. 64), and its elected organs were established by the law (art. 50). By majority decision, it could decide how to cultivate the land (art. 58) without being hampered by any of the property rights existing before the revolution (art. 59). Apart from individual peasants it might comprise agricultural Communes as well as *Artels* (art. 47), and it might vote in favour of transition to collective cultivation of the land (art. 112), allowing for the right of the dissenters to secede (art. 114). So provision was made to ensure that the dispersal of the traditional village-community—as all Russian Marxists agreed, an inevitable process—need not necessarily result in strengthening capitalism.

Another process by which, under Stolypin, the capitalist evolution of agriculture had been encouraged, was the transformation of the traditional peasant's family household into an agricultural enterprise individually owned by the head of the family. In this field the tendency of Soviet legislation to protect the rights of women and young persons restricted what otherwise might have been an advance of capitalism at the expense of primitive patriarchal relations. Although the peasant's family husbandry (*Dvor*) is represented by its head,[53] it enjoys all its

[52] Bruzkus, *Agrarreform and Agrarrevolution in Sovietrussland* (Berlin, 1925, Osteuropa Institut), interprets (p. 196) the 1922 Land Code as " a victory of the peasantry who always opposed nationalisation of land ". This Stolypinist interpretation of the development is the current with Russian White *émigrées* (see also C. Zeitzev in *The Slavonic Review*, vol. IX, pp. 560–1) but has been sufficiently refuted by events. Even in 1925 it clearly contradicted the established facts, at least as regards the peasant attitude in 1917—unless " peasant " is regarded as a synonym of " kulak ".

[53] It is rather problematic whether the ruling that men and women were equally legitimate " heads of the *Dvor* " had great practical importance under Russian village conditions at the time. But the members of the *Dvor* could appeal to the village Soviet for replacing the head by another member of the *Dvor*, if he had neglected his duties.

rights as an entity, independent of the sex and age of its members (art. 67). Its property cannot be impaired by the individual debts of any of its members, including the head of the family (art. 71). Nor can it be divided, except for the building of new peasants' households (art. 74) and then only if the viability of the latter is secured (arts. 85 ff.). Thus the main channels through which capitalism had absorbed the small farmer's husbandry were narrowed.

On the other side the framers of the Code had some conception of the alternative way in which the peasant might escape from the smallness of his husbandry. The *kollkhos* was named in article 90 as one of the alternative forms of using the land, besides the traditional village community (or individual use of the land periodically redistributed amongst the *dvors*) and parcellation, which involved permanent separation of individual peasants' holdings from the land used by their neighbours. Three forms of *kollkhos*—Agricultural Communes, *Artels*, and Associations for Joint Cultivation of the Land—were mentioned and described in articles 103 ff., but the description was hardly an advance upon the Land Law of 1919.[54] In the Agricultural Commune, as distinct from the two other forms of *kollkhoses*, the individual members had no land shares. To-day this is true of the bulk of the agricultural land even in the *Artel*, though, if interpreted as excluding individual kitchen gardens belonging to the member families, such a definition would be rejected as a "leftist deviation" even in the Commune. The authors of the 1922 Land Code certainly did not think of such extremes. Even when speaking of *kollkhoses*, they based their theories on the individual share of the individual peasant *dvor* in the village land fund. For them, Communes were collectives taking their share jointly out of the village fund. *Artels*, on the other hand, were only formed by agreement between the individual *dvors*, after the periodical redistribution of the land and held good only for the duration of each redistribution. The members of the *Artels* enjoyed fixed shares in the joint product (arts. 106 ff.). This seems to suggest that the areas submitted to collective cultivation were regarded as one economic unit for the duration of the *Artel*. It implies that as early as 1922 an Association for Joint Cultivation of the Land, as distinct from an *Artel*, was regarded as a co-operative owning merely certain means of production and employing them on the land shares of its indivi-

[54] See above, p. 51, and especially articles 124 ff. of the 1919 law.

dual members, without these shares losing their individuality, so that each earned the harvest on his individual land.

More fruitful for the future than such definitions was the provision, in a rider to article 109, that the People's Commissariat for Agriculture should publish model agreements for the various types of *kollkhoses*.[55] The authors of the Code regarded collectivisation of agriculture as belonging rather to a remote future. For the time being, they hoped that the State farms (*Sovkhoses*, arts. 160 ff.) would serve " as a scientific and technical basis for the development of agriculture and its *mise en-commune* ", by influencing the neighbouring peasant farms technically as well as culturally.

A long-term view of the prospects of private enterprise in agriculture, as well as admission of capitalism in general, seems also to underlie the Forest Code of the N.E.P.[56] which replaced that of 1918.[57] Rational exploitation and not protection of the forests dominated the minds of the authors. The main division was between forests of local interest, which were left to be exploited by village communities and collectives on condition that the exploitation followed an ordered plan (the application of which was to be supervised by the Gubernial Soviet), and forests of general public interest to be exploited by the State. In addition to their cultivation for purposes of general health and welfare which had been the focus of the 1919 legislation, special provision was made in articles 56 ff. for leasing them in part to capitalist concessionaires. It is interesting to note that the Forest Code of 1923 had to be replaced, in 1936, by a new one rather closer to the 1918 conceptions.

Whilst in the economic field the foundations of Soviet Law were established during the N.E.P. period, in all branches of Law that deal with the personal relations of the citizen, or the political structure of the State, the Law of the War-Communist period was preserved with remarkable stability. Whilst political dictatorship has continued almost unmodified during the whole existence of the Soviet State, the essential achievements of the first revolutionary period in the field of personal rights were characteristic of a democratic revolution,[58] and have remained so to the present day.

The Matrimonial Code of 1918, the most distinct expression of that tendency, was simply re-enacted in 1921. A revised

[55] See below, pp. 178 ff.

[56] July 25, 1923, S.U. 1923/564.

[57] See above, pp. 52–3.

[58] See above, p. 55.

Matrimonial Code was promulgated towards the end of the N.E.P. period, on November 19, 1926. In 1926, slight amendments were made to the 1918 Code, such as the transfer of the decision (in cases of disagreement between the parents on questions of the education of the children), from the ordinary courts to the special organs of tutelage.[59] There are only two important modifications in the institution of matrimony : the introduction of the right of either partner to demand divorce (art. 18), instead of the judicial discretion preserved for such cases in 1918, and the recognition of *de facto* marriages as having the same material consequences as registered ones. Apart from the question of inheritance, which by the 1922 Civil Code was decided in favour of the persons actually supported by the deceased,[60] this point became important in consequence of the establishment, by the 1926 Code, of a normal joint ownership by both partners of all property acquired during the existing wedlock (art. 10). The desire to protect the rights of the wife more strictly which induced this modification [61] also demanded the protection of the rights of women living in *de facto* marriage. So the latter was recognised as a legal institution throughout most of the U.S.S.R., though the eastern republics were still so dominated by the struggle against patriarchal and religious custom, including polygamy, that they avoided weakening the authority of registered marriage by taking this step. There were various forms of establishing *de facto* marriage in Soviet law : in registering a marriage at the Registrar's Office the parties might declare that the actual state of marriage had already existed from an earlier date (art. 3) ; or the judge might establish, on the demand of the abandoned wife, that *de facto* marriage had existed and that, therefore, property acquired during its duration ought to be regarded as common (arts. 12–13). The establishment of the right of either party to demand divorce at any time rendered provision for the education of the children (arts. 22 ff.) obligatory, and also the maintenance of the wife for a transitional period after the divorce (art. 13). For the very reason that the 1926 Code consistently tried to secure the emancipation of married women, it had to drop the rather negative attitude of Western

[59] Article 39. The change is rather a technical one, made to create more competent organs by division of labour between courts and educational organs. When the place where the children are to be educated—i.e. virtually the question which of the parents should have the responsibility for them—is disputed, under the 1926 Code the decision remains with the Court. But the Court also has to take its decision according to the interests of the education of the children.

[60] See above, p. 82.

[61] See above, pp. 58–9.

feminism to the economic implications of marriage which had influenced the 1918 Code. But all these modifications consistently developed the basic policy of the 1918 Code, as did the statement (art. 33 of the 1926 Code) that paternal rights are recognised exclusively in the children's interest, and can be abolished in the case of abuse. As in the 1918 Code, these are individual rights of children and parents, and not—as in Nazi conceptions—rights of some supposed entity of which the parents are mere trustees: article 31 of the 1922 Criminal Code ruled that deprivation of paternal rights should be inflicted by the Court only in cases where it was established that the convicted parent had abused these rights. Even loss of all other civic rights does not automatically involve loss of parental rights.

In Criminal Law the principles developed during the first revolutionary period were followed up, continuously, with such modifications as the very fact of codification demanded.[62] Crime is identified with socially dangerous action, i.e. according to article 6 of the Code (in the 1922 as well as in the 1926 form) as "every act or omission which is directed against the Soviet regime or violates[63] the legal order as established by the workers' and peasants' authority. . . ." The fact that it was found necessary to include the first half of the definition explicitly,

[62] See above, p. 74 ff. In the field of Criminal Law the codification of Soviet Law has proceeded under special complications. The Criminal Code of the R.S.F.S.R., of May, 1922 (S.U. 1922/153), was immediately received by the other Soviet Republics, but very soon regarded as insufficiently elaborated, and amended already in 1923. When the Soviet federation was constituted, as early as October 31, 1924 it made use of its power to establish general principles for the legislation of the federated republics in Criminal Law and Criminal Procedure. These principles caused sharp disputes with the leading authorities of the R.S.F.S.R., especially in those points where their authors had introduced the conception of fighting potential dangers threatening from an individual citizen rather than actual breaches of the Law (by the institutions of protective banishment, and of regarding the class situation of the convicted as in itself an aggravating or attenuating circumstance). The R.S.F.S.R. formally gave way to the superior authority by having its new code, of November 22, 1926 (S.U. 1926/600), enacted in the form demanded by the principles of the U.S.S.R., whilst the latter, February 27, 1927, were amended according to the demands of the R.S.F.S.R. So the latter got its way when, June 6, 1927, it could amend its Code according to the amended principles of the U.S.S.R. The amendment also included the new form of the article 58 (counter-revolutionary crimes), resulting from a new definition of the latter by the V.C.I.K. See Maurach, op. cit. (1928), pp. 55 ff. and D-ov, op. cit. In the text according to the terminology applied in Soviet literature, we speak always of the "1922 Code" (in spite of the fact that the latter was amended in the following year) or of the "1926 Code" valid up to the present day, in spite of the latter's revised form dating from 1927 (apart from various additions in the following years). But the revisions of 1923 and 1927 took the form of mere amendments, without altering the order of the established Code.

[63] The word "violates" is found only since the 1924 principles, but evidently forms a mere editorial improvement.

although attempts at overthrowing the regime might reasonably be included amongst violations of its legal order, suggests that the legislator had a two-fold approach to the codification of Criminal Law: he intended an explicit enumeration of the ordinary offences subject to punishment, whilst as to counter-revolutionary attempts the mere fact of proven counter-revolutionary intention was regarded as a sufficient basis to render an action liable to punishment, independent of whether or not it had been explicitly provided for in the Code. Such an interpretation is supported by Lenin's argumentation in favour of article 57 (now 58, 1) of the Criminal Code, containing the definition of counter-revolutionary crimes.[64] "Justice ought not to remove the terror; to promise this would be self-deception or deception. It ought to establish and legalise it by principles, clearly and honestly." The only possible interpretation of such an attitude to political opponents is to regard it as a continuation of the Civil War, judicial procedure being established in order to identify most surely the irreconcilable enemies of the regime who had to be annihilated.

So the attitude of the War-Communist period was also preserved in the description of the purposes of criminal repression. Article 9 of the present (1926) Criminal Code repeats the 1919 principles[65] when stating the threefold purpose as "(*a*) to prevent the commission of further crimes by the same offender, (*b*) to influence other unstable members of society, and (*c*) to adapt the offenders to the conditions of the community-life of the toilers' state", adding that "measures of social defence shall not have as their object the infliction of physical suffering or personal humiliation. The question of retaliation or punishment[66] does not arise". Thus, in line with earliest Soviet Criminal Law the repressive approach is supplemented by the educational, the former being emphasised in fighting the irreconcilable enemies of the regime, the latter in dealing with the ordinary offender, whose social past and attitude does not prevent him from eventually becoming a useful member of society. There is no reason to censure morally either the man who fought for what he was bound to deem right, or the man who acted asocially by reason of his bad education in a bad society.

The fact that, since 1922, at least the ordinary crimes have

[64] See below, p. 115.
[65] See above, pp. 74–5.
[66] "Punishment" meant in the moral sense. See below, pp. 111–2.

been described in a special part of the Code, does not constitute a fundamental change: for a Code drafted in such a hurry was not likely to enact anything more than principles already experienced in practice, nor was the enactment understood as a strict circumscription of all actions threatened with penalties. Article 1 of the 1926 Code of Criminal Procedure described the task of Soviet Criminal Justice as "protecting the socialist state of workers and peasants and the legal order established by it against actions threatening the common weal (crimes)". Such a definition was certainly in full accordance with the principles of 1919. No Judge is allowed to let such actions remain unpunished "for the reason that such actions are not characterised in the Criminal Code, nor under the pretext of uncompleteness or obscurity of the law, or of a contradiction between the laws".[67] According to article 10 of the 1922 Criminal Code (art. 16 of the 1926 Code) the judge, in such cases, has to apply measures of social protection analogous to those prescribed by the Code for delinquencies similar in kind and importance to the one committed. In view of such a recognition of the principle of analogy the question arises whether the codification of Soviet Criminal Law involved the acceptance of the classical principle *nulla pœna sine lege.* The wording of article 1 of the Code of Criminal Procedure may be interpreted as a mere ideological justification for criminal procedure in general, a full description of the actions threatening the common weal being contained in the special part of the Criminal Code. In such an interpretation of the Law, the principle of analogy could be admitted only in order to cover obvious technical failures of the legislator to express what he had in mind, and would be quite compatible with the strictest conception of legality acceptable to the Soviet, which, as we know, rejects any formalism and any basing of rights and duties on a merely grammatical interpretation of the Law. Or, alternatively, the Criminal Code might be interpreted as a mere enumeration of the most usual forms of actions threatening the common weal, intended to guide the judge's "revolutionary consciousness of Justice" and to show him in which way the legislator desired various dangerous actions to be dealt with, independently of whether or not the legislator had these concrete actions in his mind when shaping the Criminal Code. In the latter case the judge would have to decide whether some action, though omitted by the Criminal Code,

[67] Article 2 of the Code of Criminal Procedure.

threatened the common weal to such an extent that it ought to be punished, i.e. he would have to assume legislative functions.

This problem has remained fundamental for Soviet conceptions of Justice up to the present day.[68] By the definition of Crime in the Criminal Codes of the N.E.P. period (and by art. 2 of the 1922 Code of Criminal Procedure) the answer to the problem appears to be twofold : (*a*) in dealing with counter-revolutionary crimes, analogy is accepted as an expedient to determine the sanctions to be applied against acts regarded as criminal independent of their explicit description in the Criminal Code ; and (*b*) in dealing with ordinary crimes, it merely serves to fill gaps left unwittingly by the legislator in shaping the Code.[69] To use an expression common in continental jurisprudence, it can complete prohibitions, established by the Law, by adding a criminal sanction which the legislator might be supposed to have had in mind, according to his general attitude as expressed in the Criminal Code. For example, in 1926 a gang of Leningrad hooligans, who, acting as a group, had raped a woman, were shot,[70] as if they had jointly committed robbery. It was supposed that the legislator, who threatened the crime of rape with much more serious penalties than that of robbery and, for reasons of public order, prescribed capital punishment for the robbery if committed by a gang, would certainly have dealt similarly with the Leningrad gangsters. Any Soviet jurist would reject the reproach that the Leningrad G.P.U. had violated the principle *nulla pœna sine lege* : the principle of analogy, i.e. article 16 of the Criminal Code, covered, in the spirit of the Code, the latter's unintentional omission to establish a crime " rape, committed by gangs ".

But in dealing with political crime, the principle *nulla pœna sine lege* has been modified, to say the least of it,[71] if not abolished. The 1922 Code contained the most extreme modern example of

[68] See below, Chapter VII, pp. 225–6.

[69] See above, pp. 105–6.

[70] It was done by the G.P.U., but evidently merely with the intention of acting swiftly and to increase the deterrent effect of the punishment on other hooligans. An ordinary court might have differentiated as regards the guilt of the individual members of the gang but, under Soviet Law, it would not have approached those mainly responsible in a different way.

[71] I.e. in the sense that exemptions from the general rules of Law, as long as provided for in the Law itself, do not formally abolish the principle *nulla pœna sine lege*. But that principle is generally understood in the sense " there should be no punishment, unless explicitly provided for by the law valid at the time of the offence " : and in such a conception it clearly contradicts the principle of analogy, as described above.

*post facto* legislation.[72] If there had been any considerations in principle against it, the aim intended, annihilation of some especially despicable agents of the former regime might have been achieved by declaring certain individuals outlaws—a procedure not strange to original Soviet law. On the other hand, it has been clearly stated that the judge, in deciding the danger threatening society from the defendant, should not only look backwards, to the accomplished crime, but also forward at the eventual outcome of the future actions of an irreconcilable enemy of the regime.[73] In this case, the principle of analogy was applied in order to sentence prisoners who had obviously committed certain crimes clearly defined in the Code to much heavier penalties than those prescribed in view of their probable intentions.[74]

[72] Article 67 (58/13 in the 1926–7 Code) threatened with capital punishment persons who, as leading officials or as members of the secret police of the Tsarist regime, had participated in oppressive measures against the revolutionary movement —i.e. who had fulfilled what was then regarded as their official duty (although it ought to be kept in mind that the lower executive organs are threatened only if they have acted secretly, as *agents provocateurs*). The desire of a revolutionary movement, once victorious, to avenge atrocities committed against it by the former holders of State power is very natural, and legitimate even from a moral point of view broader than that of the revolutionary movement itself: for the possibility of such vengeance may form the only restriction against the brutalities of certain regimes. The *agent provocateur* is not the kind of person whose survival, under the cover of legality, most people desire in a revolutionary period, when sincere partisans of both sides stand up for their conviction. It is another question whether a regime that used extra-judicial procedure for destroying political enemies ought to mix the execution of such a policy with the normal functions of Justice. Besides, this kind of prosecution was ended by the amnesty on the occasion of the tenth anniversary of the October Revolution.

[73] See Krylenko, *Speeches in Court, 1922–1930* (Russian, Moscow, 1931), pp. 4 and 25–6, in the trial of the leaders of the Roman Catholic Church, March 24, 1923.

[74] Ibid. Although article 119 of the Criminal Code very unequivocally described the actions for which the defendants were convicted, and left the judge the decision between application of the penalties threatened by article 83 (incitement to demonstrations against individual measures of the Soviet regime, imprisonment from one year upwards) or by article 69 (demonstrations against the Soviet regime as such, in peace-times imprisonment from three years upwards), Krylenko demanded and got a conviction on article 59 (capital punishment for active counter-revolution). His argument was that at least the main defendants had regarded the demonstrations organised by them against the Disestablishment Laws as preparatory steps towards overthrowing the Soviet regime, and that one of them had appealed to Poland with the demand for protecting the Roman Catholic Church in Russia. The latter was certainly treason in the sense of the Law (see below, p. 115). But Krylenko demanded and got capital sentences (although they were not executed) also against persons his main argument against whom had been : " Do not deal with us as with children. Not in vain each of us has the experience of fifteen or twenty years of revolutionary struggle. You must not teach us how to prepare a revolution. We Bolshevists, too, have applied, as a political tactic your method of combining legal methods (appeal to the government) with illegal demonstrations. But we did so without juridical subterfuges. We should expect you to bear as honestly the consequences of your political defeat." (Ibid., pp. 29–30). This is not the language of a lawyer, nor of a man who intends to impress lawyers. It is the language of War and Revolution. It is true, the Bolshevists themselves (although not those convicted in Court) would not have failed to start a campaign of protest, with juridical arguments, too, if a Tsarist court had inflicted capital punishment for actions of such a character.

Thus there is a mechanism to deal more severely with a political opponent than the law in force at the time of his action provides. But article 8 of the 1926 Criminal Code excludes from responsibility a person who has committed an action which, when committed, formed an offence, if the law has meanwhile changed, and also " by virtue of an alteration of the socio-political situation or if the person who has performed the act cannot now, in the opinion of the court, be regarded as socially dangerous." Most states solve such problems by avoiding prosecutions, and similar procedure would offer no peculiar difficulties for the Soviet with its highly centralised State machinery. But to include within the law itself a rule according to which acts, that are technically offences, should not be punished if the public interest in such punishment has ceased, is certainly a more honest way of dealing with such matters. However, the application of this method supposes that there is no ideological bias in favour of strict, formal legality, and that there are no scruples about allowing crimes, at least in the political field, to be virtually defined as acts, the prosecution of which is deemed by the competent court to be in the public interest.

Another fundamental question of Soviet Criminal Law, meanwhile, has been settled by the stabilisation of Soviet society : but as long as there were recognised classes in the U.S.S.R., some ruling, some oppressed, the conception might arise that the suppression exercised by Criminal Law was not only to be interpreted sociologically in terms of class, but that it was also to be exercised against individuals simply because they belonged to a certain social class, irrespective of the seriousness of the offences committed by them against the laws enacted by the ruling class. Certain modern Western conceptions of special prevention as the main purpose of Criminal Law, directed against the " professional ", or " hereditary " criminal—although in their theoretical foundation these are hardly compatible with Marxism—might enter a strange alliance with such extremist interpretations of class-justice. Although influential in theoretical circles,[75] such conceptions did not succeed in dominating Soviet legislation : in the 1926 Code, just as in the 1919 principles, the social order is defended against actions, not against individuals. True, article 5 of the 1922 Code, in covering purely preventive measures, spoke of " protecting *against delinquencies and against elements* dangerous to the common weal ". But article 7 defined

[75] See below, pp. 208–9.

the danger involved in a person as expressed exclusively by his actual activities. The 1924 principles of the U.S.S.R., although they went further in the direction of prevention and introduced purely personal characteristics of dangerous persons, defined criminal prosecution as directed merely against *actions* threatening the common weal, not against persons as such.

But though a primitive interpretation of "class-justice" [76] was certainly foreign to Soviet legislation in all its phases, in the 1922 R.S.F.S.R. Code as well as in the 1924 principles (art. 22), preventive measures independent of actual violation of the Law were admitted. Persons who, by reason of their criminal past or of their permanent association with criminal circles, constituted a danger to society, even if they should be acquitted for lack of evidence in an actual case under consideration, might be banished from a certain locality for anything up to five years. Such an approach to the potential criminal might coincide with theoretical doubts as to whether the conception of individual "guilt" even of the actual, convicted criminal was compatible with a strictly determinist sociological theory.[77]

In the theoretical interpretation of the 1922 Code [78] the question was answered quite sensibly by the statement that a determinist philosophy excludes the philosophical (or theological) principle of retaliation, but not responsibility in Criminal Law (i.e. the objective necessity for society to protect itself against the dangerous actions of its members by influencing their decisions through suitable measures of repression). Responsibility presupposes a mental state in which the individual concerned might be influenced in his decisions by the threat of repression. This does not apply to the insane, or to children, who can be isolated or educated in suitable institutions, without any intention of exercising a deterrent influence. According to this view [79] the term "guilt" was excluded from the 1922 Code simply in order to avoid its identification with metaphysical conceptions of morals, although it might quite objectively denote the psychological relation of the offender to his criminal action in the form of intention or negligence. Accordingly the 1922 Code used the

[76] See above, p. 20.

[77] For the 1919 position see above, p. 75. The term "sociological" is here applied in the normal general sense. In present-day Soviet legal theoretical literature it is even used as a reproach against those psychological or biological theories that distinguish mainly between the occasional criminal and the recidivist, the latter being the object of special prevention. Marxism, which is certainly a sociological theory, will in all cases stress the importance of *milieu*, and the possibility of re-education.

[78] Piontkovsky, op. cit., 1924, p. 215. [79] Ibid., p. 131.

term " penalties ". But since 1924, under the influence of a relativist reaction against the conception of guilt and individual responsibility, the term " penalties " has been replaced by the more neutral " measures of social defence ".[80] But a distinction was still needed between the repression applied to the conscious law-breaker, and the protective or educational measures applied to insane or juvenile law-breakers. So, " judicial-corrective measures of social defence ", as inflicted by the courts, ranked by the side of " medical " and " medico-educational " measures (art. 7 of the 1926 Code).

As prevention is sought not only against further delinquencies by the person convicted, but also against other potential law-breakers, the preventive effect of Soviet Criminal Law, as of any other, depends on the general opinion that a prison differs from a sanatorium. This difference involves the demand that no one should be committed to " measures of social defence " without having been *proved* dangerous to society. In the 1927 editions of the R.S.F.S.R. Code as well as the U.S.S.R. principles, banishment, as a protective measure, might be applied only after conviction for a particular crime. Like any other part of the judgment, it might be contested by an appeal to the Court of Cassation. The G.P.U. also had the right to banish persons who had been convicted at least twice for certain crimes (those associated with the professional criminal in other countries), and also " activists of anti-Soviet parties " to camps of forced labour for a maximum of three years.[81] Whilst it would not be easy, by means of Administrative Law, to refute an assertion by the G.P.U. that a certain person belonged to the latter category, misuse of the powers of detention against professional criminals was restricted by the demand for at least two convictions by the ordinary court for the crime concerned. Of course, the G.P.U. might proceed mechanically once these two convictions—say for theft—had been made by a court, whilst the Court itself (or the Court of Cassation) would still have to examine whether the convicted person was indeed dangerous enough to justify protective banishment. But the Court might easily avoid such a situation by granting suspended sentence.

As regards the social interpretation of criminal prosecution, the 1922 Code, in its enumeration of aggravating and extenuating

[80] In 1922 (art. 5), as well as in 1919, it was still retained—evidently with the intention of differentiating between ".penalties " and other " measures of social defence ", and to spare the insane or young the usual associations of the term " penalty ".

[81] Decree of October 16, 1922 (S.U. 1922/844).

circumstances, avoided going beyond the position taken up in 1919[82]; the social position of the defendant formed an essential element in shaping the opinion of the Court in considering the reasons for his criminal action, but it was not in itself an aggravating or extenuating circumstance. Articles 31–2 of the U.S.S.R. principles of 1924 tried to proceed along the line of a class-interpretation of Justice to the length of recognising such circumstances based on the mere fact of belonging to the capitalist or to the working-classes. But instructions issued in 1925 by the People's Commissariat for Justice of the R.S.F.S.R.[83] explained that carrying out a class policy in the penal field did not mean the conviction of the N.E.P.-man or *kulak*, and the acquittal of the worker (which was a mass-phenomenon in contemporary Soviet justice). What was demanded was that the social danger involved in the delinquency should be clearly appreciated from the point of view of the proletariat as a whole. In 1927, on the demand of the R.S.F.S.R.,[62] the aggravating, or attenuating circumstance of the social status of the defendant was removed from Criminal Law. Since then, the term " class-justice " can be applied to Soviet justice only in the objective sense, namely (1) in that, according to the Marxists, the basic conceptions of what social relations ought to be protected by justice are shaped by the ruling class in line with its class-ideology and its class-interest, and (2) in that the working of Justice is regarded as an instrument of remorseless class-struggle, so that ruthless oppression is applied to all antagonists of the existing regime. But, apart from the interlude already mentioned, Soviet Justice rejects the primitive conception of class justice as meaning discrimination betweeen the private interests of various groups of citizens according to their social status.[76] This can be supported by the well-established fact that during the N.E.P. a member of the Communist Party involved in corruption was much more likely to be shot than a non-Communist official—for the simple reason that corruption in the ranks of the ruling party was much more dangerous from the latter's point of view than the continuation of the habits acquired under Tsarism by some minor official. Certainly, the *kulak* who demanded extravagant interest from a neighbouring smallholder would be more likely to be impeached for usury than that same smallholder if he should have the opportunity of exploiting another neighbour's difficulties. But the reason for such differentiation was not a

[82] See above, p. 75.

[83] Quoted by Zelitch, op. cit., p. 366.

sympathy for the shortcomings of smallholders exploiting their neighbours' difficulties (morally, a Marxist would take rather the opposite point of view), but the fact that the offence of usury had been established by the Soviet in order to prevent certain economic processes of which, by the very nature of things, only the *kulak* could be the subject. Specially severe punishments enacted (especially during the period of agricultural collectivisation) against *kulaks* who committed certain crimes that were less severely punished if committed by other persons,[84] ought to be considered in the same light as the demand of the Civil Code that legal transactions ought to be interpreted according to their material, economic content.[85] Apart from the above-mentioned aberration, Soviet Criminal Law, even before the stabilisation of the new society since 1936, dealt with individuals belonging to different social groups in different ways only in so far as they were the bearers of different social processes.

But interpretation of State and Law as compulsion exercised by the ruling class implied a concentration of judicial repression against political crimes. The characteristic division of the War-Communist period, between ruthless dictatorship exercised by the Revolutionary Tribunals, and a very human approach of the People's Courts to the ordinary law-breaker, and to the circumstances that had rendered him a criminal, developed further during the N.E.P. It became even more impressive after 1922 through the concentration of jurisdiction over all kinds of crime in the ordinary judicial procedure, and of all Criminal Law within the framework of one code. Attempts were still being made to interpret the extremes of revolutionary legislation as merely temporary emergency measures.[86] With the U.S.S.R. surrounded by hostile capitalist states and the fundamental internal problems not yet solved, an emergency certainly existed. And even if it were temporary it was likely to be very long, so that Soviet justice tended to go on regarding political crime as by far the most serious kind of crime, without seeming likely to reach a more tolerant attitude. The distinction between the most

[84] Article 61 of the Criminal Code (refusal to perform any public duty, especially food-deliveries) in the form as amended February 15, 1931 (S.U. 1931/102).

[85] See above, pp. 93–4.

[86] For example, in the U.S.S.R. principles of 1924, capital punishment was mentioned merely in a remark to article 13, outside the systematic enumeration of admitted penalties, and was explicitly described as a "provisional measure". On October 31, 1927, it was, indeed, repealed for a large number of crimes, and preserved only for directly counter-revolutionary acts. But very soon after the definition of the latter was greatly widened. See below, p. 209.

serious crimes for which a minimum [87] and the less serious ones for which a maximum penalty was prescribed by the Code, found further explanation in the U.S.S.R. principles of 1924. Here, the former were identified with those actions " that are directed against the principles of the Soviet constitution and which, therefore, are regarded as the most serious ones."

Amongst these main objects of judicial repression the distinctly " counter-revolutionary crimes " are a special and important group. In article 57 of the 1922 Code they are defined as " any actions directed towards overthrowing the Soviet regime, or towards supporting that part of the international bourgeoisie which does not recognise the equal status of the Communist regime, and attempts to overthrow the latter by intervention ".[88] In the 1923 edition of the Code such actions are included which, without the direct aims above described, " implied an attack on the fundamental political and economic achievements of the Revolution and thus attempted to injure, or to undermine the Soviet regime ". So the " eventual intention ", i.e. the readiness of the delinquent to admit consequences of his action which he had not directly envisaged, was introduced into the definition of the crime most severely persecuted by Soviet Law. In the 1927 edition of the Criminal Code this conception was dropped for a short time,[89] but attempts against the external security of the U.S.S.R., against the solution of the national question (for example, pogroms), and against any other socialist state even if it did not belong to the U.S.S.R., were included into the definition of counter-revolutionary crimes.

Prior to 1927 [86] the application of capital punishment was not restricted to the actions of avowed enemies of the regime. As in the Civil War, the same threat was applied to other crimes which are regarded by most people as much more contemptible than treason for political reasons, though most states which apply the death penalty for the latter would not use this sanction

[87] But article 28 of the 1922 Code, like the principles of 1919, provided a general right of the Court to mitigate punishment under the legal minimum, provided that the reasons for such procedure were explicitly stated in the judgment.

[88] Thus there was even a legal explanation for the tendency of Soviet jurisdiction to use a very topical (from the point of view of current international relations) description of the partners of a supposedly treacherous action. For it depends very much on the interpretation of the policies of a foreign power whether collaboration with it may be regarded as legitimately furthering the international relations of the U.S.S.R., or as counter-revolution. Disagreements on this point or failure of the defendants to understand at the right time changes in international policies, may explain many of the " mysteries of the purges ".

[89] See below, pp. 209–10.

against mere corruption. According to the 1922 Code, capital punishment was applicable in the most serious cases of bribery (arts. 114 and 130), appropriation of public property through fraudulent misuse of official power (art. 128), the passing of unjust sentences for reasons of personal interest by judges (art. 111) and misuse of official power (art. 110). In all these cases, as well as in that of counter-revolution proper, under the War-Communist regime the Revolutionary Tribunals, or the Cheka (the "Extraordinary Commission for Fighting Counter-revolution, Corruption and Speculation") had had jurisdiction. They had been more ready to apply "the highest measure of social defence" than the Courts that succeeded them under the Criminal Code. Knowledge of the potential dangers of the huge inheritance of corruption left by Tsarism for a regime which entrusted its officials with such large powers and depended on public trust in their honesty, seems to have dictated that catalogue of objects for the most severe repression. At the beginning of the N.E.P. the danger that capitalism might co-operate with corrupt officials, and thus thwart all legislation intended to keep the N.E.P.-man in his proper place was regarded as actual. But five years after the enactment of the 1922 Code the application of extreme measures against non-political criminals seemed superfluous.[86] Re-education now appeared as the main purpose of criminal policy, except for the convinced political opponent, or enemy agent, who could only be rendered harmless by annihilation.

In the field of non-political crime, the educational purpose prevails over the purely repressive, and the prescriptions of the Code may be regarded as a fair reflection of social values as interpreted by Soviet Justice. The personality of the citizen is granted by far the strongest protection. As in other countries, murder ranks amongst the most serious offences. But it is not regarded as necessarily the most serious one.[90] Very serious cases of intentionally inflicting grievous bodily injuries, violation of women under aggravating circumstances, and forcing women into prostitution, rank beside the most grave forms of murder. Murder without aggravating circumstances[91] gets punishment

[90] In considering this point it ought to be kept in mind that (1) the mysticism of the *jus talionis* is completely strange to Soviet law, which regards the murderer—at least if he has not acted for political reasons—as a suitable subject of re-education, and (2) that, from the latter point of view, the maximum term of imprisonment was so restricted that differentiation between serious crimes was not easy.

[91] It is true, not only motives of private interest, but even jealousy are enumerated amongst the aggravating circumstances—in addition to the usual, like cruelty, special

equal to that prescribed for violation of women, for sexual intercourse with children, intentionally inflicting grievous bodily injury, furthering and living from a woman's prostitution, professional abortion if committed by laymen under aggravating circumstances,[92] and transference of mentally sound persons to an asylum for reasons of private interest.

Property, in general, is much less protected : the *maximum* penalty for simple theft [93] is six months, for burglary two years imprisonment. Even in the 1922 Code, public property is protected by sterner threats, and the theft of a farmer's horse brings a *minimum* of two years imprisonment. Robbery under aggravating circumstances, and any kind of banditry (i.e. robbery committed by a group of persons) is threatened with capital punishment. Here it is clearly not property but State security which is the actual object of protection. Uneconomic management of State property, even by mere negligence,[94] brings a minimum of one year's imprisonment to state officials (art. 128) or leaseholders (art. 129) entrusted with the administration of this property. The N.E.P.-man who did not use a loan granted him by the State for the purpose prescribed in the agreement risked a minimum of two years, and confiscation of all his private property, unless he had risked his (and his partner's) life by collusion with a bribed State official (art. 130).

The 1922 Criminal Code was reluctant to inflict heavy penalties for violations of details of the established order. Usurpation by religious organisations of functions in the administrative or judicial field, of which they had been deprived by the Disestablishment Act (art. 123), compulsory raising of taxes for religious organisations (art. 122) and, on the other hand, the disturbance of legitimate acts of religious worship (art. 125), were threatened with forced labour at the place of normal employment (i.e. without imprisonment) up to a maximum of six months. Double punishment was risked by anyone who used superstition as a

obligations towards the victim, etc. So it is very difficult to imagine a case of "simple murder", under Soviet Law, where a Western jury would not try to avoid capital punishment.

[92] Without the consent of the woman, or resulting in her death.

[93] It ought not to be forgotten that some months before the enactment of that Code hundreds of thousands of people in the towns were forced, by starvation, to regular thefts. See Dobb, op. cit., p. 190. Of course, any Soviet court would acquit in such cases, but even so they could not remain without influence on the general moral approach to theft. In 1924, pilfering by workers in factories (i.e., as a rule against public property) was exempted from other than disciplinary sanctions (see Freund, op. cit., p. 188).

[94] Intentional mismanagement for political or private reasons would immediately put the affair on a much more serious level.

means of deceit (say by feigned miracles) or who organised religious education in State schools. For preventing the factory organisations of the trade unions from exercising their legitimate functions the punishment was forced labour from six months upwards (art. 134), and for ordinary infringements of the Labour Code mere fines or short terms of forced labour at the place of employment. It should be remembered that very serious infringements of Soviet law in these fields would have been brought within the definition of political crimes.

The commercial activities of the N.E.P.-man were restricted by penalties for usury (art. 193—there was no legal maximum for interest so that the judge had to decide the case according to its circumstances), and for cornering a market (art. 127), the minimum penalty being six months' imprisonment. Cornering by a ring was threatened with a minimum penalty of two years' imprisonment, confiscation of private property and loss of the right to future commercial activities. Similar penalties (arts. 61–2) threatened the *kulak* who tried to evade his obligations to sell his products to the public purchasing organisations, again with special emphasis against attempts to control the market by conspiration. These rulings served later [95] as a legal lever for the complete expropriation of the *kulaks*.

Under the N.E.P., many civic duties that had been theoretically accepted under the War-Communist regime were eliminated. But it is characteristic of the general tendencies of Soviet Law that very tight restrictions were imposed on the activities even of the "independent" business man, and still more that not only honesty but even some degree of diligence were demanded from everyone who had to administer public property. Most states merely demand from their citizens non-interference with their fellows' rights, although, especially in the protection of human life, certain cases of negligence are also regarded as punishable. To interpret Soviet Criminal Law in this sense is possible only by means of very general abstractions, such as the construction of a right of the public to find the market supplied with all goods which can be produced under the circumstances at the lowest reasonable prices. But Soviet Law, including that of the N.E.P.-period, can be explained much more satisfactorily by the assumption of positive duties. The above-mentioned obligations are imposed upon certain groups of citizens in consequence of the special importance of their services for the satis-

[95] See below, p. 171.

faction of public needs. But certain positive duties are imposed on everybody, even in peace-time. Article 164 of the 1922 Criminal Code threatens any citizen who does not do all in his or her power to help another in danger of life with up to six months' forced labour (at the place of employment), if death or serious bodily injury has resulted from his failure to help.[96] This might be constructed as a right of each citizen to assistance in peril. But the demand made goes beyond what is expected of the citizen in other countries, apart from cases of public emergency. In revolutionary times very great demands on the readiness of the citizen to assist his fellows seemed reasonable, but during the period of stabilisation preceding the present War the advisability of criminal prosecutions for " failure to be a hero " has become a contested issue.[97]

In the field of Constitutional Law it was only during the period under discussion that real problems arose. The One-Party-System had always rendered the statute of the Communist Party a most essential part of the real constitution of the country—and it may be said that it became complete only during the N.E.P.-period, when the danger that factions contesting within the Party might become expressions of distinct class-interests in the country resulted in the abolition of the freedom of factional contest within the Party in favour of " iron homogeneity ". But these are developments outside the proper legal sphere. In Constitutional Law the most important development was the federation of the Soviet Republics. The U.S.S.R. was founded, by agreement on general principles, on December 30, 1922. But the new constitution did not come into force until July, 1924, after much discussion.[98] Important, from our point of view, is the fact that here the principle of division of powers, rejected by Soviet ideology in its usual applications, was introduced for a certain limited purpose : protecting the autonomy of the smaller national republics which had been granted to them by the constitutional compromise from interference. To secure this in the federal constitution a two-chamber system was established, with the Second Chamber composed of a majority of non-Russians. Of course, under the One-party system it was most unlikely

[96] For medical personnel the maximum punishment is even two years' imprisonment. But this is not in principle different from professional duties established in most countries for certain groups of citizens, for example for soldiers.

[97] See Vishinsky, op. cit., 1939.

[98] See the present writer's *Federalism in Central and Eastern Europe*, published 1945, in the International Library of Sociology and Social Reconstruction, part IV, and the materials reprinted in Batsell, *Soviet Rule in Russia*, London, 1929.

that the Second Chamber would in fact exercise its powers of obstructing legislation deemed harmful to the rights of the national republics. It functions as a body where the complaints of these republics and matters especially touching their interests were discussed.[99] The actual decisions, as all important decisions in Soviet life, are taken within the Party caucus. But the purpose of the system is to bring different influences to bear upon that caucus, and to suggest compromise in certain fields where the mere working of compulsion, otherwise a normal part of proletarian dictatorship, is regarded as undesirable. These fields are mainly cultural (although they include, for example, the application of general principles of Soviet Law to local circumstances). It is important for our study that here the conception of constitutional legality came to mean something deeper than a mere matter of passing party resolutions through the established State machinery : at least in some fields of Soviet life constitutionalism was conceived as a means of compromise between interests accepted as distinct, but equally legitimate. To a certain degree this compromise coincided with the general compromise underlying the N.E.P. : the nationality question was essentially a question of relations with the non-Russian peasantry, sometimes under *kulak* influence, but it was also a compromise with the bourgeoisie of some national minorities who, because they had been oppressed under Tsarism, were inclined to co-operate with the Soviet.[100] Some people, therefore, would interpret the Soviet nationalities' policy as essentially bound to the N.E.P., but it survived the latter and, by permeating the whole conception of Soviet patriotism, formed an essential foundation of the new state. So it introduced into the otherwise homogeneous state partial conceptions of equilibrium which may be important from the point of view of its eventual constitutional evolution. It is true that, however close the connection is between the socialist character of the revolution and its successful approach to the nationalities ' problem, in solving this problem the Russian revolution had to carry out general democratic tasks. In this respect it is reminiscent of another Soviet achievement, the Matrimonial Code of 1918. Each of them proves the ability of the Russian revolution to create new Law—but neither of them can be regarded as an example of specifically socialist Law.

[99] See the example given by Batsell, op. cit., pp. 648–9.

[100] See Stalin, *Marxism and the National and Colonial Question*, Moscow, 1940 (English ed.), *passim*.

### (c) Soviet Judicial Organisation after the 1922 Reforms

The codification of Soviet law of judicial procedure served the double purpose of giving private enterprise the necessary legal security from arbitrary interference by the local authorities, and of preserving public policies, as envisaged by the central authorities, from arbitrary interpretation by a judiciary dependent on the local authorities. Lenin deemed that Soviet Russia was " living in a sea of illegality " and that the local authorities were " one of the principal, if not *the* principal, adversaries to the establishment of civilised legality ".[101] The aim of stabilising " revolutionary legality " was pursued in two different ways : the judicial functions themselves were centralised so that supervision of the judiciary shifted from the local Soviets to the supreme judicial organisations, and a special organ for " safeguarding revolutionary legality ", the public attorneyship, was established and organised on a strictly centralised basis.[102]

Centralisation of the judicial functions proceeded through the establishment of Gubernial Courts and Supreme Courts of the individual Soviet Republics, elected respectively by the Executive Committees of the Gubernial, or of the all-Russian, all-Ukrainian, etc., Soviets. The Gubernial Soviet, in its choice of Gubernial judges, depended on approval by the national People's Commissariat for Justice. The Gubernial Courts had to deal with all complicated cases in Civil Law and with the more important cases in Criminal Law, those for which a bench of the local People's Court with six People's Assessors [103] had been formerly competent, as well as those counter-revolutionary crimes [104] that had come under the competence of the Revolutionary Tribunals, and also with the more important violations of the duties of officials and managers of economic organisations.[105] For a member of the Gubernial Court two years, for the President and his Deputies three years of judicial experience were demanded, and one out of eight of the People's Assessors to these Courts had to be People's Judge (i.e. President of a local Court), so as to enable the formation of a competent

[101] Lenin, *Works*, Russian, vol. XXVII, p. 300.

[102] To achieve this, Lenin (see Ibid.) had to strive against the majority of the Communist group in the Central Executive Committee who intended to make the attorneys dependent on the local Soviets, i.e. the very authorities they had to supervise (at least indirectly, by their influence on the judiciary).

[103] See above, p. 67.

[104] See above, pp. 63 and 77. The Revolutionary Tribunals were dissolved in the beginning of 1922.

[105] Article 26 of the Code of Criminal Procedure of May 25, 1922.

bench in cases of Civil Law.[106] Both provisions meant decisive steps in the formation of a new professional Judiciary. The institution of recalling judges by the Soviet which had elected them was preserved, but lost importance—although the short term of office continued to render the judges dependent on their electors. But now the local Judges had to give judgments much more nearly in accordance with the general lines of Soviet Jurisdiction. Amongst the reasons for opening disciplinary investigation against a judge was included " cassation of a number of judgments in cases of Criminal and Civil Law which have been passed by the judicial worker if this has been done on account of these judgments contradicting the general spirit of the laws of the R.S.F.S.R. and the interests of the working-classes ".[107] To run this danger, from the local People's Judge's point of view, was certainly more risky than having, at the worst, to look for a job in another district after having displeased the local Soviet by applying the Law even though it were disagreeable for the Judge's prospective electors.

Some local bias on the part of the Judge was regarded as inevitable, and even desirable in so far as it would result in adapting the measure of punishment to circumstances.[108] But, as a counterweight, there was to be an organ that would impeach for violation of the Law, independent of local explanations of the illegal proceedings of local authorities,[109] and to preserve the unity of the Law, as distinct from Kaluga or Kasan conceptions of legality. Therefore this organ, the Public Attorneyship,[110] was subordinated merely to the central authorities, i.e. the People's Commissar for Justice as the Attorney of the Republic, and the Supreme Court on whose interpretation of the Law the attorneys of course depended.

The Soviet Attorneyship is one of the most characteristic features of Soviet jurisdiction. It is not merely a hierarchy of public prosecutors, as in other continental countries.[111] The

[106] Articles 64–65 of the Law on the Organisation of the Courts, October 31, 1922.

[107] Ibid, article 112.

[108] Lenin, *Works*, Russian, vol. XXVII, p. 299.

[109] Ibid. It is remarkable that Lenin thought mainly of Criminal Procedure (and not of the various other ways in which the legality of administrative acts might be contested) and of local officials claiming emergency interests of public policy as the typical defendants.

[110] Established by decree of May 28, 1922, S.U. 1922/424.

[111] The tendency of Soviet Criminal Law merely to punish actions dangerous to society excludes, in theory, the continental distinction between prosecutions by the attorneyship acting in the public interest for offences threatening the common weal, and other actions which are prosecuted merely in the interest of the party concerned, and even more the analogous construction current in this country which substitutes

attorneys have to see that the general working of the State machinery keeps within the framework of the Laws. Criminal proceedings against officials committing illegal acts are only one of the means by which they fulfil this general task. The procedure of " cassation by the way of supervision " (as distinct from cassation on demand of the party in question) is another means, and this expedient may be applied by the higher Soviet Courts even after a judgment has come into force.[112] Normally it is the Public Attorney at the respective Court who starts such a procedure, but the Court is entitled to take the initiative itself, and has in any case the final decision. And apart from proceedings in Court the Attorney is expected to protest against any measures taken by State organs contrary to the Law.[113] The most conspicuous amongst the duties of the Attorney-General, i.e. the People's Commissar for Justice of a Union Republic, is " supervising the legality of all actions of the People's Commissariats, of all central authorities and organisations, and proposing the abolition or amendment of orders and decrees of such authorities deemed by him contrary to the Law ".[113] In most countries the Minister of Justice is asked for his opinion as regards the legality of regulations envisaged. It is certainly easier in the U.S.S.R. than elsewhere to overcome this kind of difficulty, for the supreme administrative authority is identical with the legislative one. If its attention were drawn, by the Attorney-General, to a contradiction with existing law, it could easily [114] amend the law to accord with the decree envisaged, without interfering with formal legality. But Soviet Law brings this very normal function of the People's Commissariat for Justice into line with the functions of the local attorneys who act as checks on the local authorities (who cannot so easily rectify the legal flaws in their decrees) and with their duty to see, for instance, that no one is kept in prison without proper legal

public prosecution for a private claimant. Under Soviet Law, too, (art. 10 of the 1922 Criminal Code) prosecution for certain delinquencies (slight bodily injury, slander, etc.) depends on the demand of the injured citizen. But, if the public interest demands it (for instance, if there has been some big increase of drunkenness in the district) the Attorney is allowed to continue the prosecution even after the persons immediately concerned have been reconciled. So it may be assumed that in the normal case the dependence of prosecution on demand of the person concerned is the outcome of public interest (in avoiding unnecessary trials) rather than of a supposed interpretation of criminal procedure in slighter cases as a contest between the persons concerned.

[112] Articles 429–30 of the Code of Criminal Procedure.

[113] Article 85a of the 1922 Statute on the Constitution of the Courts.

[114] Apart from the division of powers between the federation and the individual republics. See also above, pp. 119–20.

grounds.[115] However modest may be the influence wielded by considerations of formal legality at the centre, on the periphery the very interest of the centre in homogeneous policies demands strict regard for legality. So the attorneys work as an agency of legality as well as of centralism.

The office of Public Attorney is not constructed solely to deal with the special interests of the prosecution, but with legality as such. So it may appear inconsistent to have not only a judiciary dependent on central judicial authorities, but also a special organ dependent on the same authorities which has virtually to pursue the same ends. In fact, a glance at the decisions of the Supreme Court "by way of supervision"[116] shows that the Attorney-General takes the initiative in quashing unreasonably hard judgments at least as often as he protests against sentences regarded as too lenient,[117] and that in this respect there is hardly any difference between the direction in which the initiative of the Attorney-General is exercised and that of the President of the Supreme Court. In the lower grades of the judicial hierarchy, the Attorney might be expected to take less account of local political trends and of the special circumstances of the case than the Court[108] and to regard his office as nearer to the general continental conception of public prosecutor. Repeated quashings by the Supreme Court of judgments of lower courts on account of their over-severity seems to bring less reproach upon the Attorney himself, who demanded such stern or even sterner sentences, than upon the Court which has uncritically accepted such proposals. It seems an accepted duty of attorneyship, at least in its lower grades, to stress, where there is any doubt, the case for the prosecution (its exclusive duty in other continental countries), even if there should be a strong case for acquittal through lack of evidence sufficient for conviction. If in view of the prosecutor's attitude the Court is more afraid of the possible acquittal of a guilty man than of the possible conviction of an innocent one,[117] and is inclined to rely rather on the higher courts for correcting mistakes, than to bear responsibilities itself, the atmosphere in the lower

[115] Article 89h of the 1922 Statute on the Constitution of the Courts.

[116] The most important of which can be found in *Sovietskaja Justicija*.

[117] Of course, such a state of things might result simply from a tendency of the lower courts to be rather too harsh than too lenient in doubtful cases. Certainly such a tendency exists in all cases with immediate bearings on the policies of the regime (e.g. proceedings for alleged speculation, or for failure to fulfil managerial duties). But there is no reason to assume any other approach than a purely human and judicial one to the ordinary thief or murderer.

courts may be unfriendly to the defendant at least in cases with a political interest. It has been remarked that, whilst at the preliminary and trial proceedings the wide discretionary power of the trial court frequently works against the defendant, the latter is the ultimate beneficiary in the cassational and supervisory tribunals through the application of the very same wide discretionary powers, and that the ultimate aim of the system is directed towards a thorough attempt to correct judicial errors.[118] Certainly the system works in this way if taken as a whole, i.e. if the corrective intervention of the higher instances is regarded as a normal phenomenon. Indeed, it is encouraged by the ruling (art. 424 of the 1922 Code of Criminal Procedure), that no appeal by the defendant may result in a judgment less favourable for him than that against which the appeal has been directed. Such an attitude contradicts that popular aversion to complicated judicial procedure which lay at the root of the theoretical rejection of appeal (as distinct from demand for cassation of incorrect judgments) originally found in Soviet Law of Procedure.[119] To-day it is readily admitted that the Soviet procedure of cassation is not concerned with the mere formal aspects of procedure, but that it contains also elements of what is called elsewhere revision or appeal.[120]

The concept that it is the duty of the higher courts and even of the Public Attorney to protect the legitimate interests of the defendant makes for the rather subordinate position of the advocate, not so much in Soviet Law of Procedure,[121] as in the emphasis laid by public opinion on the various elements of the judicial machinery. The formal contest of the parties to the proceedings, glorified by most Western lawyers as "the rule of Law", is regarded by Soviet opinion as a mere expedient to serve the public interest in justice. The bourgeois conception of the law suit as a private affair of the parties concerned which they can freely dispose of, is rejected.[120] Even in Civil Law the higher court is entitled and obliged in its decision to go beyond the claims of the appellant, if it regards this as justified,[122] and such procedure is recommended in order to protect the interests of claimants lacking general or juridical education.[123] With Court and

[118] Zelitch, op. cit., p. 319. [119] See above, pp. 69–70.

[120] See *S. J.*, 1939, No. 19, pp. 28 ff.

[121] Violation of his rights, or of the right of the defendant to have the advocate chosen by himself, is a compulsory reason for cassation of judgments.

[122] Article 245 of the Code of Criminal Procedure. [123] Ibid., article 5.

Attorney occupying such positions, the sphere elsewhere dominated by Counsel is bound to be restricted to the emphasis of one special side of the social interest in Justice, namely that no argument speaking in favour of the defendant, or the plaintiff, should be omitted. But the counsel is not expected to advocate all the interests of the defendant, including that of evading the legal consequences of his actions.[124] There is no reason to doubt the possibility of the Soviet advocate defending his client if he believes him to be innocent, and otherwise to emphasise all mitigating circumstances. But it is quite true that the Soviet counsel cannot support his client in the contest on the legal or moral merits of an action avowedly harmful to the regime without exposing himself to the reproach of being disloyal to it. Once the latter's policies are involved, Soviet Law becomes, avowedly, the political weapon of a dictatorial regime. But within the framework of that political and social order which the regime protects, the Law attempts to deal justly with every citizen's personal interests.

### (*d*) The Social Conditions of the Application of N.E.P. Law

Soviet Law, under the N.E.P., involved a compromise between the original socialist conceptions of the Revolution, and certain principles current in the Law of capitalist states, somewhat modified by Soviet legislation. To understand the results of that legislation, and the character of its application in practice, the social structure of the society it served must be the starting-point. Socialist and capitalist elements existed in the Soviet society of the period, just as there were socialist and capitalist elements in the Law of the period. What were the relations of these elements?

Apart from certain special institutions, Soviet Law, an admixture of both elements, was applied in its totality to the whole of Soviet economics. The N.E.P.-man entrepreneur or leaseholder of a nationalised enterprise was subject to obligations that can only be understood on the assumption that he was regarded as a kind of public trustee, whilst the State-trust had to dismiss its workers when it became insolvent—as capitalists do in any country. To understand the period, it must be realised at the outset that the very terms of "socialist" and "capitalist" may mean very different things when applied to the economic and to the legal spheres. In economics, if the

[124] Krylenko, quoted by Zelitch, op. cit., pp. 250–1.

Marxist differentiation between the lower "socialist", and the higher "communist" stages of post-capitalist development [125] is accepted, it is very difficult to define the former as anything beyond public ownership and control of the most essential means of production with its necessary implications as regards planning. There may be controversies over the interpretation of certain border-phenomena, for example, whether a peasants' co-operative is sufficiently controlled by the leading organisations of national economy to be regarded as a mere autonomous element in the socialist sector rather than as collective capitalism. But these are details—typical examples of co-operatives could be constructed that would fit both definitions. The only intelligible interpretation of State capitalism (in the economic sense) as distinct from socialism is Lenin's, namely : the State-controlled activities of private entrepreneurs, who, indeed, played a very important rôle during the N.E.P.

But in a legal system socialist and capitalist elements may have a very different significance. In a typical capitalist society the economic initiative is left to individual entrepreneurs, whether individual persons, or Joint Stock Companies, Trusts, etc. It is their right, but not their duty to work—otherwise there would be no freedom of capitalist enterprise, and no possibility for the profit motive to work as the regulator of such a society. Their duties (as well as those of all the other members of such a society) consist in non-interference with the rights that are regarded as essential for the functioning of the society. These rights include the possibility of capitalist enterprise [126] and such personal status for the various members of the society as is deemed necessary for the latter's productive efficiency, for its acceptance and defence by the citizens, etc.[127]

In a typical socialist society all economic initiative rests with the State. If the individual citizens are granted certain

[125] See above, Chapter II, pp. 24–5.

[126] Not necessarily the actual freedom of every owner of the capital necessary to start a private undertaking. Anti-trust legislation is certainly not an essential element of capitalist legality, although it may fulfil essential demands of the ideology of free competition usually covering capitalism of any type.

[127] It is the motivation and function of, say, Labour legislation within the whole economic system, not its actual content, that counts for our distinction. A country with a very high standard of protection of labour need not necessarily be socialist, nor *vice versa*. Even people who regard socialism merely from the trade-unionist point of view might be ready to compare different social systems from the point of view of their efficiency under equal conditions, i.e. in countries with similar economic resources. But it is quite conceivable that a socialist system, just because it can appeal to the self-interest of its citizens in its prosperity, may demand such sacrifices as no capitalist system could demand without risking collapse, at least in the next war.

rights (these being desirable in the interest of the internal strength of such a state), these rights may in part concern personal freedoms which can be left outside State planning without injuring the latter's efficiency. But chiefly they will concern the direction of this planning : the State promises its citizens that it will handle economics in such a way that certain accepted needs of the citizens—say preservation of forests for certain purposes,[128] or full employment,[129] or a certain minimum standard of life—will be granted. As a guarantee for the fulfilment of such promises in the way desired by the citizens the State grants the latter certain possibilities for participating in the management of national economics.[130] In order to fulfil such promises, and indeed to make socialist economics work at all, the State establishes certain duties of its citizens that go far beyond mere non-interference with other people's rights. In a socialist system the fulfilment of civic duties has to cover that decisive sector of social activities which capitalism leaves to the " automatic ", extra-legal, working of private enterprise.

If a socialist state is successful in abolishing unemployment the threat of the latter loses its efficiency in enforcing diligent management, and quite a lot of managerial duties that otherwise might be enforced by the threat of dismissal have to be included in the Criminal Code. This does not mean that the actual position of the man who holds office during the pleasure of the leading organs of the State is necessarily less free than that of his colleague in a capitalist country who holds office during the pleasure of the Board of Directors of a Trust—which may be the only potential employer of his special skill. It simply means that there are legal duties where, under a capitalist system, there would have been extra-legal dependences. In a democratic conception of socialism,[131] every duty is balanced by

[128] See above, p. 52. [129] See below, p. 221.

[130] In theory, an autocratic socialism—say on Catholic authoritarian lines—could be conceived. But, in our times, this is not a political possibility. Those ideological forces that might support planning for, but not by, the people are so closely connected with the defence of the capitalist order of society that they cannot support any kind of Socialism. And those forces that may establish a socialist society depend on mass-support that never would be forthcoming without the prospect of the individual citizen participating in running the machinery he has helped to conquer (within such limits as by modern conditions set to the influence of the individual over social processes at all). It is another question how far democratic control of State economics can be realised. See below, pp. 260–3.

[131] I.e. in a conception based on running economics with the active participation of the citizens, as opposed to an autocratic one. This question has nothing to do with the merits or demerits of some forms of parliamentarism, and the definition given certainly includes the Bolsheviks.

corresponding means of securing that it will only be enforced according to the needs of the community, without encroaching upon those individual rights which the State leaves to the private sphere of its citizens. Therefore, from the abstract socialist point of view [132] the working of civic duty is much preferable to automatisms which may or may not work in the direction desired.

Actually it is very difficult to imagine, at least in our times, a socialist state that would really direct all civic activities needed for the fulfilment of its functions in the same way that it (or any capitalist state) directs, say, the fulfilment of the duty to defend the country against external aggression. Many of its ends will be achieved by allowing the pressure of economic reality (controlled by itself) rather than by the law. For example, since the failure of the " Duty to Work ", the normal participation of the U.S.S.R.'s citizens in the national productive effort is enforced by the same mechanism as in any capitalist country—namely, by the alternative of starvation. Entry into the different professions is regulated not by compulsory direction but by increasing or decreasing the material rewards offered by the various professions according to the needs of State planning. Thus young people who, for non-material motives, prefer one profession to another which is better paid, remain free to choose, though the promise of high earnings (and, in many cases, also of external social distinction) will probably attract the necessary numbers of young people demanded by the plan. The examples given show the mistake of identifying specific socialist forms of legal regulation with socialist economics or even with the realisation of socialist ideals : most socialists—Russian and non-Russian—will agree that the last method described is infinitely preferable from the point of view of combining the needs of planned economics with the demands of personal freedom, and would regard the deviations of the U.S.S.R. from these principles enforced by the needs of the present war and its preparation, as necessary but regrettable sacrifices in an emergency. (In the period of War-Communism, as we have seen above, the attitude of the Russian Communists was different, and the theoretical demands for strictly socialist regulation were used as an ideological justification for what, in fact, were mere emergency measures).

[132] I.e. from a point of view that prefers socialist forms of regulation, for their own sake, to any others. That this point of view does not necessarily coincide with the interests of a socialist society will soon be illustrated.

In spite of occasional remarks on the " bourgeois " character of the legal institutions inherited from bourgeois society,[133] Marxism, as a socio-economic theory, is bound to regard as socialist Law all that furthers the development of a society which is socialist in the economic sense—and *vice versa*. From this point of view the distinction we have just elaborated is meaningless : the question (hotly discussed amongst Soviet lawyers),[134] whether the Law of the N.E.P. was socialist or not, might easily be answered by the historical fact that it has rendered possible the triumph of a socialist economic system. But from the point of view of analysis of the legal forms applied, it is easily conceivable that the optimum conditions for the development of a socialist society (in the economic sense) might differ from the maximum development of those juridical forms which characterise the " pure type " of socialist regulation. It may be questioned whether the " pure type " of socialist Law corresponds to any likely development of socialist reality. It may be argued that this " pure type ", like many others, is an abstraction, a mere antithesis to the " ideal type " of liberal state with a minimum of interference in economic processes. It may be pointed out that, apart from the ideological advocates of War-Communist emergency measures, it is the liberal critics of socialism[135] who have underlined that all-embracing juridical regulation of human behaviour alleged to be characteristic of the " pure " socialist state. During the development of socialism on foundations shaped by capitalism it might appear very unreasonable to drop, for the sake of mere regulations, all those mechanisms for regulating human behaviour developed by the predecessors of the socialist society. In a higher stage of development, custom and the moral pressure of public opinion may secure a very large part of those civic activities needed to make socialist economics successful,[136] with legal compulsion reduced to a rather auxiliary rôle. For our purposes it is not necessary to

[133] See above, pp. 24 and 30 ff. The argument is different from that developed above in the text, where we discussed *formally* capitalist *traits* in the law of a socialist society, independently of its material content. Marx and Lenin argued that Law, by its very nature, contains *material* elements of inequality which they described as "bourgeois ", even if found in a socialist society.

[134] See below, pp. 203 and 207.

[135] See above, p. 7.

[136] It was in this sense that Lenin (vol. VII, pp. 423 ff.) spoke of the " Communist Saturdays" as the beginning of a new, socialist approach to work. But similar movements are characteristic of all revolutionary upheavals, and sometimes even of patriotic enthusiasm during emergencies in non-revolutionary countries. If they were to be regarded as typical of a certain social formation, this would certainly not be the first stage of socialism, in the Marxian (and also Leninist) sense.

discuss all these arguments at length: it is sufficient to state that a survey of the respective importance of socialist and capitalist elements in a given society can never be based upon juridical or psychological conceptions. Such a comparison makes sense only if restricted to the clear economic facts of ownership and effective control.[137] In the course of our study we shall have the opportunity of investigating the juridical regulations characteristic of the socialist sector, once it became predominant.

In estimating the relative importance of the socialist and the capitalist elements during the N.E.P. we must distinguish between industry and commerce on the one hand, and agriculture on the other. In the former, the "commanding heights" of economics—banking, insurance, large-scale transport and the production of the raw-materials—were completely monopolised by the State. Industry was dominated by public enterprise to such an extent [138] that it might be questioned whether the private entrepreneurs, with some 5 per cent. of the total production, were significant enough to influence the working of public enterprise by their competition and thus to fulfil the function attributed to them when the N.E.P. was introduced. Private activity was really important only in commerce, where it dominated the retail trade alone. There the service offered by the private shopkeeper was evidently superior to that provided by State enterprise with its background of War-Communist rationing, regardless of the consumer's needs. According to Krivitsky [139] the amount of private activity in the total exchange of goods amounted in 1923–4 to 58·6 per cent., and, during a period when the State competed mainly on economic lines, sank gradually to 32·6 per cent. in 1926–7.

These figures include trade with agricultural products, i.e. the commercial activities of the peasantry itself. As regards professional commerce sufficiently reliable data is available from the figures for taxation, mass-evasion of which was very unlikely in view of the draconic penalties threatening the N.E.P.-man who violated his obligations towards the State. The following

[137] The latter, and not the mere fact of juridical ownership, is decisive. The problem of the economic structure of the N.E.P.-society cannot be solved by the mere statement that the land and the factories leased to private entrepreneurs remained public property. The question is how far the State retained power to control them.

[138] See above, pp. 88–9.

[139] In *Problemy Ekonomiky*, 1930, No. 3, p. iv.

schedule [140] gives the number of Trade Licences issued to commercial and industrial enterprises :

| In the Second Half of the Taxation Year. | To State. | Co-operative. | Private Entrepreneurs. |
|---|---|---|---|
| 1923–4 . . . . . | 22,400 | 71,400 | 496,400 |
| 1924–5 . . . . . | 29,800 | 112,400 | 524,400 |
| 1925–6 . . . . . | 38,600 | 119,700 | 608,300 |

The annual sales, in billions of roubles (with percentage of the total sales of the respective year in brackets) amounted to :

| Taxation Year. | State. | Co-operatives. | Private Enterprises. |
|---|---|---|---|
| 1923–4 . . . . . | 3 (31) | 2·8 (28) | 4·0 (41) |
| 1924–5 . . . . . | 5 (36) | 5·2 (37) | 3·7 (27) |
| 1925–6 . . . . . | 7 (33) | 9·0 (43) | 5·0 (24) |
| 1926–7 . . . . . | 7·8 (34) | 10·2 (45) | 5·0 (21) |

In 1926–7 the average sales by enterprise (in 1000 roubles) amounted to :

| | State Undertakings. | Co-operative Undertakings. | Private Entrepreneurs. |
|---|---|---|---|
| In Trade . . . . | 277·7 | 106·2 | 15·6 |
| In Industry . . . . | 569·4 | 112·6 | 31·1 |

In discussing this data some fundamental facts, fairly illustrated by them, ought to be kept in mind. The typical private enterprise was a small shop with none or very few employees in trade, and with a number of workers well below the legal maximum [141] in industry. The typical State enterprise in trade was a wholesale organisation—so its sales, which are relatively higher than those of the average co-operative, do not prove the latter's inferiority in the organised retail trade, which is its own field. The typical co-operative in industry was an association of a group of craftsmen, ten or twenty as a rule. So it differed greatly in its social content from the Consumer's Co-operative, which was characteristic of trade.

Progress in economic reconstruction meant an increase of the sales in each group of enterprises. But in the group of private undertakings the increase in the total sales corresponded nearly exactly to their numerical increase, and thus indicated no change in their average size, whilst not only the total, but also the average sales of the State enterprises increased considerably, and those of the co-operative undertakings increased strikingly. The simplest interpretation of the changes illustrated

[140] Quoted from J. Reingold's article in *Soviet Policy in Public Finances*, Stanford University Press, 1931, pp. 175 ff.

[141] See above, p. 88.

in the second table is striking progress of the urban Consumers' Co-operative at the relative expense of private trade. The State, dominating industry and the wholesale trade, could preserve its position independent of changes in retail distribution. If there was any progress in the relative importance of industrial co-operative production (which was virtually private production in association), this progress had evidently been made at the expense of the individual entrepreneur, not of the State.

In view of these facts, how then within a party that was accustomed to describe contemporary capitalism as the domination of the whole economic structure by some big industrial and financial monopolies, could the question of insecurity as regards its position under the N.E.P. have arisen at all? No Bolshevik would have hesitated for a moment to interpret the economic life of, say, the U.S.A. as completely dominated by a certain trust, if the latter (even without the complete control of a dictatorial State machinery) had enjoyed a position in the economic life of that country in any way similar to the dominating position of the State in the economics of the U.S.S.R., during the N.E.P. Why should the latter position be regarded as insecure simply because private enterprise dominated in agriculture and had an important share in retail trade?

The first explanation of this problem is a rather superficial phenomenon. Though the average private undertaking was small and comparatively innocuous to the dominating position of the State, their numbers were huge. From the point of view of those who had to deal with the administration of the Law, the 600,000 private holders of trade licences and the 120,000 co-operative shops whose activities were often dubious, were likely to make a stronger impression than 100,000 public and truly co-operative managements—even if those 100,000 controlled two-thirds of the total sales. It is the case as such, and not the amount in question, which interests the lawyer and the administrator. Further, the very fact that private enterprise was widely disseminated exposed quite a considerable number of people with "bourgeois" incomes and habits to the critical eyes of the observer of everyday Soviet life, especially if he was in opposition within the Party, and thus only too ready to make use of any arguments in order to criticise what he called "the bourgeois degeneration of the regime". A score of millionaires, each contesting public leadership in one important industry, would certainly have been much more dangerous for

Russian socialism. But an annual income of 167 million roubles distributed amongst 9,500 taxpayers, each with an annual income of more than 10,000 gold roubles (£1,000) [140] produced more capitalist features in everyday life (at least in the two capitals), and in that sphere of life with which the courts had to deal, than if it had been shared between a hypothetical score of really powerful capitalists.

But the possible connections which private trade in the towns might form with the still unbroken domination of private production in agriculture provided the ruling party with a much more serious problem. The N.E.P. had been introduced mainly in order to provide the peasants with articles of consumption produced by industry, at a time when State industry was unable to supply these goods and when the peasants would not deliver food without them. The private trader certainly succeeded in closing the gap by mobilising the reserves retained in private households (especially in those of the former bourgeoisie), or newly produced by small-scale industry, and also by overcoming the initial inability of the State to supply and deliver the goods produced by its industries to the consumer. And here, from the point of view of the State, the private trader's function was fulfilled. He might have continued to play an important rôle in the distribution of goods against the growing competition of State undertakings. Indeed, he had been admitted partly for the purpose of teaching the latter how to do good business. And it would have been worth while to continue this course for some more years, until the mechanism of competition between unequal partners would defeat him here as elsewhere, though the purity of Russian socialism would have been polluted with capitalist survivals for some years longer. All would have gone very well if the specific weight of agriculture had been smaller than it was, or the State had secured a certain *nucleus* controlled by itself in the countryside that could supply a minimum of food, independent of the peasant's and the trader's conception of good business.

But agriculture, employing more than four-fifths of the Russian population, was almost completely in private hands : [142] the actual issue, here, was not between public and private enterprise but, amongst the latter, between the peasant smallholder and the agricultural capitalist (*kulak*), however modest his dimensions. Agricultural co-operatives developed, but mainly

[142] See above, p. 85.

on those lines familiar enough in capitalist countries, namely as co-operation of the husbandries of private peasants, who retained possession of the main implements of production and could dispose of their respective shares in the product as they wished. It was this type of co-operative, the " Association for Joint Cultivation of the Land ", that made progress [143] as compared with the Communes and even the *Artels*, which are to-day the predominant type of *kollkhos*. Whether such a type of agricultural co-operation made the State's dealings with the peasants easier, or more difficult, depended completely on the social structure of the co-operating peasantry. In the hands of the *kulak* they might become an instrument in the struggle for political power, for boycotting the State as opposed to private trade, or at least for cornering the market to enforce more favourable conditions than the State was ready to offer.

The strength and influence of the *kulak* in the Russian village of the N.E.P.-period was the most contested of questions during the factional struggles of this time, and no authoritative data could avoid being coloured by the position which its author took in that struggle. As there is hardly any objective characteristic of the *kulak* [144] such colouring was bound to arise even without any attempt at falsifying facts : the investigator whose political convictions emphasised the danger threatening Russian socialism from the *kulak*, would find the latter, where a rather optimistic observer would see efficient and flourishing peasant husbandry, highly desirable from the point of view of developing the productive resources of the country. Stalin, during the main period of the N.E.P., co-operated with the right-wingers in his party against the left-wing critics of the *kulak* danger. But in 1928, when his main struggle was directed against Bukharin's encouragement of the *kulak*, Stalin [145] uttered his opinion about the numerical share of *kulaks* in the whole of Soviet agriculture as follows : 5 per cent. of the total agricultural population, 12 per cent. of the total agricultural production, and 20 per cent. of the grain surplus supplied to the market. On the other

[143] See above, pp. 102–3, and Kviring in *Na Agrarnom Frontem*, 1925, No. 4, p. 27.

[144] Permanent employment of waged labour would be the correct Marxist characteristic, but in view of the size of many Russian peasant families and, on the other hand, of the demands for occasional waged help even for the poor peasants' homes, a strict delimitation, based upon a single characteristic, is impossible.

[145] Op. cit., 1940, p. 208. The share of 5 per cent. in the agricultural population corresponds to the official estimation of 3·7 per cent., in 1928, of the *total* population. The fact that the two possible biases balanced each other in Stalin's position, in 1928, forms an argument in favour of his data.

side, Kamenev declared at the 1924 Party Congress that 8 per cent. of the farms possessed a quarter of the total cattle available [146] and 34 per cent. of the cultivated area. In 1925 the Central Statistical Board, dominated as it then was by the left-wing opposition, gave consecutive estimates of the *kulak* share in the marketed grain as 61, 52, and 42 per cent.—the last number being evidently that for which they risked an argument with the Party majority.[147] Evidently such numbers were intended to include not only the grain produced by the *kulaks* themselves but also that purchased by them from their weaker neighbours, and potentially cornered. In order to approach the problem uncoloured by contemporary factional bias, a start can be made from a fact only indirectly related to the contested issues and published long after these disputes had passed:[148] the peasants collectivised in 1934 possessed 101 million hectars as against 71 before the collectivisation, and at least half of the increase was land expropriated from *kulaks*.[149] Some of the latter still retained land in 1934 as individual peasants and some *kulak* land had been appropriated by State farms. So it is hard to avoid the conclusion that, in 1928, some 16–18 per cent. of the total agricultural land (and certainly not less of the total product) must have been in the hands of peasants who, during the collectivisation, were described and expropriated as *kulaks*. The interpretation of the term *kulak* must decide whether this contradiction is to be solved on the assumption of an understatement of the number of *kulaks* by Stalin in 1928 (though not so gross as alleged by the opposition), or by an expropriation, in 1929–31, of non-*kulak* peasants, or by a combination of both factors. The struggle in later years was so bitter that it is difficult to believe that it was directed against a group of producers in control of a mere 20 per cent. of the available surplus. On the other hand, the success of this struggle without extreme political complications refutes also the contentions of the 1925 opposition that in 1929–31 the State would have had to confiscate at least half of the grain needed. The *kulak* was certainly a danger to State-controlled economics in a predominantly agricultural country. But this danger was removed before it could seriously

[146] According to this latter characteristicum Kamenev's groups were constructed. So it might be doubted whether they could correctly be described as *kulak* in the general sense of the word. But certainly they were used in this sense.

[147] See Stalin (op. cit. 1928, vol. I), p. 406.

[148] See D. Levin in *Na Agrarnom Frontem*, 1935, Nos. 2–3, p. 35.

[149] See Jakovlev's Report on the XVIth Party-Congress.

threaten that control, or combine with the private capitalist traders in the towns into a factor of such economic importance as would justify an interpretation of the N.E.P. as anything more than an auxiliary institute of State economics. In the analysis of legal institutions, the *kulak* phenomenon is without importance: in consequence of the structure of Soviet Law it came outside the scope of the Civil Code. It was solved later by administrative measures and application of Criminal Law [150] without resort to the Land Code under which it came. So also the N.E.P.-man himself has passed away without troubling the Civil Code, unless article 1 is interpreted as a justification for any procedure in abolishing economic institutions that have lost their meaning in consequence of a change in public policy.[151]

The permanent result of the N.E.P. for the development of Soviet law was not the N.E.P.-man or the *kulak*, but the introduction of a new point of view into the management of public enterprise. According to a resolution of the 9th Soviet Congress "all State undertakings, whether subsidised by the State or not, must be managed on a commercial basis". The reality behind such a demand depended on whether or not the State would cover the eventual deficits of the enterprises. There were two groups of State enterprises: those that continued to receive State subventions, against an obligation to deliver their surplus product to the State, and those that were made financially independent and autonomous. Since February 6, 1922, the former category was limited to undertakings which by the very nature of their production could supply only the State, as the only potential buyer for ammunition, implements of production for railways and heavy industries, etc. The latter group, with some 75 per cent. of the total number of workers employed in nationalised industries, was organised into trusts. According to the decree of April 10th, 1923, Trusts were autonomous units with legal personality, endowed with a charter by the Supreme Council of National Economics which also appointed the members of the Board and preserved the right even to liquidate the Trust if necessary. The Trust was not owner of the public property administered by it and could not mortgage the fixed capital belonging to the State. But, according to article 19 of the Civil Code, it might incur debts that were covered by the turnover capital (funds of money, raw materials, semi- and finished products, etc.). The Trust was also protected against the State

[150] See below, pp. 171–2. [151] See above, p. 93, and below, pp. 145 and 190.

by the ruling that, apart from emergencies, no one could acquire any goods from it except by contractual agreement. But, according to article 50 of the decree, in all buying and selling transactions the Trust must give preference, wherever terms and conditions are equal, to State departments and Co-operatives. Evidently, the framers of the decree thought of possibly permanent conditions of scarcity, and feared that the "private sector" of national economics might boycot the nationalised sector without the latter being able to put into action article 1 of the Civil Code, or the various provisions of the Criminal Code applicable to such proceedings. Of the profits of the Trust 20 per cent. were directed to a reserve fund, 22 per cent. to a Welfare fund for betterment of the conditions of the employees, and 3 per cent. to premia for the Board and the employees, who were thus immediately interested in the success of their activities. The rest of the profits remained at the disposal of the Supreme Council of National Economics. As early as the summer of 1923, 478 trusts were organised, and included 3,561 factories with about a million workers. The 41 largest trusts had an average of 12,500 workers each (900 per factory), the smaller ones averaged out at no more than the number of workers per factory then allowed to the private entrepreneur.[152] So they had to compete with him on equal terms.

The degree in which the reorganised State enterprises succeeded in working remuneratively depended on the kind of produce they had to supply. In the heavy industries the degree of reconstruction needed was much larger, and the State which supervised the Trusts would also prevent prices for essential means of production from rising to heights detrimental to itself, as the main customer. In 1926–7, when the main work of reconstruction after the losses of War and Civil War was done,[153] the profits of certain industries [154] amounted to :

| Industry | Percentage of Output sold. | Percentage of Working Capital. |
|---|---|---|
| Rubber | 16·5 | 18·3 |
| Electric articles | 15·6 | 10·4 |
| Textiles | 15·4 | 10·0 |
| Oil | 9·8 | 10·3 |
| Building | 7·8 | 5·7 |
| Coal-mining | 6·6 | 1·1 |
| Metallurgy | 4·8 | 2·1 |

[152] See above, pp. 87–9, and Dobb, op. cit., pp. 198 ff.

[153] In the early years of the N.E.P. deficits in the coal-mining and metallurgical industries were regarded as unavoidable.

[154] Reingold, op. cit., pp. 229–30.

The share of the Treasury in the profits of the Trusts amounted in 1923–4 to 15·8, and in 1925–6 to 21 per cent. It was felt desirable not only for financial reasons to check the development of the Trusts into independent Joint Stock Companies, with the State as a mere monopolist shareholder. The new Statute on the State Trusts, of June 29, 1927,[155] emphasised the need to co-ordinate the profit-making activities of the Trusts with the general needs of socialist economics, and established permanent supervision of each Trust's activities by a State department mentioned in its charter. According to article 4 of the statute the central economic organs of the State were entitled to appropriate Trust property, but only on condition that the Trust was left assets sufficient to cover its liabilities, or that the decree appropriating Trust property (or liquidating the Trust) made other provisions for satisfying the Trust's creditors. Thus, at the end of the N.E.P., the juridical personalty of the Trust, as against the State, was secured no longer : but it could not be interfered with without the State taking full responsibility for all obligations entered during the Trust's existence. Deprived of all possibility of becoming an independent social reality, like the Trust in capitalist countries, the Soviet Trust was definitely described as a mere trustee of the State, administering, during the owner's pleasure, a circumscribed part of the public property. Accordingly, a new, and less equivocal, mode of distributing the profits of the Trusts was established : after paying income-tax (as a rule 10 per cent. of the gross profits), 10 per cent. of the net profits was to be kept for the reserve fund, and for the improvement of the workers' living conditions, 25 per cent. was to be spent on increasing output, and up to one-quarter per cent. for premia for the management and technical personnel. The rest—i.e. nearly 45 per cent. of the net income, and including taxation just half of the gross income—was to be paid to the Treasury. In fact, in 1927–8, the latter received 40 per cent. of the profits of the Trusts. But only part of the financial year was covered by the new legislation.

Thus the progress of the Trusted (i.e. self-supporting) State enterprises towards administrative as well as financial independence was checked. But the success of the economic principles according to which they were managed was sufficiently convincing to adapt the status of the State-subsidised, non-Trusted industries,[156] to the new methods of management. A

[155] S.U. 1927/322.

[156] See above, p. 137.

decree of September 27, 1926, conferred upon them the right to enter legal obligations, and so subjected them to principles of financial accountancy. As even the non-Trusted industries now were normally self-supporting in their current transactions (as distinct from investment), there was no more reason to waive the application of a useful expedient to check rational management. The only difference between their status and that of the Trusts was that the latter had a charter of their own, i.e. they fulfilled the condition established by the Civil Code for a legal entity. This condition had been established in order to check private capitalist companies. Once that reason " withered away " with the end of the N.E.P., the difference between the Trusted and non-Trusted State enterprises lost any but formal importance.[157]

The original intention of the Soviet in establishing the Trusts had been to secure management of the nationalised industries (apart from some of overwhelming importance for the whole system of national economics) according to those principles developed by capitalist experience, and embodied in Russia of the period by the N.E.P.-man competitor. Defence of the interests of the enterprise against other State enterprises as well as against their own workers was regarded as an essential duty of the manager of a Soviet Trust. It was in view of this very duty that the Labour Code [158] had enacted the guarantees as needed by labour when confronted with an entrepreneur looking for maximum profits. Closing down a factory, if it worked unprofitably, was amongst the legitimate functions of the new economic structure. Indeed, the first period of the N.E.P. was characterised by a series of economic crises. In the beginning of the N.E.P. the peasant market proved unable to accept the goods offered by industry, partly in consequence of the latter's inability to trade efficiently, a defect which was bridged by the intervention of the private capitalist trader, and partly in consequence of the 1921 famine. In 1923, on the other hand, the so-called " scissors " opened, i.e. it appeared that, in comparison with the pre-War level, agricultural products were much cheaper than industrial ones. There have been various explanations for the phenomenon which was paralleled in most other countries devastated by the War. To me, the most reasonable explanation seems the inevitable difference in pace between reconstruction in a very primitive agriculture on

[157] See below, Chapter VIII, pp. 247–9. [158] See above, pp. 97–9.

the one hand, and a complicated industrial machinery on the other. Once industry was reconstructed to its pre-War level (i.e. since 1925) the "scissors" closed and some kind of equilibrium on the markets was restored—apart from those disturbances caused by the *kulak's* attempts to corner the grain market.[159] In any case, during the first years of the N.E.P. there was, in the U.S.S.R., mass unemployment similar to that of any capitalist country: 160,000 on January 1, 1922, 640,000 at the beginning of 1923 and 1,240,000 at the beginning of 1924. The 950,000 of the two following years, and the much larger numbers preceding the abolition of unemployment [160] may be interpreted differently, as a mere discovery of the hitherto hidden unemployment in the villages. Once industry was restored, hundreds of thousands of young peasants came to town to find seasonal work in summer. Apart from the chance of getting a permanent job they thus acquired a claim for unemployment benefit during the winter, which was, at almost any level, higher than the average poor peasant's standard of life.

The institution of the State Trust involved the preservation of the profit motive as a stimulus to economic activities, although it did not exclude the preservation of public ownership and control in all important spheres. So far, the institution of the State Trust, under the N.E.P., had been a transitional phenomenon: a State holding all the "commanding heights" of production would certainly not tolerate a working of the machinery of "free markets" which forced its own factories to close down (unless they were really backward in technical equipment, etc.). After the first "purge" carried through by the N.E.P., the N.E.P. itself had to be purged. The short-term aspects of State enterprise under the N.E.P. may explain why people could speak of it as "State capitalism", whilst the long-term trend of State enterprise proves why they were wrong.

### (*e*) The General Legal Conceptions of the N.E.P.

The general tendencies of N.E.P.-law may be described as a continuation of the conceptions of the first revolutionary period, after the interruption caused by the emergency measures of War-Communism against which it reacted. As in the first revolutionary period,[161] we find a transformation of institutions of traditional Civil Law by the separation of those elements

[159] See below, pp. 167–8. [160] See below, p. 218.
[161] See above, pp. 80–1.

which were to be preserved from others which were abolished. On the other hand, we find a tendency to adapt public enterprise to the new conceptions of private enterprise.

As a counterpart, say, to the institution of a private entrepreneur acting under Workers' Control we find, in N.E.P.-law, the institution of the leaseholder of nationalised enterprise. In contrast to his predecessor he has achieved his status, not by the historical accident of having been a private entrepreneur when the October Revolution abolished his traditional rights and enforced Workers' Control upon him, but by voluntary agreement with the new state and in recognition of the latter's rule that nationalised enterprises are *res extra commercium* (art. 22, Civil Code), and cannot be subject of private ownership. In consequence, the leaseholder of a nationalised enterprise is subjected to limitations not only as regards the duration of the lease [162] but also as regards the use of the leased property and even of his own. Under penalty of having his contract annulled by the courts, he must continue to produce at least that minimum of products as established in the contract (art. 162, Civil Code), and it is he who is responsible for providing raw materials and for feeding the workers. In contrast to the leaseholder of private property it is he who bears the responsibility for all repairs of the leased property (art. 159, Civil Code, remark) and all improvements carried out by him belong to the owner (art. 179, remark) without the compensation normally due to the private lessee who has improved the property of a private lessor. The commentators on N.E.P.-law [163] would remark that such improvement of public property by investments of the lessee formed the very purpose of the lease. The compensation due to him took the form of the usufruct of the leased property, i.e. the right to make such profits by its use as he could without infringing the law. The State was not narrow-minded in its approach to profits reasonably allowed to a man who had invested a large part of his property in an enterprise which he had to return after six years.[164] In spite of such rather speculative

[162] See above, p. 88. [163] Kantorovich, op. cit., p. 174.

[164] Willisch, op. cit., pp. 55–6 mentions (for concessions) that transfer of profits up to 20 per cent. of the invested capital, or 6 per cent. of the turnover was allowed without special formalities, and that profits from 20–30 per cent. were regarded as normal. Further up the progressive taxation would interfere, and hardly allow more than 50 per cent. of total annual profits. A Soviet citizen could hardly go so far without risking prosecution for cornering the markets. In any case, the example shows that even those profits regarded as normal under the N.E.P. would, after six years, give a high return on investments.

traits the institution comes nearer to a trusteeship, limited in time, than to anything else. The very sanctions of Criminal Law against misuse of the public property entrusted to the lessee [165] tend to support this view. Apart from these negative privileges the leaseholder of public property [166] also enjoyed a more positive privilege which could hardly be understood without the above assumption: article 418 of the Civil Code exempts the rights on leased public property from the 10,000 roubles limit of the Law of Inheritance. True enough, the contradiction between the economic need for the capitalist trustee, and the political suspicion which his economic power drew upon him [167] meant that by the very fact of fulfilling his contract, i.e. by employing the number of workers needed to produce the contracted minimum product, he deprived himself of his political rights, even if his capitalist past had not already done so.

Much less restricted are the rights of another typical figure of N.E.P.-law, the peasant householder.[168] As compared with the pre-revolutionary status of an owner he had lost only the rights to sell, to mortgage, or to lease for more than six years the land used by him, and he had accepted the new obligation to pay a tax in kind, on an average about 5 per cent. of his marketable surplus,[169] before he was allowed to sell the rest of the product. Against these restrictions of his rights stood the fact that, in consequence of the agrarian revolution, the average peasant controlled much more land than he had done in pre-revolutionary times, while, at the same time, he was freed from all mortgages and subject to the new taxation which, except for the upper income-classes, was certainly much more lenient than the old one. The peasantry, as a whole, produced in 1913–4, 3·4, but in 1926–7, 4·0 more billion poods of grain than they brought to market.[170] This fact illustrated rather drastically that

[165] See above, pp. 117–8.
[166] As well as the concessionaire and the holder of building rights.
[167] This distrust was not always without foundation. Willisch (op. cit., p. 53), in general a defender of the concessionaire's point of view, mentions the tendency of many of the latter to employ former aristocrats and bourgeois, sometimes for most of the manual jobs, with the natural implications as regards the structure of the trade unions in their factories. Again, a Soviet citizen would be more careful—but it is at least an open question whether the best business man deserved the highest political confidence of the Soviet.
[168] See above, pp. 99 ff.
[169] Of course, it was very progressive. According to Reingold (op. cit., pp. 105–6), in 1926–7, 25 per cent. of the peasant population were tax-exempt, whilst the upper 20 per cent. bore half of the agricultural tax. The *kulaks* proper, up to 4 per cent. of the population, could be subjected to individual taxation, up to double the norm (ibid., p. 169).
[170] See D. Levin, op. cit., p. 36, and Stalin (op. cit., 1940), p. 208.

the first achievement of the agrarian revolution had been the right of the peasant to eat his fill. The loss of the above-mentioned property rights as well as the restriction of political suffrage concerned only the *kulak* minority which under Stolypin's legislation, in the teeth of violent protest of the peasant majority, had begun to establish private property rights against the traditional village community and at the expense of the other members of his family. Now the collective right of the peasant family to the homestead and the impossibility of pledging the latter for the husband's private debts was established.[171] Those members of the village community who desired to continue in it, or to transform it into a modern co-operative, were protected against capitalist infringements of their decision just as those, too, who preferred the individualist line of development were protected. But there was hardly any special trait in N.E.P. Land Law which might not be found in the land law of other progressive countries, or, at least, in the projects of land reformers with no socialist aspirations.

So, too, we find very little originality in the new shape given to public enterprise in the State Trust.[172] In many continental countries public-owned enterprises, bound by their charters to work according to the principles of economic profitability and to distribute their profits in a certain way, have been accepted as a popular compromise, long before it was introduced into this country (say in the form of the L.P.T.B.). Specific features of the Soviet Trust, under the N.E.P., are the exemption of the fixed capital from any liability for its debts, and the right of the State, as owner, to liquidate the enterprise, if desired. Both features denote the priority of the rights of public ownership, and were possible only in consequence of the nationalisation of the credit system in the U.S.S.R. : no private credit system would have financed the expansion of a publicly owned enterprise if the creditors were debarred from any chance of acquiring it, or even influencing its management. But all the legal limitations on the holders of public property, or even on the peasant homestead, pursue the merely negative purpose of preventing its disintegration in favour of private capitalism. The positive promotion of planned economics, in the Land Code, is restricted to a scheme of patterns for collective enterprise, the use or non-use of which is left to the peasants' initiative.[173] As regards industry, the planned co-ordination of

[171] See above, pp. 101–2. [172] See above, pp. 137 ff. [173] See above, pp. 102–3.

the nationalised enterprises is left completely to the meta-juridical sphere. It was the task of State planning organisations, in the development of which there had been a certain continuity since the days of War-Communism,[174] and of the Communist Party, which had *de facto* control of all public institutions, to supervise the rights granted to the various autonomous bodies administering public property, so that no anarchic competition might result from their autonomy.

Soviet Civil Law, whilst systematically protecting existing public property against the possible progress of capitalism, very carefully excluded any interpretation that might render it a protection of capitalism against the eventual progress of State-economics.[175] We have seen [175] that the economic purposes pursued by the State are included in the definition of any civil right. There is nothing fundamentally problematic in such a conception—unless some reality is ascribed to Law above the State that establishes it, and this reality is described as including the foundations of capitalist society.[176] No critic can be prevented from holding such views—but it is at least inconsistent to subject Soviet Law to them. But even if revolutionary changes are regarded as involving the abolition of civil rights, real problems arise when the State that has established such rights changes its conceptions of the economic purposes immediately to be pursued while its social structure is not subject to revolutionary changes. Such a situation, indeed, eventually arose during the liquidation of the N.E.P. Certain Soviet theoretists interpreted the rights of the N.E.P.-men as rights of property, while in trying to preserve the continuity of Soviet Civil Law, they thought that the abolition of a right in consequence of a change in policy involved a claim to compensation.[177] But such a procedure, by creating new unearned income, say in the shape of interest from State securities paid as a compensation for expropriated enterprises, might contradict the very purposes of the change intended. No Soviet politician could accept such limitations of the State's right to carry through socialist reforms—and, indeed, no Soviet N.E.P.-man got any compensation. If the former N.E.P.-man's function had been conceived as that of a semi-independent agent within the framework of State economics, his personal position would have been much better :

[174] For this point see A. I. Gordon, *The System of Planning Organs of the U.S.S.R.* (Russian), Moscow Commacademy, 1929.

[175] See above, pp. 93 ff.

[176] See above, pp. 4–7.

[177] See below, p. 154.

he would have had a justifiable claim to be employed within the new economic system according to his proven abilities, with the chance of earning an income corresponding to his former standard of life, and enjoying social security. From this point of view it may be said that the interpretation of the N.E.P. in traditional terms of capitalist enterprise not only contradicted the intentions of the legislator, when introducing the N.E.P.,[175] but also impaired the interests even of those whose function, for the moment, was enhanced. For it bound their personal future to a system doomed by history.

## CHAPTER V

# THEORETICAL CONCEPTIONS OF LAW DURING THE N.E.P.-PERIOD

The organisation of Soviet Justice during the first period of the Soviet regime demanded of its administrators common sense, political understanding, and a purely empirical knowledge of the chief decrees of the new regime, but no special theory of Law. Marxian sociology was deemed a completely sufficient guide for the " socialist consciousness of Justice " which, according to Soviet Law at the time,[1] had to fill the many *lacunæ* which remained until the latter's codification. It would, indeed, have been very unreasonable to burden with complicated professional teaching the type of man or woman then regarded as the most desirable administrator of Justice, the intelligent and socially active worker who regarded judicial functions as a social activity which he would readily exchange for another, if so " commanded " by the Party. Those juridical specialists who collaborated with the Soviet, like Hoichbarg and Reissner, stressed in their theoretical statements the negative attitude of Marxism towards bourgeois ideologies of Law rather than the positive problems of Law in the new society.[2] Law is a dope " like Religion " or, according to Reissner " a compromise between the classes ", obviously bound to be superseded, as soon as compromise ceased to be necessary. As early as 1919 Hoichbarg described Law in general as a " bourgeois fetish " and regarded its withering away as inseparably connected with the triumph of collectivism, without making the distinction between socialism and Communism as elaborated by Marx and Lenin.[3] Stuchka, who in his official activities during the period under discussion [4] did not deny the necessity for Law under proletarian as well as under bourgeois rule, was inclined to regard Matrimonial and Labour Law as the main items of socialist law—and indeed they were the only ones codified during that period.[5] Much later he described the general attitude of the War-Communist period by the sub-title " Down with the Law "—as opposed to the " Return to Law " under the N.E.P. Civil Law, under War-Communism, had survived only " underground ", as a

[1] See above, p. 68. [2] See Vyshingsky, op. cit., 1937.
[3] See above, pp. 24–6. [4] See above, p. 74. [5] See above, pp. 54 ff.

regulator of the parties dealing on the Black Market.[6] It is difficult to reconcile such statements with Stuchka's own official description of Law as an effluence of the political rule of a certain class,[4] ordering social relations according to its interests. During War-Communism itself there was no conception of Law in any but the positivist sense which is, of course, incompatible with the conception of " underground Law ". But the fact that only a little positive Law, and still less Civil Law, was codified, encouraged a utopian interpretation of the situation, in the sense that the transition from the rule of bourgeois Law to the presumably lawless regulation of the future collectivist society had already begun.

We have already noted the development, since the introduction of the N.E.P., of codified Law as well as of a professional Judiciary.[7] For the latter's training elaborate legal theory was needed. Marxism recognises the existence of purely legal ideologies, and even their influence on the real development of Law.[8] But it certainly rejects the explanation of Law by the development of legal or supposedly general ideologies. Anyone desiring purely legal theories had to look round the existing ones elaborated by bourgeois jurists, and choose those he found most compatible with a Marxist approach to sociology and politics. All the classical bourgeois theories, based on certain assumed fundamental rights, were excluded by their evident function as idealisations of the foundations of capitalist society. So Duguit's functional approach became popular amongst Soviet jurists. By its influence on Hoichbarg, who shaped the Civil Code,[9] it certainly influenced the latter's formulation. But Duguit, who was popular in the U.S.S.R. because he criticised traditional bourgeois legal theories for their metaphysical assumption of a Freedom of the Will, might easily be reproached with merely replacing these metaphysics by others, such as Solidarity, and thus functioning as an advocate of decaying capitalism.[10] However fitting Duguit's function within the society in which he lived, the argument does not necessarily seem convincing to those who read the theories of Duguit in a completely different society : the fact that in a class-divided society the interpretation of Law by solidarity might easily work as an ideological cover for class-oppression even in Fascist forms, does not exclude the

[6] Op. cit., 1931, pp. 37–8.
[7] See above, pp. 121–2.
[8] See above, pp. 21–2.
[9] See above, p. 96.
[10] Stuchka, op. cit., 1931, p. 56.

existence of solidarity of interests in another society, and the functionalist explanation of rights and duties in that society. We shall see that all present Soviet legal theory is based upon such an assumption. But, particularly in the 'twenties, a theory was regarded as refuted once its function as a bourgeois apologia was proved, however inconsistent such a conclusion may appear from the point of view of the Marxist dialectic. No theory could aspire to success in the U.S.S.R. unless it appeared to be based on orthodox Marxism.

Now any attempt at a theoretical interpretation of Law in general, and particularly Soviet Law, was bound to be influenced by the fact that the codification of Soviet Law (and the non-codified Law of War-Communism was hardly accepted as law proper) originated from the needs of the N.E.P. The Civil Code had granted the private capitalist entrepreneur a certain sphere of activities and, in order to stimulate the progress of socialist enterprise by competition, private enterprise had been granted a sphere of legal activity larger than it was ever actually envisaged as occupying.[11] The starting-point of the Soviet Civil Code had been the decree on private property rights, of May 22, 1922, "the first N.E.P.-Code", as Stuchka [12] called it. Was not this very fact a proof of the bourgeois character of Law in general, including the Soviet Law of the N.E.P. which thus appeared as a temporary retreat before the forces of capitalism? He who defended such a point of view might quote Marx who, in another connection, had described even the Law of the first stage of a Communist society as "bourgeois",[13] and had expected the withering away of Law as well as of State in the process of transition to a higher form of Communism. True enough, the quotation was not quite fitting: when speaking of the "bourgeois" character of the Law of a socialist society Marx had implied no more than the fact that even such Law was unable to realise complete Equality and Justice. What he had had in mind was certainly not a state of the N.E.P.-type, but at least something similar to the U.S.S.R. of to-day, i.e. a State completely controlling national economic life, and linked with the capitalist past by the mere fact that its citizens had grown up in an outlook inherited from capitalism. But Marx had expected even such a Law "to wither away", together with the State it served. In the middle 'twenties few Russian people

[11] See above, p. 97.
[12] Op. cit., p. 85.
[13] See above, pp. 24–5.

foresaw a long historical period of transition—and thus is was easy enough to identify the necessary transitions out of specific N.E.P.-Law (i.e. the temporary concessions made to capitalism proper), with the " withering away of Law " in general (i.e. with the transition to a classless society, based upon voluntary instead of compulsory discipline). Within such a conception there was, indeed, no place for socialist Law proper, i.e. for the Law of a State that not only aimed at overcoming capitalism, but already had complete control of economic life. It was inconsistent to quote Marx's sayings about the partially bourgeois (that is inegalitarian) character of such a law as an argument for quite another thesis, namely that in the compromise of N.E.P.-Law the bourgeois (that is capitalist) elements prevailed. But it was not the only inconsistent quotation of Marx current in Soviet theory, and in this case there were even vague sayings of Lenin in 1917 [14] to which one might refer.

In the discussions preceding the enactment of the Civil Code, Lenin had taken a very definite stand against any interpretation of this Code which might mean a return to bourgeois economic relations.

> We do not recognise any " private " thing ; with us, in the field of economics, there is only public, and no private Law. The only capitalism we allow is that of the State. . . . For this reason, we have to widen the sphere of state interference with " private " legal relations, and to enlarge the right of the State to abolish " private " agreements. Not the *corpus juri Romani*, but our revolutionary consciousness of Justice ought to be applied to " Civil Law relations ". . . .[15]

This letter of Lenin to the People's Commissar for Justice clearly decides which of the two sides of the Soviet Civil Code the legislator regarded from the first as the essential one. But for nearly ten years most Soviet legal theorists answered the question the other way round, insisting on interpreting Soviet Law as bourgeois. As we have mentioned above,[16] the immediate realities of N.E.P. life might further such an interpretation. It might also be backed by the desire to criticise the N.E.P. and its Law, together with a Utopian approach to the means of superseding it—or, in short, by what the later impeachers of Pashukanis and his school described as counter-revolutionary Trotskyism. Whatever the motives for such an interpretation

[14] See above, pp. 30–1.

[15] Letter to Kursky, *Works* (Russian), vol. XXIX, p. 419.

[16] Pp. 133–4.

of Soviet Law, once it was accepted, the last barrier to a bourgeois interpretation of Law in general was removed.

If such an interpretation was attempted, a natural starting point was provided by some of the attempts of Marx, in his *Capital*, to explain the origins of bourgeois legal ideology. Mutual recognition of Property forms the basis of commodity exchange, and this juridical relation, which expands itself in a contract, is but the reflex of the real economic relations between the two.[17] The sphere of commodity exchange is described as a very Eden of the Rights of Man—Liberty, Equality, and Property.[18] Interpretation of liberal ideologies by the objective conditions of commodity exchange have been very common with Marxists, even of the reformist school.[19] The formal principle of juridical equality is a mere expression of the formal criterion of Law as general. But if it were translated, as it is by the Natural Law school, into an ideological principle of Equality, one might say that, according to Marx, an essential principle of Law, equality of the partners, supposed exchange of commodities. But such a translation would have been rejected by Marx himself, who had sneered at Proudhon's "proof", "to the consolation of all good citizens", that "the production of commodities is a form of production as everlasting as Justice".[17] Marxism is strictly historical, and rejects any generalisation which erects the categories of a certain historical stage of development into general characteristics of social agencies working in various stages of that development. Marx's reference to commodity exchange in the explanation of the legal ideologies of a certain stage of commodity production, and especially of the period of transition from "simple commodity production" by independent small producers to capitalism, cannot be quoted in support of the explanation of Law, or at least Civil Law, by commodity exchange, as developed by the school of Soviet legal theorists we are to discuss.

Even during that period of capitalist development the legal ideologies of which Marx tried to explain in the statements of basic economic principles just quoted, it is not commodity exchange as such that forms the relations reflected by legal ideologies. As everyone can read in Chapter I of *Capital*, the real economic relation between exchangers of commodities is the social division of Labour. The conception of a commodity

[17] *Capital*, vol. I, p. 56. [18] Ibid., pp. 155–6.
[19] Renner, op. cit., pp. 2–3.

and its inherent " value " is, according to Marxism, a mere ideological reflection, a fetishistic substantiation of this real relation between members of a society whose inherent organisation works beneath their consciousness.[20] The fetish of Law, i.e. the delusion that Law could exist apart from the State, and apart from the people whose relations ought to be regulated, has been explained, by the Russian " Commodity Exchange School " of lawyers,[21] as another aspect of the fetishisation of commodity exchange. For in order to be able to exchange commodities their possessors must assume the character of subjects of Law, and appear as bearers of rights. " Before the owners of commodities recognised each other as proprietors of the latter, they were already such—although in another, organic, meta-juridical sense." [22] This last statement is confused : property—as distinct from possession—cannot be assumed prior to its juridical recognition by society. Property differs from mere possession by the fact of existing in the realm of Law, and only for the purposes of the Law. But apart from the confusion—which, if taken seriously, would imply that the author of such a statement believed in eternal, meta-juridical " Law "—the meaning of Pashukanis' thesis is clear : Commodity exchange demands mutual recognition of rights, and legal relations, which within a society based on commodity exchange are bound to reflect the needs of the latter. What is not proved by such an explanation, is (1) the non-existence of legal relations other than those produced by commodity exchange, and (2) even within the framework of a society based upon commodity exchange, the position of the latter as the only or even the main source of legal relations. As we have seen above, these two points cannot be proved without dropping two essential features of Marxism, its historical approach and its explanation of social phenomena by relations that men enter in *producing* their means of livelihood, as distinct from the distribution of the products which Marxism regards as secondary.

That scholars who described themselves as Marxists, and were not even conscious of developing a theory distinct from Marxism, should overlook these essentials of Marxism, can only

[20] This sociological explanation of the conception of a " value " inherent in the commodities, and not its ability or inability to explain the movement of prices is the test to which the Marxian theory of value ought to be subjected. It is an historical rather than an economic (in the sense of modern academic economics) theory.

[21] See Stuchka, op. cit., pp. 45 and 48.

[22] Pashukanis, op. cit., p. 78.

be explained by the pre-1917 development of Russian "legal Marxism". In a vulgarised economic interpretation of history under the title of "economic materialism" the Marxian conception of "relations of *production*" was replaced by the Buecher-Bogdanovian conception of *distribution* of products as being the really fundamental fact of social relations. Accordingly, in the field of History, most progressive Russian scholars, as well as the school of Pokrovsky which dominated Soviet historical studies during the first fifteen years after the Revolution, found the driving force of Russian history in "merchant capitalism", i.e. in the concentration on commerce during a period when productive relations were, undoubtedly, dominated by feudalism, or even by pre-feudal relations in agriculture.[23] If, indeed, it was Merchant Capitalism that had created the Russian state and the institution of serfdom,[24] and if, according to Klyuchevsky, the leading Russian liberal historian,[25] the first Russian law-books of the eleventh century (in their general content very similar to the early Saxon law-books of this country) defended capitalism and were "bourgeois" because they contained rules on merchant companies (mainly dealing in slaves), bankruptcy, etc., then there was nothing unreasonable in an explanation say of Hammurabi's Code, or of the ancient Roman Twelve Tables by the needs of commodity exchange. There was probably more of the latter in Babylon of the twenty-second century B.C. or in Rome of the fifth century B.C., than in early mediæval Russia. Such an attempt to juxtapose all the past history of civilisation to the coming Communist Utopia is hardly Marxism, and has more in common with the liberal advocates of Natural Law who describe that Utopia as a monstrosity, contrary to all the past developments of civilisation. But little can be said against such a conception if the mere fact of the distribution of the social product by commodity exchange is accepted as a sufficient characteristic of a social formation.

There have been two gradations of the Commodity Exchange explanation of Law elaborated by Soviet theorists. Stuchka [26] has described *Civil* Law as

> the result of the production of commodities for exchange and the corresponding means of satisfying human needs. It expresses

[23] See the present author's article in *Zeitschrift fuer Sozialforschung* (Paris), vol. 1938, Nos. 1–2, pp. 189 ff.

[24] Pokrovsky, *Istoricheska Nauka i Borba Klassov* (Russian), vol. I, p. 28.

[25] *Russian History* (English ed.), vol. I, pp. 163–7.

[26] In *Bolshaja Sovietskaja Encyklopedia*, vol. XVIII, pp. 737 ff.

> that formal equality between people which originates from the exchange of commodities on the base of their respective value. . . . The external expression and formal realisation of the exchange of commodities is the contract . . ., the partners to which in the process of historical evolution become formally free citizens and subjects to the Law at an ever-increasing rate.

This might be interpreted as a definition of the complex of facts Stuchka desired to be included in the conception of Civil Law—as irrefutable as any definition is so long as it is consistently applied. But it was certainly intended as an explanation: Stuchka's *definition* of Civil Law [27] describes it as "the form of organisation of social relations, i.e. relations of production and exchange, safeguarded in the interest of the ruling class by the political power established by that class". It is the form of organisation of the "bourgeois society" in the Marxist-Hegelian sense, as distinct from the organised activities of the State.[28] There can be no doubt that Stuchka explained all these relations from the very beginnings of their legal regulation up to their eventual withering away in a Communist society, on the basis of commodity exchange and its ideological expressions. And he proposed consistently to restrict the application of Civil Law in the Soviet society to the regulation of the surviving private property relations. The internal economic relations of the socialist sector of economics were to be excluded, as not needing juridical regulation.[26] On the other hand, within the realm of Soviet Civil Law, Stuchka consistently recognised the principle of the "equivalent": being based on commodity exchange, the real object of any right was a certain value. Compensation for this value ought to be paid if, by a change of policy, the Soviet State abolished the original right, without the bearer of this right having infringed the conditions under which it had been granted.[29]

The more radical aspect of the Commodity Exchange Conception of Law was evolved in 1924 in Pashukanis' "General Theory of Law". Here not merely Civil Law, i.e. the juridical regulation of economic life, but Law in general is explained by the relations of commodity exchange. Civil Law, i.e. "the description of the relations of persons who act in the market as commodity dealers", is the only true object of any general

[27] Op. cit., 1931, p. 42.
[28] Ibid., pp. 61 ff. See above, Chapter II, p. 17.
[29] Op. cit., 1931, pp. 229 and 250–1.

theory of Law,[30] all other so-called aspects of Law being mere reflections of those basic relations. " When the whole economic life is based on the principle of the agreement of intentions (between the commodity dealers making contracts), then every social function obtains a legal characteristic in some way or other." [31] The principle of Contract, which originated on the commodity market, is transferred to all spheres subject to legal regulation, including Constitutional Law where rights are constructed as analogous to the rights of the individuals to the goods in which they deal, and to Criminal Law where the principle of retribution is a mere expression of the narrow views of the commodity dealer who claims equal and just compensation if his goods have been destroyed.[32]

The explanation of legal ideologies in various fields by the economic attitudes of a society that regards money as the standard by which all social values are measured, is as old as Thomas More's critique of capitalism. Classical German legal theory had taught that the very core of the legal structure was the individual in his relations with other individuals, and that Law, in actual operation, connoted equality rather than subordination. The State as such, according to the Prussian Conservatives, is its origin, but not partner to the Law unless, for certain special purposes, it equalises its position with that of other individuals. Under a socialist regime, according to these theories, the whole national economy would become the private business of the State and, therefore, beyond Law.[33]

From such a point of view all Law based on evident relations of subordination, like Criminal Law (apart from the artificial equalisation of the prosecution with the defendant) and Constitutional Law, is not Law proper. It is strange that a Marxist, apparently bound to explain Law by class-rule, could repeat such statements, but Pashukanis did : " Conflicting private legal interests are the basic condition of legal regulation." [34] Only commodity exchange—and this is the original contribution of Pashukanis and his school to the theory—can produce such private interests within the framework of a legal system. Only as long as the State is looked upon as the guarantor of the smooth working of the exchange of commodities, does it exist within the scope of juridical analysis, as the abstract legal norm.[35]

[30] Op. cit., p. 10. [31] Ibid., p. 62. [32] Ibid., pp. 113 ff.
[33] See Dobrin, op. cit., pp. 408–9. [34] Op. cit., p. 41.
[35] Ibid., p. 92. In the field of purely juridical analysis, there is an analogy to Kelsen.

As a social organisation for class domination, or an organisation for war, the State " neither requires, nor really admits legal interpretation ".[35]

The consequences of such a conception, for the past as well as the future of Law, are evident. In the past, the development of Law has been proportional to the development of capitalism. " Only capitalism creates all the conditions necessary to enable the judicial element to obtain its highest development in social relations." [36] Once capitalism is abolished, there will be no more Law, but mere technical regulation.[37] In the transition period, the sole alternatives are bourgeois Law, or no Law. " The withering away of bourgeois Law can under no circumstances mean its replacement by some new categories of proletarian Law, but only the withering away of Law in general, i.e. the gradual disappearance of the juridical element from human relations." [37] From such a point of view, the abolition of the N.E.P. implied the abolition of Law, whether this were desired as the fulfilment of the chiliastic hopes of original Communism for a very speedy transition to a state of society based on purely voluntary discipline, or abhorred, as by bourgeois legal theorists who identify socialism with lawlessness.[38] If a Soviet writer professed the first interpretation, his N.E.P.-public was not necessarily bound to share it. And when, later,[39] Pashukanis reproached Stuchka with injuring the interests of the Soviet State by demanding compensation for expropriated N.E.P.-men,[40] it might have been replied that Stuchka did so not on the basis of his partial criticism of Pashukanis' lack of historical sense, but on that of a conception which he shared with him, namely that at least in the field of Civil Law the only alternatives were recognition of the " equivalent principle " of commodity exchange, and lawlessness.

We have already mentioned above that the commodity exchange interpretation of Law, especially in its radical form which covers the whole field of Law, is but the well-known conception of capitalist Law as the only possible, Natural Law, to which the sole alternative is lawlessness,[41] with the addition of a sociological interpretation of the historical conditions of Law and of its eventual " withering away ". Within the realm of Law the adherents of the Commodity Exchange conception are

[36] Op. cit., p. 21. [37] Ibid., p. 23. [38] See above, p. 7.
[39] Op. cit., 1936, p. 9. [40] See above, p. 154.
[41] For a recognition of this proximity, see above, p. 4, note 10.

merely adherents of Natural Law. Any argument based on the historical evolution of Law that can be put forward against the Natural school is, at the same time, an argument against the Commodity Exchange conception. A glance at any ancient law-book—English, German or Russian—shows that long before they found elaborate regulations for commodity exchange, people regarded each other, for example, as the possible subjects and objects of blood feud. In a state of society where commodity exchange was a rare exception, Wergild was certainly not paid to compensate the bereaved family for the loss of a potential producer of commodities, nor even for the loss of a producer of goods. Pashukanis might answer that such Law was not Law proper, but this would merely beg the question. At least in theory one can imagine a well-functioning juridical machinery that, in a pre-capitalist society, protected what was felt to be most important within that society. There was a well-elaborated feudal Law in the mediæval village, and its study makes a much larger contribution to the understanding of contemporary Criminal Law than could an analysis of the growth of commodity exchange in the towns. Unless one is ready to analyse the past in the light of the present, as the early Soviet historians avowedly did,[23] there is no reason to assume that in all conceivable circumstances within a society needing and evolving legal regulation, it must be simply and solely the relations on the commodity market which exercise the predominating influence over conceptions of Law. Certainly there is no reason for such an assumption within the framework of Marxist sociology, which analyses ideologies as they are conditioned by the social relations which men enter with each other in *producing* their means of subsistence.

It may be alleged, although it is not proved, that Law, in order to be secure, supposes some actual equality between its partners.[42] But even if this be supposed there is no proof that these partners must necessarily be individuals more or less equal in power : the Law of the mediæval village contained very elaborate mutual obligations between lord and serf, although it was based upon the subordination of the latter to the former. There was some equilibrium, it is true, though not between the lord of the manor and any individual serf, but between

[42] We speak here of equality of actual social power to prevent the judicial machinery from being biased by overwhelming influences from one side—not of the mere formal " equality before the Law " that is merely another way of expressing its claim for generality. See above, Chapter I, pp. 4–5.

the lord and the village. On the other hand, the commodity market, and especially those institutions which correspond to it, like the Labour market prior to the organisation of Labour, in no way secure the actual equality of power of the partners to the Law.[43] The advocates of the Commodity Exchange Conception and its counterparts in bourgeois Natural Law cannot have it both ways: either they must restrict themselves to an analysis of ideologies—in which case it cannot be proved that those elements of legal ideology likely to be developed by commodity exchange are necessarily the foundations of any legal system. Or else they speak of the sociological likelihood of the legal machinery working "justly", i.e. equally applying the established norms to all cases fulfilling the established conditions.[44] But to-day, even avowed advocates of capitalism will hardly contend that the existence of commodity exchange grants that equality in actual social power which is needed to prevent violations of Justice.[43]

To a Marxist, for whom class-rule is the fundamental explanation of State and Law, the assertion that Law supposes co-ordination rather than subordination is but another way of saying that Law is a mere phraseology with no reality behind it—apart, perhaps, from the few cases where the partners to the Law are actually equal in social status (e.g. legal contests of trust versus trust, small entrepreneur versus small entrepreneur, worker versus worker, etc.). But there is not the slightest proof for such an assertion. Class-rule does not exclude a strong interest on the part of the ruling class in the regular and predictable working of the judicial and legal machinery, including its predictable working against individual members of the ruling class who violate its common interests.[45] In this sense every legal system is a system of co-ordination. But this does not exclude class-rule, i.e. subordination, as the basic phenomenon of the social structure protected by the Law. Certainly Pashukanis was right in stating that the very phenomenon of the State as class-rule neither admits nor demands legal explanation. It is a meta-juridical fact, to be explained by sociology and history, that, say, buying products of agriculture or industry destined for mass-consumption, in order to sell these again at a profit, is regarded in the U.S.A. as a contribution to national prosperity, and in the U.S.S.R., since 1932, as the crime of speculation,

[43] See above, Chapter I, p. 7. [44] Ibid., p. 4.
[45] See above, Chapter II, pp. 19–20.

according to article 107 of the Criminal Code. But within the legal system of the U.S.A. it is perfectly possible to distinguish honest commerce to be protected by the Law from violation of the anti-Trust laws, and within the legal system of the U.S.S.R. to distinguish the crime of speculation from the actions, say, of a housewife who has bought some article for her own use, but later, in consequence of personal circumstances, sells it at a profit.[46] Unless the question is avoided by including capitalism in the basic definition of Law it is hardly conceivable that the social machinery protecting honest trade in the U.S.A. against unfair competition should be described as Law, and the machinery protecting the socialist way of production in the U.S.S.R. against speculation should not.

Pashukanis has stated that, whilst private legal interests in conflict demand legal regulation, the condition of technical regulation is unity of purpose.[34] But there is no unity of purpose between the Soviet State and all interested in the functioning of its economics on the one hand, and the speculator on the other: the very fact of the existence of a Penal Code proves the existence of conflicting private interests. Not all of them are legal, it is true—but this is merely because there is a law, distinguishing legal from illegal private interests. Certain functions of private trade, regarded elsewhere (and also in Russia during the N.E.P. period) as normal, were made an offence by the Soviet law of 1932. In the U.S.A., a man may be interested in not fulfilling his contract. But this is not a legal interest, although it may become the subject of a legal decision. The Soviet legal system, since 1932, is interested in preventing speculation. But no less legal is the interest which housewives have in not risking criminal prosecution if by chance they should have to re-sell articles of domestic use, let us say under conditions of monetary inflation, when a " profit " on paper may easily result. By deciding a case in any court, in the U.S.A. as well as in the U.S.S.R., it is established that only one of the conflicting interests was legal: in fact, had both been legal, there could have been no decision. To speak of distinct conflicting private legal interests does not make sense unless it be understood as " private interests conflicting in the Courts of Law ". And this is what happens in any state that has a judicial system other than Public Law.

[46] The issue has formed a very important item in the explanation of the Law by the Supreme Court of the U.S.S.R. See *S. J.*, 1939, No. 1.

Of course, the question can always be begged by including in the definition of Law, if not capitalism *expressis verbis*, some ideological expressions of "free enterprise".[47] A critic of Soviet Law[48] has stated that "a contract between two Soviet organisations is much more in the nature of a plan, of an estimate of what each party can, and, therefore, must do in the common interest than an agreement of wills", and that, in realising those contracts "the bourgeois idea of the sanctity of contracts is replaced by contract discipline: State organisations must act in accordance with their contracts because discipline requires it. . . ." Apart from the fundamental question[47] whether as the recognition of such an institution as contract is a preliminary condition for recognising a system as legal, it is evident that—unless *a priori* "will" is defined as "will of a private entrepreneur, acting in his private interest"—a Soviet contract is based upon decisions of partners both of which have enjoyed a certain amount of freedom to decide whether they will make this contract, or another. A Soviet factory is bound, by plan to produce, let us say, a certain amount of nails, at certain prices, and another Soviet enterprise is bound, by plan to build, let us say, a certain number of houses. But the enterprise is to a very great extent free to decide for itself how to organise its working, and thus economise nails, and whether to buy the nails at this or that factory, which may offer quicker delivery. Unless the Soviet State had desired to leave its management freedom of decision in such matters, there would have been no sense in constructing its economic enterprises as separate legal entities, and preserving such a form of organisation up to the present day.[49] Whether entrepreneurs in a capitalist country, in fulfilling contracts, act out of respect for the "sanctity of contracts", or for any other ideology, can be left aside in a discussion of Law. For, in so far as they act on similar considerations, their actions would come under the title of Morals, and not of Law. Law begins at the point where a certain discipline is *enforced* upon them: i.e. at that point where the non-respect for the "sanctity of contracts" results in certain material acts of compulsion, ordered by the Courts. The manager of a Soviet enterprise may have concluded a contract with a certain partner and with a certain content merely because he was ordered to. He may

[47] See above, Chapter 1, p. 6.
[48] Dobrin, in *Law Quarterly Review*, vol. 49, pp. 260–1.
[49] See above, pp. 139–40 and below, pp. 193–4.

fulfil this contract in view of the disciplinary consequences arising if the Soviet Civil Court ordered his factory to pay the conventional fine established by the contract for non-fulfilment, and if, in consequence, the balance-sheet should show a deficit. But the very same reasons will determine the conclusion and fulfilment of contracts by the salaried manager of an American factory belonging to a certain trust, and even by the "independent" continental "owner" of a factory, completely dependent on a certain bank, that orders him to do business with other factories under its control. This bank, by making him bankrupt, could bring social sanctions to bear upon him as heavy, and much more serious for his family, than the Soviet Criminal Court would, if disciplinary dismissal of a manager should be followed by a trial for mismanagement. It is not difficult to prove that, in these times of organised economics, there is but little correspondence between the social reality and the legal ideologies of the heyday of "free" capitalist competition. But, unless the question is begged by a definition of Law according to those ideologies, there is no reason to assert that Law can exist only in the incomplete stages of the organisation of social economics.

Pashukanis' most serious argument is, that in a society based upon unity of purpose, legal regulation would be replaced by technical regulation.[34] This is merely another form of Engels' saying [50] that, with the gradual abolition of classes, rule over men would be replaced by the mere administration of things. Such an assertion is acceptable if it implies no more than an interpretation of the vast majority of the cases of compulsion necessary in the capitalist and also in the transitional society as a consequence of present or recent class-divisions. It may be expected that the abolition of such divisions would be followed by a marked reduction of the number of cases in which compulsion would be applied. If a rather utopian mind follows such an argument to its ultimate conclusions it may visualise a complete unity of purpose amongst the members of such a society (at least in their economic activities) where, in consequence, regulations would have a purely technical character. But it is completely wrong to quote, as Pashukanis and his German Conservative predecessors do,[33, 34] a modern railway by-law as an example of "purely technical" regulation (unless it is meant in the sense that the various departments of a railway

[50] See above, p. 24.

organisation do not deal with each other as with distinct legal entities, as Soviet enterprises do).[49] These so-called " technical regulations " always mean commands to *men* (for the rails and engines, unhappily, do not understand either English or Russian). Whether it works as mere technical advice which the engine-driver, to whom it is addressed, follows because he is convinced of its reasonableness, depends on the general character of the society in the framework of which this railway works. Apart from disciplinary sanctions—which, if brought into an orderly system, are no less Law than the Law of the Manor—neither the Soviet, nor any capitalist state refuses to back the " technical " regulation by its Criminal Code. Non-compliance with technical rules is in serious cases followed up by penalties more serious than those which the management of the railway could inflict upon its employees. In the U.S.S.R., where great demands are made on somewhat backward villagers to master the complicated working of a modern railway system, and where there is no threat of unemployment to back the disciplinary powers of the management, the scope accorded to Criminal Law is rather wider than elsewhere. In view of the highly technical character of the questions generally met in this field, it was regarded as necessary to establish special Railway Courts, headed by a " Transport Bench " of the Supreme Court of the U.S.S.R. But experience has proved that these courts, by virtue of their connection with the practice of management, work out as another aspect of the Railway Management—backed by all the enormous powers of Soviet Criminal Law—rather than as organisations mainly concerned with doing Justice to the individual citizen.

It is quite a natural working hypothesis for a railway management that any accident must have a cause removable by human endeavours, and that, therefore, in every case there must be someone responsible—with responsibility graduated according to the seriousness of the consequences of the supposed misbehaviour. It is, on the other hand, an elementary demand of Justice, including Soviet Justice, that no one should be punished but for acts or omissions committed when he might reasonably have been expected to act in another way, so that his punishment may serve as a deterrent for him and other people who may eventually find themselves in similar situations. And the punishment must be appropriate to the danger to society which the delinquent represents, i.e. to the malignity of his intentions, rather than to the actual consequences which his action had for reasons partly independent of him.[51] The first part of this demand clearly contradicts the working hypothesis of the railway management. If there has been an accumulation of inexplicable accidents the management may be inclined, by the threat of exemplary punishment, to impel employees to do even more than can reasonably be expected of them, even if some who are innocent from the legal point of view may suffer.[52] The second part of the demand of Justice should seem acceptable from the point of view of an ideal railway management as well. If some catastrophe occurs to focus public interest, actual railway management, as it exists on earth, will be naturally eager to find a few culprits and if possible to interpret their action as criminal neglect of duty rather than to recognise that the method of organisation (established by the management itself), imperfect rolling stock, etc., were such that a minor failure by a junior official could precipitate a catastrophe. In any case, there is some difference between the approach of the railway management and that of the judiciary, or, to speak in general terms, between the social interest in avoiding railway accidents at any price and the other, broader, social interest in securing any citizen employed by the railways from imprisonment unless he has really and intentionally committed some crime. Soviet Law recognises this difference, and tries to solve it judicially by subjecting the sentences of all railway tribunals to special supervision by the Plenum of the Supreme Court [53] as is the case with Courts-Martial in peace times. Practice shows that there is ample scope for such supervision. The Plenum of the Supreme Court has to quash many convictions, including some which are almost incomprehensible to the judicial mind, which have been passed over even by the Transport Bench of the Supreme Court

[51] We have here, as fits our investigation, expressed that judicial interest in terms of Soviet conceptions of Justice (see above, pp. 74–5 and 111). It could be expressed also in the terms of other theories of Criminal Law, apart from the primitive talionic theory.

[52] For example, if a skilled railwayman, to whom some beginner has been apprenticed, goes on holidays after his pupil has taken over independent work, and is arrested on his return from holidays because the novice has meanwhile, by a technical mistake, produced a collision. See *S. J.*, 1939, Nos. 4 and 10.

[53] Article 75 of the 1938 Statute on the Constitution of the Courts. So every defendant in a special Bench of the Supreme Court of the U.S.S.R. is granted an appeal to the Plenum of that court, whilst in general jurisdiction judgments even by the Supreme Courts of the individual Union Republics are definitive, unless contested by the Attorney-General of the U.S.S.R., or the President of the Supreme Court itself, in the course of the procedure of supervision (see above, pp. 123–4).

itself.[54] As long as technical regulations must be backed by sanctions against violators of "technical" duty, to speak of the purely technical regulation of the behaviour of the citizen of a socialist state means simply to grant the technical managements unlimited powers against their subordinates. If the State, which has amongst its other functions a broader social interest that all citizens should be dealt with in a way that they can accept as just, should "wither away" in favour of managerial omnipotence, a truly lawless state of affairs might ensue. But this is no argument in favour of the Commodity Exchange Conception of Law which explicitly demands such a procedure, once commodity exchange ceases to be the economic foundation of society. It is simply an argument in favour of looking for foundations of Law broader than those provided by capitalist ideology. Certainly, serious problems are involved in the State's checking the natural trends of socially important parts of its own organisation, by preventing railwaymen from being imprisoned for having had bad luck and worse judgment in the choice of sufficiently able apprentices. But there is no inherent contradiction in a solution of these problems. In preventing engine-drivers, who have quite correctly refused to drive unsafe engines, from being convicted for sabotage,[55] the State may impair the immediate concern of railway managers to fulfil their plans with whatever equipment is available. But it certainly serves the long-term interest not only of the State in general, but also of the railways. But there is an inherent contradiction in the conception that the power of the individual enterprise, in the U.S.A., is a guarantee that the anti-Trust laws will be duly applied. This very conception is implied in the Commodity Exchange conception of Law, and in the explanation of Law by the rights of private enterprise in general.

It is not difficult to understand why the Soviet dropped a theory which could only be interpreted as an apology either for capitalism or for lawlessness, in the sense of anarchy or arbitrary rule. Its temporary success can only be explained by the deep-felt dissatisfaction with the capitalist features of the N.E.P., together with the impression which the apparent revival of

[54] In fact, that Bench is composed of specialists promoted in the hierarchy of Railway Courts and, evidently, tends to support their judgments. So the real supervision of special justice from the point of view of general conceptions of Justice is carried out within the framework of the Supreme Court. See the examples given in *S. J.*, 1939, Nos. 4 and 10.

[55] Supreme Court of the U.S.S.R., *S. J.*, 1939, No. 4, p. 72.

capitalism made on many Soviet intellectuals. Both trends worked together in furthering the acceptance of a theory open to very ambiguous interpretations, according to whether the necessarily capitalist character of any Law, or the desire for its quick " withering away ", was stressed. With the downfall of the N.E.P., the latter interpretation seemed to approach its heyday.

## CHAPTER VI

# THE CRISIS OF THE N.E.P. AND OF THE COMMODITY EXCHANGE CONCEPTION OF LAW

### (a) The Victory of Economic Collectivism

Development of public enterprise in competition with the private entrepreneur, and the use made of this competition in overcoming the dangers of bureaucracy inherent in State-administered economics, had been amongst the major purposes of the N.E.P. In the industrial and commercial field [1] the inherent advantages of large-scale enterprise, backed by the State's control of the "commanding heights" and systematic planning of economics, did not fail to produce the desired results, that is, gradual progress of public enterprise, with private enterprise just able to continue its competition and thus to check the efficiency of State-management. The percentage of the annual increase of the total invested capital amounted to :[2]

| In the years | State Enterprise. | All Enterprises Together. |
|---|---|---|
| 1923–4 | − 1 (disinvestment) | + 1 |
| 1925–6 | + 3 | + 4 |
| 1926–7 | + 6 | + 5 |
| 1928–9 | + 11 | + 7 |

In 1926–7 the State did not restrict its private competitors artificially. But already the rate of growth of State economics surpassed the increase in the private sector. The marked discrepancy in 1928–9 may be interpreted as a partial transfer of capitals accumulated in the private sector to State-owned industries. Concentrating on the expansion of its own enterprises the State ceased to grant private entrepreneurs credits, but continued to take increased toll of their profits in form of taxation. Thus extreme shortage of money occurred in the private money market, with consequent enormous rates of interest even up to 80 per cent. per annum. Private capital, deprived of an increasing part of its own specific functions, escaped into investment in public loans, and private enterprise in industry and commerce dwindled, long before it was formally deprived of its

[1] See above, pp. 131–2.

[2] Kritsman, in *Problemy Ekonomiky*, 1930, Nos. 4–5.

legal foundations. In theory, another way of absorbing the private sector might be visualised : the State might have used its dominating position and the shortage of money which threatened private enterprise, to subject the latter to its full control by granting credits under certain conditions.[3] Political considerations originating from the general situation to be discussed below, and the need to concentrate all available means of the State on expanding its own industries, prevented such an approach from being followed. However, from the point of view of industry and commerce, the N.E.P. undoubtedly fulfilled the functions designated to it, and by its own mechanism provided the conditions for gradual transition to full public control of economic development.

The real difficulties arose in the field of agriculture, where the lack of really efficient State or collective enterprise allowed the kulak to dominate the market.[4] Periodical difficulties in spring, when the kulaks had cornered most of the grain, were paralleled by similar periodical discussions within the Party caucus on the policy to be applied in the village. True, there was no absolute grain shortage, if measured by the standards of the first years of the N.E.P. : the public purchasing organisations raised in 1925–6, 434, in 1926–7, 596, and in 1927–8, 574 million poods,[5] and this was far beyond the 300 million which the State had unsuccessfully tried to raise during the last period of War-Communism. In 1925–6 123, and in the following year 153 million poods were exported. Thus 311 and 443 million poods respectively remained for internal consumption. But this was not sufficient for the increasing needs of expanding industry, at a time when defence, and the collective development of agriculture [6] demanded an increased tempo in industrial expansion. At the same time, this very expansion rendered certain grain exports highly desirable in order to pay for industrial imports. In 1927–8, confronted with a rise to 549 million poods in internal consumption, the proceeds of the public grain-purchasing campaign allowed for only insignificant grain exports. The situation was critical.

There were only two possible solutions. Either the Government could continue the New Economic Policy in the village, restrict the increase of industry so that its needs did not go beyond

[3] See Kozlov, op. cit., pp. 79 ff.

[4] See above, pp. 134 ff.

[5] Stalin, op. cit., 1940, p. 205. 60 poods correspond to about a ton.

[6] See below, pp. 171 ff.

what the individual peasant or kulak would sell, and then concentrate industrial development on such articles as would induce the peasant, and especially the kulak, to sell his grain; or else industry could be developed according to the needs of defence and of a development of agriculture in such a way as to render the State independent of the kulak's whims. In the latter case, provisional measures were needed to enforce the delivery of the grain that the kulak would not voluntarily sell—in fact, without such measures not even the restricted deliveries of 1927–8 would have been accomplished. But the experience of War-Communism had shown that these were only short-term solutions: one could not indefinitely go on confiscating grain or applying the respective articles of the Civil and the Criminal Code on usury, speculation, and failure to fulfil public tasks, as it was politely termed, without destroying the economic incentive to grain production and relegating Soviet agriculture to that state of self-sufficiency which would certainly destroy any hope of developing industry.

In order to solve the agricultural problem, industry had either to produce those goods that would satisfy the kulak, or those goods that would render him superfluous, so that he could be expropriated without destroying the foundations of industrial development. Soviet industry would have to produce agricultural machinery in any case: either jointly with articles of mass-consumption, as an incentive to the agricultural population to sell their grain (the kulak buying machinery, the middle peasant textiles, etc.), or jointly with all those other implements of large-scale production which would render the country independent of possible boycott by its capitalist neighbours, and secure its defence in the case of war. The answer to this question decided whether the U.S.S.R. was to be socialist or capitalist in character. For had the kulak bought agricultural machinery, he would have developed into an agricultural capitalist; and by the same mechanism that enforced this decision, he would have become the actual master of the country and its economics. But the answer also decided whether the U.S.S.R. was to remain politically and economically independent or not. For a restricted speed of industrial development, and the concentration of industrial production on those articles which the farmer desired, would have excluded the development of the essentials of economic self-sufficiency and even the satisfaction of the most imminent needs by any other way than the export of those surpluses which the peasants would sell. Thus, the rôle of the U.S.S.R. would have been restricted to that of an exporter of raw materials and importer of foreign capitals, with the resultant dependency on foreign capitalists. Quite apart from this, the country would have been condemned to a very modest existence : the very dismemberment of the pre-War large-scale landlord enterprise involved a restriction of the marketable surplus of agriculture. Unless Russia's industrial standard of life was to be restricted to a level compatible with what small-scale peasant husbandry would spare after the peasants had eaten their fill,[7] Russia could not be able to continue in the social structure established during the N.E.P., with the agricultural compromise dominated by peasant's family husbandry. It only remained to decide whether to reconstruct large-scale agriculture on the basis of private capitalist enterprise, or on that of some form of State control or collective.[8] Furthermore, the State's increasing demands for food deliveries made it likely that a co-operative solution would include strong elements of State control. The following figures [9] illustrate the problem and the way in which it was solved :

GRAIN PRODUCTION IN 100 MILLION POODS (IN BRACKETS THE PART OF THE PRODUCT MARKETED)

| Enterprises of | Before the First World War. | 1926–7. | 1934. |
|---|---|---|---|
| Landlords | 6 (2·8) | — | — |
| *Kulaks* | 19 (6·5) | 6 (1·25) | — |
| Small and middle peasants | 25 (3·7) | 40 (4·66) | 6·6 (1·22) |
| State and collective farms | — | 0·8 (0·4) | 48 (14) |
| Total | 50 (13) | 47 (6·3) | 55 (15) |

Both agrarian revolutions, that of 1917–19 as well as that of 1929–31, are well illustrated by these figures, as is the fact that only the second definitely restored and surpassed the pre-War standard of general productivity and of the ability of agriculture to cater for other needs than those of the agricultural producers themselves. In the pre-War period part of these needs were for export—in 1934 Russia had completely ceased to export grain and used the increased marketable surplus of agriculture merely to support an industrial population which had nearly doubled. The main social result of the first agricultural revolution, the possibility of the small peasant eating his fill, was not

[7] See the table below. [8] Stalin, op. cit., 1933 (vol. II), p. 337.
[9] Based on Levin, in *Na Agrarnom Frontem*, 1935, Nos. 2–3, p. 36.

reduced by the second : that part of the agricultural product consumed by the peasants themselves remained stable, and fed a farming population reduced by the migration of many millions to industrial centres. From the point of view of Russia as a whole, the farming as well as the industrial sector of her people, the two agricultural revolutions, taken together, were fully successful : but the first itself, the triumph of small-scale peasant enterprise, failed to satisfy the needs of the country as a whole. Thus the second revolution was inevitable : Stalin's success against the right-wingers within his party turned what otherwise would have become a restoration of capitalism in the most important field of Russian economic life, into a triumph of collectivism in agriculture, supplementing the nationalisation of industry during the 1917–19 Revolution. Originally,[10] the N.E.P. had been a compromise between the State, dominating industry in consequence of the 1917 Revolution, and the individual peasant who, in the consequence of that very revolution, had become the complete master of agriculture. Once collectivisation of agriculture was achieved, the N.E.P. lost its meaning, apart from introducing methods in the management of State enterprise more efficient than the ordinary capitalist War-economics and bureaucratic emergency measures which War-Communism had taken over from its predecessors.

The real difficulty arose from the fact that, by the very nature of things, the solution, collectivisation of agriculture, was not ripe when the question became urgent. As long as the kulak was strong in the village, the crisis in food deliveries was an unavoidable consequence of the very expansion of industry. Even if industrial expansion could have been completely devoted to the production of modern agricultural machinery (which was impossible owing to the needs of defence, and the insufficiency of raw materials) some time would have had to elapse between the expansion of industry and that outflow of agricultural machinery which might have convinced the peasant that large-scale farming, and therefore collectivisation, was superior to the traditional individual peasant's husbandry. Therefore methods of enforced collection of grain from the kulak had to be applied at a time when agricultural collectivism was insufficiently developed to replace the kulak as a producer, and the first steps in the development of collective agriculture had to be taken before its superiority was a purely technical matter. In conse-

[10] See above, pp. 85 ff.

quence, oppressive administrative measures against the kulak and his possible influence on other peasants played a larger part in the new agricultural revolution than would have appeared reasonable to those who, in the days of the N.E.P., relied upon the inherent merits of modern agricultural methods gradually to convince the peasants of the advantages of collectivisation. As early as 1928 article 107 of the Criminal Code was applied on a large scale for confiscating from the kulaks the grain which they declined to sell. The poor peasants who helped in finding and confiscating the grain were granted a share of 25 per cent.[11] In 1928–9 658 million poods, and in the following year 1·3 milliard poods, were collected. On this second occasion State farms participated, supplying 2·4 per cent., and collective farms (kollkhoses) 9·1 per cent.[12] The State farms and kollkhoses together now delivered as much grain to the market as the kulaks had delivered in 1927, and four times the amount they themselves had been able to sell in that year. But evidently the enormous expansion of the State purchases of grain, in 1930, was partly due to confiscation of the stocks of the kulaks, i.e. to a non-economic expedient the application of which could not be repeated.

> Prior to 1929, the Soviet Government had pursued a policy of restricting the kulak, but at the end of 1929 it turned to the policy of eliminating the kulak. The Laws on the renting of land and the hiring of labour were repealed, and the peasants allowed to confiscate farm inventory from the kulaks for the benefit of the collective farms. The kulaks were expropriated, just as the capitalists had been expropriated in the sphere of industry in 1918, with this difference, however, that the kulak's means of production did not pass into the hands of the State, but into the hands of the peasants unified in the collective farms.
>
> This was a profound revolution, a leap from an old qualitative state of society to a new qualitative state, equivalent, in its consequences, to the revolution of October, 1917. The distinguishing feature of this revolution is that it was accomplished *from above*, on the initiative of the State, and directly supported *from below* by millions of peasants. . . .[13]

After such an explanation from the most competent source, under the personal editorship of Stalin, it is hardly necessary to dwell upon the formal fact that, being carried through by a

[11] *History of the C.P.S.U.*, p. 292.

[12] Leikin, in *Na Agrarnom Frontem*, 1931, No. 1, p. 9.

[13] *History of the C.P.S.U.*, pp. 304–5. The decisive resolution, by the December Plenum, 1929, of the Central Committee of the C.P., has been published in *Pravda*, January 6, 1930 (English in *Slavonic Review*, vol. X, pp. 202 ff.).

government uniting in its hands full dictatorial powers, the abolition of the rights hitherto granted by the Soviet legal order was formally legal.[14] " A leap from an old qualitative state of society to a new qualitative state " is a meta-juridical fact, and the legitimacy of revolutions is not measured by their compatibility, or otherwise, with the legal order previously existing. Being a revolution *from above*, the transformation of Soviet agriculture was carried through, or at least regulated, by decrees, the most important of which was that of the V.C.I.K. and Soviet of People's Commissars of February 1, 1930,[15] which enacted the chief measures resolved by the December Plenum of the Central Committee of the C.P. But being *a revolution*, i.e. a co-ordination of mass-movements varying greatly according to local conditions, that transformation could hardly include the generality and predictability which legal measures demand: even such distinctly legal measures as the repudiation of parts II and III of the Land Code, permitting the renting of land and employment of hired labour in individual peasant households, were ordained only for " the districts of wholesale collectivisation ", and even within these limits, exceptions were made in respect of middle peasant holdings which were to be regulated by the District Executive Committees.[16] In the districts of wholesale collectivisation, the Regional Executive Committees and the Governments of the Autonomous Republics were granted the right " to take all the necessary measures for combating the kulaks up to complete confiscation of their property and their deportation of the confines of the Region in which they live," independent of any violation of the existing laws committed by the kulaks. The confiscated property of the kulaks, with the exception of such parts as were needed to pay their debts to the State and co-operative organisations, " must be given over to the indivisible funds of the kollkhoses, as the share of the poor peasants and agricultual labourers who join the kollkhos ".[17]

The last phrase was of essentially ideological importance, intended to refute the reproaches to which formerly poor members of the kollkhos had been exposed from the middle peasants who had had to renounce part of their property when joining the kollkhos. From the Marxist point of view it expresses a

[14] But see below, pp. 200–1.
[15] Reprinted in *Slavonic Review,* vol. X (1930), pp. 209 ff.
[16] Ibid., article 1.
[17] Ibid., article 2.

mere truism : as it had formerly been the poor peasants and labourers who, under the kulak's control, had toiled with his implements of production, the transfer of the former kulak enterprise to kollkhos management involved the transfer to the kollkhos of the former kulak property in means of production as well as the transformation of his former labourers into members of the kollkhos. From the point of view of the latter's individual rights the phrase is meaningless ; no one but the kollkhos as such can dispose of indivisible funds, and to join a kollkhos no one needs to have any property unless he formerly owned implements of agricultural production. The latter ruling was disappointing from the point of view of the former middle peasant, who was bound to regard the kollkhos as a union of individual properties at least as much as of individual labours. So the State intervened and explained to the kollkhos-member that the collective property was increased by the kulak's former means of production, under the condition that those who had toiled on the kulak's fields were accepted as equals. Should the middle peasants fail to join the kollkhos, or leave it, the poor peasants and labourers, i.e. that part of the village population most likely to be in sympathy with the Government's purposes, might work on co-operative lines with the former kulak's implements of production, and they were firmly induced to do so since they were not allowed to use the property expropriated in their favour in any other way.

So far this " revolution from above " depended not on legal acts, but on revolutionary transformations. But by being a revolution *from above* and by being a part of the general transition to planned economics, it seriously threatened one feature essential to the economic and political content of that revolution. In the Communist Party of the U.S.S.R. it was generally agreed that if the enormous changes involved in transition from individual to collective husbandry were to take place in the peasant's life and conditions of labour, if the peasant must renounce his rights to individual property in means of production in exchange for participation in the fruits of collective endeavours, then voluntary action of the peasants themselves was the only possible basis if the estrangement of the strongest class of the people was not to result in the downfall of the Soviet regime. But the projected " wholesale collectivisation " in certain regions at a certain time, as expressed in the December resolution of the Central Committee,[13] involved the danger that local organisations which had failed to convince the peasants with the necessary speed, would replace consent by administrative pressure. There is certainly no *a priori* contradiction between planning, understood as foresight applied to the development of human relations [18] and the voluntary character of decisions which carry out the development as foreseen. The advantages of the application of modern machinery, possible only in large-scale enterprise, together with such inducements as the State might offer in the field of taxation, credits, etc., might suffice to induce a considerable percentage of the peasantry voluntarily to enter the kollkhoses, without any pressure being exercised upon those who were not yet ready to make such a decision. But it was only in 1931 that the new factories could begin large-scale output of modern agricultural machinery, and the December resolution of the Central Committee of the C.P. had provided for complete collectivisation of grain production rather earlier. Moreover, " Socialist emulation " between the local organisations might easily result in attempts to " surpass " the tempo and the degree suggested at the expense of the voluntary principle : some dozens of Regional Committees might attempt to achieve " wholesale collectivisation " as soon and as completely as possible, not only by forcing the peasants into collectives, but also by forcing such a structure on the collective that the sphere of activities left to the individual member would be reduced to a minimum. Not only cattle, but pigs and even poultry might be " collectivised " and any private husbandry (including private cooking) might appear highly suspect in such a " Commune ". These " applications " of the principle of " wholesale collectivisation ", not to speak of the " interpretations " of " combating kulaks " as an attack on all individual peasants who for some reason disturbed the local plans,[19] were not rare. In other places besides the Urals [20] it might happen that some kollkhos, eager to surpass all former experiments, would transform itself into a Commune (i.e. absorb all the private husbandry of its members, apart from the private household), and would absorb nearly

[18] See K. Mannheim, *Man and Society in an Age of Reconstruction*, London, 1940, p. 193.

[19] A drastic example from the Orenburg district is quoted by Zarov, op. cit., pp. 114–15 : on the basis of article 61, Criminal Code, twenty-seven out of the sixty-seven peasants' households of a village, for " non-fulfilment of their economic duties ", were characterised as " kulaks " and re-settled, twenty-four miles away, on a soil unsuitable for their vegetable-growing activities. Besides, they were soon joined by their other forty neighbours who were removed from their land " to make place for a Sovkhos " (communal farm). The local Soviet " explained " these proceedings by the argument that individual peasants, even if there was no proof of any illegitimate activities, would certainly raise the prices on the local vegetable market !

[20] Whence this story is reported by Uralsky, op. cit., p. 14.

all the other kollkhoses of the district, so that the new " giant " could proudly claim to embrace 700,000 acres and 66,000 members—whose actual participation in the so-called " co-operative " management was, of course, impossible. They also would declare illiteracy in the district abolished, and all churches closed !

Such proceedings might easily undermine the position of the regime amongst the peasantry. As early as January 30, 1930, a resolution of the Central Committee had to prohibit enforced transformation of Agricultural Artels into Communes, as well as collectivisation of houses, poultry, and cows not producing for the market, etc., against the will of the peasants concerned. On March 2, 1930, Stalin published his article, " Dizzy with Success ", and, one month later, his " Reply to Comrades of the Kollkhoses " [21] on the questions raised by the first article : whilst strictly rejecting any attempts at enforcing collectivisation, and granting all peasants, who so desired, the right to leave the kollkhoses, the government would support those peasants who continued to work on collective lines, against the current of withdrawal that followed as a reaction against the wave of " wholesale collectivisation ", and would grant them facilities and advantages which the individual peasant would not enjoy. A decree of April 2 established these privileges, for kollkhoses and their members, mainly as regards taxation and cancelling debts incurred by the kollkhos or by the kulak whose land had been handed over to the kollkhos. Another decree, that of April 12,[22] explained that these privileges fully applied to Societies for Joint Cultivation of the Land, and their members, only under the condition that draught animals and machinery were collectivised, i.e. only to such Societies for Joint Cultivation as differed from Artels merely by the formal preservation of the claim of each peasant to the harvest from a certain part of the land cultivated by common efforts. All other Societies for Joint Cultivation of the Land, i.e. the typical representatives of this kind of co-operative enterprise, enjoyed only part of those privileges. There were still kulaks in the regions not subjected to wholesale collectivisation, as evident from the rules on the assessment for agricultural tax in 1930–1 : provision was made for a special group of kulak enterprises (along with kollkhoses, kollkhos-members, and individual small peasants). Their taxa-

[21] Reprinted in Stalin, vol. II (1933).
[22] Both reprinted in *Slavonic Review*, vol. X, pp. 344 ff.

tion was hard, but not prohibitive, even the part of their annual money income in excess of 6,000 roubles being burdened with no more than 30 per cent. In these regions the kulaks were only gradually eliminated, whilst in the regions originally laid down for "wholesale collectivisation" the only economic units left to compete were kollkhoses and small-scale individual peasant holdings.

In his "Reply to the Comrades of the Kollkhoses," Stalin [23] had described the original estimate of a 60 per cent. collectivisation in the grain-producing areas as "obviously exaggerated", and had expressed the hope that, after the withdrawal of those peasants who made use of the freedom granted to withdraw, the kollkhos movement might be stabilised at an average level of 40 per cent. of the peasantry in the grain-producing areas. Such expectations proved as much an under-estimate as the original hopes of the winter of 1929–30 had been an over-estimate: once the attitude of the Government towards the collectivisation was made clear, and support of the *Artel* was clearly established, the number of kollkhoses continued to rise. The Artel favoured by the Government, strongly surpassed the Communes, which were rejected as going too far, as well as the Societies for Joint Cultivation of the Land, which were rejected as insufficient steps towards collectivisation. The number of the kollkhoses of the different types (in thousands) amounted [24] in the years 1919, 1928, 1929, 1930, and 1933 to the following:

| | 1919. | 1928. | 1929. | 1930. | 1933. |
|---|---|---|---|---|---|
| Communes | 1·9 | 1·8 | 3·5 | 7·2 | 4·8 |
| *Artels* | 3·6 | 11·6 | 19·2 | 60·1 | 216·0 |
| Societies for Joint Cultivation of the Land | 0·6 | 19·9 | 34·3 | 14·2 | 6·3 |

The Communes, although never represented in any considerable numbers in comparison with the total strength of the Russian peasantry, played a certain rôle in the period of War-Communism [25] as well as during the first wave of enforced collectivisation. The Societies for Joint Cultivation of the Land, i.e. a type of agricultural co-operative similar to that prevailing in many capitalist countries (for example Central and Northern Europe), was in Russia a product of the N.E.P., but continued to prevail during the first stage of collectivisation. After the extravagances of premature "wholesale col-

[23] Op. cit., p. 300.

[24] According to Uralsky, op. cit.

[25] See above, pp. 51 and 85.

lectivisation " were dropped, the advance from 1929 to 1930 remained not so much a quantitative one (although an increase of the total number of kollkhoses in one year by 40 per cent. is certainly remarkable), but mainly an advance in quality: replacement of inadequate types of collectivisation by more efficient ones. This change and the improvement in management resulting from a clearer conception of the type of kollkhos desired, along with the output of the new factories producing agricultural machinery, made possible the eventual triumph of collectivisation.

From the point of view of the evolution of Soviet Law, it is not the expropriation of the kulaks by revolutionary measures, but the establishment of the new order of collectivised agriculture, and of the mutual relations between kollkhoses and individual peasant husbandry, that is important. Apart from the Sovkhoses, i.e. State farms that in their type of organisation did not differ from any industrial or commercial State enterprise, the drafters of the Land Codes of 1919 and 1922 had already known the three main types of kollkhoses, i.e. of co-operative agricultural enterprise.[26] But the distinction was rather vague:[27] in 1919 the term " Common Cultivation of the Land " embraced the traditional village community, the Artel, and the Society for Joint Cultivation of the Land in the later sense. In 1922 the only strict distinction was between the Commune, which did not allow individual land shares to its members, and the Artel and the Society for Joint Cultivation, which did. In both last mentioned types of co-operative, part of the land was cultivated in common, but in the Artel, as distinct from the Society for Joint Cultivation, each member was allotted a fixed share in the product of the joint efforts. This share was determined partly by the contribution which the individual member could make in draught animals and implements of production, and partly by the traditional peasant assumption that each member of the Artel, or rather each member of his family capable of working, would contribute equal personal efforts to the common work.

It is not difficult to imagine the consequence of such arrangements on the intensity of labour, especially once the Artel was no longer an association of a small minority of peasants who had volunteered for an experiment of whose inherent merits they

[26] See above, pp. 51 and 102–3.

[27] Therefore, the correspondence of 1919, 1928, and 1933 data (see the schedule above) is always somewhat problematical.

were convinced, but a body uniting virtually the whole village, or at least all those who could not withstand the inducements offered by the State to kollkhos members. On the other hand, in the Society for Joint Cultivation of the Land each member retained a certain share of the land, the product of which he enjoyed. Only certain agricultural operations were carried out jointly, as a rule by joint use of implements of production belonging to the individual members. Under these conditions, the individual member of such a co-operative was more interested in that part of his work individually done on his private land share, than in that part executed jointly with other members whose individual share in the joint effort (say, ploughing all the land belonging to the co-operators on a certain day) could hardly be distinguished.

The Plenum of the Central Committee of the C.P.,[13] in its resolution of December, 1929, demanding wholesale collectivisation of grain production, also resolved " to replace the Society for Joint Land Cultivation, in which only the labour of the members is socialised, whilst the private property of means of production remains intact, by the Agricultural Artel, in which the essential means of production (draught animals, machinery, building, cattle) are socialised ". As we have seen above,[28] the distinction between these two main types of agricultural co-operative was still so vague that the government, in official enactments, could speak of such " Societies for Joint Land Cultivation " that, in essentials,[29] corresponded to the definition given by the Central Committee of the C.P. for the Artel. In fact, by now it had been accepted that the Artel was characterised not only by joint ownership in the above-mentioned means of production, but also by a joint land fund to be used only collectively : according to article 3 of the Model Articles for Agricultural Artels, published in 1930 by the People's Commissariat for Agriculture,[30] the land belonging to the Artel was in no circumstances to be reduced. All means of large-scale production were to be collectivised, and only one cow was to be left to each farm, to cover the private consumption of the family. Small livestock, such as pigs, sheep and poultry, were to be partly

[28] P. 175.

[29] The differences concern buildings and cattle, apart from draught-animals. But it ought to be kept in mind that, during this whole period, grain production was regarded as the essential field of collectivisation.[5] So the difference was rather unimportant.

[30] Reprinted by Burns, op. cit., pp. 278 ff.

collectivised where this branch of agriculture was highly developed. So it might pay for the kollkhos to have, in addition to its large-scale grain production and cattle-holding, special farms of that kind. The remuneration for the work done by the members in the collective enterprise was to be graded according to the skill needed, and the amount of work done : just as in State enterprises a scale of hours (or days) to be worked, as well as of remuneration for the work done, was established. So, too, in a State farm the individual worker might be granted a private kitchen-garden, a cow, pigs and poultry for private use. Thus the distinctive features of the kollkhos were restricted to (1) a more democratic form of management, the members of the co-operative themselves deciding on the management and the plan of work to be done, and (2) a lack of that security of income which a State enterprise offered, in so far as the State met the wage bill, a procedure inapplicable in a self-governing co-operative. According to the Model Articles of 1930, only 50 per cent. of the earned wages were to be paid to the kollkhos-members during the agricultural year, and the rest after the realisation of the harvest. Unless the working discipline of the kollkhos-members was very strict so that all work was done efficiently and in due time, or the scales of remuneration were established at a miserably low level, the kollkhos-member was not likely to receive the full second half of his earnings after the harvest. Such experiences were no more likely to better working discipline than low wage scales. In an inefficient kollkhos, i.e. in one that could not duly recompense its members for their participation in the collective work, the latter was likely to be reduced to a formality, " fulfilled " in order to secure the privileges in the field of taxation, etc., which the State granted to the kollkhos-member. Whatever the phraseology, the " auxiliary private husbandry " of the kollkhos-member was likely to remain his main source of income, and the focus of his activities. Little interested in the prosperity of the collective, the kollkhos-members would make use of kollkhos-democracy to distribute the collective product to their own advantage, for example by starving the cattle in the collective farm to get more food for their private cows. On the other hand, if the influence of the Communist members of the kollkhos, and of the administrative machinery, was exercised in order to distribute as little as possible of the product, and to invest as much as possible, the inducement to the members to participate actively in the collective work would be reduced, too. So the acceptance of the Artel as the preferable type of kollkhos, described a mere framework, within which the real problems of the co-ordination of private and co-operative interests had to be solved.

The double purpose of restricting the private husbandry of the kollkhos-member so that it left the bulk of his labour for the collective work, and of determining the remuneration for that work in such a way that it might appear attractive to the kollkhos-member, might have been achieved easily enough had it been possible to pay the kollkhos high prices for the delivered products, and to supply the market amply with such consumer's goods produced by industry as the peasant desired. Under such conditions the collectivisation of agriculture would have been merely another expression, corresponding to the ideologies of the former small property-owner, of his transformation from a primitive husbandman who regarded money as a mere complement of his income in kind, into a partner in national productive activities, who gave labour in order to receive a claim in money form to whatever goods he desired. The fundamental difficulty in the development of agricultural collectivism was just the same as it had been in its foundation. Needing huge reserve funds of agricultural products, and being forced to devote the bulk of its industrial investments to armaments and to those means of production necessary for armament, the State could neither pay very high prices for grain, the main agricultural product at the time, nor use the profits made from the low agricultural prices to produce those industrial products the peasant needed. In consequence the double problem mentioned above would have been insoluble, unless the Soviet had succeeded in rendering the private " auxiliary economy " of the kollkhos-member which competed with the kollkhos for his or her activities, the main incentive to his active participation in the collective work. Stalin in his speech to the Kollkhos-congress of January, 1935, described the Artel as " a co-ordination of the private with the public interest."

This solution was feasible at a certain stage of the development of agricultural collectivisation : that in which the solution of the grain problem (apart from the supply of certain industrial raw materials, like cotton, sugar-beet, etc.) appeared as the main problem to be solved by collectivisation,[5] a stage at which the State was very glad to have part of the burden of supplying the industrial markets with meat, butter and similar products left to the peasant's initiative. Under such conditions it was not very relevant to the peasant member of a kollkhos whether his share in the money collective earnings was high or not : what counted most was that as large as possible a part of the collective product should be distributed in kind, and supply the feeding-stuffs upon which the peasant, or his wife, might develop cattle-holding in his " auxiliary husbandry " sufficient to supply the necessary money income. Since 1932 the State encouraged this tendency by opening the " kollkhos-markets ". There not only the kollkhoses as such, but also their individual members,[31] after making those deliveries to the State which were needed to supply the industrial population with a certain minimum for ration-books, might sell their surpluses in meat, butter, vegetables, etc., at prices fixed by the play of supply and demand. Once the main difficulties of industrialisation were overcome, and the fulfilment of the Second Five Year Plan secured, the State, in 1935, abolished all rationing and, competing with the kollkhoses and their members, supplied the industrial population at prices somewhat below the former free " kollkhos-market ", but above the former ration level. Being the only middleman and the owner of powerful Sovkhoses, many of which specialised in producing the very foods which the kollkhoses might bring to market, the State could prevent any cornering of the market and any unreasonable rise in prices of the kind which had characterised the corresponding periods of the N.E.P. At this time as at an earlier occasion [32] the opening of the markets encouraged peasant enterprise. But, by now, the kulak and the private trader were eliminated and the " commanding heights " in agriculture as well as in industry were secured by the State. Now, free trade in foods encouraged not only the activities of the kollkhoses as such, which tried to supplement the distributable money income from grain by selling vegetables and meat, but also the activities of the individual members of the kollkhoses who could not profit from these markets without earning the necessary feeding stuffs by participation in the collective work.

On these foundations the Soviet succeeded in making that compromise between private and collective husbandry, the Agricultural Artel, a great success. Four fundamental problems of organisation had to be solved, and this was done in the interval

[31] The possibility of granting to kollkhos-members facilities in marketing the products of their " auxiliary husbandries " formed another inducement to membership in the kollkhos.

[32] See above, p. 86.

between the Model Articles of 1930 [33] and the new ones of February 17, 1935.[34] These problems were (1) the establishment of such a form of participation by the individual kollkhos-member in the collective earnings that his or her maximum participation in the collective work was encouraged ; (2) the limitation of his private " auxiliary husbandry " in such a way that the inducements to participation in the collective work were increased to the maximum in the sense that the very interest of the peasant in his private husbandry demanded increased earnings from participation in the collective work, without absorbing too much of the labour of the peasant's family ; (3) the distribution of the collective earnings as between the individual member's shares on the one hand, and the collective investment funds, etc., on the other, in such a way that the collective farm as well as the interest of its members in active work would be promoted ; (4) the establishment of such forms of leadership inside and outside the individual kollkhoses that, in spite of the market and the play of market prices being used as a main incentive to the kollkhoses' as well as to the kollkhos-members' activies, the State interest in securing a certain supply of essential products and in controlling the markets would be satisfied. Closely connected with these four fundamental problems of internal structure there was a fifth : the position of the remaining individual peasants had to be regulated. For on its solution depended whether some strengthening of intra-kollkhos discipline would not simply result in withdrawals, or whether kollkhos-members would readily risk expulsion for not fulfilling their duties.

In 1930–1 [35] the first of these problems was solved by the establishment of the " Labour-Day " as the basis of the distribution of the collective product. Each kollkhos-member has a book in which are entered the working-days spent in collective work. Skilled work is multiplied by a certain coefficient (up to 2), whilst the least skilled kinds of work are counted as less than one " Labour-Day " (to a minimum of 0·5) for one

[33] See above, pp. 178–9.

[34] Reprinted in *Slavonic Review*, vol. XIV, pp. 188 ff. The document was published as an official enactment (S.U. 1935/82) and is certainly regarded as law (see below, pp. 197–8. But its description as " model " statute denotes that it can be realised only by the incorporation of its suggestions in the concrete statutes of individual kollkhoses.

[35] See the Decree of the People's Commissariat for Agriculture and Kollkhos Centre, of July 12, 1931 (reprinted in *Slavonic Review*, vol. XI, pp. 711 ff.), where the opposite practice is criticised as a deviation from established rules.

working day actually spent in the fields. Thus payment by "Labour-Days" (which, more correctly, may be described as "Labour-Units") depended on the degree of skill exercised by the kollkhos-member. In addition to this, as in all Soviet enterprises, piecework remuneration was made dependent on fulfilment of the established norm. For example, a tractor-driver who ploughed only half the number of acres regarded as normal in his region, would receive only half the normal remuneration (i.e. in spite of his high qualification, only one instead of two "Labour-Days"), and he might earn less than, say, an unskilled woman who has spent the same day in destroying weeds over more than twice the area allotted to her.[36] On the other side, the difference in income between a highly successful tractor-driver, and an inefficient unskilled worker, is far more than the established average of 4 : 1. These Labour-Units do not represent a certain amount of remuneration, but a claim by the kollkhos-member who has earned them to a proportionate share in that part of the collective product to be distributed amongst the members. So the "value of the Labour-Day" consists in a certain number of pounds of grain, vegetables, milk, and whatever products in kind the kollkhos may have to distribute amongst its members, after it has fulfilled its obligations towards the State and itself sold on the free market what may be best realised there, plus a certain amount of money, the proceeds from the sales to the State and on the free market. It is just this compound of earnings in kind and in money that is desired by the peasant who, at least under pre-War conditions, could make less use of a high money income[37] than of a sound basis for his private "auxiliary husbandry". The "value of the Labour-Day" is regarded as a standard by which the efficiency of the Administrative Board of the Kollkhos ought to be measured.

In fact, this holds true in so far as economy in spending Labour-Days, i.e. making the most profitable use of the labour

[36] As piecework in the U.S.S.R. is remunerated progressively, the fulfilment of the double norm would involve much more than double the normal earnings—so the woman, with a normal coefficient of 0·5, would earn more than one Labour-Unit for each day actually spent on the fields. It is another question how long the kollkhos would employ a tractor-driver who could fulfil only half his norm.

[37] This is unavoidable in kollkhoses the produce of which is unsuitable for immediate consumption by the members—say cotton. Therefore the "millionaire-kollkhoses" prevailing in these regions, although much advertised by Soviet propaganda, are not necessarily the most flourishing ones. A money income of, say, 2,000–3,000 roubles per average member (which would correspond to some millions total income of the average kollkhos) need not necessarily mean more than, say, one ton of grain plus some hundred roubles.

force available, and in realising the product, is concerned. But, once the most urgent needs of the members are satisfied, it may appear sound policy to invest an increasing part of the collective income in enlarging the future output, and creating cultural amenities, etc. Such a policy, for reasons of socialist ideology, might be carried even further than is rational from the long-term point of view of the community. But even within the limits of the long-term interest of the kollkhos, such a policy might impair the average peasant's readiness to participate in the collective work, little inclined as this peasant might be to consider other than his short-term interests. It might appear that the working of intra-kollkhos democracy, together with the strong influence of the Communist Party on the decisions of the kollkhos, would form a sufficient guarantee that both points of view were given due consideration. But in reality, the Soviet authorities never did trust the working of this mechanism : evidently they expected either the individual feelings of the kollkhos-members participating in the decisive meeting, or the pressure exercised by the local Party and State authorities, to carry decisions to one or the other extreme.

Therefore, year by year, since 1931,[35] decrees of the supreme State authorities have, according to actual public policy, established the general framework within which the decisions of the kollkhos-assemblies on the distribution of the annual income ought to be kept. On September 20, 1931, a resolution of the "Kollkhos-Centre" [38]—which was, however, at least formally the supreme authority of Kollkhos-self-government—went to the length of cancelling not only those resolutions passed by individual kollkhoses that provided for distributing grain according to heads of the kollkhos-members' families irrespectively of the work done, but also those that attributed too large a share of the collective earnings to stocks or general public purposes, at the expense of the dividends distributed. Whilst cancelling the former type of resolution might still be interpreted as safeguarding an essential characteristic of the Artel, i.e. the distribution according to work done, the latter clause definitely involved a restriction of the freedom of the kollkhos to pass resolutions at least immediately furthering its own prosperity. (Of course, the reason for such a procedure was to protect the actual freedom of the kollkhos-members against pressure brought upon them "in the interest of the community", with the ultimate result of

[38] Reprinted in *Slavonic Review*, vol. XI, pp. 193 ff.

reducing the incentive to work.) A decree of the Soviet of People's Commissars and the Central Committee of the Communist Party, of April 19, 1938, amended article 12 of the Model Articles of 1935 to the effect that no more than 10 per cent. of the monetary income of the kollkhos could be spent for capital purposes, and no more than 2 per cent. for economic and administrative expenses. At least 70 per cent. was to be distributed amongst the members on a Labour-Day basis. This decree was combined with another prohibiting expulsions from the kollkhoses except in the most serious cases and granting the expelled member the right to appeal to the District Executive Committee. A third decree provided for increased taxation of individual peasant's horses and stricter supervision of their fulfilment of all their duties to the State. The coincidence of these decrees, all published April 20, 1938,[39] explains their political meaning : when the regime proceeded to make the position of the peasant remaining outside the kollkhos less desirable, conditions inside the kollkhos had to be acceptable even for the more backward type of peasant, however unaware he might be of the common interest.

More distinct are the restrictions on the scope of the individual husbandry which every kollkhos is allowed and encouraged to grant to its members. Articles 2 and 5 of the 1935 Model Articles for Artels gave very elaborate rules, varied according to the conditions of various regions, as to how much land and how much cattle of various kinds was to be allowed to the individual kollkhos-member's auxiliary husbandry, and only the details of these matters are left to decision by the individual kollkhos. A decree of the Central Committee of the Party, and the Soviet of People's Commissars, of May 27, 1939,[40] further emphasised the maximum limits established for the kollkhos-member's private husbandry, in order to secure that the latter, indeed, remained a mere auxiliary, and did not distract him from the collective work. So also certain minimum amounts of Labour Units—varying according to the conditions prevailing in various types of kollkhoses—were established, which every kollkhos-member was obliged to perform, on pain of expulsion from the kollkhos for failure to participate in the common work. To render this alternative less desirable, the taxation of the individual peasant was once again increased. Whilst a certain gradual

[39] S.P. 1938, Nos. 115 and 116, reprinted in *Slavonic Review*, vol. XVII, pp. 219 ff.
[40] S.P. 1939/235.

absorption of the kollkhos-member's activities by the collective was enforced, the government did not refrain from interfering with traditional kollkhos organisation in order to secure that sphere of private husbandry which they felt desirable : a decree of the Soviet of People's Commissars, of May 25, 1934, entitled agricultural Communes to transfer up to a third of their cattle-holding to the individual use of their members, against payment by instalments. So these " Communes " (i.e. organisations that originally had gone to the length of collectivising even poultry, and reducing their members' house-gardens) no longer differed much from the Artels. It may be regarded as established, that the form of organisation of collective agricultural enterprise, apart from details, is regulated as a matter of public policy.

This does not exclude a high degree of autonomy which central regulation allows to the kollkhos, nor does it exclude guarantees of a truly democratic decision on such matters as are left to kollkhos autonomy.[41] But from the very moment that the collectivisation of agriculture became virtually complete, and all possible resistance to government policy was thus concentrated within the kollkhoses themselves, political leadership by Party and State towards the kollkhoses was regarded as essential if that form of agricultural organisation created by the Soviet itself was not to turn against it.[42] Such leadership is exercised by the political influence of the Party which has its cells in the kollkhoses as well as elsewhere, and by a competence of the Agricultural Departments of the Regional and District Soviets to supervise, in certain regards and within certain limits, the exercise of kollkhos autonomy. In the economic field, the State can regulate kollkhos activities by its virtual control of the markets as well as by its strong position as owner of the Machine Tractor Stations,[43]

[41] For example, part VIII of the 1935 Model Articles demands all important decisions to be taken in a full Assembly of the kollkhos-members. (Cf. that of 1930, which provided for delegate meetings for reasons connected with the current tendency towards giant kollkhoses. See above, pp. 174–5.)

[42] See " On the Class Struggle within the Kollkhoses ", Stalin's speech on the Plenum of the Central Committee, June 11, 1933, op. cit., 1940, pp. 441 ff.

[43] Originally (see, for example, the contract of the first Machine Tractor Station, reprinted by Burns, op. cit., pp. 201 ff.), this point was not so clear—eventual acquisition of the Station by the peasants, once collectivised, being envisaged. It ought to be kept in mind that in that agreement, concluded with 238 individual peasants, in the name of the Ukrainian Union of State Farms, the actual rôle of the peasant partners is much more dependent on the directives given to them by the engineers of the M.T.S., than in the present state of things, when the kollkhoses as organised bodies deal with the M.T.S. On the other hand, once the State found out that to encourage kollkhos activities a very high percentage of the visible kollkhos earnings had actually to be distributed amongst the members, it might appear advisable to keep the most expensive kinds of investment outside the kollkhoses' balance-sheets,

upon the services of which the kollkhoses depend. This influence is exercised in the form of contracts following certain standard types elaborated by the authorities, between the State-owned Machine Tractor Stations and the kollkhoses served by them.[44] In such a contract the Machine Tractor Station undertakes work enumerated in detail of a certain agreed quality, and supplies agrotechnical help, etc. The kollkhos undertakes to supply the labour needed (apart from some specialists sent by the Machine Tractor Station), to send a certain number of its members to the courses established at the Station to qualify as tractor-drivers, etc., and to grow certain products on the fields prepared by the Machine Tractor Station at certain minimum standards of cultivation. The payment for the services rendered by the Station is made in kind. Of course, the Machine Tractor Station looks for payment in such kind as the State happens to need, just as its general influence and technical suggestions will influence kollkhos production in the desired direction. These influences, along with the State's power of making the prices of the most-needed agricultural products favourable to the producer, will virtually suffice to keep the free decisions of the kollkhos within certain well-defined limits as regards the general direction of its production and organisation. Apart from details of this kind, kollkhos autonomy covers the management and the internal discipline of the working community, together with the disposition of that strictly limited part of the collective product that is not bound to be distributed amongst the members. In any case, the latter's income depends so much on the efficiency of kollkhos management that all members are warmly interested in the functioning of kollkhos democracy.

It may be asked how far the agricultural organisation just described is co-operative at all. Agricultural collectivisation has succeeded only on voluntary lines, and on the eve of this war there were still 6 per cent. of individual peasant's holdings, whose very survival formed some corrective to the application of too severe a discipline within the kollkhoses. However preferable the position of the kollkhos-member may be, he is not the only one who can earn his living in Soviet agriculture (apart from the State farms). And however strong the influence of the State on the direction of the kollkhose's productive efforts, it certainly

although, of course, they are partly paid out of the profits which the State makes in marketing the kollkhoses' products.

[44] See Ribalko and Lovkov, "The contractual relations between the M.T.S. and the Kollkhoses", in *Na Agrarnom Frontem*, 1934, No. 10.

does not work as it does upon the industrial factory, which is ordered to produce this or that commodity. A certain freedom of local initiative and experiment is not only allowed but encouraged. Public recognition is earned by that kollkhos which establishes a number of various special farms for distinct purposes, ranging far beyond those suggested by the State to the average kollkhos, and which has increased its total income as well as its income for distribution far beyond the average. Since 1935 the kollkhos has enjoyed the Right to Use the Land, occupied by itself, " for times everlasting "[45]—the nearest approach to ownership of land established since the Soviet revolution. This guarantee holds true also against the individual members of the kollkhos : according to the decree of May 27, 1939, an increase in their number (and also claims of former kollkhos-members to individual farmland) should be met by resettlement in other parts of the Union, and not by distributing land hitherto worked collectively into new members' " auxiliary husbandries ". Of course, the kollkhos' Right to Use the Land does not exclude a right of the State to approximate kollkhos organisation still further towards that centralised type of socialist organisation represented by State enterprise, or—say, by way of taxation—to participate in the advantages of kollkhoses cultivating especially good soil.

But these are distant perspectives : actually the kollkhos-member enjoys a virtually complete guarantee that he or she may follow his traditional occupation in his traditional surroundings if he desires, under a discipline exercised by his appointees and controlled by himself and his fellow-members by means of genuinely democratic procedure. Further, he will be rewarded for his efforts in a way easily understood and proportional to those efforts. What he does not enjoy is individual control of his means of production. For the portion of the originally private means of production left outside the indivisible fund [46] is rather insignificant in comparison with that

[45] Article 2 of the 1935 Model Articles, Decree of the Soviet of People's Commissars of July 1, 1935 (S.U. 1935/300), and article 8 of the 1936 Constitution.

[46] According to the 1935 Model Articles, from a quarter to a half of the socialised means of production (according to the previous income of the kollkhos-members, the details of the scale to be left to the decision of the individual kollkhos) are to be regarded as the kollkhos-members' contribution to the indivisible funds, which would not be refunded in the case of his leaving the kollkhos. There is a theoretical inconsistency with the legal explanation (see above, pp. 172–3) of the contribution made in the name of the poorest peasants, which is of no value for them unless inside the kollkhos. Once the contribution of the individual member to the kollkhos funds has become unimportant in influencing his income (see the next note) the issue becomes purely academic.

accumulated in the kollkhos itself, not to speak of the Machine Tractor Stations. Even if the individual peasant were granted better chances than he actually is, of leaving the kollkhos, it would mean that he would have to part with most of the fruits of his efforts during the years of his membership. Nor has the kollkhos-member's former ownership of socialised means of production any influence on his actual earnings, at least since collectivisation became complete :[47] this would contradict the theoretical description of expropriated kulak property as a contribution made in the name of the former poor peasants and labourers entering the kollkhos [48] and, even more, the fact that by far the larger part of the kollkhos' working capital has been accumulated since the average member joined it. Contributing one's individual property in certain means of production was a preliminary condition to the right and the duty [49] of contributing one's labour and enjoying its fruits. As the latter, in Soviet Law, is the only legitimation of property in means of production, there was no expropriation of the peasants joining the kollkhos. On the contrary, in consequence of the enormous investments made by the State, the former individual peasants, now kollkhos-members, can apply their labour more productively, and earn more than before. According to capitalist conceptions of ownership, there has certainly been an actual, although not a formal, abolition of property. For the former individual peasant's right to dispose of his collectivised property has disappeared. If, therefore, the right of the member to dispose of a share which is still regarded as his private property, is said to be the characteristic of a co-operative, then the kollkhos is certainly not one. If, on the other hand, a co-operative is defined as a form of socialist enterprise distinguished from others by its greater degree of autonomy and financial responsibility, the kollkhos certainly comes within the definition. It must be added

[47] The decree of July 12, 1931,[35] provided for 5 per cent. of the kollkhos income to be distributed in accordance with collectivised property, but only in those districts where collectivisation was not complete. Evidently, disposition and even usufruct of the property contributed by the peasant to the kollkhos funds was regarded as dependent on his actual alternative of husbanding as an individual peasant. Indeed, whilst most natural under such conditions, these rights contradict the basic attitude of the kollkhos, which tends to recompense every member according to his or her contribution *in labour*. In considering the share in the kollkhos income temporarily distributed amongst the former owners of means of production, it ought to be kept in mind that, according to Yakovlev's report on the XVIth Party Congress, 40 per cent. of the total fixed capital of the kollkhoses were contributed by the State, 15 per cent. out of the property of expropriated kulaks, and only 45 per cent. by the kollkhos-members themselves.

[48] See above, pp. 172–3.

[49] See above, p. 185.

as a rider, however, that State ownership of the essential means of production restricts the degree of autonomy enjoyed by the organisation of producers, who control only the less important, although the more visible, part of the means of production used by them. Soviet ideology has been inclined to describe the Commune [50] (i.e. a kollkhos which more completely than the Artel embraces the peasant activities) rather than the State farm (Sovkhos) [51] as the highest form of agricultural organisation ultimately aimed at—without making a sensible distinction between these two conceptions. The Commune, i.e. absorption of the "auxiliary" private husbandry of the kollkhos-member, puts an end to those elements of private production for the market which still survive, while emphasis on the superiority of State farms denotes the superiority of stricter planning. Hitherto, such prospects have remained purely theoretical: in the field of agriculture the advantages of co-operative initiative over the hierarchy of State administration, which attracts the less efficient type of agricultural worker and, amongst the co-operatives, the advantages of those granting the individual member a larger scope for personal interest, have proved superior. So the tendency has been to transfer as much land as possible from Sovkhos to Kollkhos management, and to transform all surviving Communes into Artels. Complete as the triumph of collectivism has been, in the field of agriculture it has been a triumph of the State-controlled co-operative, not of direct State management.

Whilst Soviet agriculture, during the period of the Five Year Plans, acquired a completely new outlook, and developed new forms of organisation, there has been no new qualitative development in industry. As had been expected when the N.E.P. was introduced, private enterprise in industry and commerce "withered away", partly because of pressure by the State and excesses by administration and judiciary,[52] but essentially in consequence of its inferiority in comparison with the State's overwhelming economic power. Certainly the process was accelerated by the State's need to concentrate all available resources on enormous investments to make possible agricultural collectivisation as well

[50] Stalin in "Dizzy with Success", in op. cit., 1940, p. 336.

[51] Which has been described as the leading factor which directed the peasant masses on to the path of collectivisation" (Stalin, op. cit. 1933, p. 339).

[52] Cp. Zarov, op. cit., for the attempt of the Moscow Regional Court to introduce —evidently in copying the procedure applied against the kulaks—by its own jurisdiction "the elimination of the (urban) bourgeoisie as a class", without any authorisation by the legislative authorities.

as rearmament,[53] but it would certainly have proceeded without these special circumstances, as it had done since the beginning of the N.E.P. When in the economic field the elimination of private enterprise was virtually complete, the Law of August 22, 1932, firmly established the change by amending article 107 of the Criminal Code, so that purchasing agricultural products, or industrial products destined for mass-consumption, with the intention of reselling them at a profit, was defined as the crime of speculation, to be punished with no less than five years' imprisonment. Ridiculous, but occasionally also very serious, misuses of this law [54] had to be corrected repeatedly by the Supreme Court. But in essentials, since 1932 the position is clear : the production and sale of goods for luxury consumption is the only field left to the private entrepreneur. All other trade [55] is State, or co-operative monopoly, black marketing being suppressed with all the vigour of revolutionary law.

Interesting progress was made during this period in the administration of industrial State enterprise. The enormous expansion during the First Five Year Plan could not be met out of the profits of the enterprises concerned, and even the State could grant the necessary credits only at the price of monetary inflation and the resultant undermining of the stability of balances. These facts, like the corresponding developments during the period of War-Communism, resulted in a temporary popularity of theories on the " withering away of the Credit from the State sector ",[56] i.e. on the lack of responsibility felt by the enterprises for the economic use of money granted them by the State for purposes of investment. But, this time, such theories could not prevail : the experiences of War-Communism acted as an efficient inoculation against all leftist nonsense. The government took just the opposite course. The resolution of the Central Committee of the C.P., of December 5, 1929,[57] accepted as a general policy also during the period of reconstruction the " placing of enterprises on a separate accounting basis ". This

[53] See above, pp. 170–1.

[54] Amongst the former an interpretation of the law as including trade in such agricultural products as guinea-pigs and white mice (*S. J.*, 1939/4, pp. 22 ff.) may be included. More serious is the fact (*S. J.*, 1939/3) that the Supreme Court has very often to intervene to protect simple housewives—maybe with some speculative vein—against the application of fierce measures aimed at the professional profiteer.

[55] Apart from trade in self-produced commodities by small craftsmen (for example tailors in the town), and especially by kollkhos-members and other peasants (see above, p. 181).

[56] See Kozlov, op. cit.

[57] Reprinted in Burns, op. cit., Appendix, pp. 261 ff.

policy had already been well developed during the N.E.P.,[58] and later became popular as *Khosrazchot* (Economic Accountancy).

> Independent accounting shows the real position of the enterprise, facilitates the rationalisation of production, and the proper organisation of supplies and sales, whilst it also creates a force which runs counter to bureaucratism and intrigue. At the same time, the placing of each enterprise on an independent financial basis makes it easier to form a correct idea of the productive work of the enterprise and to keep the workers informed of the results of their work.

Independent accounting entails, of course, a certain amount of economic autonomy : subject to the strictest observation of the plan, and within the limits laid down by it, the productive enterprise must be independent, and its manager bears full responsibility for its working. A definite sum, the amount of which is to be fixed annually, must be placed at the disposal of the enterprise, and the contracts which it concludes for the delivery of its products must be based on the estimated costs of production. The difference between these and the actual costs of production is the main test of the successful work of the enterprise : if positive, it forms the profit of the enterprise, part of which is left at its disposal, and spent on the improvement of the conditions of workers and employees, on paying premia to efficient members of the staff, etc.

The only way the attitude of this document differs from later policies is its rather lenient approach to current cases of enterprises failing to fulfil contracts on time and at the agreed price : in such cases adjustments in the conditions were to be made. For this purpose a special organ, the State Arbitrage, was established in 1931 [59] to settle conflicts between State enterprises. In due course it became a kind of special Civil Court regulating the intercourse between these enterprises (i.e. virtually by far the most important part of Soviet economic relations) and considerable conventional penalties were provided against unpunctual fulfilment of contracts. These penalties as well as an eventual deficit arising out of a difference between the estimated and the actual costs of production were recovered from the current account of the enterprise at the State Bank. Thus the latter became a main regulator of the fulfilment of plans.

The Decrees of the Soviet of People's Commissars, of January 14 and March 20, 1931, had already stopped the auto-

[58] See above, pp. 139–40.
[59] S.U. 1931/203. See Shkundin, op. cit.

matic supply of credits to State enterprises. Not the plan, but its fulfilment were to form the basis of granting credit to the enterprises. The account of any enterprise was to be credited for goods delivered only after the purchaser had acknowledged the receipt of the goods in due quantity and quality.[60] In order to assist those enterprises which were burdened with the enormous investments demanded by the Five Year Plan in fulfilling their contractual obligations, a Decree of the V.C.I.K. and of the Soviet of People's Commissaries, of May 3, 1931, reduced the obligatory delivery to the Treasury from 85 per cent. of the profits to 10 per cent. for all State enterprises likely to need State subventions. Only those enterprises that had no claim to State subventions—i.e. virtually those producing consumer's goods —had to continue delivering to the Treasury their 85 per cent. which had been introduced as a means of centralising all State resources for financing the Five Year Plan. Like the analogous steps taken during the last stage of the N.E.P.,[58] this change meant increasing the autonomy of those enterprises where accountancy was unlikely to express profitability in the current sense of the word. By these measures accountancy was clearly reduced to a standard of economic efficiency and made applicable to the whole of national economics whether actually yielding profits or not. The more decentralised the responsibility for efficient working, the more likely was economic accountancy to function as a check on the efficiency of management. By the laws of February 18 and July 23, 1931, the right to enter contractual obligations on their own responsibility was granted to those enterprises that belonged to a Trust, thus reducing the latter to a rather supervisory organ. On the other hand, the position of the leading organs of national economy themselves has been gradually approximated to that of superior planning and supervising organs. The Supreme Economic Council has been replaced by a number of People's Commissariats competent for various branches of national economics ; and since 1936 these People's Commissariats have been further split till each of them corresponded rather to a single big trust administering a distinct industry. With the disappearance of the need to compete with the N.E.P.-man, and to make proper commercial decisions, the Trust of the N.E.P.-years [61] had lost its importance : what counts, to-day, is, on the one side, economic leadership of a branch of industry—whether exercised by one of the bigger

[60] See Khavin, op. cit. [61] See above, pp. 137–9.

Trusts or, as is the rule, by a special People's Commissariat—and, on the other hand, efficient technical management of the individual factory. Management of enterprises and Trusts is checked by the "control by the rouble", that is to say, by the individual accounts that are credited and debited according to the fulfilment of contractual obligations which they enter into, in the most important cases, with other State enterprises. With the end of private capitalism, the possibility of transferring its surpluses to the socialist sector *a fond perdu* had ceased, and this fact enforced strict economy within the socialist sector itself. So the triumph of planning increased rather than diminished the rôle of credit and of the contractual obligations forming its basis.[62]

(*b*) The Soviet Legal System during the Second Revolution

It is a highly interesting question whether the continuity of the Soviet legal system was preserved during the revolutionary changes in the social relations regulated by it. This question is quite distinct from that of the preservation of legal continuity, i.e. from the question of whether the changes effected, however contradictory to the former prevailing law, were carried through according to the rules of Soviet constitutional law. This is certainly the case. The most serious infringement of Soviet legality happened before the Soviet was ready definitely to replace the policy of restricting the kulak by that of eliminating him as a social factor,[63] and to authorise the corresponding revolutionary action: and indeed, a very wide interpretation of article 61 of the Criminal Code was needed to confiscate the property of people who continued to do business in the manner that had been customary and even officially encouraged during the N.E.P. In 1925, Bukharin had advised the kulaks to enrich themselves and thus also to serve the community But to declare this kind of business illegal and to replace it by that new order which has always been proclaimed as the ultimate purpose of the Soviet, was certainly within the legal competences of the government, and it was even in the spirit of the fundamental ruling of the Civil Code according to which Civil rights were

[62] See Molotov on the industrial conference of 1931, and Grinko on the XVIIth Party Conference, February 2, 1932 (reprinted in *Finance and Socialist Economics*, 1932, Nos. 8–9). For the opposite point of view, i.e. for an explanation of Plan-credits by mere redistribution of the former funds of the private capitalist sector, with the resulting "withering away of credit", see Kozlov, op. cit.

[63] See above, pp. 171 ff.

protected only so long as their exercise served certain economic and social purposes, for the sake of which they had been established.[64] To claim a right to compensation when the Soviet deemed those rights to have outlived their useful function was possible only on the basis of the Commodity Exchange Conception of Law,[65] never accepted by the Soviet government. To re-settle Soviet citizens in an emergency, according to their social position and to their danger to reconstruction, was certainly within the powers of the Government, at least prior to the abolition of all social distinctions by the 1936 constitution. On the other hand, the decrees " eliminating the kulaks as a class ", however much these were within the legal competences of the government, were distinctly revolutionary measures [63] and lacked the elements of generality and certainty demanded of any law in an established social system. The whole procedure might be used as an argument for the theory that Law is unfit to serve as an instrument of social change,[66] unless it were not evident that the extreme speed and ruthlessness with which the " de-kulakisation " of the U.S.S.R. was carried through was a consequence of an extraordinarily difficult external situation, which enforced a quite abnormal speed of industrial reorganisation. Apart from those special conditions other slower but more regular means of carrying through the change would have been available.

But this argument has nothing to do with the question of whether the legal order, after the transformation, was the same as before, and it does not even help to answer it. Some legal systems, for example the Common Law, have survived quite a number of social changes which any Marxist sociologist would describe as social revolutions, independently of whether or not all changes in property, etc., such as the confiscations during the Wars of the Roses and the Reformation, proceeded according to the rules of Law. The institutions survive, and serve a social system completely different from that out of which they were developed, although, of course, changing their function in Renner's sense,[67] including the transformation of connex-institutions into essential ones, and the withering away of those originally essential. The very fact that after the enormous social changes since 1927 the 1922 Codes are still in force, proves that something similar has happened in the U.S.S.R. But

[64] See above, pp. 93–4.
[65] See above, p. 154.
[66] See above, Chapter I, p. 6.
[67] See above, Chapter II, pp. 27–8.

how has this change been achieved, and what is the actual function of the institutions of 1922?

For industry and commerce, the question may be answered in a relatively simple way: those institutions of Civil Law established for the sake of regulating the competition between private and public enterprise, now that the former is abolished, are applied in order to secure the economic efficiency of the latter, and its compliance with the plans for whose execution the individual public enterprise has been granted a certain amount of autonomy. For example, article 30 of the Civil Code,[68] originally established in order to prevent the private entrepreneur from evading the Law, is now used by the State Arbitrage [69] to invalidate transactions of State enterprises that provide for investments not foreseen by the plan. This is done even if, in view of the lack of State credits for the intended investment, its costs are covered in some other way, for instance, by the surplus profits of the enterprise. A new problem arises in this connection: when granting an increasing number of State enterprises [70] the right to enter such legal transactions as are needed to transfer their management to a basis of Economic Accountancy, the government did not bother much about article 19 of the Civil Code, according to which only those State enterprises are recognised as subjects of Civil Rights that enjoy a certain degree of autonomy which is not exercised by all enterprises subject to the regime of Economic Accountancy.[71] But these are details: the State could easily avoid theoretical difficulties by amending article 19 in a suitable way. In such a case, the Civil Code would still have been essentially that of 1922, with some important parts rendered obsolete by the withering away of private enterprises, and with other parts having changed their function.

The position as regards agriculture is much more complicated. The function of legislation proper in carrying through the great transformation was rather restricted. It included preparatory measures, like the Law of December 15, 1928, modifying the regulations of the Land Code on the periodical redistribution of the Land, in such a way as to facilitate the establishment of kollkhoses. It authorised the revolutionary changes by the Decree of February 1, 1930.[72] It has protected the new order

[68] See above, Chapter IV, p. 94. [69] See *S. G.*, 1939, No. 4, p. 70.
[70] See above, pp. 139–40. [71] See below, pp. 247–9.
[72] See above, p. 172.

with determination by the Law of August 7, 1932, which introduced extreme measures, in the most serious cases including capital punishment, in order to protect socialised and especially kollkhos property against plunder, destruction and appropriation. But it was not legislation proper that established the foundations of the new order, apart from the provision, in article 109 of the Land Code,[73] for Model Articles for the various types of kollkhoses which were to be elaborated by the People's Commissariat for Agriculture, and from the various ensuing modifications of the Model Articles of a semi-legislative nature.[74]

The reason for such a state of affairs is the co-operative construction of the new order. Being, at least in theory, based upon voluntary association of its members, the kollkhos had to be organised on a basis which might be supervised and supported, but not ordained, by the State. The legal basis of each kollkhos is its own articles, enacted by its Assembly. In theory, the Model Articles (and, in consequence, all their amendments carried by legislative procedure) are no more than advice by Party and State as how best to organise the kollkhoses. The articles are perhaps also a legal condition of their enjoyment of those privileges which are granted to the Artels for reasons of public policy. In view of the decisive rôle of these privileges in the existence of the kollkhos, the difference between such an authoritative advice, conditioning the very foundations of the kollkhos, and a law regulating its internal structure, might appear of little importance. Indeed, few kollkhoses will trouble to enact special amendments to their individual articles in order to embody amendments to the Model Articles enacted by the supreme authorities and, in spite of this omission, no judge will fail to enforce the observance of the new modified articles with the same energy as he would enforce the observance of some rule enacted by the kollkhos in a matter left to its autonomy by the Model Articles. But, in spite of this, there is some official consciousness of the fact that, the Kollkhos being a co-operative, its foundations cannot be regulated from above as might be done

[73] See above, p. 103.

[74] See above, pp. 182 ff. As, in the articles of the kollkhoses, there is no provision for a constituent authority of delegates' meetings, etc., in matters of Statute, the participation of kollkhos activists in enacting such Model Articles certainly does not imply more than a demand by the State for competent advice from the people immediately concerned. The C.P., although in fact all-powerful, is no legislative authority—its signature under the Model Statute does not involve more than an order to its members to support corresponding changes in the individual Kollkhos Articles. So the legislative character of the Model Articles is based upon the signature by the Soviet of People's Commissars.

by the State in the case of its own factories : when, in 1939, big changes in the working order of the kollkhoses in the direction of strengthening the collective and reducing the private element in their economics were felt desirable,[75] the State and the C.P. confined themselves to enforcing, by decree, amendments which kept within the general framework of the Model Articles, whilst *advising* the kollkhoses to expel members not participating in collective work up to the established minimum. They also provided for a new Delegates' Meeting which should further amend the Model Articles in the direction required. It might be said that this is a matter of policy, not of Law : a state which feels entitled to set limits to the freedom of the kollkhoses in distributing their income, or in exercising their discipline over members not fulfilling their duties, could, from a purely formal point of view, just as well abolish the private " auxiliary husbandry " and the private cattle-holding of the kollkhos-members. The fact that it certainly would not do so without seeking the assent of representatives of the kollkhoses may be regarded as a political, not a legal fact, as an interpretation of the actual constitution of the U.S.S.R. rather than of Kollkhos-Law. But even so it is a fact which cannot be regarded as irrelevant for the interpretation of the latter. In any case, the Model Articles of the Artel, which was only very loosely connected with the Land Code still theoretically in force, are generally recognised as the basic law regulating the economic life of the majority of the people.[76]

It is quite evident that the bulk of the Land Code has become obsolete. Only parts II and III which formed the foundations of kulak (capitalist) enterprise have been explicitly repealed : but the parts dealing with the individual peasant's Right to Use the Land, with the latter's periodical redistribution (VII–IX), etc., have lost all importance except for an insignificant minority. The same may be said of the rules on the rights and duties of the village community (part IV). For all practical purposes the latter has been absorbed nearly everywhere by the Kollkhos-assembly. Although the peasant *dvor* still forms the basic of the kollkhos, and is envisaged in the Land Code as the very foundation of the latter, the regulation of its legal status by the Land Code [77] is hardly applicable any longer, especially since

[75] See above, pp. 185 and 188.
[76] Vishinsky, op. cit., 1938 (Constitutional Law), p. 181.
[77] See above, pp. 101–2.

May, 1939, when membership in the kollkhos was made dependent on a certain minimum participation in the collective work by each individual member. If, with the *dvor* still recognised as an indivisible economic unit, the wife of a non-member belonged to the kollkhos, the result might be that the rights of the kollkhos-members, for example to use the kollkhos horse, would be used to further the private enterprise of a non-kollkhos-member, at the expense of, and sometimes even in competition with, the kollkhos. Dividing up a *dvor* prior to the entry of some of its members into the kollkhos [78] was regarded as a normal measure when accepting new members, and it might be applied also in the case of some members of the *dvor* voluntarily leaving the kollkhos, whilst others remained in it. But how would this be done if some member of the family were expelled for not fulfilling his duties within the kollkhos? Dividing up the *dvor* cannot be enforced against the will of all the members of the family concerned. Besides, it would not be difficult to cover continued joint ownership of the implements of agricultural production by continuing joint ownership by husband and wife of the means of consumption, according to the Family Code. The logical conclusion would be to put the kollkhos on an individual membership basis, i.e. to abolish the *dvor* as an agricultural unit on the ground that it goes beyond that joint family ownership of the means of consumption which is normal also in the towns. But the question is still undecided.[79] Even if, say for reasons of the public interest in strengthening family life, or in establishing collective responsibility of the peasant family for all its members participating in kollkhos work, it should be decided to preserve the *Kollkhos Dvor* as the lowest unit in Land Law, this would no longer be the *dvor* in the sense of the 1922 Land Code, but something new. It is clear that there has been, in Soviet Land Law, not only a change in the social functions of institutions formally preserved, but, to use Renner's terminology, a connex-institution of the Right to Use the Land, that is to say, the collective mode of exercising this right (more correctly, a certain sub-species of this mode, namely the Artel-form of the Agricultural Co-operative) has absorbed the main institution, and in fact the whole Land Code.

[78] Not a rare event, as very often the younger members of a family understood the advantages of the Kollkhos before their elders. Dividing up the *dvor* means, of course, merely terminating the joint ownership of its agricultural implements—not necessarily physical separation of the members.

[79] See Dembo in *S. G.*, 1939, No. 4, pp. 54 ff.

### (c) The Theoretical Conceptions of Law during the Second Revolution

The official Soviet view on the legal aspects of the Second Revolution has been explained in the contemporary writings of Vishinsky.[80] The illegality, in terms of previous Soviet Law, of essential measures carried through in the process of " de-kulakisation " is recognised, and defended (with references to Stalin's statements at the time), on the grounds that the interests of proletarian dictatorship were superior to its own laws, and that the solution of the problems of revolutionary transition within the framework of any fixed legal system were impossible.[81] This assertion, while contradicting Lenin's opinion according to which Soviet legislation was sufficiently elastic to meet changing needs,[82] seems to support those bourgeois theorists who regard Law as essentially an element of conservatism, opposed to social change.[83] But it should be remembered that Vishinsky uses for his argument such definite emergency measures as those taken during the anti-collectivisation risings in the North Caucasus : his whole argument seems to question the compatibility of strict legality rather with swift revolutionary changes, than with change in general. From the point of view of Soviet legality, Vishinsky's recognition of emergencies, which most states would deal with by emergency measures, is less serious than his tendency to introduce the element of elasticity, and " revolutionary expediency " into the working of Law, or at least of Justice itself—naturally at the expense of that generality and predictability of the working of the Law which we are used to regard as essential. During the mass revolutionary movement itself, he regards it as a task of Justice to check excesses,[84] from the point of view not of the former legal order—the breakdown of which is supposed—but of the desired political framework of the movement.[85] Even apart from the needs of revolutionary situations, the freedom of decision left to the Soviet Judge [86] is regarded as characteristic of revolu-

[80] Op. cit., 1933, and article " Revolutionary Legality " in *Bolshaja Sovietskaja Encyclopedia.*

[81] Op. cit., 1933, pp. 55 ff.

[82] See above, p. 92.

[83] See above, p. 6.

[84] Vishinsky, op. cit., 1933, p. 58.

[85] For example, against the application of anti-kulak measures, in themselves illegal but politically necessary, in such a way that they hit middle-peasants too, or against atrocities committed in the course of anti-kulak upheavals.

[86] For example, by the principle of analogy, and by the right of the Soviet Judge to apply the remark on article 6 (which excludes criminal responsibility for offences of little importance and without harmful consequences), or article 8 of the Criminal Code (see above, p. 110), as well as by the wide range of punishments allowed by some articles of the Criminal Code, so that the Judge was left a very wide freedom of decision.

tionary Law, i.e. of Law serving the needs of revolutionary developments as opposed to formal and conservative legality. But in contrast to the followers of the Commodity Exchange Conception of Law, for whom the abolition of the N.E.P. implied the withering away of Law in general,[87] Vishinsky did not doubt the emergence of a new legality corresponding to the new state of Society: Revolutionary Legality and Revolutionary Consciousness of Justice are described as the correct application of the Law in the sense intended by the revolutionary state and as the use of that freedom of decision granted to the Judge by the Legislator in the sense intended by the latter. Thus Vishinsky's observations on the needs of emergency situations and periods of revolutionary transition could be set aside; for, in spite of some muddle in his terminology, they would not have affected his conception of the normal working of Law, had he not had a tendency to introduce " elasticity " into the latter, and to regard as revolutionary Law the Law of a state which not merely aims at a thorough transformation of society, but which frequently changes its legal policies while carrying through that transformation without troubling to amend its laws.

According to Vishinsky,[88] revolutionary legality contains oppressive elements like any other legality, but also educational elements, which are lacking in bourgeois legality and which create a new discipline. Theoretically this statement does not make sense unless it is interpreted as meaning that, while bourgeois legality is by its very nature merely negative (" you must not interfere with other people's rights "), and while it leaves the positive evolution of social life to the working of anonymous economic forces beyond the Law, Soviet Law must itself enforce the requisite positive behaviour of the citizens if socialist economics are to prosper. In this sense the argument is correct. But, although it is an argument in favour of a certain flexibility (for, in socialist Law, all desirable evolution of the economic life must find its expression), it is also an argument against the instability of the Law and against too frequent changes in judicial behaviour according to changing political needs: how could certain social habits be developed by the working of a judicial system which itself frequently changed its habits? In this sense there *is* a contradiction in Vishinsky's conception of

[87] For a polemic against the " leftist " conceptions that collectivisation of agriculture had ended legality, see Vishinsky, op. cit., pp. 72–3.
[88] Ibid., pp. 70 ff.

" revolutionary legality " : not in the sense that a revolutionary state is bound to be lawless, but in so far as the desire to carry through revolutionary changes by educational influences (i.e. by the development of certain social habits enforced by the legal system) presupposes a certain degree of stability in the new order, and even the occasional rejection, for the sake of stability, of certain measures that might be desirable from the purely political and economic point of view.

Instead of looking for new forms of Law fitting the needs of the revolutionary state when the N.E.P. broke down, the adherents of the Commodity Exchange Conception of Law found themselves delivered from having to bother about Law at all. Once capitalism had become incompatible with the survival of the Soviet, the latter had to drop Law, as an essentially capitalist institution. According to Pashukanis, as we have seen above,[89] the withering away of the categories of Bourgeois Law implied the withering away of Law in general, that is to say, the gradual disappearance of Law from human relations. Evidently, this change was already proceeding. Students discussed whether it was worth while continuing to study Law, and some local administrators suggested abolishing the Village Soviets (with whose working they evidently disagreed) once all the local peasants were included into the Kollkhos. For the latter might fulfil the functions of the political as well as of the economic organisation. So the theory of " withering away of the Law " was made to imply the immediate possibility of the withering away of the Soviet State—in the face of the greatest crises in its history ! When Mr. Pritt visited Russia in 1930, he was told by some high officials of the People's Commissariat for Justice that all litigation, civil or criminal, would disappear within the next six or seven years, and those who disagreed with such a prediction found it only " much too short ".[90] In 1927, Nemzov had expressed the opinion that formal and codified Law was necessary only in consequence of the shortage of administrators sufficiently prepared to decide each individual case according to its merits and the interests of the Soviet State.[91] Any conception that the State—not to speak of its individual citizens—might have a primary interest in the certainty and predictability of its reaction to certain social facts, was obviously lacking. The Moscow Regional Court [52] regarded even the regulation of the social structure of society as within the scope of judicial initiative.

[89] P. 156. [90] Pritt, op. cit., p. 165. [91] See Zarov, op. cit.

Pashukanis himself, even much later, when he had to drop his original conceptions,[92] excused them as an alternative to Stuchka's attitude according to which the expropriated kulaks and N.E.P.-men should be compensated.[93] This was indeed a logical inference from the alternative between capitalist Law and lawlessness, as established by both the moderate and the more radical advocates of the Commodity Exchange Conception of Law. But to choose the alternative of lawlessness was hardly an argument in favour of a theory which allowed such an alternative.

For the adherents of the Commodity Exchange Conception, Law was a mere automatic reflection of the existing economic relations.[94] So for them, as for their counterparts in bourgeois legal theory,[83] Law was an essentially conservative agency, and the only alternatives to the preservation of the existing social order were anarchic mass-initiative, or purely arbitrary exercise of dictatorial State power. During the collectivisation of agriculture the Soviet encouraged mass-initiative from below, while at the same time its own interference with the kulaks' rights did not always conform to the demand for generality and predictability which even revolutionary legality must meet. But the State desired to pass out of the period of revolutionary disturbances as quickly as possible, and was bound to reject a theory that prevented the consolidation and the legal protection of any non-capitalist order.

So the Commodity Exchange Conception of Law, in its radical form which included Law in general, had to be dropped from 1930 onwards. Pashukanis agreed that the derivation of Law from relations of exchange, instead of production and the class relations based on property in means of production, was non-Marxist, and in the practice of Soviet life was bound to result in putting the Economic Accountancy principle of socialist enterprise on equal footing with the remnants of private trade, thus encouraging leftist theories of the "withering away" of trade and money in that stage. He also rejected his former explanation of State, Morals and Law as essentially bourgeois institutions, unable to achieve a socialist character and bound to wither away once socialism was achieved: the withering away of State—and, therewith, of Law—could only begin once Labour lost its character as a duty, enforced by Society.[92]

[92] Op. cit., 1936. [93] See above, p. 154.
[94] See Bratusz, op. cit., 1937, pp. 50–1.

Prior to Pashukanis' retreat, Stuchka[95] had attacked the dependence of his conception on exchange instead of production, and its failure to explain pre-capitalist Law, or Soviet Law after the abolition of capitalism. Between Pashukanis' interpretation of existing Law as bourgeois, and Hoichbarg's as socialist, Stuchka tried to find an intermediate way by calling it simply " Soviet Law " and interpreting it as a " bourgeois law without a bourgeois society ".[96] This would imply the survival of Soviet Law, as long as there was need for distributing the national income according to the participation of the individual citizen in the work done (i.e. on inegalitarian lines) and a need to preserve the State. But Civil Law would be gradually absorbed by Public Law.[97] After the withering away of commodity exchange the basic economic relations would be governed by a Law distinct from Civil Law, which was described as " Economic Law ".[98] In general, it was an application of Administrative Law to economics. So it implied the abolition of all initiative granted to the administrators of public property by the application of Civil Law forms of exchange even within the socialist sector, and of Economic Accountancy as an expedient to secure the latter's efficiency. Amfiteatrov, in 1932, distinguished between " Plan contracts " and " Civil Law contracts ", the latter being restricted to that sector of national economics not directly subject to planning. Thus they were bound to be gradually replaced by the former. To deny the Civil Law character of the contracts concluded between State enterprises meant restricting their binding force, for it was very difficult to understand by " Plan Contracts " anything fundamentally different from those " contracts for socialist emulation " concluded by many shock-workers with their mates on the next bench " to fulfil and overfulfil the plan " to a certain degree. Such " contracts " might have a certain moral, but certainly no legal force ; and to compare the relations between the State enterprises with propagandist devices for socialist emulation between workers was not the most suitable device for insuring the punctual delivery of raw materials and finished products. Some representatives of Soviet legal theory,[99] indeed, expected that after the withering away of capitalist production all Soviet Law would be reduced to the

[95] Op. cit., 1931, pp. 50 ff., 67 ff., 72.

[96] See above, p. 32.

[97] Stuchka, op. cit., p. 74.

[98] For a criticism of these conceptions, see Bratusz, op. cit.

[99] Liebermann, in *S. G.*, 1930/8.

Law of Labour, to which Stuchka might add Matrimonial Law and Criminal Law.

In such discussions much depended on the definition of the "Civil Law" which, as alleged, was bound to wither away. In his exposition of the subject [100] Stuchka, the main representative of the moderate wing of the Commodity Exchange school, could even then mention all those attempts at defining Civil Law which became current in later Soviet legal theory: (1) defining Civil Law as that which concerned property, as distinct from Public Law, which dealt with other subjects; (2) Civil Law as what is protected by the Courts in the interest and on behalf of individual persons, as distinct from Public Law which is protected by the State itself in its own interest; (3) Civil Law as what deals with the mutual legal relations of individuals, as distinct from the relations of these individuals to groups and to the State which is regulated by Public Law; and (4) Civil Law explained as decentralised Law, the realisation of which is made dependent on individual initiative—whilst the State takes the initiative in realising the norms of Public Law. It was not difficult to refute all these definitions of Civil Law. All of them, with the possible [101] exception of the third, include characteristics appropriate to other fields of Law, and on the other hand, with the possible exception of the first,[102] exclude from Civil Law certain fields which are undoubtedly to be ascribed to it. The Soviet state in particular has clearly [103] established that Civil rights are protected in the public interest at least as much as in the interest of the persons immediately concerned, and in cases where the public interest so demands, it has made provision for the public attorney to take the initiative in realising Civil rights if the interested individual fails to do so.[104] As regards the third attempt at definition, it excluded such elementary facts as legal entities, and the appearance of the State as a party in Civil Law suits.

Stuchka [105] rejected these definitions and based his own definition of Civil Law on the Marx-Hegelian conception of

[100] Op. cit., pp. 58 ff.

[101] In the codification and in the current teaching of Soviet Law, Matrimonial as well as Labour Law are distinct from Civil Law. The theoretical justification of at least the first exception is, up to the present day, hotly contested.

[102] The existing Soviet Civil Code does not include the protection of such non-proprietary personal interests as an author's name, the recognition of his priority in developing an idea, etc., unless material damages have been caused. But there is a strong tendency among present Soviet theorists to include, *de lege ferenda*, such matters into the new Code, and no one regards this question as one of theoretical principle.

[103] See above, p. 93. [104] See above, p. 95. [105] Op. cit., pp. 61 ff.

Bourgeois Society [106] as distinct from the organised activity of the State. Such a definition is exposed to the objection that the organised activities of the State are themselves the main factor in Soviet economic life, i.e. in what would correspond to the " basic structure " in the Marxist sense. From this fact the conclusion may be drawn—and is being drawn by the majority of present Soviet legal theorists [107]—that, under Soviet conditions, any clear distinction between Civil and Public Law is bound to be artificial. Stuchka [97] defended the distinction for the time being by the argument that in consequence of the disfranchisement of capitalist elements there was still a distinction between the subjects of Civil and of Public Law, and that even after its abolition (which meanwhile has been accomplished) the social division of Labour and the survivals of class distinctions would preserve a Bourgeois Society,[96, 106] as distinct from the political community. This is hardly an answer to the objection mentioned above. Even if we had to discuss the legal relations within a capitalist system consciously interfered with by an undemocratic state, it would be difficult to bring its activities under the title of " Bourgeois Society ", a term that has been coined in order to express the difference between the automatisms of economic life and conscious State interference. As long as private capitalism is the predominating element in such a society, the term could still be defended by explaining that the State, whatever its delusions about its rôle, is bound to express the predominant forces of capitalist anarchy. But in the Soviet system all such interpretations lose their meaning : if Law, as an ideological superstructure, is to be derived from the economic foundations, it follows that within the realm of Law all its branches, including the Civil Law relations between individual citizens, are to be derived from the basic fact of State ownership in means of production, which is certainly not in opposition to Public Law.

So it was quite logical that the attempts of Stuchka and his school to preserve socialist Law outside the sphere of Civil Law, which they continued to explain by Commodity Exchange, resulted in the conception of Economic Law, i.e. some glorified

[106] See above, pp. 17 and 23. In Russian (and German) this conception, and some misunderstandings possibly connected with it, lie much nearer than in the English language if " Bourgeois Society " is applied, the first words in *civic* Society and *Civil* Law being identical. With Hegel's *buergerliche Gesellschaft* the meaning bourgeois as distinct from " civic " only enters the orbit.

[107] See below, pp. 252–3.

Administrative Law. Even Pashukanis and his school, when accepting the possibility of socialist Law, were bound to explain it as essentially Public Law. As long as one started from the Commodity Exchange Conception, Law, in a socialist society, was reduced to the distribution of the social product in accordance with each citizen's participation in the social work, i.e. in exchange for his labour. But whence, then, a pupil of Pashukanis [108] asked, the evident strengthening of the Soviet legal order during a period when private property in means of production was reduced to a minimum, and commodity exchange had lost its central importance? The only possible answer, he deemed, was a derivation of socialist Law, including the principle of distribution according to the work done, from the fundamental institution of socialist property in means of production. Yet in 1936, Pashukanis [109] had defended the formally bourgeois character of the Law of a socialist society in the field of distribution (although it had nothing to do with a bourgeoisie), as being a mere expression of the incomplete realisation of Communist principles.[110] Dozenko was of the opinion that Soviet Law was using the institutions created by bourgeois, or even pre-bourgeois law as organic elements of the new socialist legal system. From the point of view of a formal analysis of the genesis of the single articles of the Soviet Civil Code, such an interpretation might appear justified. But from the point of view of the spirit of the interpretation which its authors desired the Civil Code to have, it was certainly not; [111] whatever use they had made of the current formulas of bourgeois Codes, these words had certainly been deprived of their original meaning. Dozenko's thesis fits only if by "legal form" is understood the formal, verbal construction of the individual articles of the Code, but not their meaning within the framework of the legal system. Renner's conception of the "change" in the function of legal institutions may well cover continuous evolution, within a bourgeois as well as within a Soviet system. But it can hardly be applied to direct and consciously revolutionary change, when the application of inherited institutions is explicitly limited in order that they shall fit into the new framework.

[108] Dozenko, in *S. G.*, 1936/3. [109] Op. cit., p. 7.

[110] Such a conception certainly corresponded to the application of the term by Marx and Lenin (see above, pp. 24 and 30). But when used by Pashukanis it was generally regarded as a mere residuum of his original denial of the possibility of socialist Law.

[111] See above, Chapter IV, pp. 92 ff.

In the field of Criminal Law the revolutionary changes of 1929–30 were accompanied by an academic discussion of principles.[112] It had been a logical implication of Pashukanis' General Theory of Law [113] that, as long as there were antagonistic classes, and Criminal Law was still needed, it was bound to be dominated by the principle of "equivalent"—or to use the current term, taliation. Otherwise Criminal Law, in an attempt to do justice to the individual criminal, would lose its predictability and its general preventive efficiency. The other, rather utopian side of the Commodity Exchange Conception of Law was expressed by theorists like Krylenko and also by Pashukanis himself. In their draft of 1930, for a new Criminal Code they revived tendencies which we found in 1924–6,[114] and carried them to an extreme. "Bourgeois legality" ought to be replaced by the application of repressive measures according to considerations of expediency, without any claim that these repressive measures should correspond to individual guilt, and that they should express more than revolutionary expediency.

> Measures of class oppression, and of enforced educational influences, may be applied to persons who have committed a certain delinquency as well as to persons who, in spite of not having committed a definite crime, justify the serious apprehension that they eventually may commit delinquencies, in consequence of their relations to criminal surroundings, or of their own criminal past.[115]

If something of this kind had become law, it would, indeed, have been irrelevant for a man with a suspicious past, whether he committed further crimes or not. Once such standards were introduced, even if they only applied to a small suspicious minority, the security of Law enjoyed by the average Soviet citizen (quite apart from the political antagonist, who is openly regarded as an object of suppression according to considerations of expediency) would have been destroyed. Piontkovsky and some of the other older representatives of Soviet Criminal Law theory tried to avoid both extremes of the new theories by explaining that, without any resort to bourgeois principles of taliation, fixed punishments for certain crimes could be justified by the degree of the danger threatening society from this or

112 See Maurach, op. cit., 1933, pp. 183 ff.

113 Op. cit., 1925, p. 118.

114 See above, Chapter IV, pp. 110–13.

115 Article 6 of the Draft Krylenko-Pashukanis, of 1930.

that kind of crime. A glance at the Soviet Criminal Code [116] should, indeed, suffice to let such an explanation appear simple common sense. But, in the atmosphere of 1930, there was not yet sufficient place for common sense, and Piontkovsky had to retreat from his " deviation ".[117] Swimming with the current, without giving way to it completely, he duly expressed all the tendencies of Soviet Criminal jurisprudence of those years : elimination of the conception of guilt, and all the related conceptions like the distinctions of intention, negligence, attempt, participation, etc. For this he was reproached by Vishinsky,[118] when the current had turned again to the stabilisation of social relations, and security of the Law was felt desirable. But more serious tribute than that of university teachers of Criminal Law was paid to the fashion of making the protection of society independent of the individual guilt of those who endangered its working : in 1928 the 18th Plenum of the Supreme Court introduced the conception of " eventual intention " into the definition of such a serious crime as counter-revolutionary sabotage (art. 58, 7 of the Criminal Code). Actions seriously threatening the whole working of Soviet society were to be regarded as counter-revolutionary even if an actual counter-revolutionary intention had been lacking, provided that the defendant could foresee the danger for the State involved in his action or inaction. Thus, negligence was virtually subjected to the heaviest sanctions provided by the Law for a crime the essential element of which is intention. There was, and still is in spite of all recent efforts of the higher Judiciary and legal theory to elaborate a clean conception of guilt, a strong tendency in Soviet Justice to convict according to the action, instead of according to the criminal intention, or otherwise, of the defendant. Even since the Supreme Court repealed the above-mentioned ruling on sabotage,[119] lack of foresight is a very common indictment against functionaries of socialised agriculture [120] or the railways, and it is favoured by judges who in cases of ordinary crime feel that their consciousness of Justice demands a heavier punishment than that provided for by the Criminal Code Thus the exposure of children, even on the territory of a foundling-hospital, or the breach of relations with a woman in such a way as to upset her self-confidence, if resulting in the accidental

[116] See above, pp. 115–18.
[117] In *S. G.*, 1931/1.
[118] Op. cit., 1937.
[119] See below, p. 225.
[120] See S. Lifshitz, in *S. G.*, 1940, No. 4.

death of the child or the suicide of the woman, may result in convictions for murder which have to be quashed by the Supreme Court.[121] At present, such judgments have to be interpreted as aberrations from, rather than expressions of, the spirit of Soviet legal thought. They are relics of an earlier period, when the conception of guilt was impaired by a conception of Law in mere terms of class rule and actual expediency. When the Law could be explained as representing the interests of all strata of the new society, its violation appeared as an act of individual guilt, in the moral as well as in the legal sense.[122] For this very reason the citizen might claim that only the guilty should be punished, according to the degree of his guilt.

[121] See *S. G.*, 1940, Nos. 8–9, and Goljakov, in *S. G.*, 1940, No. 2.
[122] See below, pp. 236–7.

CHAPTER VII

# SOVIET SOCIETY AND LAW AT THE END OF THE SECOND FIVE YEAR PLAN

## (a) The Economic and Social Structure

The enactment of the Kollkhos Model Statute, the abolition of the ration books in 1935, and the enactment of the new Constitution and of quite a number of important changes connected with it in 1936, mark the end of the transitional period that had been opened by the "Second Revolution" in 1929–30. By this time, the triumph of the socialist section of Soviet economics was complete, and nearly all the population depended for its livelihood on this section. The following schedule shows the evolution of the social structure of the population :[1]

| | Percentage in the years | | | |
|---|---|---|---|---|
| | 1928. | 1934. | 1937. | 1939. |
| Workers and salaried employees | 17·3 | 28·1 | 34·7 | 49·7 |
| Amongst them workers of State farms and Machine Tractor Stations | 1·5 | 3·3 | 3·2 | 3·6 |
| Kollkhos peasants | 2·9 | 45·9 | 55·5 | 46·9 |
| Individual peasants | 72·9 | 22·5 | 5·6 | 2·6 |

From this schedule of the two main changes, industrialisation of the country as a whole and collectivisation of agriculture, it is quite clear that there has been no transformation of peasants into State farm workers, and no more increase of the number of workers of Machine Tractor Stations than immediately necessitated by the progress of collectivised agriculture, but that there has been a big migration even of kollkhos peasants into State industries. In consequence Russia, on the eve of this war, had ceased to be a peasant country, even in terms of population statistics.

Still more impressive is the distribution of the means of production,[2] for, here, the somewhat ambiguous position of the kollkhos-members appears split up into the various economic elements which determine their social position. These are : State property in some essential means of agricultural production, as administered by the Machine Tractor Stations, co-operative

[1] Source : *Bolshevik*, 1939, Nos. 15, 16 ; 1940, No. 10.
[2] Source : Vishinsky, op. cit., 1938, p. 176.

property proper, and the private " auxiliary husbandry " of the individual kollkhos-member.

PERCENTAGE OF THE TOTAL IMPLEMENTS OF PRODUCTION

| Owned by | 1928. | | | 1936. | | |
|---|---|---|---|---|---|---|
| | Industry. | Agriculture. | Total. | Industry. | Agriculture. | Total. |
| The State | 96·6 | 62·6 | 76·5 | 97·4 | 76·0 | 90·0 |
| Co-operatives | 1·3 | 1·0 | 1·2 | 2·6 | 20·3 | 8·7 |
| Individual kollkhos-members | — | 0·1 | — | — | 3·1 | 1·1 |
| Individual craftsmen or peasants | 2·0 | 31·9 | 19·6 | 0·05 | 0·6 | 0·2 |
| Private entrepreneurs (kulaks) | 0·1 | 4·4 | 2·6 | — | — | — |

In consequence, there can be no economic exchanges in the field of production and wholesale exchange, except between enterprises and organisations owned or controlled by the State. The only important legal transactions entered into by the individual citizen are (*a*) the sale of his labour, by labour contract or by membership of the kollkhos with a dividend strictly proportional to the work done, and (*b*) the purchase of consumer's goods on the market. For a section of the kollkhos-members [3] a third important relation, sale of part of the products of their auxiliary husbandry on the urban market, enters the picture, but it ha been recent Soviet policy [4] to reduce this function of the kollkhos-member's private husbandry to a minimum, and to give him his dividend in the shape of money which he may spend on consumer's goods in State or co-operative [5] shops, like any other citizen. In view of these changes it is regrettable that no more statistics on Soviet Internal Trade are available [6] since those of 1935 (i.e. immediately after the abolition of rationing). In that year, the total money income of the population amounted to 101,000 million roubles, 57 per cent. of which came to the

[3] In many regions all the efforts of the auxiliary husbandry are needed for the peasant's family consumption, and in still more there is no suitable market available.

[4] See above, p. 185, and below, p. 214.

[5] In 1936, the State transformed its rural retail stores into co-operative stores, whilst in the towns the Consumer's Co-operatives were transformed into State stores. Experience had shown that only under rural conditions was there sufficient interest in co-operative self-government, but that, under those conditions, it proved far superior to direct State management.

[6] U. Chernarsky and S. Krivetsky in *Planovoe Chosaistvo*, 1936, No. 6.

urban, 43 per cent. to the rural population. After covering all expenses outside the commodity markets (subscription to State loans, expenses for transport, housing, etc.), 47 milliards roubles (all from wages or salaries) remained in the hands of the urban population, nearly 10 milliards of which were spent in purchasing foods on the kollkhos market. The village could dispose of 38 milliards, half of which (19·3 milliards) came also from wages and similar earnings. 10·8 billions were earned by sales on the kollkhos market, and 8·8 by direct sales of agricultural products to the State. In the market for consumer's goods produced by industry, the rural and urban population appeared with some 37 milliards purchasing power each. It may be assumed that this equilibrium has continued, for the reduced percentage of the rural population has certainly been compensated by its increased wealth and increased dependence on the markets in consequence of the progress of money economics. Since 1935, the rural population (which includes an increasing number of people working in neighbouring factories, and of highly skilled workers in Machine Tractor Stations, etc.) has certainly become even more dependent on wages and salaries as their source of income; but of the respective sales of agricultural products to the State, and in the kollkhos market, we remain in ignorance, for want of more recent statistics. In view of the energetic efforts of the State and the offer of higher prices as a premium on larger deliveries of the most needed goods, there can be no doubt that the kollkhos market has proportionally lost importance.[7] Whether the private sale of his individual produce has ceased to be a factor determining the outlook of the peasant and his conception of private interest, cannot be stated on the basis of the material available. Certainly it has ceased to be the predominant factor. Since we have to deal with the spirit of Soviet Law, not with the possible incompleteness of its realisation, it can be definitely stated that the sale of labour by wages contract or kollkhos membership to the organs of socialist economy, and the purchase of consumer's goods from these organs, are the typical exchange relations which the Soviet citizen enters.

The 1936 Constitution takes a differentiated attitude to the various kinds of individual property. Personal property in means of consumption, i.e. the remuneration the citizen earns for his participation in national production, is protected without any

[7] We speak, of course, of pre-War conditions.

restriction (art. 10). Private property of the individual peasant or craftsman in small means of production "is admitted by the Law" (art. 9)—evidently as a transitory phenomenon. The individual "auxiliary husbandry" of the kollkhos-member is dealt with in a special clause (art. 7, 2) and described as "personal". From this contemporary Soviet legal theory interpreted it, along with personal property in means of consumption, as a mere by-product of the growth of socialist economics bound to develop with them.[8] Since the May decrees of 1939,[9] there has been some tendency to hint at the possible contradictions between the interests of the "auxiliary husbandry" and the truly socialist kollkhos economy and the prospect of an eventual reduction of the former, so that the agricultural Artel would gradually be transformed into a Commune, absorbing all the labour of its members and satisfying all their needs by the co-operative dividend.[10]

Whilst the sphere of individual ownership protected by the Law has always been recognised as a central problem of legal theory, the limits within the sphere of socialist property (apart from the fundamental distinction between State enterprise and kollkhoses) are rather vague: the State did not bother about taking over urban co-operative property in retail shops [5] and dwelling-houses.[11] As the needs of the interested consumers were catered for rather better than before, there was no protest against what, at least formally, amounted to another act of expropriation. As regards the kollkhoses, their Right to Use the Land "for time everlasting" [12] is strictly observed, in so far as the kollkhos movement as a whole is concerned—for no other reason than that the State is convinced of the superiority of co-operative management in agriculture over any alternative, including its own State farms. But the protection of the property of the individual kollkhos is much more problematic: if some of its members leave for resettlement in other parts of the Union,

[8] See Vishinsky, op. cit. (1938), pp. 186 ff.

[9] See above, pp. 185 and 188. [10] See *S. G.*, 1939, No. 4, pp. 11 ff.

[11] The housing legislation of 1936 abolished the many house-building co-operatives, established since the N.E.P., and municipalised the buildings. The members got their subscriptions refunded, unless the houses were already built, in which case they got a priority claim for accommodation. In this case, although being formally expropriated, they certainly did good business: they got the flat (although merely as tenants) without having to pay the whole costs of its construction, and with the likelihood of having to pay a rent lower than the repairs (charged to the individual member of the housing co-operative) would have been. If they got their money back (sometimes after some depreciation of the rouble) they were much worse off: they were not expropriated, but the desired flat had vanished.

[12] See above, p. 188.

the kollkhos has to part with a corresponding amount of its funds, including those which are " Indivisible ".[13] So, too, ti has to part with the land fund attributed to it " for time everlasting " if there is no likelihood of its making proper use of the land (for example, if new settlers arrive in the eastern regions and desire to establish new kollkhoses, at the expense of older ones which have more land than they can use for many years to come).[14] Such procedure is not unreasonable from the point of view of planned economics as well as from that of the citizens concerned: the question is whether it is advisable to proclaim principles which, although pleasing to peasant ears, are bound to conflict with the needs of planned economics. As for the " property " of the individual State enterprise, as distinct from the State, this is a mere problem of legal theory, which we are to discuss later.[15]

The mutual relations between the State enterprises, i.e. the organs administering the bulk of national economics, are regulated by the plan, although they are realised by mutual contractual obligations the observation of which serves as a check on the fulfilment of the plan and the efficiency of management. If complementary tasks are attributed to each of two enterprises concerned by the competent planning organs (for example, if the plan provides for a coal-mining trust to deliver coal, at certain costs, to some metallurgic trust) the very enactment of the plan constitutes mutual contractual obligations between them, amongst which is the duty to conclude a contract settling the details of the transaction.[16] If there has been no such strict assignment (and, especially in the case of all commodities whose production is planned only on general lines as, for example, all consumer's goods), the State enterprises concerned enjoy a higher degree of autonomy, and themselves decide what agreements they will conclude with what partners in order to fulfil their plan and to earn maximum profits.[17] According to an enactment of April 20, 1936, half of the surplus profit in excess of the planned profit (which goes to the Treasury) forms the " Director's Fund " to be spent for rewards for employees and workers who have contributed to the achievement, and for general betterment of living conditions of the staff (half of this fund has to be spent on domestic building). Disputes between the State enterprises

[13] S.P. 1940/2. [14] Kazancev, in *S. G.*, 1940, No. 7, p. 137.
[15] See below, pp. 247 ff.
[16] For enforcing the conclusion of such a contract, demanded by the Plan, there lies a " pre-contractual " suit at the State Arbitrage.
[17] Shkundin, op. cit. (1940), pp. 90–1.

as regards the fulfilment of their contractual obligations are settled by the State Arbitrage. Starting as an organ of equity which had to concern itself with the interests of the common owner of both disputants rather than with formal law, the State Arbitrage evolved a special and rather elaborate procedure.[18] Its decisions play a part in Soviet legal life elsewhere played by leading cases decided by the ordinary courts (which, in the U.S.S.R., are prevented from dealing with property disputes between State enterprises—i.e. all really important ones—if more than 1,000 roubles is contested).[18a] In spite of all attention paid to the formal claims of the individual State enterprise, i.e. in checking the profitability of its working, there are no restrictions on the right of the State to deal with this, its property, however it seems fit, for example to reorganise State enterprises, or to transfer State property from one of them to another, without compensation. In order to preserve the " control by the rouble " the State, in such cases, will see to it that the obligations of a dissolved enterprise towards other State enterprises are met, although certainly the State Arbitrage would not give judgment for the creditor (i.e. the State) against the debtor, i.e. another State enterprise, so as to enforce its liquidation. Claims of individual citizens are covered by the responsibility of the State for all its directly owned enterprises. It is true, according to article 19 of the Civil Code, the Trusts with independent management are solely responsible for their debts, without backing by the State. But the State can expropriate Trust property only if provision is made for the settlement of its debts.[19]

Whilst the internal organisation of State economics, as developed since the N.E.P., was brought to its logical conclusion, the position of the individual citizen, as a producer, was dominated by the fact that by now, apart from the kollkhoses, the State had become the only employer of Labour. This fact has affected the working of the 1922 Labour Code, although the latter's essential institutions have remained in force, at least up to the War-economic measures of 1938–40.[20] During the N.E.P. there had been a clear differentiation between the tasks of the trade unions in the privately-owned enterprises and those in the public, and support of the efficient management of the latter had always been regarded as a main obligation to the socialist

[18] See Shkundin, op. cit., 1936.

[18a] But by a law of Aug. 21st, 1927 (S.P. 1937/240) all law-suits of the kollkhoses have been restored to the competence of the ordinary courts.

[19] See above, Chapter IV, p. 139.

[20] See below, pp. 219 and 239.

State.[21] But the basic conception of the Collective Agreement, the central institution of the Code, was that of an agreement between different, although not necessarily irreconcilable interests, the trade union representing one side of the social interest, the Management another. But the industrialisation of the country and the preparation for war had to be carried through by heavy sacrifices by the workers themselves. The transformation of backward peasants into efficient workers in modern mechanised industries demanded an approach differing widely from trade-unionist traditions ; not only had work to be intensified, but skill and industry had to be stimulated by an increased differentiation of earnings. In 1929–30 the former leaders of the T.U.C., adherents of the right-wing opposition within the Party, were removed, and the furthering of socialist competition, i.e. intensification of work, as well as encouragement of the most productive workers by higher earnings, i.e. increased differentiation within the working-classes, became a main task of trade-union leadership. The remuneration of work, which is the central content of any collective agreement, ceased to be a contested issue since the wage fund available for each industry was fixed by the plan, and since it was agreed between both Trade Unions and Management that the distribution of this wage fund amongst the workers employed was to be regulated with a view to maximum stimulation of production. The Trade Unions were compensated for the loss of most of their traditional tasks by the complete transfer of Social Welfare Administration to their management : in 1931 the People's Commissariat for Labour was abolished and its function, the administration of all Social Insurance, was transferred to the T.U.C. Thus the functions of Soviet trade unionism were changed from a sectional representation of the workers, as opposed to other social interests, into workers' welfare self-government in the factory. The leading representatives of this self-government participated in the establishment of the plans, and thereby also of the material foundations of the individual worker's conditions. Soviet practice, though not yet Soviet Law, has succeeded in developing the Labour Contract from private into public Law, as has been the tendency in most countries. At the same time, maybe in consequence of specifically Russian conditions, the basic character of that contract fundamentally changed.

One of the main achievements of socialist reconstruction in

[21] See above, p. 98.

the U.S.S.R. was full employment. During the year 1930 unemployment sank from 1·3 millions—i.e. the average standard since the N.E.P.[22]—to nil. The needs of reconstruction and rearmament were so heavy that since then not even the enormous migrations of peasants into industry [23] have been able to prevent labour shortage from becoming a chronic disease of Soviet industry. As opposed to a policy that tried to subordinate the collective representation of workers' interests to the needs of industrial development, labour shortage gave the individual worker a very strong position *vis-à-vis* the management. Migration from one State factory to another became the worker's most usual expedient in order to profit from the competition between managers who needed him and his like for the fulfilment of their plan. The average manager had to choose between violating his duties to the State by upsetting the Labour market and enticing his " competitor's " staff, or being unable to fulfil the plan ; and he had to endure this dangerous dilemma if he was not able, or diligent enough, to kill both birds with one stone by making more efficient use of the available labour force, and thus achieving the surplus profits necessary to improve the housing and other conditions of his staff and so secure some stability. From the long-term view of the State, migration was quite an efficient mechanism for eliminating incompetent managers. Even the constant migrations of workers, however undesirable for the individual factory that lost a worker just when it had trained him, might prove as fruitful as the institution of journeymen had been in other European countries in producing a class of skilled workers out of a semi-illiterate peasantry. But the State, needing increased output of machinery and armaments, could neither restrict the pace of industrialisation in order to keep the labour shortage within reasonable limits, nor indulge in a long-term view of the possible positive results of workers' migrations. " Birds of passage " became a term of abuse, along with idlers and saboteurs, long before the legal freedom to change employment was restricted. Administrative practice and propaganda had certain effects on the more highly qualified workers who might be induced to remain by better housing conditions and by the chances of professional schooling and promotion. But the average semi-skilled worker migrated simply because the average Soviet enterprise was unable to offer him attractive housing conditions.

[22] See above, p. 141.

[23] See above, p. 211.

Since Munich, when the danger of war had become imminent, the Soviet gradually dropped the legal freedom to change employment. The decree of December 28, 1939, made the amount of Social Insurance dependent on the duration of employment in a given enterprise, and ordered that the loss of housing-accommodation provided by the management should follow the quitting of employment. On June 26, 1940, after the fall of France, the right to quit employment without the assent of the management (apart from certain specified cases, where the latter was bound to give its assent) was abolished. This was clearly explained as a consequence of the imminent war-emergency,[24] and so it may be wrong to regard it as a standard of Soviet legal theories. The fact that the U.S.S.R., in spite of a far greater shortage of labour than could be expected in other countries attempting socialist reconstruction, has managed up to the very eve of war without restricting the freedom to enter and to quit employment, may rather appear as a refutation of those who regard such restrictions as the inevitable consequences of planned economics and full employment.

## (*b*) The 1936 Constitution and the Conception of Legality

The avowed[25] intention of the 1936 Constitution was to describe the political and social structure achieved, not to develop a mere programme, nor to detail that structure by concrete legislation. There was no change in the political structure of dictatorship. Only wishful thinking by Western Constitutionalists could overlook the fact that[26] the freedoms of association, of the Press and of public meetings are only granted "in order to strengthen socialist society" and that (art. 126) the Communist Party is recognised as the organisation of the politically leading citizens, working in the key positions of the State. Consequently, those critics were bound to construct alleged contradictions between the content and the working of the Soviet constitution. In fact, the State has proceeded along its traditional lines, confirmed by the 1936 Constitution: granting political rights to those who support the regime, and to no one else. If there has been a change, it has been towards more open treatment of the One-Party system which formerly, like the multi-Party system in most Western countries, had not been recognised in the written

[24] See N. Alexandrov in *S. G.*, 1940, Nos. 8–9.
[25] Stalin, op. cit., 1940, p. 569.
[26] Articles 125–6 of the Constitution.

constitution, though it formed a most important element of the actual constitution. The official recognition of the Party as a fundamental element of government involved making the Party open to all citizens on the same terms as other organs of government. Indeed, the Party Congress of 1939 removed all distinctions between various groups of citizens as regards the conditions of admission to the Party.

In general, the only important change brought about by the 1936 Constitution was the legal recognition of the fact that, after the elimination of the private capitalist section of economics, the former differentiations between the political status of various groups had lost their meaning.[27] The description of the regime as a " Workers' and Peasants' Government " implies no more than emphasis on continuity with the 1917 Revolution, and a certain sociological explanation of the functions of this government. But there is no differentiation in political and social status according to the present or former social position of the citizen, nor any difference between the position of the two groups described as leading.[28] The only political differentiation recognised is the leading rôle of the members of the Communist Party, which ought to be confirmed by winning the citizens' support in general elections. The only social differentiation recognised is the difference in income resulting from the quantity and quality of the work done.[28a] The actual value of the guarantees of the inviolability of the Soviet citizens' person [29] may be questionable in the case of potential political opponents, but differentiation in the attitude of the State towards individual citizens for other reasons than their individual behaviour has become impossible, and so has class-justice in the sense in which it was seriously discussed formerly.[30]

If " every state is known by the rights that it maintains " [31]

[27] In most important regards, for example the access to higher education, such differentiation was abolished as early as 1934.

[28] This is the true political meaning of the introduction of equal suffrage and secret ballot in constituencies delineated according to territorial, not occupational, principles. There is certainly no more freedom than before to oppose candidates supported by the Party, and only a very restricted freedom to register a protest-vote. But there are no more differentiations between the respective representation of workers and peasants, and the deputy when acting as representative of local grievances is expected to advocate the interests of all his electors, independently of social status.

[28a] Also the prizes paid to successful inventors and the royalties earned by scientific and literary authors, are regarded as compensations for extremely highly qualified work—although, in these cases, the recompense is measured rather by the benefit to society than by the amount of labour actually involved in achieving it.

[29] Articles 127–8 of the Constitution. [30] See above, p. 113.

[31] H. Laski, *A Grammar of Politics* (ed. 1934), p. 89.

the main characteristic of the 1936 Constitution is indeed the recognition of certain social rights, according to the realisation of which the Soviet desires its working to be evaluated. The central of these is the Right to Work, that is to say " the right to guaranteed employment and payment for work in accordance with its quantity and quality ".[32] Thus it concerns normal productive work, under the general conditions regulated by collective agreements or by the kollkhos statutes. It is not (as in some fascist or semi-fascist states which in theory recognise the right) a mere claim to emergency work compensated independently of its productive value on purely maintenance lines, and it is not (as in the Constitution of the Weimar Republic) a mere circumscription for the right to Unemployment Benefit (which, in the U.S.S.R., does not exist any longer, except for invalids). The State undertakes to maintain full employment, i.e. to conduct its economic and educational policies in such a way that there is always a demand for labour of any available qualification, so that no applicant for work in his own profession can be rejected, or " temporarily " be transferred to less skilled and lower-paid work, as provided for in the 1918 Labour Code.[33]

As already explained correctly by the first commentators on the 1936 Constitution,[34] the other basic Social Rights, to Social Security (in the case of incapacity for work), to Leisure and to Education, are complementary to the Right to Work. As regards the first two, the connection is self-evident. As regards Education, equality of opportunity to acquire higher professional qualifications is an obvious condition of " payment of work . . . in accordance with its quality " if new class divisions are not to arise. But these commentators were wrong in interpreting article 130 of the Constitution in the sense of a " Duty to Work " corresponding to the Right to Work, as in the 1918 Labour Code, although that article speaks only of a duty " to maintain labour discipline ", i.e. to fulfil Labour contracts once entered. To enact a Duty to Work in this part of the Constitution would have implied depriving the Labour contract of its voluntary character—something which the Soviet legislator, at least prior to the 1940 emergency measures,[35] certainly desired

[32] Article 118 of the Constitution.

[33] See above, p. 57.

[34] Alexandrov, in *S. G.*, 1937, Nos. 1–2. Krylenko, op. cit., 1936, emphasises the complementary character of the other social rights, including those of equality of the sexes and the nationalities, but fails to see the special qualification of the Soviet Right to Work by promise of payment according to quantity and quality of the work done, and the ensuing connection with the Right to Education.

[35] See above, p. 219.

to avoid.[36] The Duty to Work is explicitly named in article 12 of the Constitution, amongst the general principles of the social structure, in connection with the basic principles of socialism that " He who does not work, shall not eat " and " From each according to his abilities, to each according to his work ". These are moral principles, involving a general obligation of the State to maintain a social structure which excludes unearned incomes, and therewith the possibility of anyone living without fulfilling his moral Duty to Work. In many households in the U.S.S.R. the interest on savings form some addition to the family income, or at least a partial compensation for the deductions from current income connected with new savings campaigns. It is possible to live temporarily on one's savings, or for a woman, even if she has not very much to do in her home, to live on her husband's earnings. Temporarily living on savings is regarded as quite normal and, in the absence of unemployment benefit, in many cases forms a condition of actual freedom to choose the best available job. As long as there is no actual [37] possibility of a new *rentier* class evolving (and public opinion would discourage everyone who tries to live on savings longer than for a transitional period needed to find a suitable occupation), no danger for the socialist structure of society can arise from such a possibility. As regards the position of wives, recently more recognition has been given to the services rendered to the community by the housewife and mother, while the activities of the wife of the officer, factory-manager or engineer, who does useful welfare work at her husband's place of employment, has found official encouragement, even at the expense of the former conception that she was only accepted as a useful member of society if she did some normal, paid work.[38] In any case, there can be

[36] Cp. *S.J.*, 1939, No. 4, where the necessity of preserving the right of the employee to give notice, if desired, is emphasised even in an article discussing the possible incitements to discourage him from exercising this right.

[37] Certainly, there are in the U.S.S.R. a few people (mainly successful authors or inventors) with savings (invested, of course, in State loans or Savings Bank accounts), the interest on which, after deduction of the Inheritance Tax, would suffice to maintain their children without seeking employment. But the really interesting question is whether, in view of public opinion and the actual dependence of the satisfaction of many needs on a certain position in social production, etc., such a position of *rentier* rather near to a bare subsistence-level, would be preferable to anyone, especially the heir of a famous name, whose professional chances would be likely to be good in any career to which he brings some talents of his own.

[38] It should be remembered that such " Wives' movements " were encouraged, after 1936, only among professional groups where the employment of a wife, say, as a typist in some Moscow office, was likely to interfere with her husband's services, say, in some frontier garrison or pioneering in Siberia. The remarkable fact is that even in such cases what was encouraged was some kind of social work, although not necessarily normal, paid employment.

no question of the " Duty to Work " being interpreted in peacetime as other than a moral obligation of the part of the citizen to do some work useful for society.

There is no special guarantee of the social rights granted by the Constitution, i.e. there is no procedure by which the individual citizen can secure their satisfaction,[39] although reference to these constitutional rights would certainly form an impressive argument in, let us say, a complaint by an injured citizen or his deputy against an administrative act interfering with those rights. Each article of the Constitution granting a certain social right enumerates those actual features of Soviet society and legislation which secure the realisation of this right. The socialist organisation of national economy, and consequent abolition of unemployment, mentioned in article 118 as a guarantee of the Right to Work, could not be abolished short of a counter-revolution destroying the whole structure of the Soviet system. But amongst the individual laws mentioned in the articles 119–21 as guarantees for the Rights to Rest, to Social Security and to Education, there are many not necessarily bound to the Soviet structure, and two of them [40] were indeed abolished or restricted by the legislation of 1940, under pre-War conditions. The only possible inference from such facts is an interpretation of the Social Rights not as a constitutional guarantee of those laws mentioned in the Constitution which safeguard their realisation, but as a description of the aims pursued by Soviet legislation, whatever its concrete content, just as the Fundamental Rights of the Weimar Constitution were interpreted by the German Supreme Court. The most favourable interpretation of these rights, from the individual citizen's point of view, is as a direction for the administrative application of the existing laws.

The attitude of the Constitution towards Justice is described by article 112, according to which "the Judges are independent and shall be subordinate only to the Law ". In other words, there is a certain division of powers : the Judicial hierarchy cannot be directly interfered with in its working by the Adminis-

[39] There are, in recent Soviet publications (e.g. Dogadov in *S. J.*, 1939, Nos. 19–20), proposals to introduce such procedure in the form of a suit against any enterprise which declined to employ any citizen in a job for which he is qualified, if there is a corresponding vacancy. But the very fact that such proposals, *de lege ferenda*, are deemed necessary proves that, *de lege lata*, such guarantees do not exist. In so far as they are alleged to exist, the enactments are of a special character, to protect certain groups of citizens against personal discrimination for reasons of their social origin (S.U. 1936/276) or for having been dismissed from the Party.

[40] The seven-hours day, and free education extending to the university.

trative State Organs. This independence has been emphasised by the direct popular election of the People's Judges, instead of the former election by the local Soviets,[41] and by the centralisation of the right to give directions of general binding force on the decision of judicial problems in the hands of the Plenum of the Supreme Court,[42] instead of the former practice according to which any Court of Cassation, as well as the People's Commissariat for Justice of any of the republics, could issue directions binding within its special sphere. With all due regard to the One-Party system, which prevents divergences on serious political issues, the Supreme Court has a far stronger position than the corresponding administrative organs. The Union's People's Commissariat for Justice secured [43] for itself the right to participate in the supervision of the Judiciary by the process of drawing the attention of the Supreme Court to violations of the Law, or to the need to issue some general directions according to article 75 of the Statute on the Constitution of the Courts, or to move disciplinary action against judges at the competent Soviets. The 1938 Statute on the Constitution of the Courts (arts. 17, 18), as distinct from the 1922 Statute,[44] does not allow for disciplinary action: judges can only be removed from office if recalled by their electors or if criminal proceedings are opened against them by the Attorney-General of the Union Republic concerned with the assent of the Supreme Soviet of the Republic. The latter procedure would not work except in the case of intentional violation of the Law, and the former could be applied only against judges of the higher courts who are elected by the corresponding Soviet (the People's Judges are directly elected by the people, and there is no law providing for the recall of any functionary by his electorate, although the procedure is theoretically provided for in the Constitution). Recall of a member of a Court of Cassation by the Soviet which has elected him is unconceivable unless it is either carried in consequence of frequent disagreement with the decisions of this judge by the Supreme Court, i.e. on the same basis as under the former law,[44] or as a

[41] But it ought not to be forgotten that the same party-caucus controls the local Soviet and recommends candidates for the Judiciary to the electorate. On the other side, even if in cases of conflict the local Party caucus should back the local administration, the Judge has behind him the judicial hierarchy to back him, and only the supreme organs of the Party could force the latter to change their attitude.

[42] Article 75 of the Statute on the Constitution of the Courts of August 16, 1938, reprinted in *Slavonic Review*, vol. XVII, pp. 452 ff.

[43] By its own statute of September 15, 1939.

[44] See above, p. 122.

result of open conflict between the Soviet concerned (or the People's Commissariat for Justice that had to instigate the recall) and the Supreme Court of the U.S.S.R. The latter would certainly have its way, unless the People's Commissariat for Justice were backed by the supreme Party organs, who, by their control of the Supreme Soviet, could in any case also control the Supreme Court. Short of this, a change in the personnel of the People's Commissariat for Justice could be effected much more easily than a change in that of the Supreme Court. Corresponding to the recognition of the need for a Judiciary independent of the whims of the administration (although not of the policies of the party ruling the State [45]) there has also been increasing recognition of the need to strengthen the authority, hitherto often lacking, of the barrister as representative not only of the personal interests of the defendant, but also of a very important side of the social interest in Justice.[46]

Stronger emphasis on legality implied overcoming the traditional " elastic " application of the Law. The December, 1938, Plenum of the Supreme Court repealed the definition of the Crime of counter-revolutionary Sabotage, issued in 1928 and repeated even in Soviet text-books on Criminal Law published in 1938.[47] It was firmly established that no one could be convicted for counter-revolutionary actions unless his intention to overthrow the Soviet regime had been proved. So also the Supreme Court waged a consistent struggle against all kinds of convictions that had been carried according rather to the objective consequences of some action or negligence, than to the individual guilt of the convicted.[48] The Railway-Courts in particular, including the Transport Bench of the Supreme Court itself, provided ample material for its supervisory activities.[49]

By this time, the undermining of the security and predictability of the Law for the sake of changing political needs was regarded as an evil, the roots of which went deeper than certain decisions of the Courts, or directions issued by the Procuracy, which the Supreme Court could overrule if it desired. In 1938, Tavgasov published an article under the characteristic title " The Incompatibility of the principle of Analogy with the new Soviet

[45] See below, pp. 227 ff.

[46] See Elkind, op. cit., Chelcov, op. cit., and also *S. J.*, 1939, No. 4, for a criticism of the attitude of the courts.

[47] Strogovich, op. cit., p. 123.

[48] See above, pp. 209–10.

[49] See above, pp. 162–4.

Constitution " [50] and the Editors of *Sovietskaja Justicija*, the organ of the People's Commissariat for Justice, evidently supported such views. Goljakov, the President of the Supreme Court, declared [51] that the principle of analogy was frequently applied by the Courts in cases clearly provided for by the Law, with the intention of inflicting a penalty heavier than that provided for by the Law.[52] Another school of Soviet lawyers,[53] based on the authority of the Chief Attorney, Vishinsky, defended the institution of analogy, and desired its continued application against all actions threatening " the social and political structure of the U.S.S.R., as established by the Constitution . . . the socialist system of economics, and the socialist property ",[54] i.e. against political and economic actions dangerous to the State, unless they were specially provided for by the Law. But this school too had to admit that, in former judicial practice, the principle of analogy had been grossly misused,[55] and that part of the responsibility for that misuse lay in directions issued by the Supreme Court and the Procuracy themselves. A third group of lawyers suggested that the institution of analogy should be preserved for cases where it was really needed to fill lacunæ of the Law,[56] but that the limits of its application be strictly circumscribed.[57] Officially,[58] the Judges are seriously warned against basing their judgment on their own personal impression of the defendant and the punishment deserved : the correct way is to set out from an analysis of the action committed, and its legal qualification according to the Criminal Code. It is clear that such a procedure would prohibit the application of the principle of analogy unless it were to fill obvious gaps in the Code, i.e. in order to punish offences according to the intentions of the legislator himself, in spite of some technical omission.

[50] *S. J.*, 1938, Nos. 23–4.

[51] In *S. J.*, 1939, No. 1, p. 10. On the original conception of the principle of analogy, see above, chapter IV, pp. 107–10.

[52] It may be remembered that, in 1923, the Attorney-General could defend just such a course, and carry the Supreme Court. See above, p. 109, note 74.

[53] See *S. J.*, 1939, No. 3.

[54] Article 2 of the 1938 Statute on the Constitution of the Courts.

[55] For example, in twenty months the Courts of the Moscow region applied " by analogy " fifty-three articles of the Criminal Code (i.e. a third of its total special part !) to offences not strictly provided for by these articles.

[56] An example would be the punishment of falsification of passports by analogy with the crime of falsification of money. Evidently the legislator who threatened the latter, in grave cases, with capital punishment, started from the probable counter-revolutionary intentions of large-scale falsifications of Soviet money. In the case of falsifying passports, such intentions were even more likely.

[57] See, for example, Trainin, in *S J.*, 1940, No. 7.

[58] *S. J.*, 1939, No. 4, p. 23.

But the problem with which the Soviet lawyers are confronted in striving for the security of Law, is deeper than they have hitherto dared to admit. It is the problem of whether judicial policy is a mere aspect of the general policy of the day. So long as an enactment that does not explicitly claim retrospective application, is suggested for application to conflicts originating prior to the enactment of the law, and so long as people rejecting such a procedure are described as " narrow-minded formalists ",[59] there can be no security of the Law. People who are afraid of giving judgment formally contradicting the actual policy of the regime, are unable to fulfil the special function they have to fulfil *qua* lawyers within the framework of the regime, namely to look after the regularity and predictability of the working of the State machinery, whatever the actual political tasks it has to fulfil. A man who serves the Soviet regime as a Judge—as distinct from someone who serves it, say, as a Factory Manager—must understand that the special side of the public interest he has to defend is to make sure that a citizen is punished only for actions that were illegal at the time when committed. It is not his function to allow the dismissal of the worker who has been late, beyond certain allowed limits, though he may have committed his offence prior to the enactment of the law that allowed the management to take such a course. There are various sides of the public interest, but there can be no stability of Law unless the lawyer understands what *his* special functions are, and is ready to fulfil them. But it is in this particular aspect that Soviet practice falls short of its functions *qua* judicial machinery.

There can be little guarantee that a judicial system will secure a proper approach to the individual defendant if the latter is prosecuted in an atmosphere of general excitement, and of " campaigning " against certain kinds of crime deemed specially serious for society. Admittedly Soviet Criminal Law aims at the ruthless repression and elimination of all conscious enemies of the regime, and political propaganda being amongst the avowed purposes of public trial it is not astonishing that, in such cases, it is propaganda against the defendants. On the other hand, even if a general campaign is opened against a certain kind of crime and if the guilty are exposed to public contempt, Soviet Justice never assumes that the defendant is guilty merely because he himself acted suspiciously enough to be committed

[59] Moskalenko, in *S. J.*, 1939, No.5, p. 10.

for trial. As the experience of the U.S.A.[59a] shows, no judicial system, not even the Anglo-Saxon, is immune from the danger of miscarriages of Justice, especially during periods of excitement, if the convicted may be supposed to be an enemy of the ruling interests. No reference is needed to extreme cases, like those of Sacco-Vanzetti or Tom Mooney, in order to demonstrate the problems involved in any alleged separation of Justice from political struggle. The interesting question is rather whether and how a given system may be able to correct mistakes once made, even if powerful political interests have identified themselves with a miscarriage of Justice. The U.S.S.R. is a dictatorship which admittedly prevents that public criticism which opposed the working of the American judicial machinery in the cases mentioned above. But it is also fair to admit that within this setting the U.S.S.R. provides for correctives against miscarriages of justice. The very dependence of the judicial on the political machinery that may make possible a miscarriage of justice against mere suspects (as distinct from the ruthless application of repressive machinery against real enemies of the regime, a policy openly accepted by the Soviet) will, in the U.S.S.R., also promote a reaction against judicial errors, when once committed, and the extreme severity of political justice will in such cases turn against those who had misused it. Thus it happened after the purges. People who had stressed the conception of "eventual treacherous intention" to the utmost had no right to complain when the boomerang turned against themselves. Certainly the purges as well as the reaction against them are phenomena better suited to a political than to a juridical explanation: but the existence of a system of emergency measures once taken for granted, it is evident that security against its misuse must be looked for within the workings of this system itself.

Prosecution and conviction of innocent people for political reasons happens under systems very different from the U.S.S.R. in times of general political excitement, and we have just asserted that the latter has certain means of correcting mistakes. It is more doubtful whether the Soviet system can protect the citizen who has committed a rather slight offence from being inflicted with the penalties for more serious ones, if the latter happen to be in the focus of political campaigning. During the purges, "the conception of ordinary delinquencies in office, or

[59a] See D. W. Brogan, *The American Political System*, London, 1943, *passim*, and especially Chapter II and p. 295.

in economic administration, was completely lost in some places, and any offence was regarded as sabotage ".[60] When a representative of an outlying republic more exposed to these dangers uttered such a criticism, the Attorney-General of the U.S.S.R. himself demanded " a more responsible attitude to the question of what is embezzlement and what is bad accountantship, and also to the question of what is sabotage and what is a delinquency in office ".[61]

But " purges " do not take place every day in the U.S.S.R., and after such extraordinary happenings a strong reaction is likely to correct the errors committed as far as possible. But the Government is continually concentrating public opinion and judicial activities on some campaign against shortcomings. An official who has failed to understand the whole importance of such a campaign, and has committed mistakes of a rather trivial character, is very likely to risk a penalty quite disproportionate to what would be regarded as adequate perhaps one year after his conviction, when the new law is generally accepted, but when its violations are seen in the proper light. Probably he will by then have served his sentence, and there will not be much public excitement because a man who has certainly violated his official duties was sent to prison for a year instead of having to pay a fine. In view of the circumstances the Soviet government may have been right in demanding [62] the dismissal of employees who failed to work the prescribed hours without sufficient explanation. We must assume it expected that the very conditions which made such a decree necessary, the extreme shortage of labour, would result in many managers trying to evade the Law by inflicting no disciplinary penalties, or very slight ones, on employees whom they ought to have dismissed according to the new decree. So it was very natural to mobilise public opinion, especially the Press, against managers failing to fulfil their duties under the new law. An accepted expedient to warn managers who were lucky in that their failure to execute the law was not the first observed by the Press, is the organisation of a public trial by way of demonstration.[63] Under such circumstances, it was very natural that the prosecuting attorney, and the trade unionist appointed as " public

[60] The Attorney of the Kalmyk Republic on the Union conference of Attorneys, see *S. G.*, 1939, No. 4, p. 85.

[61] Ibid.

[62] By the decree of December 27, 1938, and its explanation of January 7, 1939.

[63] See *S. J.*, 1939, No. 5, pp. 41 ff.

impeacher " for this special occasion, did their duty, and that the Judge sentenced the unhappy manager to one year's imprisonment, the minimum term of imprisonment he then could inflict without assuming extraordinary attenuating circumstances, and stating them in the judgment.[64] Under such circumstances, it was also hardly surprising that the advocate who had to take over the defence, did not appear very eager in the affair and failed to discuss the juridical qualification of the offence committed as well as the general merits of the defendant, apart from the failure for which he was impeached. More astonishing is the fact that the Soviet journal which, with general approval, reports this " exemplary trial ", is surprised by those failures of the advocate. They were hardly avoidable under the circumstances. As long as trials even of defendants whose offences would not prevent them from remaining useful members of Soviet society are carried out as a means of public propaganda for certain administrative measures, they are certain to be dominated by the merits of the decree violated not by the personal circumstances of the violator, nor even by whether his behaviour was below the general level of Soviet officials at the same time and under similar circumstances. The application of judicial propaganda for popularising new government policies prevents anyone—including even a defendant who is sincerely loyal to the regime—from making the full case for the defence. Such propaganda, therefore, is bound to fail in fulfilling the normal functions of judicial procedure.

To assert the incompatibility of Justice and propaganda for actual political needs in one and the same procedure,[65] does not mean advocating the isolation of the Judicial Machinery from actual social life. One of the most impressive feats of Soviet Justice [66] is the way in which many Judges fulfil their duty to

[64] Besides, the incommensurability of one year's imprisonment for that type of offence was later recognised by the Supreme Court, which, altering the sense of the Law, by an " explanation " allowed, in such cases, imprisonment for less than the legal minimum of one year and " suggested " terms of three to eight months (*S. J.*, 1939, No. 10).

[65] Here I am referring only to the question of making truly judicial decisions, as regards the guilt or otherwise of a defendant, and the right measure of punishment, etc. If the guilt of a prisoner is evidently established (as in the Krasnodar Trial, of the summer of 1943, of Soviet citizens who had been collaborators of the Gestapo during the German occupation) one can hang him with whatever procedure is desired, and there is nothing to be said against a public trial as an efficient expedient of propaganda, and of increasing the general preventive effect of the hanging. But this is simply a procedure of annihilating enemies of the common weal—and not a standard by which the average citizen can be re-educated if he somehow has violated his social duties.

[66] *S. J.*, in a special rubric, presents a large amount of material on such reports.

report their activities periodically to their electorate, on a territorial basis as well as in the factories, kollkhoses and barracks of their district. From the questions put by the audiences it is evident that the main public interest, and also the report of the Judges, centres round such questions as fighting hooliganism or juvenile delinquency, protecting public and private property and, especially in the eastern republics, the position of women. Even if the fight against some "topical" offence, as in the above example, should be the subject of the Judge's report, Justice to the individual defendant would not be imperilled, for amongst the various cases that have come under his purview, the Judge could always choose those of an evidently exemplary character without linking up the problem of the individual guilt, or otherwise, of some individual defendant, with the pros and cons of the government's policies. There is nothing to be said against, and very much to be said in favour of, submitting judicial policy in general to the judgment of public opinion. But when the general and stable application of a certain judicial policy, once accepted, is recognised as a primary interest of the State (and this seems to be the case since the enactment of the 1936 Constitution and the legislation which followed on the Constitution of the Courts), the individual case has to be judged by Courts independent not only of local administrators, but also of the organs of public opinion.

There is no law superior to the interests of society ; society has certainly the right to establish whatever law is regarded as serving its purposes. But the social interest is to be safeguarded by the content of the law, not by interference with the way in which it is applied to the individual case. Unless one believes in some *a priori* sanctity of the law-books, the social interest in legality is an interest in the predictability of the Law. There is no reason for the Judge to let a scoundrel escape the consequences of his actions for a mere technical failure of the legislator to enact parts of what was evidently the judicial policy of the land. For there is no social interest in encouraging anyone to evade the Law by making use of its technical shortcomings. Thus it is certainly the duty of the Judge not, as often has been said, to legislate, but to establish the recognised content of the legal order. But for the Judge, *qua* Judge, the social interest exists in so far as it is embodied in the legal order, and nowhere else. Unless a state is ready to purchase the evident advantages of stable social relations, at the cost of the inevitable delays involved in adapting its judicial policies to changing social needs (and Soviet legislation is presumably elastic enough for this purpose),[67] it cannot achieve that normality and smoothness in the social machinery which may be demanded of any political system, once it has outgrown the initial difficulties of its revolutionary origin. In this sense the enactment of the 1936 Constitution was certainly a mere beginning.

### (c) The Stabilisation of Social Relations

In the discussions of Soviet legal theorists, there are trends resisting the strict establishment of a rule of Law in the Western sense, i.e. an unconditional binding of the State machinery in general and of the Judiciary in particular to the laws enacted by the State. These trends represent the traditions of the revolutionary emergency out of which the present U.S.S.R. arose, and the needs of which, in many critical periods, seemed superior to any other consideration. The increasing demand for strict legality, with the adjective " revolutionary " merely describing the origin of this legality, arises from considerations of expediency in the working of the State apparatus. The very success of the Revolution has created a new order of social values and a new social hierarchy, which is distinguished from the pre-revolutionary by the fact that higher income and social prestige is derived exclusively from a larger contribution made by the particular citizen to the national economic effort. But for this very reason it is enjoyed with much better conscience as regards the legitimacy of property and social position. The fact that the completion of the great social transformation has been due to what is now officially recognised as a " revolution from above "[68] has destroyed the traditional association between the revolutionary ideology and a destructively critical approach to the social institutions established and protected by the State—and has also destroyed the advocates of this traditional association, the Trotskyists and similar opposition groups. This general tendency can be observed in any field of Soviet ideology, including even art, and dominates the whole evolution of Law, where the latter deals with the everyday life of the citizen. For purposes of illustration we shall take two of the most important examples: Matrimonial Law and Criminal Law.

Very naturally the Soviet attitude towards family links has changed since the time when they were regarded, if not as veiled

[67] See above, p. 92. [68] See above, p. 171.

forms of serfdom (especially as regards the position of women), then at least as an agency by which the influence of the elder and backward generation might restrain the revolutionary activities of the younger one. Although, especially in the eastern republics, the great task of the emancipation of women is not yet fully accomplished, the average Russian family is regarded by now as a bulwark of the new order, which should be strengthened in the interest of strengthening that order itself. Responsibility for his family is regarded as a powerful inducement to the citizen to play his part in the productive effort. The State has not ceased to encourage the productive activities of women wherever their personal qualifications allow (it could never have won the present war without doing so), but it regards the fulfilment of the mother's functions as no less important for society and would not want them to be impaired by considerations for the interests of the woman as a participant in social production. The need to increase the population after the ravages of the present war has certainly contributed to the 1943 abolition of co-education in the Soviet schools in favour of educating both sexes for their special needs and has explicitly been stated as amongst the reasons for the legislation of July, 1944, which granted material privileges and social distinction to large families as well as to unmarried mothers with a large number of children. The care of children born out of wedlock has been removed from the shoulders of the fathers to those of the State, and practical measures for easing the position of mothers, including those unmarried and divorced, have been taken beyond those contained in the law of June 27, 1936, which had prohibited abortion, an operation already discouraged by the very law of 1920 that legalised it.[69] The law of 1936 made certain formal changes in the procedure of divorce which preserved the freedom of either partner to the marriage to get a divorce if he or she desired it and which merely stressed the need for a serious approach to marriage, as propaganda had done before. The laws of 1944, apart from abolishing the long-contested institution of *de facto* marriage,[70] have increased the moral and material difficulties of divorce, and returned the

[69] Text reprinted in H. Sigrist, *Socialist Medicine in the U.S.S.R.*, London, 1937, pp. 264–5. The fact that this law, whilst abolishing the criminal sanctions against abortion, developed a programme of measures for gradually liquidating abortion, at that stage of the Soviet development of course rather theoretical, must be kept in mind in order correctly to appreciate the position of the law of 1936 within the framework of Soviet development—as distinct from Western leftist propaganda.

[70] See above, p. 104, and next page.

decision to the courts. Whilst the legislation of 1936 had implied a mere transfer of influence, hitherto exercised by propaganda and organised public opinion, into the very content of the Law,[71] that of 1944 signifies a change in fundamental principles, both by increasing the barriers against divorce till they may become hardly surmountable for certain strata of the population,[72] and by replacing the former claims of the unmarried mother against the father of the child by a right to support out of public funds—or, if so desired by the mother, to having the child admitted to a public educational institution.

As we have seen above,[72a] the recognition of *de facto* marriages, in the 1926 Matrimonial Code, had been caused not by any disregard for the stability of matrimonial relations in the sense of leftist conceptions of " free love ", but by the desire to protect the woman's share in the joint economic efforts of the couple, in the event of the link being dissolved or of the husband's death, and to extend this protection to all women living in actual matrimonial relations. The measure, which involved dropping the original feminist conception of strict division of property, was certainly not intended to discourage the registration of marriages. It was not introduced in the eastern republics of the U.S.S.R., where the struggle for Civil Registration of marriages as opposed to religious or tribal custom, and the ensuing female slavery, continued with an intensity still surpassing that of the corresponding struggle against ecclesiastical regulation of marriage that had dominated the first Matrimonial legislation of the Russian Soviet Republic. But the fact that the institution of *de facto* marriage had only a limited aim, and the fact that its validity was restricted to part of the U.S.S.R., did not prevent it from being regarded as a symbol of the ultimate tendencies of Soviet matrimonial legislation. Consequently, a very large part of the discussion on the re-codification of Soviet law centred round this question, and those who simply defended

[71] Hoichbarg's assumption (in a discussion article in *S. G.*, 1941/1) that the law of June 27, 1936, implies *de lege lata* the abolition of *de facto* marriage (because otherwise the precautions of that law against concealment of former divorces would lose their stringency), cannot be regarded as typical of present Soviet legal theory. But there can be no doubt that *de lege ferenda* this hostility to the institution of *de facto* marriage was already very widespread.

[72] The lower-paid strata of the industrial and agricultural population, in comparison for whose income the new divorce fees are prohibitive, as well as those who depend on official public opinion and prefer not to face announcement of the divorce in the local newspaper and public proceedings in Court at least through two instances.

[72a] Pp. 104–5.

the institution formed a distinct minority. Yet even they,[73] in the case of conflicting claims, suggested strict priority for the wife [74] of the registered marriage, unless the Court should find that the latter has been dissolved *de facto*.

The opponents of the institution of *de facto* marriage [75] regard stricter distinction between legitimate and illegitimate matrimonial relations as a condition of strengthening family life. From the same point of view they suggest, for the new codification of Soviet Law, broadening the Law of Inheritance by extending the circle of relations entitled to be heirs, and granting the testator freedom to dispose of the estate in his will, under the sole condition that a certain minimum share should be granted to the next relations dependent on the deceased, especially, of course, to minors. It is interesting to notice the features of present Soviet Matrimonial Law that were regarded, in this connection, as essential and to be preserved. Mikolenko enumerated seven points : monogamy ; complete equality of rights between husband and wife ; absolute freedom to enter or not to enter wedlock ; freedom of divorce ; equality of rights between " legitimate " and " illegitimate " children ; parental rights to be realised exclusively in the children's interest and only in so far as they are exercised in the children's interest ; mutual obligation to maintenance, if necessary, between husband and wife, parents and children, brothers and sisters. This statement, by an advocate of the tendency in Soviet Matrimonial Law that would be regarded as reactionary by most Western leftists, still preserved all the essential tenets of the democratic revolution in this field.[76] On the other hand, he sought the answer to the population problems mainly in strengthening the institution of marriage—which involved lowering the standard of the unmarried mother. In so far as the bonds of wedlock are strengthened, the decrees of 1944 follow such suggestions to something of an extreme. But alongside with the stabilised family, the position of the unmarried mother is transformed from a rather abnormal by-product of the institution of wedlock into an institution of its own, rather emphasised in its importance by the fact that public support and honours are granted to the mother (married or unmarried) who makes child-bearing her main profession.

[73] E.g., Asknasy, in *S. J.*, Nos. 15–16.

[74] The complete equality of the rights of all *children* was undisputed.

[75] Cp. Mikolenko, op. cit., 1939, Godes in *S. J.*, Nos. 19–20, on the Law of Inheritance, also Rabinovich in *S. G.*, 1940, Nos. 5–6.

[76] See above, pp. 59–60.

Whilst childless men and women over 20 years are burdened by increased taxation, the Russian woman is offered two different ways of fulfilling her natural functions and, by doing so, achieving material security. Whether unmarried motherhood, as an alternative to the status of the housewife, bound to her position by the increased difficulties of divorce, will prove more than a makeshift to overcome the ravages of the war, will depend on the general evolution of Soviet society and morals, and also of Soviet public expenditure for child welfare. In any case the feminist conception of the woman's material position being independent of household and motherhood has been restricted to skilled workers and specialists who can face the spinster's tax and to those unmarried mothers who prefer all their children to be educated in public institutions.

Even more distinct were the ideological changes in the field of Criminal Law. Here, the Marxist conception of the State as the product and instrument of class-struggle, and the legacy of the pre-revolutionary period when the revolutionaries had to justify their infringement of the existing laws, had resulted in a relativist conception of Crime as something that could not be evaluated by any moral standards generally acknowledged. In view of the great majority of crimes, and of the attitude of the revolutionaries themselves during the establishment of the Soviet regime,[77] this was certainly an exaggeration, foreign to the actual spirit of Soviet judicial policy at any period. But, as already shown,[78] it had acquired a theoretical foundation in the shape of the Commodity Exchange Conception of Law which, *inter alia*, interpreted the conception of guilt as fundamentally bound to a bourgeois outlook, and alien to a socialist community. In consequence, we find very sharp attacks on the conceptions prevailing since the U.S.S.R. Leading Principles of 1924.[79] Articles on fascist conceptions of Criminal Law [80] deal with the "sociological school" of Criminology, and the tendency to pay attention rather to the criminal than to the crime, in a way which leaves little doubt that it is the past history of Soviet criminology itself that is being attacked, and that it is not only against fascists that the classical liberal theories of criminology are defended. In official opinions uttered in the discussion on

[77] See above, Chapter III, pp. 62 and 74. [78] See above, p. 208.

[79] As regards the 1922 Criminal Code it is rather recognised that it accepts the conception of guilt, although not using the term. See Makharin in *S. J.*, 1939, No. 10.

[80] A. Trainin in *S. G.*, 1941, No. 1.

the recodification of Soviet Criminal Law relativist conceptions, especially as regards political crime, are decisively rejected,[81] whilst, on the other side, the essentially educational approach to non-political crime is defended.[82] But the educational aspect is no longer regarded as central : the law of April 7, 1935, introduced normal criminal responsibility for juveniles who have committed thefts, assaults, injuries, murders, and attempts to murder—i.e. crimes specially dangerous to public order—in place of the purely pedagogical measures hitherto exclusively applied by the organs of the People's Commissariat for Education, instead of by the Courts. Procedure in the Courts as well as the regime in the educational institutions where sentences of imprisonment on juveniles are served, are organised with special regard for the educational purpose of criminal procedure against youths, and the general purpose of the law was at least as much protection of youths against misuse by adult criminals [83] as protection of society against criminal youths. But, in any case, the latter purpose is now clearly recognised in a field where the purely educational approach was naturally strongest. In other branches it is definitely regarded as merely one side of criminal policy : Soviet Justice, says article 3 of the 1938 Statute on the Constitution of the Courts, " does not merely chastise criminals. It also aims at reforming and re-educating them ". In any case, chastisement, which always existed, is openly avowed now. Unless it is accepted that the purpose of punishment is not only to educate but also to deter the conception of general prevention of Crime, as accepted by all Soviet Criminal legislation since 1919, makes no sense. But, in any case, stress on this point has been avoided by the earlier [84] basic Soviet documents.

[81] Vishinsky, op. cit., 1939, p. 19, in a polemic against the draft of the new Criminal Code as elaborated by the Institute for Legal Theory of the People's Commissariat for Justice (in any case, also an official institution), for making a difference between armed counter-revolutionary insurrection, and invasion by armed gangs supported from abroad. V.'s argument is that there was no more possibility for treacherous activities against the Soviet but based upon foreign interventionists. The implication is that any counter-revolutionary is a foreign agent, and ought to be dealt with accordingly.

[82] Ibid. Vishinsky rejects the proposal of introducing long terms of imprisonment (up to 25 years, as introduced in 1938 for counter-revolutionary crimes) also for murder : V. deems that this crime ought to be fought by progress of Communist education, not by increased repression.

[83] A main argument in favour of the law was the prevention of the previous habit of adult criminals using children and youths who could not be imprisoned and who, at worst, could easily escape from an educational home, as their tools in gangsterism. Any adult who induces a youth to commit a crime of any kind (also one for which the youth himself is not responsible), to prostitution, etc., is threatened by the law with imprisonment of not less than five years.

[84] See above, p. 75.

More important than the terminology in which the purposes of Soviet Justice are explained, is the conception of the interests which are protected by it. In all former documents, since 1919, this was simply the social interest in general—with the implication that violation of individual interests is punished merely when, and in so far as, it implies a violation of the interests of the whole society. But article 2 of the 1938 Statute on the Constitution of the Courts enumerates, along with " the social and political structure of the U.S.S.R. as established by its Constitution ", also " the political, labour, housing and other personal and property rights and interests of the citizens of the U.S.S.R. as granted by the Constitution . . ." and " the rights and legally protected interests of public institutions and enterprises, kollkhoses, co-operations, and other social organisations ". Personal rights are, of course, granted by Soviet Law because the legislator deems that their realisation is in the social interest, for a conception of personal rights as superior to the rights of the Community is completely foreign to Soviet legal theory, and Soviet ideology in general. But, for all that, present Soviet Justice is expected to protect the public interest by protecting the rights of individuals, as well as of the various organisations administering socialist property, the latter's rights being safeguarded in the same way as those of the former. There is still some difference between the intensity with which both kinds of interests are protected : and it may be argued that fierce measures like the law of August 7, 1932,[85] should be avoided in the interest of the humanisation of Criminal Procedure. The Soviet may point to the fact that, once a certain public interest protected by such measures is generally recognised, partially as a result of these measures, and, for example, sabotage against kollkhos property becomes a rare exception, the application of such measures recedes in favour of the more lenient articles of the Criminal Code : the number of convictions, in the R.S.F.S.R., under the above law dropped in 1935 to 9·2 per cent., and in 1937 even to 1·3 per cent. of the 1933 level.[86]

In evaluating the actual development of Soviet Criminal policy we are confronted with the play of contradictory tendencies. The stabilisation of the new society makes for a reduction in crime, but also for less readiness on the part of the Courts

[85] See above, p. 197.

[86] Vishinsky, op. cit., 1939, pp. 16–17, and Mankovsky, in *S. G.*, 1939, No. 3, pp. 88 ff.

to recognise attentuating circumstances based upon the defendant's lack of understanding of the new conditions. Criminality in general recedes, but the State, under the strain of enforced rapid preparation for war, finds itself forced to make more and more actions into offences, subject to increasingly heavy penalties, instead of the former disciplinary sanctions, or mere counter-propaganda. As early as February 15, 1931,[87] a law was published which threatened " any breach of labour discipline by transport workers . . . if it has led or might have led to damage . . . or any other act involving a breach of the transport plans of the State " with imprisonment up to ten years—the maximum being applied, of course, only against negligence resulting in serious catastrophes. In 1940, i.e. under the immediate threat of war, it became an offence, punishable by imprisonment, to leave one's place of employment without consent of the management, to be more than twenty minutes late, or, as a manager of a State factory, to supply goods of lower quality than prescribed in the contract. It would be wrong to infer from such tendencies, arising out of emergencies, the fundamental attitude of the Soviet towards the rôle which the Criminal Code should, normally, play in enforcing the working discipline of a socialist society. Certainly this rôle was magnified by the fact that there was not only full employment, according to the principles of this state, but a permanent and extreme shortage of labour, which suggested the application of the Criminal Code to managers failing to enforce Labour discipline with sufficient sternness.[88]

These contradictory trends are expressed in the statistics [86] of crime and punishment during the period of the stabilisation of Soviet Society after the " Second Revolution ". As a percentage of the number for the first half-year of 1935, there were convictions in the R.S.F.S.R. as follows :

| | First Half-year : | | |
|---|---|---|---|
| Crimes Against | 1936. | 1937. | 1938. |
| Property . . . . . . | 79·9 | 80·6 | 52·0 |
| Duties of Officials . . . . | 73·3 | 46·1 | 51·0 (purges !) |
| Public order . . . . . . | 86·6 | 61·1 | 68·7 |
| Amongst them, hooliganism [89] . . | 90·4 | 72·5 | 98·7 |
| Murder . . . . . . . | 93·6 | 90·3 | 68·7 |
| Grievous bodily injury . . . | 92·0 | — | 79·2 |

[87] Article 59, 3c of the Criminal Code, enacted by S.U., 1931/103.

[88] See above, pp. 229–30.

[89] Sentences for hooliganism reflect rather the criminal policy applied than the actual movement of social facts. For the classification of certain actions (whether mere disorder, to be administratively punished by the police with a fine, or hooliganism) depends upon whether the authorities feel the need for a drive against the latter, as they did in 1938.

Amongst the sentences inflicted for all offences by the Soviet Courts were (in percentage of the total) :

| Year. | Imprison-ment. | Disciplinary Work.[90] | Other Punishment (fines, reprimands, probation, etc.). |
|---|---|---|---|
| 1928 | 31·2 | 22·0 | 46·8 |
| 1929 | 11·7 | 50·8 | 37·5 |
| 1930 | 9·6 | 56·9 | 33·5 |
| 1931 | 12·6 | 57·5 | 29·9 |
| 1932 | 18·9 | 54·2 | 26·9 |
| 1933 | 29·0 | 49·7 | 21·3 |
| 1934 | 25·7 | 56·9 | 17·4 |
| 1935 | 36·3 | 50·1 | 13·6 |
| 1936 | 39·3 | 46·8 | 13·9 |
| 1937 | 44·6 | 40·4 | 15·0 |
| 1938 (first half) | 38·4 | 43·7 | 17·9 |

From the point of view of the general development of the U.S.S.R. it is interesting to note that there is nothing like a sharp rise in the heavier sentences, corresponding to the " purges ". Instead we find gradually increasing severity of sentence after a minimum that corresponded not to the N.E.P., but to the " Second Revolution ", connected as the latter was with a more lenient approach to small thefts, etc. There is little tendency, in recent development, to carry out Lenin's suggestion, that there should be less imprisonment, and more disciplinary work, probations, reprimands, etc. But this shortcoming is recognised.[91] The period under observation may be too short, and too strongly dominated by pre-War conditions to form a basis for a definite judgment on the tendencies towards stabilisation in Soviet society.

As in the case of Matrimonial Law, it would be most valuable to state what definitive achievement remains, after the exaggerations of the first revolutionary period were dropped. A nearer approach of Justice to the life and actual conditions of the citizen is one such achievement, and consideration for the personality of the offender and the possibility of returning him as a useful member of society rather than for formally classifying the crime committed, is another. In the spring of 1937 a peculiar " movement " was started by letters to the editor of *Isvestija* from some former professional criminals, members of the " underworld "

[90] Mostly " forced labour at the place of employment ", i.e. prohibition for the duration of the sentence, to change the latter, and obligation to pay a certain percentage of the earnings as a fine.

[91] See Mankovsky, op. cit., where the Georgian law on factory-fellowship courts which, by dealing with nearly all kinds of lesser offences, spare the offenders normal criminal prosecution, is mentioned as an example to be recommended to the other republics.

who asked what treatment would be afforded to them if they surrendered to get papers and normal employment. The Attorney-General answered in a number of articles, and also reported his conversations with those criminals whom he had invited to meet him. The gist of his statement was as follows : even if the crimes committed were of such a character that more than a formal sentence was inevitable, the fact of voluntary surrender would form a serious attenuating circumstance and, together with good behaviour in the Labour Camp where the sentences were to be served, it would be an argument in favour of early reprieve. In fact, some hundred members of the Moscow " underworld " found their way into the Attorney's consulting room and from there to the Criminal Court. They did not, indeed, act under conditions of completely free decision : at that time, in connection with the increased drive against foreign agents and members of subversive organisations, the authorities had begun a more thorough campaign against the use of falsified passports, etc., and men who were ready to risk some years of imprisonment as recidivists, larcenists or house-breakers might be more afraid of coming within the reach of that chapter of the Criminal Code dealing with the counter-revolutionary crimes. But in any case, had they not seen some hope in returning to normal civil life, they might just as well have tried to continue living in the " underworld " without falsified papers. The fact that they surrendered seems to prove that the criminals themselves, not only some legal theorists, seemed convinced in 1937, i.e. at the height of the purges, that Soviet Justice still inquires into the likeliness of the prisoner again becoming a useful member of society rather than into the formal qualifications of the crime, and that in any case the offender, once he has served his term, is granted complete rehabilitation without regard to his past.

It would appear that, in the two fields investigated, the stabilisation of Soviet society involved a stabilisation of those features of Soviet legislation which were characteristic of non-socialist democratic movements as well, whilst some extreme leftist conceptions, advocated outside the U.S.S.R. even by non-socialists, were dropped after they had enjoyed some encouragement under War-Communism and especially under the N.E.P. Official Soviet ideology regards conceptions of " free love ", or, in the criminal field, the negation of individual guilt, as " lower-middle-class radicalism ", to use the most friendly description. It stresses the special Soviet achievements in so far as they are consistent realisations of original democratic conceptions rather than in the assertion of fundamentally new principles (for example, equal status of women exists not merely in the formal legal, but also in the material sense of free access to all professions, while the re-education of criminals into useful members of society is taken very seriously, etc.). It seems apparent that socialist economics create the most favourable conditions for the realisation of the original democratic conceptions, and this is easily understood as resulting from conditions of full employment. But there seem to be no specific socialist answers to problems other than economic ones, at least at the present stage of socialism as realised in the U.S.S.R.

CHAPTER VIII

# PRESENT PROBLEMS OF SOVIET LEGAL THEORY

On the eve of the present war, which concludes the revolutionary period, Soviet society was in a state of transition. No definite answers to the fundamental problems of Law can be expected at such a stage : no elaborate theory has yet filled the gap left by the dropping of the Commodity Exchange Conception of Law. But the general direction in which Soviet legal theory is developing can be illustrated by discussing its attitude to some fundamental problems. These problems are chosen from Civil Law, or at least they are connected with it. For it is in this field that a new economic structure has to solve the fundamental tasks of finding adequate legal expression. A socialist economic structure, in particular, finds itself confronted with the problem of how legal regulation, supposing a plurality of partners to the Law, is possible once all economic life is controlled by a monopolist organisation.

There has been no fundamental disagreement between Soviet theorists as regards the definition of Law in general. In 1938 Vishinsky [1] defined it as " the corpus of rules of behaviour expressing the will of the ruling class, established by legislation, and also of custom sanctioned by the State, and secured by its coercive power in order to protect, to strengthen and to develop such social relations as are favourable for the ruling class ". Against this definition it has been objected that it neglects the all-national character of the Soviet State where no differentiation between ruling and ruled classes remains, and also that, by including Custom, it obliterates the distinction between Law and Morality : that those customs recognised by the State, and included into the system of norms established by legislation, formed itself part of the latter, while other customs were irrelevant from the legal point of view. [2] Vishinsky [3] answered, but himself corrected his definition by applying it concretely to the conditions of the Soviet State : " Socialist Law during the accomplishment of socialist reconstruction and the gradual transition from Socialism to Communism " is defined as a " system of norms established

[1] In *S. G.*, 1938, No. 4, p. 27. [2] Goljakov, in *S. J.*, 1939, No. 1.
[3] Op. cit., 1939, p. 10.

by legislation by the State of the Toilers, and expressing the will of the whole Soviet people, led by the working classes headed by the Communist Party, in order to protect, to strengthen and to develop socialist relations and the building of a Communist society ".

An interesting problem is presented by Vishinsky's continued attempt to include class-leadership, if not class-rule; in the definition of a Law claiming to express the will of the whole people. The point is even stressed by his including " gradual transition from Socialism to Communism " into the tasks of the Law so defined, an inclusion which, from the point of view of the actual tasks of Soviet Law, is certainly unnecessary. The need for State and Law even under a completely communist [4] regime (as long as the latter is threatened by a capitalist environment) and the compatibility of a communist [4] order of society with the continued existence of State and Law forms, since Stalin's letter to the propagandist Ivanov and his report on the 1939 Party Congress,[5] a recognised part of the Bolshevist creed. This concept of a communist state raises serious difficulties, for example, how distribution according to needs is compatible with enormous expenditure on defence, and how the contribution of every citizen to the national wealth simply according to his abilities is compatible with strict working of a State machinery completely organised for preparing defence. But apart from these problems raised already by Stalin's thesis of communism (as distinct from socialism) in a single country, Vishinsky's introduction of this thesis into his definition of Soviet Law produces the additional difficulty of attempting to visualise the transition to such a society whilst remainders of the former class-divisions still survive, and one part of the people still needs leadership by another. In Vishinsky's mind the problem may be easily solved by an interpretation of Communism as a system of increased social security by free distribution of the most important means of consumption, the participation of every citizen in national production according to his abilities being secured by the coercive powers of the Law. Such a conception of Communism would be easily compatible with the need for continued class-leadership in the sense described above. The need for such leadership, and the

[4] This means, of course (see above, pp. 25 and 31), not the mere rule of the Communist Party, but a regime that asks the citizens to help in production according to their abilities, and distributes the consumable part of the national income according to their needs.

[5] Stalin, op. cit. (1940), p. 662.

coercive character of the State might even be expected to grow within such a system, unless social education has succeeded in replacing the economic pressure to work [6] by purely moral incitements. It is another question whether this kind of Communism would be quite the same as that envisaged by Marx and Lenin.[7]

Such speculations apart, Vishinsky's definition of Soviet Law, if restricted to Soviet society as it actually is, implies a sociological statement, namely that the common interest of the Soviet people in building a socialist society can only be realised under a leadership originating historically from the Labour Movement [8] and organised in the Communist Party. In this sense it is a circumscription of articles 1–3 and 126 of the Constitution. But if the definition is interpreted in a proper legal sense, it would mean that the validity of Soviet laws, apart from their being passed by due procedure, would be conditional on the explicit consent of the Communist Party, quite apart from the latter's dominating position in the legislative bodies. Such an interpretation would certainly be alien to the spirit of the 1936 Constitution, and also to the actual policy of the Communist Party which is increasingly [9] directed towards leading the State by means of the personal rôle played by its leading members within the leading State organs, and not by a parallel machinery competing with that of the State for supreme authority.

The definition of the subjects of Soviet Law, especially Soviet Civil Law, is a rather more complicated problem than the co-ordination of the Marxist theory of State and Law as class-conditioned with the claim of the U.S.S.R. to represent her whole population. It is no more difficult in Soviet Law than anywhere else to describe the rights and duties of a physical person. But those transactions in the U.S.S.R. which are economically

[6] During the transitory period there would still be an economic incitement to work, in the shape of all those needs not yet satisfied by Communist distribution and accessible to the consumer only in proportion to the work done. But these incitements could hardly influence the most backward strata of the population.

[7] See above, Chapter II, pp. 25–6 and 31–2.

[8] To say more would be incorrect. It is an established Communist principle that short-term sectional interests of the workers must be overruled in the common interest of socialist society as much as any other sectional interests. Since 1939, workers no longer enjoy any privileges in joining the Communist Party. The latter, to-day, is an all-national organisation, representing all-national interests—as conceived by an ideology originally supported (although not created) by the radical wing of the Labour movement.

[9] The assumption by Stalin, during the present War, of the office of Prime Minister and as Commander-in-Chief, with a corresponding military rank, can hardly be explained in another sense but in that of consciously increasing the authority of the State as such,

most important, take place not between physical persons, but between the various organs of the State, administering distinct enterprises and organisations. To supervise the efficiency of management, the State prefers to let its various agencies deal with each other on the basis of Economic Accountancy, and in the forms of Civil Law contracts. This supposes a certain autonomy of these agencies at least as regards the details of the fulfilment of the plans established by the central authorities.[10] But the State does not desire an autonomy which will make its various managements independent of the central plan. With the approach of actual War, and increased need to prepare for it, all the " rights " of State enterprises became strictly conditional on their exercise being likely to further the fulfilment of the plan, and this was emphasised even more than before.[11] So there can be no doubt that " what we call the transition of the right of property from one State enterprise to another, is in fact a new distribution of the competence to exercise the State right of property, a transition of the responsibility for exercising these functions from one organ of the State to another ".[12]

As no economic transaction between socialised enterprises of any kind is valid unless fitting into the plan,[13] even co-operative " property " [14] can hardly be interpreted as more than the autonomous administration of part of the public property (although it has, of course, a much higher degree of autonomy than any State enterprise enjoys). The authors of the *Textbook on Civil Law* of 1938 [15] deem that the shares of the individual co-operators like all other funds of the co-operative enterprise " belong to the co-operative on the basis of socialist property, and do not constitute a joint property of its members, in which each of them participates ". Therefore, an obligation to return the shares of individual members exists only where these, as individuals, leave the co-operative, but not where the latter is transformed into another organisation for administering socialist property. There can be no doubt that such an explanation corresponds to the realities of Soviet life,[16] although the transformation of the kollkhoses into State farms, for instance, would be likely to be a more difficult process than the nationalisation of

[10] See above, p. 215.
[11] Compare, for example, an article by Lipecker and Shkundin on the problems of Soviet Civil Law after the XVIIIth Party Conference, in *S. G.*, 1941, No. 4.
[12] *Textbook*, vol. I, pp. 184–5.
[13] See above, p. 196.
[14] As distinct from the claims of the individual co-operator to the co-operative.
[15] Vol. I, p. 221.
[16] See above, p. 214.

urban co-operative shops, or the municipalisation of co-operative dwelling-houses. But apart from such prospects, as long as a co-operative administers a certain part of the national wealth, there can be no doubt that, although the co-operative may act as a mere trustee of the community, the co-operative fulfils this function autonomously, and that its members have an immediate personal interest in the way in which these functions are fulfilled. The difficulty with State enterprises, subjects of Soviet Civil Law, is that their managers, appointed and subject to recall at any moment by the State, enjoy a very limited degree of autonomy in entering or not entering into contracts,[10] and that their personal interest, and that of the other employees, in the use of this autonomy is restricted to what may be properly described [10] as premia added to an income that depends on " quantity and quality of the work done ", but not on commercial success.

The Soviet Civil Code, originating from the N.E.P., gives rather a clear answer to the problem of legal entity in Soviet Civil Law. Article 13 defines a Legal Entity, and article 14 establishes definite conditions for its recognition as such, namely a charter and registration by the authorities, with the evident intention of checking private collective enterprise, as a potential competitor of the State. Later, article 19 deals with something distinct from an ordinary legal entity, namely with " State enterprises and unions of such, placed under a regime of autonomous management and not financed out of the State budget ". As we know,[17] this description refers to the Trusts. They " participate in economic exchange as independent legal entities, not connected with the Treasury. Their debts are backed only by the funds at their free disposition, and not by those that are *res extra commercium* " (namely the nationalised factories themselves). The rule, when enacted, aimed at preventing State property in factories, etc., coming into the hands of their private capitalist competitors in case of bankruptcy. But it could as well be applied under present conditions for the intercourse of State enterprises with each other : when executing a judgment given by the State Arbitrage in favour of one of its enterprises against another the State does not confiscate the latter's buildings and machinery, but withholds credits, attaches the current banking accounts and, in extreme cases, stops the supply of new raw materials—in addition to the probable reorganisation of the management of the factory that has failed to fulfil its obligations.

[17] See above, pp. 137–9.

All these functions of current application of Soviet Civil Law are completely covered by article 19. But the difficulty is that only in a few cases is the State ready to grant those of its enterprises which participate in Civil Law intercourse a degree of autonomy which is normal with the Trusts. From such a state of affairs the conclusion may be drawn that the State, if it desires its enterprises to act under their own responsibility, ought either to amend the Civil Code, or to fulfil the conditions of article 19 as regards all enterprises the autonomous participation of which is desired in Civil Law intercourse. Being afraid of too great an independence of its managers the State does neither, and regards the whole business of Civil Law as a practical method of supervising the efficiency of its employees. But the lawyers, who are bound to explain the legal personality of their clients, are confronted with complicated theoretical problems. In principle, as regards private corporations, the conception of a body allowed to enter certain legal transactions but denied the general rights of a legal entity is not strange to Soviet Law (this, for example, is the status of the Churches according to the second Disestablishment Law of 1929, which explicitly denies them the character of legal entities, whilst allowing them to enter those legal transactions needed for exercising their functions of worship, for example, repairing the churches). But most present-day Soviet theoretists [18] are not inclined to apply similar differentiations to the status of State enterprises which are subject to Economic Accountancy without fulfilling the conditions established in the Civil Code for a legal entity. They either regard them simply as legal entities, or (Bratusz) distinguish two degrees of subjectivity in Civil Law. Their argument [19] is that too narrow a definition of a legal entity would threaten that very public policy of securing efficient management of the individual enterprises, for the sake of which Economic Accountancy was introduced. This argument does not seem very convincing : if interpreted *too* broadly, i.e. by applying to all those entities in State administration of economics, the checking of the efficiency of which by special accounts is regarded as desirable, the conception of a legal entity might easily be reduced *ad absurdum.* The initiative and responsibility of the leaders of a big State Trust might be reduced to a level not fundamentally different

[18] See review of the 1938 *Textbook on Civil Law* in *S. J.*, 1939, No. 6, and Venediktov in *S. G.*, 1940.

[19] *S. J.*, loc. cit., p. 63, as opposed to that of the authors of the *Textbook*, vol. I, pp. 77–8.

from that of an engine-driver and his assistant, whose successes in economising fuel are marked and encouraged by keeping a special account on their consumption and performances,[20] premia in the shape of participation in the " profits " of such enterprise forming part of their remuneration. In order to avoid such generalisations and to win a theoretically defensible approach to the problem of State enterprise proper, subject to rights and obligations in Civil Law, it seems necessary to get a definition of it establishing its personality—although, as is generally recognised, the State is the very subject of all its rights and duties, so that lawsuits between these " legal entities " are actually lawsuits of State *versus* State.

Venediktov[21] tried to solve the problem by defining the Soviet State enterprise as " the collective of the workers and employees, headed by the manager ". They have to fulfil certain functions within the State Plan. In order to enable them to do so, the State has transferred to them certain elements of its right of property : to some, who enjoy only a very limited degree of autonomy (and who are, therefore, subjects merely in Administrative, not in Civil Law), the rights of possession and usufruct are granted, and to others the right of disposition, which they may use in Civil Law transactions within the limits established by the State. Property is defined, by Venediktov and others, as " the right to appropriate the natural opportunity of labour and the products of labour ".[22] Clearly this right, in the U.S.S.R., belongs to the State, exclusively with regard to the first branch of the definition, and primarily with regard to the second. But Venediktov assumes that, whilst disposition is realised by the State establishing the general plan, yet leaving to its executive organs a certain autonomy in details ; usufruct, in Marx's conception of " productive consumption "—i.e. employment of the means of production for productive purposes, can be transferred to a trustee without the State losing its original right of appropriation ; whilst possession is identical with the actual use of the stocks. Property, if understood as the right to appropriate the fruits of production by one's own right and in one's own interest, could still exist even without possession, disposition

[20] Since Stalin, in his speech to the leading *fonctionnaires* of industry, June 23, 1931, had described Economic Accountancy as a main foundation of efficient planned economics, the term, indeed, has been applied equally to all these examples.

[21] Op. cit., 1940, and in a report to the Civil Law Section of the Juridical Institute of the Academy of Science, March 20, 1941, reported, with the discussion, in *S. G.*, 1941, No. 4.

[22] Venediktov, op. cit., 1940, and Bratusz in *S. G.*, 1940, No. 11.

and usufruct [23]—a conception which Venediktov's opponents repudiated as emptying completely the conception of ownership, and reducing it to a mere fiction. So, too, Venediktov's conception of the collective of the employees as the subject of the Civil Right personality of the enterprise was sharply criticised: it would imply an interpretation of the position of the management either as an executive organ of the State as opposed to the collective (and this would be incompatible with Venediktov's definition), or as a representative of the collective as opposed to the State. Either conception would be incompatible with the principle of subordination of the management to the leading State organs and of the employees to the management. Confronted with Venediktov's dilemma either to accept his (or some similar) interpretation of Soviet enterprises as semi-independent entities, with division of the functions of ownership between the State and these entities, or else to regard most Civil Law transactions as fictive, as business done by the State with itself, most Soviet legal theorists [24] clearly choose the latter alternative. Indeed, the former would not solve the problem unless interpreted in a sense really incompatible with organised State control of economics. Usufruct for productive purposes and possession in Venediktov's sense are transferred not only by the Soviet State, but also by any factory owner in any capitalist country to his employee, without the latter thus becoming a subject of rights distinct from those of his employer. Disposition may mean very little or very much, with the result that, when applied to the U.S.S.R., ownership of the Soviet State would be reduced to something analogous to the position of a feudal overlord, with the real owners under him. The only possible conception of the rights for which the litigants in actions between Soviet State enterprises contend, is that of functions in the service of a common employer. This is in principle analogous to the action, in Administrative Law, of a Civil Servant against unjustified deposition, but with the difference that the contested object is not the function as such, but the extent of the State property as regards which this function is to be exercised. In such a conception the management itself would be the subject of the lawsuit. But, evidently, the lawsuit would belong to Administrative, not to Civil Law. Few Soviet lawyers would be ready to accept such an interpretation, with its inferred separation of

[23] Venediktov's report in the Academy of Science, op. cit., p. 139.
[24] In this discussion Venediktov was supported only by Bratusz.

true Civil Law relations between individuals (or between the State and individuals) from mere pseudo-Civil Law relations between State enterprises. The characteristic of the relations between State and co-operatives would form a problem in itself, but with the currently accepted description of co-operative "ownership" [25] it would come nearer to the type of a legal contest for the right to exercise functions, although in this case the personal interest of the litigants, on the co-operative side, would be incomparably stronger. From the practical point of view it would be inconvenient to make a fundamental legal distinction between, for example, the liability of the mill to the store and that of the store to the individual purchaser, or, still worse, between the liabilities of the same mill to a State-owned retail store and a co-operative retail store. But from the theoretical point of view these relations undoubtedly deserve different sociological descriptions: Soviet Law and legal theory both regard the sociological characteristics of a transaction as essential elements of the legal norm itself, and on this basis it is clear that the internal working of the State concern, and the interrelations between it and the citizens *qua* consumers, belong to different sets of norms.

From the point of view of the citizen's ownership of his earnings such a separation might not be undesirable. The dropping of the Commodity Exchange Conception of Law and of its interpretation of any Law as dependent on capitalist relations, worked as a strengthening of personal ownership, which thus ceased to be associated with an institution which every Socialist is bound to abolish. The public interest in securing the efficiency of management "by the rouble", i.e. by Economic Accountancy realised in the form of Civil Law transactions, is much more stable than the public interest in the N.E.P. has been. But, in any case, it is less stable than the interest in securing the citizen's personal ownership of his reward for his share in social production, and is likely to develop in the opposite direction. If the tendency to interpret all Civil Law transactions as conditional on the Plan were to spread from the relations between State enterprises to Civil Law transactions in general, the rights of the citizen would lose much of their security, and certainly the citizen would lose freedom in realising them.[26] From the point of

[25] See above, p. 246.

[26] For example, State enterprises, once they have entered a contract (even if this has not been an automatic consequence of the Plan), are not allowed to modify

view of the social interest in securing prompt fulfilment of the mutual obligations of State enterprises it is difficult to see how the public interest in stabilising private property in means of consumption can, by analogy, further the stability of the contractual relations between the big State Trusts ; indeed, these are defended in another court—the State Arbitrage—which is distinct from that in which the property disputes of individual citizens are settled. The main Soviet argument against a dissociation of " Civil Law " relations between State enterprises from truly Civil Law relations in which individuals are concerned, would be the danger of the former being absorbed, to the detriment of Economic Accountancy, by Administrative Law, where considerations of expediency and changing circumstances are more prominent, and where the character of the obligations is less strict.[27] But the prevailing [28] tendency of Soviet lawyers to absorb Civil Law into Public Law, or even to grant Administrative Law priority over Civil Law,[29] involves just the same danger. It could certainly be overcome by making a division within the Law for administering State economics, between Administrative Law proper, concerning the organisation of State enterprises, and the Law regulating the latter's mutual intercourse, which might include as many institutions of traditional Civil Law as were felt expedient.

The definition of Civil as distinct from Public Law, and especially from Administrative Law, has been ceaselessly contested by Soviet legal theorists, without any definite solution having been hitherto reached. There have been few really original solutions, and most recent proposals are still on the lines advocated in the late 'twenties.[30] But during the late 'thirties, the discussion was to some extent focused along certain main lines : the definitions advocated were divided into those that set out from the subject-matter of Civil Law, and those starting from certain methods of realisation, allegedly characteristic of it. As no field of economic life stands outside the purview of Soviet Public Law, the representatives of the former trend are bound

it by mutual agreement, without the consent of the planning organs. It is not difficult to see the consequences likely to arise if this principle were applied also between consumer and retail stores.

[27] Besides, the very fact that Civil Law disputes between State enterprises come before the State Arbitrage, which is bound by Statute to consider not only the legal merits of the case, but also the interests of both contesting parties, involves an important concession to the Administrative Law point of view.

[28] See below.

[29] See below, pp. 253–4.

[30] See above, p. 205.

to reject any fundamental division between Civil Law and Public Law. The advocates of the second point of view may insist that, although every kind of Law emanates from the State and serves the public interest, the State may use essentially different methods for giving effect to this interest : " centralist " methods that work " from above " through the machinery of Public Law, and " decentralist " methods working through the autonomous initiative of individuals and collectives interested, which form the body of Civil Law.[31] From this point of view a fundamental division between the two branches may be defended—its only shortcoming being its failure to coincide with the traditional delimitations between the various branches of Law which it claims to explain. Every citizen who claims and exercises his suffrage against an official denying this claim forms a counter-argument against a purely centralist interpretation of Public Law, whilst the participation of the Public Attorney in Civil Law cases even beyond the claims of the immediately interested party, and the right of the Judge to give judgment even beyond the amount claimed, form a strong argument against the purely " decentralist " explanation of Soviet Civil Law, even when dealing with the rights of individuals. To explain contractual obligations between State organisations entered automatically in consequence of the plan, and unalterable except with the consent of the planning organs,[10] as if they were the result of the " autonomous initiative " of those undertakings involved, seems an artificial construction, to say the least of it.

Amongst the definitions based upon the subject-matter of Civil Law by far the broadest is that by Godes,[32] who identifies Civil Law with the regulation of economic relations in general. Such a definition has many obvious shortcomings. Only one of them, the inclusion of the Law of Labour,[33] is put right if Civil Law is defined as Amfiteatrov defines it,[34] as the regulation of property relations on the basis of socialised property in the means of production. The inevitable and admitted consequence is the inclusion of the whole of the administrative regulation of economic life. Vishinsky [35] excludes from the sphere of Civil

[31] Kechekian in a lecture in the Juridical Institute of the Academy of Science, June 25, 1940.

[32] In *S. J.*, 1939, No. 1.

[33] In the U.S.S.R. it is enacted in a special Code, as distinct from the current approach in most bourgeois countries, where it is regarded as a branch of the Law of Contract. From the Marxist point of view there are reasons of principle for the Soviet approach.

[34] Op. cit., 1940, pp. 94 ff.

[35] Op. cit., 1939.

Law *expressis verbis* those property relations that are regulated by Administrative Law—without giving any theoretical explanation of what kind of social relations belong to the proper sphere of the one and the other system of norms. From his point of view, evidently, Civil Law is simply that part of the legal regulation of property relations as not yet absorbed by Administrative Law.

Some adherents of a subject-matter definition of Civil Law avoid this defect by attempting an economic characterisation of those property relations that come under Civil Law, as distinct from those to be regulated by Administrative Law. According to Genkin,[36] Civil Law regulates the circulation of property, whilst Administrative Law, by organising enterprises and establishing the general rules of the Plan, shapes the preliminary conditions for this circulation. According to Benediktov [37] the payment of an equivalent and the usually contractual character of the transactions regulated are characteristic of Civil Law, whilst those transfers of property for which no compensation is paid (for example, the absorption, by the Central State Economic Organs, of the funds of the subordinated enterprises not needed for covering the latter's obligation,[38] are regulated by Administrative Law). These definitions cannot explain the inclusion of family rights (e.g. payment of maintenance), and claims for torts (e.g. for payment of damages for bodily injury), in Soviet Civil Law, unless at least the historical assumptions of the Commodity Exchange Conception are accepted, in the sense that such claims have been assimilated into the circulation of property. In general, these attempts to define the subject-matter of Civil Law may be regarded as an inversion of the Commodity Exchange Conception of Law (and so not exposed to the same objections as the latter) : for whilst that conception explained Law in general or at least Civil Law by the exchange of commodities, then according to the definitions discussed only those legal transactions that involve exchange against an equivalent, or that can be assimilated into such exchange, belong to the realm of Civil Law. Consequently, it would appear that with the progress of planning, Civil Law would be bound gradually to lose importance. In contrast to the Commodity Exchange Conception, this would not involve any withering away of Law in general. In this respect the logical implications of the definitions

[36] In *S. G.*, 1939, No. 4. [37] Op. cit., 1940, pp. 27 and 38.

[38] According to the laws of April 29, 1935 (S.U. 1935/221) and February 15, 1936 (S.U. 1936/93).

of Benediktov and Genkin are very near to those of Vishinsky, nor do they differ fundamentally from those of the representatives of the moderate version of the Commodity Exchange Conception.[39]

Apart from Kechekian [32] there are few completely consistent attempts to define Civil Law by the method of regulation applied. The nearest approach is that of Bratusz,[40] but a certain concession is made to the subject-matter definition by stating that the autonomy of the partners to Civil Law is " a legal form of giving effect to, and safeguarding personal interests ". By implication, the most important civil relations in the U.S.S.R., i.e. those between public undertakings, are merely analogous to genuine, i.e. inter-individual, Civil Law relationships, an implication accepted by Bratusz. In consequence, this special variant of the explanation of Civil Law by the autonomy granted to its subjects is less open to criticisms based upon the rather doubtful " freedom " enjoyed by public enterprises in entering their contractual obligations.[10] It remains exposed to criticism based upon the importance of the initiative of the interested person in Public Law as well, for example in claiming suffrage. But such cases might be explained away as actions which, as claims by the person concerned to be allowed to act on behalf of the State, are in the direct public interest, as opposed, say, to claims for personal property.

An attempt was made to combine the subject-matter and the methodological approach to the definition of Civil Law in the *Textbook on Civil Law*, published collectively in 1938 with Mikolenko and Bratusz as the leading participators. It starts by making a rather doubtful connection between Civil Law and the sociological concept of the " bourgeois society ".[41] In order to avoid confusion with the sphere of Administrative Law, the authors further proceed to a definition of Civil Law by the methods of its realisation, namely the greater amount of initiative granted to the parties, and the equality of their position in the legal contest, as distinct from the subordination characteristic of Public Law in general, and of Administrative Law in the economic field. The authors of the textbook were reproached by their critics for giving two different definitions. But actually these

[39] See above, Chapter VI, pp. 204–5.

[40] In *S. G.*, 1940, No. 1, pp. 36 ff.

[41] See above, pp. 205–6. A main reproach by the critics of the textbook (Kareva in *S. G.*, 1939/4, and Vishinsky, op. cit., 1939) was that, under Soviet conditions, the connection between " bourgeois society " and Civil, as opposed to Public, Law was artificial.

definitions make sense only in combination, i.e. if taken to mean " Civil Law embraces those legal regulations of the relations in the economic basis of society which are realised by the initiative of the parties concerned, and without formal subordination of the one to the other ". In isolation, each part could be easily refuted by the above-mentioned arguments. But if they are combined in one " mixed " definition, they prevent Civil Law from being interpreted as one of the fundamental branches of Law. It would be a sub-species of the genus " legal regulation of economic life ". This implication seems to have defeated the authors, who fought out the discussion with their numerous opponents on this very point of whether or not Civil Law as opposed to Public Law could be defined as a distinct branch of Law. In a joint article [42] they left out the whole " bourgeois society " section of their definition—certainly its weakest part if taken alone—and characterised Civil Law merely by the equal initiative granted by the State to both parties when entering the legal relation. It was not difficult to argue that, in the most important case, contractual relations between State undertakings entered into on the basis of the plan, the initiative of both parties was equally dubious, and that, on the other hand, formal equality of the parties (for example, the citizen who claims the suffrage and the official who has rejected his claim, or the prosecutor and the defendant) is a condition of truly legal procedure in every field. But the critics themselves begged the question, as, for instance, when Genkin [43] argued that, according to the Mikolenko-Bratusz definition, there could have been no Civil Law during the period of War-Communism. Certainly there was none in the decisive economic field :[44] the whole discussion on the definition of Civil Law is only intelligible as a defence of a method of securing effective management, the lack of which had been amongst the reasons for the failure of War-Communism. The real problem is that in the decisive field of intercourse between State enterprises the reality has a certain slight correspondence with the traditional conceptions of Civil Law that have grown under completely different conditions. This reality is incomparably weaker than that from which Civil Law has originated and Soviet Civil Law has borrowed its institutions : it is no longer the autonomy of the agents

[42] In *S. J.*, 1938, No. 16.

[43] In *S. G.*, 1939, No. 4, p. 33.

[44] Between individuals there were thousands of Civil Law suits on private property decided by the Courts according to Equity (as there was no valid Code).

of production, limited only by the extent of their business success, but merely one of the agencies by which the actually responsible direction of national economics secures the efficiency and initiative of its managers. Civil Law as between Soviet State undertakings is, indeed, part of Public Law—for it is a mere instrument of the most important part of State Administration. With what actually survives of true Civil Law, i.e. the protection of the citizen's share in the means of consumption produced, it has no more in common than some external forms, which have completely changed their function.

CHAPTER IX

# THE GENERAL ASPECTS AND PROSPECTS OF LAW AS A REGULATING FACTOR IN A SOCIALIST SOCIETY

Our investigation has now gone far enough to allow our returning to the problem stated in the introductory chapter of this book, and discussed once again in the fifth. On the basis of the Soviet experiences we must try to find out whether Law as an agency for regulating human relations can serve this purpose in a socialist society, and what shape the Law of such a society is likely to take. It is hardly necessary to explain exhaustively that such a question does not concern the fundamental merits of the social systems striving for the leadership in the next stage of human civilisation : Law is no more than a social technique, with some advantages and disadvantages in comparison with other possible ways of regulating human behaviour, but it is certainly not superior to what it should regulate. Socialism may be right or wrong independent of whether or not it is compatible with the application of the legal form of regulation : people may reject socialism in spite of its compatibility with the rule of Law, because they fear that legal regulation in a socialist society may become too strict. On the other hand, people may accept socialism in spite of its assumed incompatibility with the rule of Law, because they hope that a socialist society, in its higher stages, may apply forms of social regulation superior to Law, by avoiding the mechanical legal approach to cases formally equal, but materially different, in their merits.[1] No one who knows anything about the historical development of ideologies can avoid the suspicion that most of those who regard " the rule of Law " as the central standard according to which the problems of our days ought to be decided, are speaking not of Law in general, but of a certain *type* of Law, the only one which they can imagine ; in other words they are, by implication, discussing the alleged merits of a certain type of *society*. No fundamental answer as regards the merits or demerits of a certain type of society can be framed by finding out what types of formal regulation it needs, but for this very reason an unbiased answer to the

[1] See above, p. 25.

question should be possible, whatever attitude is taken to the great social issues of our time.

In attempting to decide whether a socialist society needs and is capable of legal regulation of its working, we enjoy a great advantage over Renner, who, starting from a reformist conception of Socialism, answered it in the affirmative, and over Pashukanis, who, starting from a revolutionary conception of socialism, answered it in the negative. We are in a position to start, not from abstract conceptions of socialism, but from the practical experiences of socialism in the U.S.S.R. This enables us to include in our answer not only the compatibility, or otherwise, of the legal form of regulation with the socialist form of economics (a question we have already tried to answer in the fifth chapter when discussing the opinions of Pashukanis' school), but also the other, much more intricate question of whether socialism is likely to be realised under conditions that allow for the establishment and maintenance of a truly legal system. Our advantage in being able to start from some concrete historical experience might turn into a handicap if we were to allow our approach to the problem to be influenced not only by the character of the Soviet experience as a practical attempt in socialism outside the textbooks, but also by some specific features of the Russian revolution which would not necessarily be repeated in other countries. So we have to ask the preliminary question, to what extent are the Russian experiences conditioned by the special circumstances under which the Russian revolution succeeded and was defended, and how far they may be regarded as typical of any attempt to establish a socialist society, wherever it may be made.

Even Communists will not deny that Russian experience contains many elements which are typical of Russia, and perhaps of some other Eastern European and Asiatic countries, though they are not typical of the Central and Western European countries. To these elements belong the overwhelming importance of the peasantry, the need to catch up with more advanced countries as swiftly as possible, and the predominance of the nationalities problem. At least the first and the third of these have not only put additional difficulties in the way of the attempt to lead the Russian revolution into socialist channels ; they were also amongst the main weaknesses of the old regime out of which the successful revolution came. The original Marxist ideology originated on the eve of the 1848 German revolution. A case can and has been made out [2] for the interpretation of the successful Bolshevist revolution as the work of a young working-class which was the only class able and ready to carry the democratic revolution to its logical consequences. From this point of view, the Russian experiences may be important for eventual developments in China or Spain, but certainly not for highly developed capitalist countries. Socialism of the Russian type may be a historical expedient by which nations held back under a *capitalist* [3] regime may catch up with those more advanced, and thus secure national independence and a rôle in international relations commensurate with their numerical strength. From this point of view, the Russian dictatorship may be explained and justified in the same way as most Western Liberals are inclined to justify the Turkish or Chinese dictatorships. Its legal system would be of little importance. For, clearly, the main justification for such a dictatorship is the solution of certain transitory problems, after which it should render itself superfluous as soon as possible.

Conversely, many non-Marxists would agree to-day that, apart from the special needs of hitherto backward nations, there is a strong case for securing full employment, social security, and social equality by national planning, based upon public control at least of the essential means of production. An adherent of this point of view might share the above attitude towards many specific features of the Russian experiment. However this may be, the fact remains that, whatever the reason, the Soviet State is the first socialist [3] system to be established. Whatever special features its legal system may have in common with dictatorships established for other purposes, whether progressively capitalist in backward countries or reactionary and imperialist, it is bound to show certain specific socialist features which it has in common with any other socialist system, wherever and however it was established. The only open question is how far these analogies may go.

Socialism, in the U.S.S.R., has been established under conditions of war and civil war. At least original Communist theory and many non-Socialists assert, the " dictatorship ", or, more concretely,[4] the One-Party system, is a necessary condition for realising socialism under all conceivable conditions. If this should

[2] In A. Rosenberg, *A History of Bolshevism*, English ed., London, 1934.
[3] For the question of definition see above, Chapter IV, pp. 126–7.
[4] For the term " dictatorship " may be used as a mere sociological explanation for the fact of class-rule, something, according to Marxist teaching, not peculiar to the " dictatorships ".

be so, we should have to include amongst the essential features of a socialist legal system all those features arising in the U.S.S.R. out of the political dictatorship of the Communist Party, apart from some specially severe restrictions that may be explained by the need of the U.S.S.R. to prepare its defence against a hostile world. These specifically Russian features might include most of those features of the U.S.S.R. which are alien to the Western Socialist Democrat : the restriction of freedom of dissent even within the ranks of a ruling party consisting of undoubted supporters of the regime, the brusque methods used in the collectivisation of agriculture and generally throughout the " Revolution from above ", and the restriction of the freedom of the contract for Labour.[5] All these features have evolved gradually since the beginning of the N.E.P., and it would not be difficult to prove that each of them originated from the isolated position of the U.S.S.R. and her need to prepare for the grave test which she has since so successfully withstood. But unless it can be assumed, *a priori*, that every socialist state is bound to fight for its survival against similar odds—an assumption refuted by the very existence and international position of the U.S.S.R.—it is impossible to say that these features are bound to be repeated in any other socialist system.

But apart from these extremes there remains the fact of the One-Party system, with all its implications. Lenin's case for " proletarian dictatorship " has a narrower, more specific meaning than the simple assertion that any regime which attempts to establish socialism is bound to be based on the working-classes, and to have to fight capitalist resistance. It is based upon a comparison between Russian and Central European experiences, especially that of Germany and Austria.[6] The upshot of the comparison is that, under similar conditions, a Labour movement that fails to break the old State machinery and to replace it by a new one from its own ranks, is bound to be defeated by the inevitable alliance of capitalist reaction with the old military-bureaucratic machinery. All the dependent ideologies developed by Marx and Lenin on the eventual " withering away " of the State in general, may be left aside, as refuted by Russian experience, and eventually dropped by the

[5] See above, p. 219.

[6] The experience of the Austrian republic seems to provide an even stronger argument than that of Germany. For the Austrian failure could not be explained away by splits in the Labour Movement, and the resulting policies of the contesting working-class parties.

U.S.S.R. herself.[7] But leaving aside utopias, the fact remains that the Russian Socialists were victorious because they were able and ready to destroy the old State machinery and build a new one, while the German and Austrian Socialists were defeated because they failed to do so, by regimes which preserved the worst features of capitalism and destroyed those civil liberties for whose preservation the Central European Socialists had refrained from applying energetic measures. In consequence, it would seem that there is no possibility of establishing socialism except by a regime which has learnt from the Russians not only its technique of economic organisation, but also of suppression of political antagonists with all ensuing consequences for the concept of Law applicable within such a system. The same case is made from the other side by contemporary American advocates of capitalist enterprise [8] who contend that democracy is incompatible with the existence of strong social reform movements, even if the latter should try to achieve their ends by purely constitutional means : for the very fact that these ends are opposed to the basis of capitalist property, entitles the capitalists to break constitutional legality in order to preserve their natural rights which stand above formal and constitutional Law. If these views should prove correct, they would be the basis of a very strong argument against the compatibility of socialism with normal conditions of legality : not on account of some inherent contradiction between socialist economics and a strict legal order, as has been wrongly asserted,[9] but simply because the realisation of socialism would be impossible except by the application of measures bound to result in Civil War and the establishment of a regime more concerned with its own survival than with legal niceties. Even in such a case, a new legality might arise in a later stage. But, in a Western country, this concept of Law would certainly owe little to the U.S.S.R. to-day. The question of the eventual socialist legal order would have to be dissociated from the needs of the transitional period, and it is in the latter field that the U.S.S.R., including its One-Party system, would make its main contribution, a political rather than a legal one.

But the case we have just made out is not of such general validity as appears from the arguments advanced in its favour from opposite sides. There is no justification for the prediction

[7] See above, p. 244. [8] See McIver, *Leviathan and the People*, pp. 160 ff.
[9] See above, Chapter V.

that the U.S.S.R. will remain the only country where socialism had to be introduced by dictatorial means applied by a victorious revolution. But it would also be no truer to assert that the development of the rest of this century will see no other forms of social transformation. Marx very carefully restricted to the European continental countries [10] his statement of the necessity of breaking down the traditional State machinery [10]—indeed it is not just from civil servants, or from the technical intelligentsia, that socialism, let us say in this country, would have to expect the most serious opposition. The readiness particularly of the capitalists, who by the very nature of things form a minority of the electorate, to subordinate considerations of formal legality to what may appear to them principles of moral justice, may be unquestionable : but between such a theoretical readiness and its realisation in the form of actual counter-revolution lies the fact that even in defending their property people do not risk their lives unless they have a certain minimum chance of success. That powerful combination of vested interests and traditional State machinery which, according to Marx and Lenin—and also, it seems, to Professor McIver [8]—can be broken only by civil war and revolutionary dictatorship, will not come forward in every country in sufficient strength to encourage experiments on the Franco or Dollfuss pattern, nor are they likely in the future to enjoy that external support without which neither Franco nor Dollfuss could have acted.

The aftermath of World War II has produced Communist-led revolutions in China and in all the countries of Eastern Central Europe. With the exception of China, Yugoslavia and Czechoslovakia, Soviet Russian influence on these events was conspicuous, and even Czechoslovakia was soon brought into line with the other " People's Democracies ". At the moment, China's backwardness makes an immediate socialist transformation of society impossible ; all the other People's Democracies, including Yugoslavia where the simultaneous resistance of the right-wing and of Cominform supporters makes conditions rather more tense, are One-Party regimes in essence if not in form. On this side of the " Iron Curtain ", the lead taken by U.S.A. in economic reconstruction has removed the French and Italian Communist parties from government coalitions ; since these parties are the only ones supported by the broad masses of the working-classes, in parts of Europe the present alternative appears

[10] Letter to Kugelmann, of April 12, 1871.

to lie between Catholic-led right-wing coalitions with a policy of Free Enterprise, or Communist-led revolutions.[11] But quite apart from the very different position in Britain and Scandinavia, it would be preposterous to draw general conclusions from such local and temporary conditions.

Further, even the most convinced Socialist will not deny that in some countries the necessary social changes will be carried through by sections of the ruling classes themselves, in adapting national economics to the needs of changing surroundings. We need not discuss here whether such a regime would be truly socialist in a higher sense than the Japanese economic regime, for instance, which originated in a similar way, is truly capitalist. But it cannot be denied that, unless a utopian definition of socialism is applied that would not even fit the Russian example,[3] such a regime and its legal order would contain socialist elements. From the point of view of our investigation such a statement is completely sufficient. What we have to prove is the mere existence of the possibility of elements of socialist Law quite apart from the One-Party system and dictatorship in the narrower sense.[4] So we can eliminate from our consideration features of the Soviet legal system such as an attitude to political justice that can only be interpreted as a continuation of the civil war; the acceptance of the principle of analogy in an interpretation hardly compatible with the principle of the security of the Law; the intermingling of political propaganda with justice, even in everyday cases,[12] and, in Constitutional Law, a balance which results solely from the co-ordination of distinct social interests within the party caucus. It would be incorrect to describe such features as caused by specific Russian circumstances: they are caused by the conditions of a regime emerging from civil war and able to survive in a hostile environment only by "legalising the Terror by clear and honest principles".[13] Our task is to discuss the legal principles of a socialist system *not* subjected to emergencies of this kind.

Under these conditions, what are the lessons to be drawn

[11] In the first edition of this book I wrote: "To say that in Czechoslovakia or France far-reaching social reforms could not be achieved except by the establishment of a dictatorial regime, bound permanently to apply emergency measures, is not a sound realistic view of the internal political forces working in either country—it is simply the expression of extreme pessimism as regards the international post-War order." I must confess that this pessimism has proved justified; but generalisations made from conditions prevailing in 1950 may prove to be as mistaken as were those which I made from conditions in 1944.

[12] See above, pp. 229–30.

[13] See above, p. 106.

from our analysis of Soviet Law for the Law of any other socialist society? From the foregoing it is clear that we must leave Constitutional and the bulk of Administrative Law [14] aside, and restrict the discussion of Criminal Law to some general problems arising out of the needs of any socialist society. In addition, we must give some consideration to the fact that in any realistic investigation a certain amount of political opposition to a new social regime must be assumed, whatever the latter's popular support. Soviet Matrimonial Law, however interesting, may be left aside for the reason that [15] its general features correspond rather to a consistent bourgeois democratic revolution than to a socialist one. The only thing to be said, in this connection, is that a socialist society, at least at the stage reached by the contemporary U.S.S.R., does not appear to need new conceptions of Matrimonial Law beyond those carried through by consistent democratic reformers in non-socialist countries: i.e. completely equal status of women, freedom of divorce, etc. But Soviet developments give us no reason to doubt that, for the present, a main part of the responsibility for educating the future citizens will remain with the family. Therefore, the State will be interested in the latter's stability so far as it is compatible with the social equality of women. The main aspects of Law we are concerned with, in the present chapter, are Civil and Labour Law.

Now it seems evident that, of the various stages of Soviet developments which we have studied, the social structure and the Law of the N.E.P.-period must form the starting-point for any ultimate generalisation. As early as 1928 it was recognised by the programme of the Communist International that, far from being a mere compromise forced upon Soviet Russia by its extreme backwardness and the overwhelming peasant majority of the population, the principles of the N.E.P., i.e. the concentration of the nationalisation of industries at key-points, and the gradual absorption of the rest of the national economy by the influence exercised from those "commanding heights", is most likely to be accepted by any socialist Revolution [16] wherever it may arise.

[14] A large amount of Administrative Law is clearly needed for any planned economy. As we have seen above (p. 254), jointly with Civil Law, and with precedence over the latter, it forms the basis of the Law of Soviet economics. But, beyond stating this general need, there is no sense in dwelling on special features of Soviet Administrative Law once we have resolved to regard its essential basis, the One-Party regime, as a non-essential condition.

[15] See above, pp. 59–60.

[16] It ought to be kept in mind that such terms, in a Communist programme, refer to states of the Soviet type, i.e. even to a field much narrower than that considered by us at this stage.

We have seen (Chapters III and VI) that the N.E.P. was much nearer to basic Bolshevist conceptions on the eve of the Revolution, and after the complete victory of collectivisation, than might appear from the fact that emergency forced upon the Bolshevists the episode of War-Communism, and a speed of agricultural collectivisation much greater than was desirable from purely economic considerations. Should the need for socialist reconstruction arise in some country on the basis of a political regime with a basis broader than the original Soviet regime, there would be an even stronger desire to concentrate nationalisation at certain key-points, and to let the majority of the middle-classes and lower middle-classes pursue their traditional way of life. This argument ought not to be overstated ; it is evident that the black-coated worker, and especially the engineer with a real interest in planned economics, is bound to form a major element in the non-working-class support of any socialist regime. But the other extreme of " technocracy " should also be avoided, not only because successful attempts at socialist reconstruction are most likely to arise in continental countries with a very large peasantry, but also because the whole case for socialism has shifted noticeably from considerations of equality of income to those of full employment, social security, and equality of opportunity. Following the experiences of the U.S.S.R., the egalitarian appeal of socialism and, therefore, the claim for a speedy elimination of all capitalists simply because their higher income-level is regarded as unjust, is not likely to be very forcible. On the other hand, the failure of private capitalist enterprise to secure full employment and the threat to individual freedom originating from capitalist monopolies, have rendered socialist measures popular even amongst people who would hardly be inclined to accept planning on its own merits, or to regard equality of income as a desirable aim. Whatever the post-War reaction to the extreme restriction and bureaucratic control of the distribution of consumer's goods will be,[17] it will not impair the claim for social control of those key-positions on which the whole working of national economy depends. But even should it

[17] After the last War so prominent a leader of Central European Socialism as Otto Bauer (in *The Way to Socialism*—Vienna, 1919—in German) deemed that Marx's emphasis on planning was a mere reaction against the anarchy of primitive capitalism, and that future socialism would evolve rather on libertarian principles, in the sense of Guild Socialism, as opposed to the bureaucratic restrictions of war economics. After the great depression of 1929, Otto Bauer would hardly have repeated such a statement.

do so temporarily, the first post-War crisis is bound to revive the call for planned economics and for nationalisation of the key-industries (including banking, transport, etc.) as a guarantee that planning shall work in the interest of the community, as opposed to the alternative of planning by monopolies. A society arising out of the realisation of such demands would not, apart from differences of national economic standards, be very far from Russia of the N.E.P.

The main positive lesson which such a society could draw from the Russian experience, would be a functionalist approach to the position of the remaining private entrepreneurs and of co-operative organisations administering part of the national wealth. Once the advantages of planning are exalted over the egalitarian argument [17] in the socialist case, there is, in principle, no more to be said for the freedom of the co-operative to disturb the plan than for the private entrepreneur. On the other hand, once socialism has ceased to be regarded as belonging exclusively to the working-classes—and this has happened in the U.S.S.R.—and premia for managerial success are regarded as a normal form of " payment according to the quantity of the work done ", there is no reason of principle why this remuneration, in the case of the remaining private entrepreneurs, should not take a shape very similar to what they have been accustomed to. There is only one conception incompatible with socialist reconstruction : namely, that anyone may own means of production when ownership means, in the classical Roman sense, that he can do what he likes with his property. In the non-nationalised industries, trusteeship would take the place of property in means of production. The right of the citizen holding such trusteeship would be any citizen's claim to be employed and remunerated according to his abilities, but not to continue to hold that trusteeship even if Society should deem that it has ceased to be necessary. Had this been clearly stated at the beginning of the N.E.P. to merchants and kulaks instead of playing with an alleged " freedom of Trade ", which the Soviet could never seriously accept, much human tragedy would have been avoided. But the reproach must rather be aimed at the popular Soviet propaganda of the time than the Civil Code, which, as we have seen, very clearly describes the framework within which all private rights are granted.[18] Indeed, the fundamental conception of the 1922 Code has stood the test so well that, although many of its

[18] See above, Chapter IV, pp. 93–5.

institutions have become obsolete with the disappearance of private enterprise, the general tendency among Soviet legal theorists after the exaggerations of the " Second revolution ", is " Nearer to the Civil Code ".[19] We saw, in the last chapter, that Soviet Civil Law, in its most important field of application, is inaccessible to rational theoretical interpretation unless a functionalist conception is substituted for " property " in means of production. This would be not the first time in history that a legal institution, formally preserved, had changed its social meaning. Unless one starts from capitalist ideology there is not the slightest reason to ascribe to such institutions as obligations and contracts any metaphysical sanctity beyond the changing needs of society. But the experience of the U.S.S.R. makes it clear that, until better methods to secure and control efficient management have been found, the formal application of these institutions is the only available expedient to prevent State economics from wasting the national wealth. The application of these methods—whether or not their continued description as " Civil Law " is correct—supposes formal equality of the partners to the contract, and a formal approach to the fact of contract independent of what may appear to be the economic merits of the case. This very fact answers the assumption that a socialist society—at least in any form that could be envisaged at present —might be " lawless ".

In general, the question of the legality of a socialist order is not simply whether some other mechanism for automatically ensuring the regular working of its economic management is needed. The question normally asked is whether the individual citizen can enjoy at least as much stability and security for his claims as in a capitalist society, with due allowance for the actual adulteration of the latter's legal ideologies by the interference of economic, especially monopolist, power with the working of its legal machinery. It seems to me that the fundamental question is not one of socialism versus capitalism, but one of the modern organised society versus the original—though always somewhat imaginary—liberal structure of " independent " individuals balancing each other. The individual worker is no

[19] See the *Textbook on Civil Law* of 1938, as well as the generally critical reviewers in *S. G.*, 1939, No. 4. The only contested issue is the question of what specific institutions are to be regarded as obsolete. The tendency of the reviewers and many other contributors to Soviet legal periodicals is rather to strengthen the protection of private property in means of consumption, the Right of Inheritance, etc., in comparison with the 1922 Civil Code.

more powerful in comparison with the American Steel Trust than with the U.S.S.R., and whether he can secure his rights depends upon the power of his organisations and their share in running the State. Even in War-time Britain there were Essential Works Orders, etc., but apart from emergencies there is no reason why sectional organisation could not develop in a socialist regime sufficiently strong to anchor whatever rights the latter grants. And even in its emergencies the U.S.S.R. shows that the State as such has an interest in giving its citizens the feeling that their rights are secure. Law, as distinct from arbitrariness, supposes a certain balance—but this can be a balance between various sides of the social interest, represented by distinct organs of the community, just as well as between individuals, whose actual power to "balance" each other may be rather questionable under modern conditions of large-scale monopolies, whether State or private.

What this Law would be is another question. Until confronted with the actual threat of war, the U.S.S.R. managed without interfering with the freedom of the citizen to choose his profession and to change his place of employment whenever he desired, and it has regulated the supply of the various kinds of labour by its wages and educational policy. Unless other socialist states—without the international conditions that made such a course unavoidable in the U.S.S.R.—were to exaggerate the policy of securing full employment to the point of creating a scarcity of labour, there is no reason why the normal mechanisms of an organised Labour market should not work, and freedom of the contract for labour be preserved quite apart from the economic pressure exercised by the fact that "he who does not work, shall not eat". To enforce Labour discipline by the Criminal Code, as the U.S.S.R. does,[20] is necessary only once the threat of dismissal has quite ceased to be effective, and under conditions of scarcity that reduce the amount of privileges that can be granted to the average diligent worker. But it seems to be a clear lesson of Soviet experience that wherever sanctions against a breach of economic discipline are applied, they ought to be decided by Courts dominated by the general interest in preserving the security of Law, and not by organs of the management, whose natural tendency is to look after the working of its undertaking.[21] The balance between the social interest in every citizen feeling

[20] See above, p. 239.

[21] See above, pp. 162–4.

that Justice is done to him, and those other social interests that may be endangered by failures of the citizen to fulfil his duty, exists only within the community as a whole: sectional self-government, if carried too far, is a danger to Justice, whether, for reasons of collective solidarity with the offender, it deals with him too leniently or, in the sectional interest of fulfilling the allotted plan, it deals with him too severely.[22]

The experiences of the U.S.S.R. show that socialism does not make the classical conceptions of Criminal Law obsolete. It was amongst the merits of the Commodity Exchange Conception of Law that it pointed to the connection between the principle of retaliation and a commercial conception of Morals and Law. But this is all. Without preserving the strict conception of individual guilt, as the condition of punishment, the desire to appreciate the merits of each individual case to the full is bound to result in arbitrariness. The true place for sociological understanding is in the decision of the legislator as to which actions should be punished and according to which measure the penalty should be meted out, and in the decision of the Judge (and the directors of the re-educational institutions) to how far it is necessary to apply the legal penalty to the convicted offender. But, as regards the conviction itself, sociology must enter the legal decision only in so far as it helps the Judge to understand the true intentions of the legislator. So also the construction of criminal proceedings as a contest between parties has proved to be a necessary guarantee for equal consideration of both sides of the public interest, that no offence should remain unpunished, and that no innocent citizen should be punished. Present Soviet legal thought rejects the conceptions of Krylenko, who regarded that construction of trial as a necessary but temporary evil.[23] The true merits of socialism, in the field of criminology, do not lie in the invention of fundamentally new principles of Criminal Law. They lie in the fact that, by securing full employment and freedom from want, socialism is able not only to remove an essential cause of crime, but also to shape the indispensable conditions for a true, and not merely formal, approach to the

[22] This is no argument against institutions of the type of the Georgian factory fellowship courts (see note 91 in Chapter VII) which, at the risk of giving less guarantees for duly legal procedure, spare the smaller offender a formal conviction in Court. Such institutions are supposed to dispose only of very limited penalties, and their influence is based upon public opinion in the factory rather than upon a real preventive influence of those penalties themselves. They are institutions of collective discipline, rather than of Criminal Law.

[23] See Strogovich, in *S. G.*, 1938, No. 4, p. 81.

re-education of the offender. A socialist society needs the former criminal as a collaborator, not merely as an implement to deter other potential " social refuse ".

As regards the organisation of the Courts the Soviet example is valuable in bringing Justice, in the issues touching the every-day life of the citizen, near to the people and its understanding.[24] The sacrifice of formality involved in such a structure of Justice is tolerable (*a*) because of the construction of the Courts of Appeal, and their extremely far-going right to supervise the inferior courts and to revise their decisions, even after they have become valid, and (*b*) because of the transfer of the most complicated issues of Civil Law to a special organ, the State Arbitrage, which deals with them under consideration of economic expediency as much as of formal law. The latter is possible in the U.S.S.R. because the most important " Civil Law " issues are disputes between what actually are mere departments of an identical combination, contests of the State with itself, which only the State can win. What is decided, in fact, by the State Arbitrage, are the principles according to which public property ought to be administered by the various agents of its owner. A society where important enterprises were in other than State hands, whatever its fundamental conceptions of the functions of private " entrepreneurs " and co-operatives as mere trustees of the community, would be bound to grant them a higher degree of security by normal Judicial procedure, particularly in the most important Civil Law issues. In such a case the Soviet principle of identical courts for all branches of Law (with specialised benches in the higher instances, it is true) would hardly work. If a society wishes to have the advantages of an elected lower judiciary, regularly reporting to the electorate and keeping continual touch with the citizen's life, then it must be paid for by the centralisation of Justice which is involved in the necessary supervision of such a Judiciary by higher courts with specialist qualification. But this is a political issue, fundamentally independent of the relative merits of socialism and capitalism. In general, the regular working of planned economics, and the securing of a stable legal order in a system dominated by a monopolist State entrepreneur, demands a high degree of centralisation. Under socialism, the rule of Law is granted by the public interest embodied in Public Law, and by nothing else. The advantages

[24] See above, pp. 230–1.

of planning and social security cannot be combined with those of extreme decentralisation. But there is no reason why they should not be completely compatible with the security of the rights granted to the individual member of such a society.[25]

[25] In his review of this book in *The Modern Quarterly*, autumn, 1948, p. 85, Mr. A. Rothstein took exception to my statement (p. 267) that certain hardships of the "second revolution" could have been avoided if N.E.P.-men and *kulaks* had been told, from the very start of the N.E.P., that the "freedom of trade" was provisional, that no ownership but only trusteeship was possible in a society moving towards socialism, and that the citizen properly fulfilling such trusteeship would be rewarded, not by private ownership in means of production but by suitable employment fitting his abilities. This chapter deals with lessons to be drawn by other countries from the Russian experiences on the road to socialism; I did not intend to reproach the Bolsheviks for not having known, in the 'twenties, what now is known because of their very experience; nor would I suggest that they, in 1922, could expect the average N.E.P.-man or *kulak* to take the survival of their system for granted. All this simply points out that a certain phraseology about "free trade", however inconsistent with the facts and with the actual intentions of the Soviet leaders (a point implied by Mr. Rothstein in his critique of my book, see above, Preface, p. x), may have been conducive to the survival of the Soviet state. But as we are here discussing problems of a socialist transformation of society without reference to the specific climate of Russia, 1922 (i.e. to the belief of the Russian middle-classes that the Soviet regime would not survive), I may answer—or rather, allow a person more competent than I am to answer—his question "why the town middlemen and commercial agents who came into being during the first phase of the N.E.P. . . . would have been more reconciled to being squeezed out of existence or expropriated, when large-scale socialist planning began in 1929, if they had been told they were only 'trustees, not owners'". In a conference of representatives of the Chinese C.P. with industrial employers in Tientsin, Lin-Shao-chi, Vice-Chairman of the Chinese Government and of the World Federation of Trade Unions, answered the doubts of the entrepreneurs about their and their families' future after the end of the Chinese counterpart of the N.E.P. as follows: "If you do a really good job in developing your business, and train your children to be first-class technical experts, you will be the obvious people to be put in charge of nationalised enterprises, and you may find that you earn more as managers of a nationalised enterprise than as owners" (quoted by M. Lindsay, in *The New Statesman and Nation*, December 10, 1949).

I should not deny that, on such an occasion, Mr. Lin-Shao-chi was likely to make more of the promise of equality of opportunity for former *bourgeois* than of the implications of equality of opportunity in general (including former workers), for competitors for the best jobs; my point is simply that a Socialist state which is firmly established (so that there is little sense for the middle-classes' dreaming of a capitalist restoration) can make an honest case for inviting their co-operation by calling things by their proper names.

## CHAPTER X

# THE SOVIET CONCEPTIONS OF INTERNATIONAL LAW

The co-ordination of different social systems in one international order is a fundamental problem of present-day International Law. Yet the very possibility of such co-ordination was disputed during the period between the two World Wars, especially outside the U.S.S.R. For the state representing a new social order, which sets it apart from all the other members of the international community, denial of the possibility of such co-ordination is simply an assertion that International Law is irrelevant to it—and the Bolshevists have always been too realistic to deny that compromises with the outside world are possible and occasionally desirable. But amongst the lawyers representing what is still the majority of the international community it is a matter of dispute whether the outsider should be boycotted, or collaborated with—or, to express this dilemma in legal forms, whether International Law should be regarded as essentially bound to certain general principles of internal order which are characteristic of the majority of states, or interpreted as "system-neutral" so that there is a place within its framework for any social structure known at the present time.

From the former viewpoint one might argue, for example, that amongst the generally accepted principles of all civilised nations was "the right of aliens to possess and deal with property, and the inviolability of such property in the sense that expropriation is only possible for public purposes and then only on payment of full compensation by the State".[1] Here the underlying assumption is that the desire of a state to abolish certain kinds of private property in general [2] is not a legitimate public

[1] Fachiri, in *British Year Book for International Law*, vol. 1925, p. 169.

[2] This is no reference to discrimination, as regards property rights, against aliens or members of certain nationalities, which certainly contradicts International Law. Schwarzenberger (*Die Kreuger-Anleihen*, Muenchen-Leipzig, 1931, p. 42) is certainly right in stating that a state (such as Rumania after World War I), when defending its policies on the basis of the alleged need to defend the institution of private property against Bolshevism, thereby waived the claim to have interference with property rights of certain national groups interpreted as social reform, and not as national discrimination.

purpose, and that the adequacy of compensation ought to be judged, not by the standards which the state in question deems right in dealing with its own subjects,[3] but by the standards accepted by states which differ from its fundamental outlook on social issues. Such an argument may be based upon the alleged general validity of existing " standards of right and duty which enlightened humanity has prescribed for itself in its domestic affairs "[4]; or it may be based upon the sociological contention that certain standards of municipal order provide the only firm basis for that economic intercourse upon which the international community rests. An advocate of private capitalist enterprise may argue, for example, that, without accepting his standards of private property, investment of surplus capital in foreign countries would be impossible.[4] But both arguments could be used by the advocates of the new system : they may contend that the existing majority is not enlightened at all, and that international planning, realisable only in a world federation of socialist republics, forms the best foundation for international economic intercourse. But International Law is not concerned with the alleged superiority of either system, and in any case the argument involves the negation of its international validity.

From the second point of view " it is surely impossible, whatever may be our views as to the relative merits of socialist and individualist doctrines, to assert that modern civilisation required all states to accept so unreservedly the theories of one side in the great economic dispute " and " it would surely be rash to erect any one set of those views into an international law which is to limit the national freedom of the members of the international society ".[5] The argument in favour of this point of view is evident, for its rejection implies the negation of the task of International Law to establish an international peace-order. But its opponents may criticise it for restricting International Law to very few abstract and general rules acceptable to both capitalist and socialist states, not definite enough to regulate the most important issues of present international intercourse.

There is a third possibility which might appear able to avoid

[3] See Sir J. Fisher Williams, in *British Year Book for International Law,* 1928, pp. 21 and 25–7.

[4] Ch. W. Anderson, in the *American Yearbook of International Law,* vol. XXI, pp. 525 ff. It is characteristic of the *petitio principii,* by the advocates of this point of view, that the Tsarist constitution of 1906 is quoted as a proof of Russian participation in the alleged international consent, ten years after the 1917 revolution !

[5] Sir J. Fisher Williams, op. cit., pp. 20–21.

both the presumptuous claim of the former and the abstractness of the latter approach. It has been stated "that there is a plurality of communities of International Law, and that a fundamental change in the social structure of a state results in its losing the status of a subject of International Law within that international community to which it formerly belonged".[6] Such a statement bears a comparison with certain original propagandist Soviet conceptions asserting the alleged impossibility of co-operation between states of differing social structures,[7] and it is an exaggerated form of early Soviet theories of International Law [8] concerning the partial change necessitated by internal revolution in the obligations of a subject of International Law. Like the first theory, this one rejects the possibility of legal relations between states whose social structures differ fundamentally, and it provides no explanation of how the U.S.S.R. has re-entered the International Community without dropping her attitude to property in the means of production, including the former property of foreigners, and to the debts incurred by the Tsarist regime.

Up to now the explanation has been based on the opinions of Western lawyers, for the problems are identical from both capitalist and socialist viewpoints. But a consideration from the latter point of view meets an additional difficulty: whilst, within Western legal ideology, an approach like that of Sir John Fisher Williams quoted above is simply that of a broad-minded lawyer, who is ready to purchase universality of the Law at the expense of its completeness, for a Marxist the additional difficulty arises as to how Law as a "superstructure" can have a common existence upon fundamentally different social foundations.

From the start the problem was complicated by bringing a sociological argument into the legal analysis. Marxism explains the State, *qua* social institution, as an instrument of class-rule.[9] This is not necessarily a description of the State, *qua* subject of International Law, as a class-organisation dealing, in its international relations, with other class-organisations of different type. But such was the assumption during the first stage of the develop-

[6] Schwarzenberger, op cit., p. 41. See also W. Friedmann in *Modern Law Review*, 1939, pp. 213–14.

[7] There is the difference that the Soviet propagandists conceived of the Soviet world coming into existence as a federation. So its Law would be Public, but not International Law.

[8] See below, pp. 277–8.

[9] See above, Chapter II, pp. 19–20.

ment of Soviet jurisprudence.[10] Certainly, during the early existence of the Soviet republic important facts might lead to a description of its international relations essentially in terms of class. There was the fact of intervention against which the Soviet defended itself by means of an appeal to all working-class forces throughout the world. Then, too, the Soviet, in its first international treaties, made stipulations as to the fate of revolutionaries in foreign prisons,[11] and even as to the legal possibilities of propaganda by the Communist parties in countries with which it concluded treaties.[12] All these facts might prove that class was a highly important element in international relations, especially of the U.S.S.R., and they might also prove that organised states were not the only forms of political organisation with which the international policies of the U.S.S.R. had to reckon. But they certainly did not prove that social organisations other than states could be subjects of International Law, as asserted by Korovin,[13] nor could they ever prove that states, when dealing with each other under International Law, acted merely as class-organisations. For antagonistic class-organisations could never recognise one another as legitimate representatives of their respective states. They could only fight one another —and thus International Law would give place to intervention and counter-intervention. In fact, the very existence of international relations between states of different social structures seems to prove that class, however important, is in the long run only one of a number of aspects of these relations.

Although the identification of the State, as subject of International Law, with the State, as an organisation of the ruling class, was illogical and insufficiently supported by the facts, it seemed to have one big advantage, from the point of view of the new State: by denying the continuity of State personality before and after a revolution involving change of the ruling class, it very simply solved the problem of the Tsarist debts by declaring them a *res inter alios gesta* [14] outside the responsibility of the Soviet

[10] See Korovin, op. cit., 1925, especially pp. 293 and 295, where a realist conception of State personality in Duguit's sense is accepted with the correction that not the ruling personalities but the ruling classes are to be taken as characteristic of the State personality.

[11] Ibid., pp. 294–5.

[12] See the secret treaty with Georgia, reprinted by Batsell in *Soviet Rule in Russia*, London, 1929, pp. 253–4. This case of a border state, formerly belonging to the Tsarist Empire and exposed to Allied intervention, may be not quite conclusive, as the alternative to toleration of the Georgian Communists was a distinctly anti-Soviet foreign policy.

[13] Op. cit., 1924.

[14] Ibid., p. 30.

government, without having recourse to the general *clausula rebus sic stantibus* that might endanger the binding force of all international commitments, including those entered by the new state. On the other side, the negation of a continuous State personality never corresponded to the political practice of the Soviet. The latter, even where it considered the preservation of rights acquired by the former Russian regime incompatible with the principles of new Russia (as in the case of capitulations in Iran and China), abandoned these rights only by special agreement. And it has never ceased to protest against the annexation by Rumania of Bessarabia, a former Russian territory where the Soviet power had never been established. True, in this case the Soviet argued that, as it had no popular support, the " National Council " established by the Rumanians in 1919 was in no way entitled to exercise the right of national self-determination as recognised by the Soviet decrees. But this argument also presupposes the automatic validity of the Soviet decrees in all territories belonging to the former Tsarist Empire, or at least of those decrees which allowed secession of territories where the population demanded it.

Apart from his direct negation of State-continuity, Korovin has expressed his fundamental attitude in a second theory,[15] which kept nearer to the realities of Soviet policies and still avoided that broad interpretation of the *clausula rebus sic stantibus* so frequently misused to cover imperialist aggression: State obligations remain absolutely binding as regards the political regime that has entered into them. But they lose their binding force once the social structure of a state changes so categorically that the fulfilment of the obligations of its predecessors, or the enjoyment of the rights acquired by them, contradicts the fundamental principles of the new regime. Thus, argued Korovin, the Soviet would be clearly wrong in demanding from Horthy's White Hungarian regime the fulfilment of the alliance treaties which it had concluded with Horthy's Soviet predecessors: in concluding a treaty of alliance which a White Hungarian regime was bound to reject, the Russian Soviet had accepted the risk of losing its partner in the event of a counter-revolution in Hungary. So, too, when in face of the public protest of the Russian socialist opposition, foreign creditors provided loans to the victor of the 1905 revolution, they had to accept the risk that the regime of

[15] Op. cit., 1924, pp. 106–7, and op. cit., 1928, p. 763. To this point see also Hazard in *The American Journal of International Law*, vol. 32, pp. 250–1.

their debtor might be followed by one which would not recognise capital investments at all, and certainly not those used in defeating the Russian revolution. From the theoretical point of view this theory of Korovin involves a combination of the second and the third of the theories enumerated above [16] concerning the validity of International Law between states of different social structures. It asserts that a truly International Law, binding for all members of the international community, should consist of a certain number of norms, including the admission of all obligations whose fulfilment is compatible with the social structure of a state, and the right of every nation to decide upon its own internal regime. But, in addition to this general system, there would also be particular systems of International Law having application to the rights and obligations of states with compatible social structures and binding for them only so long as they preserved that structure. Thus, a state can only get rid of its debts by carrying through a social revolution aimed at the abolition of private finance, and there is little danger that insolvent financiers would use this expedient for getting rid of their obligations.

But what is International Law itself? The answer to this problem has changed with the evolution of Soviet international policies during the years between the end of the Civil War and the beginning of World War II. From the outset the question arose as to what kind of legal relations were possible between antagonistic classes, acting under the title of states, once, in the description of the subjects of International Law, class and State were identified. Korovin, the main representative of that identification, was doubly mistaken in his views of the legal relations existing between the subjects of International Law : he assumed that a community of ideology such as might exist between members of identical classes in various countries was a necessary basis of International Law,[17] and he described the legal relations between states as direct relations between the ruling classes of these states, with the strange result that the existence of legal relations between Germany and the U.S.S.R. presupposed the existence of an ideology common to both German capitalists and Russian working-classes. Such a description of international legal relations between antagonistic social systems would reduce them to the application of general humanitarian standards quite independent of the respective class points of view ; [18] though it might include virtually the whole Law of

[16] Pp. 273–5. [17] Op. cit., 1924, p. 6. [18] Ibid., p. 15.

War,[19] it was quite insufficient to cover the actual international relations of the U.S.S.R. Thus Korovin and other Soviet theorists [20] very soon evolved an interpretation of the International Law of the transitional period as a compromise between antagonistic classes. This interpretation is a clear reflection of the situation existing within Russia at that time under the N.E.P.

But when the N.E.P. was superseded within the U.S.S.R., the criticism of the theoretical conceptions which had accompanied it began to crop up everywhere. It was not difficult to demonstrate that the identification of class and state broke down where the State, whatever its class-structure, acted in the name of all classes. Nor could Korovin deny that his supposition of a common ideology as a basis for International Law implied either a denial of differences between the legal ideologies of the U.S.S.R. and capitalist states, or an ultra-radical attempt to construct a specifically socialist system of International Law which could have no bearing upon the existing relations between the U.S.S.R. and the capitalist states surrounding it. As early as 1929 Korovin had to acknowledge that his original theories had been wrong.[21] In 1935, Pashukanis published his textbook on International Law where the above criticism of Korovin's and his own original position was developed into the theory that International Law was not the expression of a common ideology but, on the contrary, an instrument in the struggle between rival states, including those of differing economic and social systems. Therefore, although the forms of International Law are identical for all states, opposing social systems can avail themselves of these legal forms for their own ends.[22]

During the evolution of the Soviet policy of collective security in the years which followed, this theory of Pashukanis was subjected to very sharp criticism,[23] which, however, must be understood as a part of the criticism of the general theories of

[19] For this point see the statement of an opponent, Mirkine-Guetzevich, op. cit., pp. 331 ff. The differences mentioned there are not important nor do they cover the specific field of the Law of War : special interest in the fate of prisoners who, by virtue of their social position, were regarded as close to the Soviet was then a normal element of Soviet politics. And in these days of "ideological wars", the Soviet is certainly not the only state that rejects the obligation to preserve, during a military occupation of enemy territory by its armies, the political system which existed there prior to that occupation.

[20] Including Pashukanis, later one of the main critics of Korovin's position, in his contribution to the *Soviet Encyclopedia of Law*, vol. II, p. 862.

[21] See Makarov, op. cit., pp. 485 ff.

[22] Op. cit., p. 17.

[23] For a survey, see Hazard, in *The American Journal of International Law*, vol. 32, pp. 244 ff., and the present writer, in *Zeitschrift fuer Sozialforschung*, 1938/3, and in *Modern Law Review*, December, 1942.

Pashukanis discussed above.[24] As we have seen,[25] at a certain stage in the disintegration of the Commodity Exchange Conception of Law, it was asserted that the socialist content of Soviet Law was realised through forms which were originally bourgeois. We have already given [26] the very strong arguments against such an interpretation of the Law of the N.E.P., let alone its application after the complete triumph of State economics. But, in the international field, systems which are socially different meet without having any superior political order set above them. Thus it may not be equally wrong to describe Law as identical forms serving antagonistic purposes. In order to refute Pashukanis' view it is not sufficient to state [27] that in international conflicts of an undoubtedly social character—as in most international conflicts—each side can use this or that theory of International Law as its own weapon. This fact merely proves (*a*) that, in international society, there are conflicts, including class conflicts, and (*b*) that present-day International Law is not a system free of all contradictions and able to answer any issue arising without ambiguity. Marxists may explain the latter fact by saying that International Law has grown historically under changing social circumstances, so that its different elements represent distinct trends in international relations. But these different elements are either jointly recognised by all members of the international community, or they are not. In the latter case they are not binding as International Law at all, and a dispute fought out by the various sides using arguments accepted as law by only a part of the international community would be no legal dispute at all. In the former case (the only one which is interesting from the point of view of legal analysis), the very acceptance of such a contradictory system by states having very different interests may in itself be a compromise, as Korovin had stated, while Pashukanis (in his later point of view) might still be right in saying that the class struggle in the international field took the form of using the international legal system for antagonistic purposes.

In criticising the views of Pashukanis, Rappaport [28] has stated

[24] Chapter V, and section (*c*) of Chapter VI.

[25] See above, p. 207.

[26] See above, pp. 130–1.

[27] See Hazard, op. cit., p. 247. Recent Soviet theory (see Kozhevnikov, op. cit., p. 103) regards application of some isolated institution of International Law as opposed to its fundamental rules, not as a proof of the latter's ambiguity but simply as a form of violating international obligations.

[28] Op. cit., 1937, and op. cit., 1940, p. 139.

that present International Law is not homogeneous in its class character but comprises two distinct lines, the imperialist and the Soviet, of International Law, which are in conflict just as the international policies of the two systems are. Such a statement is not clear, for the " two lines of International Law " may be interpreted in three different senses. First, it may mean distinct policies, advocated within a common legal framework—in this case Rappaport only repeated in a different form the statement of Pashukanis which he criticised. Or it may mean that two conceptions of what is right and wrong are in opposition to each other [29]; in which case they are not the international *legal* system that by definition must be common to all the states linked by it, but conceptions of International Justice or moral principles realised in national policies. Or, thirdly, the " two lines of International Law " may mean two competing systems of particular inter-state Law, each recognised by a section of the international community. If these contested norms are to embrace the whole system of International Law, this would simply imply the negation of International Law linking distinct internal systems, in the sense of the third view discussed at the beginning of this chapter.[30] Thus the assertion of a contest of " two lines in International Law " only makes sense if there is a certain amount of common ground, accepted by all partners to the Law, and apart from this, a number of particular norms, accepted only by some states, the contest being a political one for the universal recognition of norms advocated by the one or the other of the contending groups of states. Indeed, pre-War Soviet theory [31] tended to regard the relations between the Soviet and its capitalist neighbours as a combination of competition and co-operation, and the content of existing International Law as a mixture of three groups of norms, distinguished by their social origin, namely (*a*) those elements of traditional International Law which reflected its bourgeois democratic origins, or were a

[29] Op. cit., p. 144. Rappaport's argument, in 1937 as well as in 1940, that amongst the institutions of traditional International Law rejected by the Soviet were treaties forced upon the weaker partner by external force, makes sense only within the framework of a conception of International Justice. If taken in its proper legal meaning it would imply the invalidity, say, of the treaties concluded in autumn, 1939, with the Baltic States, and in 1940 with Finland. Certainly Rappaport did not intend such implications—what he desired to say was that the U.S.S.R. regards a state of international affairs in which pressure against weaker states is a recognised and (of course for every partner) inevitable expedient to create international security, as immoral, and deserving abolition.

[30] See above, pp. 274–5.

[31] See Antonov, op. cit., p. 72, Kozhevnikov, op. cit., pp. 110–11, and Vishinsky, op. cit., 1939, p. 12.

further development from them (such as the League of Nations and possible improvements upon its conceptions), and were accepted by the Soviet, in accordance at least with progressive bourgeois opinion, (*b*) specifically imperialist institutions, like Mandates, which were rejected by the Soviet, though they formed elements of International Law within the bourgeois world,[32] and (*c*) new elements of International Law introduced by the Soviet practice, and as a result of political pressure by the Soviet, recognised at least by an increasing number of bourgeois states (for example, the principle of juridical equality of the two competing economic systems, the specific legal status of the Trade Delegations of a state with a monopoly of external trade, etc.). More recently, International Law has been described as " a stage for the struggle of two tendencies, the progressive-democratic, and the reactionary-imperialist ".[33] Obviously, a stage is a platform on which certain things are taken for granted : there can be as little common ground between a derivation of all rules of International Law from the interests of socialism and capitalism respectively as there can be one stage for a theological argument between Fundamentalists and Agnostics. The common ground—that is, the type of public opinion to which the Soviet appeal is made—may be characterised by Korovin's description of the Soviet trend as " progressive-democratic ", and of the opposite trend as " reactionary-imperialist " : the Soviet authors assert that, today, only Socialists can consistently support the original *bourgeois*-democratic principles on the international stage, while supporters of monopoly-capitalism (imperialism in the Communist terminology) are bound to betray them.

Since the War, the long-standing controversy about the essence of International Law has died down.[34] Korovin clearly maintains his former attitude when he states, in the main organ for Party activists, that each of the states representing different socio-economic structures " while pursuing its own policy, may be interested in the preservation and support of certain norms in international relations binding all of them. Thus, for example, capitalist Britain, feudal Afghanistan, and the socialist Soviet state are all concerned that their frontiers should not be violated by other states, that there should be no interference in their internal affairs, no violations of international obligations by other

[32] See Litvinov's speech at the occasion of the admission of the U.S.S.R. to the League of Nations, op. cit., p. 104.

[33] Korovin in *Bolshevik*, October, 1946.

[34] Cp. John N. Hazard, in *Soviet Studies*, vol. I, No. 3, p. 191.

states, no killing of prisoners of war, no plundering of the civilian population, etc." [35]

It is remarkable that the Soviet argument in favour of the existence of International Law continues to turn on the most elementary conditions of the community of nations [35]; the difference in socio-economic structure can hardly affect any one of the issues mentioned by Korovin, except the possible *forms* of interference with the internal affairs of another state. Clearly, it is impossible to reach agreement as to, for instance, the qualification of credits linked with some implicit influence of the creditor upon the composition of coalition-governments in the debtor-country, or of the failure of a revolutionary country to disown sympathies with revolutionary movements in other states (though it is comparatively easy to establish limits where implicit and moral influences turn into technical intervention). But even a minimum of accepted rules of behaviour incurs the *petitio principii* so current in the traditional defence of International Law. Students of Municipal Law face the fact (illustrated by every conviction for theft) that persons presumably interested in the preservation of *their* private property are not necessarily interested in the preservation of private property *in general*; but they take the formation of an overwhelming weight of social power against the individual lawbreaker for granted. By a process of ideological identification that weight is even used to secure the protection of types of property more or less artificially assimilated to those in the protection of which the average citizen may be supposed to have an interest: to some extent the general aversion against theft serves as an argument against nationalisation (at least without proper compensation). But it is impossible to derive from sociological characteristics common to the feudal,

[35] I find little support in the evidence available for the suggestion of my critic in *The Times Literary Supplement*, December 29, 1945, "that the degree to which common ideologies are a necessary foundation of International Law is exactly commensurate with the degree to which International Law proceeds from the formal and diplomatic sphere to the social and economic sphere". Just as in the days of the League of Nations, so now collaboration between ideologically different states appears to proceed better in institutions such as E.S.O.C.O. than in the purely political organs of U.N.O. (cp. *The World Today*, February, 1950, p. 72). This does not refute my critic's remark: it may simply mean that, while the "formal" political issues such as frontiers, recognition, intervention, etc., have to be decided one way or another, there is still ample space for the exchange of information on issues of welfare, education, etc., which have no direct practical implications. Their value lies in that they may preserve contacts which might help to overcome some political deadlock. Things would look very different if issues such as the Marshall Plan would appear in negotiations between the representatives of the two systems in a capacity other than as material for propaganda; but obviously it is taken for granted that such issues belong to the "internal" system of each "ideological" group.

capitalist, and socialist systems a natural propensity of states representing those systems to resist *every* violation of frontiers, of international obligations, no matter who committed them and against whom they were committed : the formation of an overwhelming weight of public opinion against thieves even would be difficult if the latter disposed of such means of influencing public opinion concerning their needs and the supposed moral (as distinct from legal) merits of their case against their neighbours as states interested in some violent change of frontiers possess not only within their own country but even in all the other countries belonging to the same international camp. For example, the effective obstacle to an occupation of the " Northern Epirus " by Greece is not right-wing public opinion in that country, Britain, or the U.S.A., etc., but the risk of having to face Albania and her allies without American support ; and in the decision upon the chances of such support a comparatively small part would be played by the possibility that a considerable part of British and American public opinion might oppose the Greek adventure to the point of accepting an intervention by Bulgaria and the U.S.S.R. as its self-invited punishment. But it is just this comparatively minor part which gives specific weight to International Law as an independent agency, as distinct from a mere formulation of the actual balance of power.[36] Its actual weight is blurred by the introduction, in statements such as that of Korovin, of clearly humanitarian standards about prisoners and wounded, less controversial than the Greek claims to Epirus. The reaction of public opinion against those violations of humanitarian standards which are published and which are usually those committed by members of the opposite coalition may be taken for granted ; it would be difficult, however, to prove that such a reaction had played an essential part in rallying the anti-Nazi coalition and bringing about its victory. During the last war, different standards in the treatment of prisoners of war could be applied against nationals of the various allied countries without arousing much criticism from the camp of the " more favoured " allies. In view of the habit, now current in both the camps of the " cold war ", to ascribe to the potential opponent all conceivable atrocities it may even be doubted whether, in case of war, the accepted humanitarian standards would form an obstacle to the acceptance, as allies, of regimes which obviously

[36] For an interpretation of public opinion as the main force backing International Law in the Soviet view, see also Hazard, in *Soviet Studies*, vol. I, No. 3, pp. 198–9.

depended upon the continuous and systematic violation of these standards.[37] Soviet publications leave no doubt that concensus as to the contents even of the Law of War is restricted to generally acknowledged humanitarian standards and is unlikely to exceed the point where the differences between the parties' political potential may come in.[38]

However, the whole argument of Soviet lawyers as to the system of International Law valid between the U.S.S.R. and non-socialist states [39] operates upon the traditional rules with the mere rider that they ought to be subjected to a scrutiny from the point of view of eliminating (1) all rules fitting the capitalist system only, now that it can no longer claim a monopoly, and (2) as many as possible of those concrete treaty regulations which contradict conceptions of International Justice on which socialist and progressive non-socialist opinion agree, and chiefly the principles of equality of states and of national self-determination. On the first set of rules to be eliminated the Soviet point of view does not differ essentially from that of Sir John Fisher Williams mentioned before.[5] The second of these, however, excludes an acceptance of the existing treaty material as the essential source of International Law, a source whose importance the U.S.S.R.

[37] The Soviet case against the plea of " superior orders " on behalf of war criminals who had taken an active part in establishing the rule of the gang to the discipline of which they were subject was based upon the characteristic of Nazism as a regime operating upon the assumption that " war crimes " were not deplorable, or unavoidable, incidents, but useful means of strengthening coherence and realising its basic distinction between " men " and " undermen ". (Boris Glebov, in *Sovietskoye Gossudarstvo i Pravo*, 1946, No. 1, p. 53, answers the plea of superior orders by the statement that relations between commanders and executives arose only when they were carrying out a common conspiracy in which both of them freely participated.) In dealing with the alleged right of neutral states to grant asylum to war criminals Soviet lawyers distinguished between the right of asylum implied in the co-existence of political systems within the international community, with different systems of social values so that political offences against one of them may appear as legitimate defences of social values from the point of view of others, and, on the other hand, the aggressive policies of the fascist systems, which were directed against the international community as such (cp. N. N. Polyansky, *International Justice and War Criminals*, published 1945, in Russian, by the Academy of Sciences, pp. 114–15).

[38] Cp. I. P. Trainin, " Problems of Partisan War in International Law ", in *Izvestia Akademii Nauk S.S.S.R.*, 1945, No. 3. This contains an interesting summary of the long-standing dispute between the Germans and most other powers upon the legality of popular levies, and the suggestion that all special demands made by present International Law upon partisans other than that for discipline and regard for International Law should be removed. Ultimately (p. 24) Trainin restricts the whole argument to that of " just war "—which would be interpreted by every belligerent power in its own favour.

[39] Rappaport (op. cit., 1940, p. 145) introduces, besides, a conception of " socialist International Law " applicable between socialist states which for one reason or another prefer not to federate, and between them and what today would be described as People's Democracies. At the time of Rappaport's writing, only the example of the Mongolian People's Republic was available. Today, the concept would be of greater practical interest.

herself has often emphasised in opposition to " International Custom ", with the danger of implicit acceptance of principles derived from and applicable solely in a capitalist society.[40] On the other hand, those critics of Pashukanis who went very far in distinguishing between those institutions of traditional International Law which the U.S.S.R. accepts, and those which it rejects,[41] have proved mistaken when they included, among the latter institutions, not only Concessions, International Settlements, Capitulations, and similar instruments of imperialist policies renounced by the Soviet, but also, say, military garrisons outside its territory. Even in 1929–31, Korovin's critics [42] gave a warning that a " purely socialist " construction of International Law, however attractive, might have little in common with the actual policies forced upon the U.S.S.R. by a hostile world. In any case, the internationally valid minimum of International Law can be described quite independently of these controversies over its interpretation. Even the *bourgeois* theorist will be inclined to regard those fundamental rules on which he and the Soviet lawyers agree as general law that cannot be presumed to be restricted unless this be done by special rulings. This holds true, especially of the principle of State sovereignty,[43] fundamental in Soviet conceptions of International Law. To say that the U.S.S.R. rejects certain institutions of traditional International Law as infringing the principles of State sovereignty and of equality of nations [44] simply amounts to saying that those institutions are reduced to the position of partial law valid only between those states which recognise them. In U.N.O., the U.S.S.R. makes theoretical reservations as regards Mandates similar to those she held when she entered the League of Nations [32]—but it was certainly not those reservations which prevented the success of her collaboration in the League. What is essential for a future international order is not the amount of

[40] See Korovin, op. cit., 1928.

[41] See Jakovlev-Petrov in *Pravda,* April 27, 1937, Rappaport (1937), and Kozhevnikov, op. cit.

[42] See Makarov, op. cit., p. 485.

[43] See *Permanent Court of International Justice, Judgements,* series A, No. 9, pp. 18 ff.

[44] A characteristic example of this attitude is the treaty with the Mongolian People's Republic, discussed by Korovin, op. cit., 1925, p. 298. When dropping the former extra-territorial rights of Russian citizens, the Soviet desired to protect its citizens against the application of the barbaric methods of old Chinese Justice still current in Mongolia. But, in order to avoid " unequal treaties ", the revolutionary Great Power undertook equally with the semi-barbarian dwarf-state the mutual obligation not to apply cruel methods of investigation and punishment against the other partner's subjects !

rules covered by agreement, but whether the rules agreed upon may be considered as stable.

Whilst elaborating theories to explain the change in the rights and obligations of a state which undergoes a radical change in its internal structure,[45] Soviet international lawyers have from the very beginning tended to emphasise the strict binding force of agreements entered into by a certain regime.[15] There was only a short-lived interruption in this attitude when in his *Textbook* of 1935, Pashukanis tried to introduce the *clausula rebus sic stantibus* in a broader sense than that accepted by Korovin,[45] for example, in order to justify the annulment of the Brest-Litovsk treaty which the Soviet government itself had concluded with the Germans in a moment of extreme weakness.[46] This implied an acceptance of the *clausula* in the sense that a change in the relation of power which had conditioned the original agreement rendered it invalid. But this was clearly the very same manner in which the *clausula* was used as a cover for fascist aggression, and therefore, since 1937, Pashukanis' standpoint has been subjected to very sharp criticism in the Soviet Press.[47] Criticism of the use of the *clausula* as a pseudo-juridical pretext for the imperialist practice of violating treaty obligations continued [48] even during the period of the Soviet-German non-aggression treaty, a period which was interpreted quite wrongly in the West as a period of Soviet-German collaboration. It would be surprising if the Russians were ashamed of having renounced the Brest-Litovsk treaty half a year after its signature—for they can, if they desire, defend their attitude in this case by moral principles overriding legal forms, or by an appeal to the principles allegedly professed by the post-revolutionary German government itself. But they exclude such extraordinary cases from being used as standards for the interpretation of International Law itself, and for the legally binding force of obligations entered by the Soviet government.

The reality of International Law is indisputably recognised by contemporary Soviet theory, and regarded as based upon (1) the economic interdependence of the states, (2) the interweaving of their international relations and their mutual political dependence, (3) the influence of public opinion, in which Soviet policy plays a very important part, especially amongst working-

[45] See above, pp. 276–8.
[46] Op. cit., pp. 160 ff. [47] See Jakovlev-Petrov, op. cit.
[48] See Rappaport, op. cit., 1940, p. 153.

class and other progressive trends.[49] The emphasis laid, not only in Rappaport's explanation, but also in the practice of Soviet foreign policies, upon public opinion as an essential factor making for the reality of International Law, suggests that conceptions of International Law are interwoven with conceptions which most Western lawyers would regard as belonging rather to the realm of International Justice, or Morals. While the first and second of the factors mentioned above as real foundations of International Law may add some strength to the strictly legal relations of states, the public opinion upon which the U.S.S.R. counts, will not be likely to support formal conceptions of Law if they are contrary to what is regarded as just. Soviet international lawyers would scarcely recognise such a juxtaposition of International Justice and International Law : for the common principles of International Law which they accept are the very conceptions of formal equality which were elaborated by the bourgeois advocates of " Natural Law ".[50] In consequence, the difference between arbitrariness and Law is found not merely in the formal existence of a norm, but also in the agreement of the norm with the supposed fundamental principles of Law ; while arbitrariness could be found in the content of the International Law usually embodied in imperialist treaties, as well as in the violation of that law.[51]

As the whole argument is based on agreement between socialist and progressive non-socialist opinion, it follows that the principle of national self-determination, as the clearest expression of the bourgeois democratic conceptions in the field of international relations,[46] must form the standard of Justice in International Law. Rappaport would not go all the way with such an argument : " formal principles " ought to be subordinated to the overriding interests of the socialist revolution, and only where there was no conflict between them would the application of national self-determination find wide support in the U.S.S.R.[52] But, in fact, the partners of the U.S.S.R. can hardly be expected to apply the principle of national self-determination in cases where its consequences contradict the supreme values for which *they* stand. In most of the seriously contested cases there is a national-cultural division corresponding to the social one, so that any argument actually based upon the merits of the

[49] See Kozhevnikov, op. cit., p. 100, and Rappaport, op. cit., 1940, pp. 146 ff.
[50] Kozhevnikov, op. cit., p. 105, Rappaport, op. cit., 1940, pp. 140–1 and 149.
[51] Rappaport, op. cit., 1940, pp. 149–51.
[52] Ibid., p. 142.

latter may be expressed in terms of self-determination, either of the popular majority, or of what may be described as " the bearers of civilisation ". So the practical application of the principle by which the merits (in Rappaport's formulation [51] even the validity) of the rules of existing International Law ought to be measured seems to be reduced to cases where the application of the principle of national self-determination cannot be regarded as retrograde, by either liberal or socialist opinion. Certainly the U.S.S.R. would support any national claim, where the enforcement of self-determination does not affect her own international power position, because she is likely thus to strengthen her ideological influence, especially on the smaller nations. The practical difference between the probable attitudes of the U.S.S.R. and other Great Powers is thus reduced to the fact that the former regards her special influence on the colonial peoples as an important source of general political influence.

The most controversial aspect of the Soviet point of view on International Law is the emphasis laid now as from the very beginning upon State sovereignty. Restriction of that sovereignty for the sake of preventing wars which might result from the arbitrary policies of the individual states is regarded by many Western lawyers as an essential element of a stronger peace-order. During the pre-War decade, the U.S.S.R., while declaring her readiness to undertake binding obligations on the use of her forces within a system aimed at the prevention of wars of aggression, rejected any conception of International Law that would restrict the freedom of the members of the international society to shape their internal system according to their own standards. As early as 1925 Korovin stated that " as long as the Soviet republic has to preserve its position of a Communist island encircled by capitalism, any restriction of Soviet sovereignty would involve major or minor concessions to political and economic principles opposed to its own, and to social groups dominated by such principles ".[53] It is clear that, under the circumstances, any restriction of the right of smaller nations to choose their own regime, for reasons of " international order ", would be more likely to prevent socialist revolutions than capitalist restorations, and thus decrease the number of potentially reliable allies of the U.S.S.R. In 1940, Rappaport [54] attacked the tendency of Western lawyers to drop the principle of State sovereignty and the principle of consent by the states concerned

[53] Op. cit., 1925, p. 299.

[54] Op. cit., pp. 152–3.

as a condition of peaceful change, and to assume instead that the practice of the Great Powers—possibly on the Munich pattern—had some special binding power. From the very beginning [53] the Soviet conception of State sovereignty in International Law was identified with the political principle of national self-determination. This identification, which is also shared by most non-Soviet students of Soviet conceptions of International Law,[55] may not be quite correct from the point of view of legal theory: the legally unrestricted autonomy of the existing subjects of International Law is one thing, and the political claim of existing nationalities, hitherto not subjects of International Law, to form independent states of their own, is another. In Soviet theory (sociological, not legal) these two conceptions are linked together by the internal connection (often found in Eastern Europe and Asia) between social and national [56] emancipation, and by the supposed antagonism of capitalism, in its imperialist stage, to both of them. "To drop sovereignty or any other guarantee of national independence," says Korovin,[33] "in a world where there are exploiters and exploited, weak and strong states, motherlands and colonies, will serve the interests of the strong, and never those of the weak." The U.S.S.R. hardly claims to belong to the weak; so Korovin's argument makes sense only (*a*) as an answer to the assertion, made by the Australian and some other delegations at the Paris Peace Conference, that majority decisions overruling State sovereignty would be in the interest of the small states because they are more numerous, and (*b*) as an assertion of the importance of economic dependence, which may be at its greatest in the very atmosphere of formal equality of political rights, and determine the way in which the votes of the many dependent on the few may be polled. Whatever their subjective intentions the advocates of restriction of State sovereignty are suspected of promoting the submission of the world to monopolist Big Business control by sacrificing the right of each people to decide upon its own internal regime, as well as the independence of the smaller and colonial peoples in general. It cannot be denied that some advocates of international federation do, in fact, feed these Soviet suspicions.

Popular controversy about the Soviet insistence on national

[55] See, for example, Taracouczio, op. cit., pp. 28 ff. and 34.

[56] Here, the term "national" is used in the Eastern European and Asiatic sense, i.e. for describing a racial-cultural unit that claims political emancipation, but need not necessarily have achieved it. In the Western sense, i.e. as a synonym for political allegiance already established, the term would beg the question.

sovereignty centres around its defence of the Unanimity principle in the Security Council of U.N.O. Actually, there is no reason to speak of a Soviet " veto " in U.N.O. any more than to speak of a farmers' veto in U.S.A. or in any other federation whose constitution (say, by the establishment of a Second Chamber) protects important social groups from being outvoted because they happen to be less numerous than others. The difference lies in the fact that agricultural member-states of a federation, for instance, are protected against an excessive application of the rule, " a man, a vote ", which is a basic concept of democracy, while the U.S.S.R. is protected in U.N.O. against the application of the assertion that all the Luxemburgs and Nicaraguas are states in the same category as herself or China. The issue, on the international stage, merely becomes sharper, and the prevention of majority votes the more desirable, as controversies do not only touch on sectional group-interests but on basic issues of social life, with implications as to which members of the international community conform with the proper standards of social morality and are entitled to participate in the voting. The merits of some domestic event in Ruritania, and of the sympathies shown, say, by the Great Power Aquitania, to one of the struggling parties in Ruritania, is a question of political philosophy, and one—though not the only—possible answer to the question may be based upon the consideration that there are more peasants than landlords in Ruritania ; but it is preposterous to decide such an issue on the ground that the majority of " sovereign states " in Central America happens to favour the landlords. The very function of an international peace-order, as distinct from an organisation for preparing " ideological war ", consists in preventing the outvoting of one " ideological " camp by the other, and in thereby forcing them to use the organisation as a platform for compromise.[57]

Even more interesting are the theoretical implications drawn by Soviet lawyers from their assertion of the principle of state-sovereignty as to the validity of International Law in relation to national legislation. The Soviet Union's reluctance to be subject to controls by a U.N.O. majority bound to be dominated by its opponents has obvious political causes ; as regards the theoretical problem it is firmly asserted, against international lawyers such as Triepel and Anzilotti, that municipal law does

[57] I have dealt with this issue in my article " Veto and Collaboration ", in *The Fortnightly*, November, 1945.

not form a sphere of its own independent of International Law but embodies all the acknowledged rules of International Law. It is precisely because this is taken for granted as regards the ordinary members of the international community—and atrocities committed by individual soldiers are therefore supposed to have been committed in opposition against the national as well as against the international legal order—that the sovereign states appear in International Law as the representatives of all their citizens and are expected to enforce the rules of International Law against them; the direct prosecution of Crimes against Humanity by International Courts was the necessary result of the rise of a certain type of states (or rather gangs) differing from the others not merely by differences in political and socio-economic systems (which, in the Soviet view, is the normal condition of the present international community), but by being based upon the needs for aggressive war and its preparation in forms incompatible with generally accepted humanitarian standards.[58] There is, therefore, no need to explain the Soviet preparedness to try crimes committed by the Nazi regime against German nationals by the International Tribunal by considerations of external expediency[59]; the Soviet point was simply that the Nazi regime did not belong to one of those types of states upon whose collaboration International Law can be based.

In contrast to the Soviet viewpoint it may be objected that the conditions for the real independence of smaller nationalities have disappeared, and that if they are not integrated into larger units, they may simply be forced into practical dependence on their stronger neighbours, such as the U.S.S.R. herself. But the Soviet may answer that because this integration into some larger unit has become inevitable, and because it may involve a definite decision as to the future basis of the national civilisation in question, the recognition of State sovereignty and self-determination must precede the choice which the smaller states may have to make as to the system for which they are willing to waive their " sovereign " rights.[60] It may be objected that this point of view is likely to result in the perpetuation of

[58] M. Y. Rappaport, " On the International Trial of the Japanese War Criminals ", in *Uchenye Zapiski*, Leningrad State University, Juridical Section, vol. I, pp. 166–9. The article is based upon the general instruction given by Rappaport, in November, 1946, to the Soviet lawyers working on the Tokio International Military Tribunal. See also note 37 above.

[59] As suggested by Prof. Hazard, in *Soviet Studies*, vol. I, No. 3, pp. 195–6.

[60] See the article in *Izvestiya*, November 18, 1943, quoted in *The Times*, November 19.

a plurality of international systems, linked together, at best, by agreements on collective security and commercial intercourse. To this the answer is that, during a period of historical transition, this is the only alternative to a chain of world wars unavoidable if each system attempts to establish universality upon its own specific foundations. In 1934, Litvinov described the essential conditions for the association of the U.S.S.R. with states having a different political and social system as follows : " firstly the extension to every state belonging to such an association of the liberty to preserve . . . its State personality and the economic and social system chosen by it—in other words, reciprocal non-interference in the domestic affairs of the states therein associated —and, secondly, the existence of common aims." [61] The second condition must, in some degree, be fulfilled if any international order is to be possible : but he who without fulfilling the first condition tries to base such an order upon a higher degree of consent than exists at present will, by the inherent logic of his attitude, be forced to face intervention from both sides—as the only instrument to enforce such consent prematurely, i.e. before the organic development of the various parts of human civilisation has produced consent as regards the desirable social foundations of its future.

[61] Op. cit., p. 105.

# POSTSCRIPT TO THE SECOND EDITION

Since this book first went to press, there have been no major changes in the structure of Soviet Justice ; the occasional attempts to claim for the Courts a position as a source of law [1] seem, to me, only to illustrate their complete subordination to the legislator who is identical with the centre of political power. The position of those who claim some place for judge-made law appears to be backed by the supporters of the institution of analogy [2] as well as by some of its opponents who regard judicial power to interpret criminal statutes in an extensive way [3] as the minor evil. The limitations of the part played by the Judiciary in shaping the actual content of enacted legislation are amply illustrated, not only (as we shall see below) in the application of new criminal statutes but also in issues such as the establishment of " essential cases " in which, according to the law of 1944, divorce is admitted.[4]

There is now general agreement that all Soviet Law is Public Law,[5] and that its subdivision has to proceed according to the subject-matter of regulation : Kechekian, once a main representative of division between the different fields of Law according

[1] Cp. the report on the Session of the Section of Law of Procedure of the Juridical Institute of the Academy of Sciences, September 4, 1946, in *Sovietskoye Gossudarstvo i Pravo,* vol. 1946, No. 10 ; V. Y. Kamenskaya's article, ibid., vol. 1948, No. 6 ; and John N. Hazard's paper, " The Soviet Court as a Source of Law ", in *Washington Law Review,* vol. 24, No. 1, February, 1949.

[2] See above, pp. 225–6. In 1947 it appeared that the opponents of analogy had won their case in drafting the new Criminal Code, but, now, the issue appears to be in dispute again. Cp. the textbook *Criminal Law,* vol. I (General part), ed. 1948, pp. 246–7, where the arguments of both sides to the dispute are summarised, and the dangers of recognising a law-creating capacity in the Courts are regarded as one of the arguments speaking against the preservation of analogy in the new criminal codes.

[3] A. P. Trainin (*The Theory of the Definition of an Offence*—in Russian—Moscow, Yurizdat, 1946, p. 135) rejects the application of the principle of analogy in order to bring convicts who exercise responsible functions under art. 109 of the Penal Code (which deals with offences committed by responsible officials) as unnecessary, because a sufficiently extensive interpretation of that article would correspond to the legislator's intentions.

[4] The initial court-practice in granting divorce was definitely liberal (cp. G. M. Sverdlov's article, reprinted in *The Modern Law Review,* April, 1948, and also in my *Changing Attitudes in Soviet Russia,* vol. I, " The Family "). But a recent Directive of the Supreme Court (reported by *Tass,* October 3, 1949) instructs the courts to deny divorce even in cases of mutual consent if, according to the Court's investigation of the circumstances, the matrimonial conflict is not of a serious character.

[5] Venediktov, loc. cit. (1945), pp. 111–12 ; Kechekian, loc. cit.

to the method of regulation applied,[6] now recognises that this method makes sense only in *bourgeois* Law where it backs the division between Public and Private Law (which corresponds also to a real distinction in subject-matter). In Soviet economics, the autonomy of the parties to a Civil Law contract is always very relative and conditioned by an act in Public Law[5]: "although each link disposes of some degree of autonomy, and provision is made for contractual relations between our economic organs, such autonomy is kept within a comparatively narrow framework. In a considerable number of cases it includes neither the choice of the other party, nor the fundamental stipulations of the contract such as quantity, term of delivery, prices, etc."[7] This statement reflects the negative effect of the very strict planning of the war-period upon the use of the contractual form by Soviet enterprises: after the War it proved, indeed, necessary to order the resumption of contractual relations so that the details of the execution of the plans could be settled between the enterprises concerned.[8]

In a division of the diverse fields of Law according to the subject-matter, Kechekian[5] sees the difference between Civil Law and Administrative Law in that the former deals with those property-relations in which the principle of exchange of equivalents is applied.[9] Land Law and Finance Law are excluded by their specific subject-matter from the field of Administrative Law, which would thus be left with the ideological superstructure and political administration as its subject-matter of regulation. Alexandrov and Genkin[10] realise that relations in Labour Law (and *a fortiori* in Civil Law so far as State enterprises are concerned) may be created by Administrative Law; but Labour Law deals with living labour in the process of application while

[6] See above, p. 253. [7] Kechekian, loc. cit., p. 43.

[8] Cp. I. Baranov's article, in *Planovoye Khozaistvo*, 1949, No. 5, English translation, in *Soviet Studies*, vol. I, No. 4. As the reluctance of the potential contractors to allow their fulfilment of the Plan to be checked by the State Arbitrage may be supposed to be mutual, great emphasis is laid upon the specific Soviet institution of the "pre-contractual suit" in which the State Arbitrage, on the basis of the Plan and the argument of the two enterprises which, according to the Plan, have to enter exchange-relations, decides upon the detailed conditions of the planned supplies, conventional fines, etc., to be stipulated in the contract. The State Arbitrage, when having to decide ordinary law-suits arising from non-fulfilment of the contracts, has an opportunity to check the correctness of its pre-contractual decisions (Mozheyko-Shkundin, loc. cit., p. 6).

[9] Loc. cit., p. 46. Characteristically, Kechekian refers to the recent Soviet economic publications in which the concept of *value* is applied to Soviet economics. (On this point, see my *Marx, His Time and Ours*, in this Library, London, 1950, pp. 157 ff.)

[10] Loc. cit., pp. 15–16.

Civil Law deals with the objectivised results of labour. There is, indeed, no reason why exchange-relations as a characteristic of Civil Law [9] should not come into their own again since the public character of *all* Soviet Law is recognised. In the theoretical interpretation of Civil Law, Venediktov's definition of the State enterprise subject to Civil Law [11] has found almost general acceptance. On the other side, he has recognised that, in Civil Law suits, these State organs appear not as owners but only as representatives of the single owner and that the issue of their contest is the right to administer State property.[12]

By decree of March 14, 1945, the circle of potential intestate heirs was broadened to include parents, brothers, and sisters of the deceased, the right to make a will in favour of some of the legal heirs, and in absence of such even in favour of other persons, with guarantees for the rights of children under 18. Already in 1943 the inheritance taxation had been reduced to a maximum of 10 per cent (on estates over 10,000 roubles value). Although they were directly caused by the War, these changes correspond to trends noticeable at an earlier period,[13] and also to the increased protection given to private property in Criminal Law.

Kollkhoz-law has been definitely recognised as a special branch of Law, with the Model Articles of 1935 as the central institution, on agreement with which the validity of all earlier enactments depends.[14] After a first stage during which the pre-War rules, such as the established minimum of labour-days to be worked by kollkhoz-members and the maximum size of the auxiliary husbandry,[15] were restored, further progress of post-War organisation has been directed towards a stricter dependence of the kollkhoz-member's remuneration on the results of his work [16] and towards an increase of collective cattle-holding and other branches of kollkhoz-economy bound to result in an increase of the kollkhoz-member's money-income at the expense of that in kind. The obvious tendency is towards an assimilation of the status of the kollkhoz-member to that of a worker in a State enterprise, or at least towards an assimilation

[11] See above, p. 249, repeated loc. cit. (1949), p. 591.
[12] Loc. cit. (1945), p. 104. See above, pp. 256–7.
[13] See above, p. 235.
[14] A. F. Mikolenko and N. A. N. Nikitin, *Kollkhoz-Law* (Textbook), Moscow, Yurizdat, 1946, pp. 10–12. See above, pp. 197 ff.
[15] See above, p. 185.
[16] Cp. M. Kraev's article, " The Collective Farm Labour Day ", *Voprosi Ekonomiki*, vol. 1949, No. 3, English translation, in *Soviet Studies*, vol. I, Nos. 2 and 3.

of the Agricultural *Artel* to the *Commune* type of organisation [17]; and this is reflected in general developments of Soviet ideology.[18] Ultimately such a tendency is bound to result in an absorption of Kollkhoz-law into the general framework of Labour Law.

Developments in the field of Labour Law were, perhaps, the most important of the period : what had at first appeared as a reflection of an external emergency, after the removal of some special hardships of wartime legislation has proved to become a more permanent framework. Collective agreements, which had been in abeyance since the Second Five Year Plan, were restored in 1947 ; but it has now been definitely stated that they do not establish wages-scales (which are regulated by the Plan) but merely the mutual obligations undertaken by workers and management respectively as regards increases of production and social improvements.[19] With the increased importance of the State Labour Reserves (that is, the output of skilled workers by the Public Technical Schools, whose pupils, if necessary, are recruited by conscription, and—like young doctors, etc.—are directed to their first place of employment) the origin of labour relations by Administrative Law instead of by contract has become a widespread phenomenon.[20] On the other side, the identity of the labour relations, thus established, with the ordinary (contractual) type, and especially the right of every worker to remuneration and other benefits established in the general regulations, is strongly emphasised.[21] The restrictions of the right to change employment, established before the War,[22] have proved final ; on the other hand, because of the shortage of labour the right of the management to dismiss employees has become obsolete.[23] Legal theorists continue to search for other than the obvious economic guarantees for the constitutional

[17] Cp. the materials published in *Soviet Studies,* vol. I, No. 4. See above, pp. 186 and 214.

[18] See the Preface, pp. xi–xii.

[19] Cp. V. M. Dogadov's article, in the *Bulletin of the Academy of Sciences* (Economics and Law), 1948/2, partial translation in *Soviet Studies,* vol. I, No. 1.

[20] N. G. Alexandrov, " The System of the Origin of Labour Relations in Soviet Law ", in *Bulletin of the Academy of Sciences,* Section Economics and Law, vol. 1945, No. 5.

[21] Ibid., pp. 51–2. See also A. E. Pasherstnik, " Legal Problems of the Workers' Remuneration " (*Pravovie Voprosi Voznagrazhdeniya za trud rabochikh i sluzhashchikh*), Institute of Law of the Academy of Sciences of the U.S.S.R., 1949.

[22] See above, p. 219.

[23] The Government even omitted its mention amongst the disciplinary measures open to the management, in its Model Regulation of Factory Discipline, of January 18, 1941 ; so the gap had to be filled by an explanation by the Presidium of the Supreme Court, of December 25, 1941.

Right to Work,[24] but they have only produced the obvious guarantees against unjustified dismissal and against discrimination in employment or promotion (i.e. violation of the equal rights of all citizens).

The Penal Code plays an increasing part in the regulation of social relations. " In the development of Soviet society it may be noticed as a general law that with increasing consciousness of the masses infringements of labour discipline become increasingly rare phenomena whilst, on the other hand, the struggle of society against the individual breakers of discipline and disorganisers of social production becomes increasingly sharper. The treatment of the violations of discipline is dictated by the actual conditions." [25] This is especially true of the distinction made between disciplinary and criminal offences.[26] On August 10, 1940, a fixed criminal sanction (one year's imprisonment) was introduced for petty thefts and cases of hooliganism in the factories [27]; it had been noticed that anti-social elements were committing petty offences in order to enforce their dismissal and were thus circumventing the restrictions on the mobility of labour.[28] In June, 1947, drastic penalties were enacted for offences not only against public but also against private property, starting with five to six years for a simple larcency committed for the first time and culminating with ten to fifteen years' internment in a labour camp for robbery committed with violence, and ten to twenty-five years for theft of public property committed on a large scale or for a second time.[29] Indeed, the measures contradicted the traditions of earlier Soviet Justice [30] to such an extent that an article in

[24] Alexandrov-Genkin, loc. cit., p. 27, Alexandrov,[20] p. 42. See above, p. 223.

[25] A. E. Pastershnik, " Some Questions of Soviet Labour Law ", *Sovietskoye Gossudarstvo i Pravo*, vol. 1946, Nos. 5–6, p. 41.

[26] Alexandrov-Genkin, loc. cit., p. 37.

[27] See above, p. 240.

[28] I. Golyakov, " 25 Years' Soviet Justice ", in *Scientific Notes* (*Uchenye Zapiski*), Moscow State University, vol. 76, Faculty of Laws, Moscow, 1945, p. 48.

[29] The extreme penalties for large-scale thefts of public property, or for robbery combined with violence committed by a gang against private property (banditism in the earlier terminology, up to 20 years according to the Decree of June 4, 1947), are not more severe than before (capital punishment before, 25 years' imprisonment since 1947).

[30] Before, the *maximum* penalties for theft of private property varied, between the various Republics, from one (R.S.F.S.R.) to eight years' imprisonment, for theft of public property from five to ten years. Suggestions published in *Socialistichesкaya Zakonnost*, 1947, No. 6 (i.e. at a time when the need for increasing penalties, at least in the R.S.F.S.R. the largest Republic, was already felt), agreed on a maximum of one year for simple theft committed for the first time and without conspiracy with other persons, and of five years for the most serious cases.

*Socialisticheskaya Zakonost* (1947, No. 10) which was evidently intended to help the Judiciary towards a milder interpretation was officially answered by the President of the Supreme Court. Such an approach to one of the most common offences seems more characteristic of present penal policies than the vacillations between abolition, in 1947, and re-introduction, in 1950, of capital punishment for treason committed in times of peace, which may easily have been caused by different assessments of the international situation.

While penalties have become more severe, there is a definite insistence on the security of the law and on strengthening the guarantees against judicial arbitrariness. Even during the War emphasis was laid upon the need to preserve strict legality and to avoid convictions based upon the social harmfulness of some action rather than upon the offender's intentions ; tribute has been paid to this principle not only by those theorists who are known as defenders of security of the Law and opponents of institutions such as analogy [31] but even by those who used the circumstances of the War as an occasion for the justification of concepts such as Eventual Intention and Retroactivity of Criminal Laws [32] and who emphasise the fact that the punishment of Nazi War criminals has reintroduced the element of retaliation into Soviet Criminal Law.[33] The presumption of the innocence of the defendant, as a basis of Soviet Criminal Procedure, has been defended by authorities such as Vishinsky and Strogovich, notwithstanding the fact that in accordance with recent general trends in Soviet ideology, their argument in favour of strict legality has been dissociated from the Western tradition.[34]

[31] M. Shargarodski, " Problems of the General Part of the Criminal Code in War-time Conditions ", in *Scientific Notes* (quoted in note 28), p. 101.

[32] B. S. Mankovsky, " Soviet Criminal Law in the Period of the Patriotic War ", *Scientific Notes* (*Uchenye Zapiski*), Leningrad State University, Legal Section, vol. I, 1948, pp. 338–40. Characteristic of the obstacles which representatives of that point of view still have to face is the fact that Mankovsky has to oppose an (evidently current) description of Eventual Intention as a German invention, and that in arguing against the assumption that there can be no guilt without consciousness of illegality he refers to art. 58/13 of the Code (see above, note 72, on p. 109).

[33] Ibid., p. 341. This statement, as distinct from those mentioned in the preceding note, can hardly be regarded as controversial within present Soviet legal theory.

[34] Vishinsky, op. cit., 1946, and Strogovich, op. cit., 1946. See also *Soviet Studies*, vol. I, Nos. 1 and 3.

# BIBLIOGRAPHY

The following bibliography has been compiled for the double purpose of indicating (*a*) all works which I found specially helpful in this work, and (*b*) all those I would suggest to any fellow-worker in the field covered by this study as relevant sources of information. These two purposes are not identical, since war conditions have prevented my direct access to many important books. These have certainly contributed to forming my views, although it was not possible to quote them in the footnotes. The author could not even avoid omitting from this bibliography some books that were not available at the time when this book was written and, in particular, many articles published in periodicals which were not available in London, 1943. To prevent an unreasonable extension of this bibliography, no book that is not of immediate importance as a source for Soviet legal theory has been included : in so far as they have been used, they will be found quoted in the footnotes. For the sake of consistency I have avoided including in the bibliography even the most important of the sources used for the first and second chapters of this book, as well as any collections or studies on Soviet laws that are not of immediate importance for the theoretical problems studied. The alternative would have meant giving a general bibliography on Jurisprudence and Marxism, as well as on all fields of Soviet Law ; lack of space as well as the desire to make the bibliography useful for the special student of the subject excluded this. It is hardly necessary to explain that the decision as to what legal materials are relevant for legal theory, and what are not, can hardly avoid being influenced by my conception of legal theory—although I have tried to conceive the latter's field as broadly as possible. In any case it is necessary to warn the reader that the following bibliography does not claim to cover Soviet Law as such.

The bibliography is divided into three parts : the first one contains the immediate sources, as regards the content of laws, in so far as they are relevant, and the official pronouncements of the legislator—i.e. virtually the C.P. of the U.S.S.R. ; the second contains studies by Soviet authors on the subjects and on issues immediately connected with it ; whilst the third mentions studies by non-Soviet authors, including Russian *émigrées*. Within either part, after asterisks, the most important sources which became available since the first edition of this book have been added. References in the Postscript usually refer to the added parts of the Bibliography. As regards the language, in the second part, unless otherwise stated, the publications quoted are in Russian, whilst in the third part they are usually in English.

As the most important foreign language of the sources used is Russian, the knowledge of which can hardly be assumed, I have given the titles of all publications, independently of their original language, in English. The abbreviations used in the notes are given in the bibliography, and those of general importance at the end of its first part.

## *A. Soviet Laws and Official Political Theory*

The official collection of Soviet enactments, from 1917 to 1936, was " Sobranje Usakonnenye and Kasporasheniye Rabochiye Krestianskovo Pravitelstsva " (Collection of the Laws and Decrees of the Workers' and Peasants' Government), which we quote abbreviated as

" S.U. Year/No. (of the Decree, or Law) (e.g. S.U. 1918/492) ;

the abbreviation " S.U.R." refers to a collection of the first decrees in 1917–18, published Moscow, 1918.

Since 1936 the official collection is described as " Sobranye Postanovlenye . . ." (Collection of Resolved Enactments) and, therefore, abbreviated as " S.P." Year/No.

There are, of course, many official editions of the Soviet codes, which include all amendments enacted up to the day of publication. It depends entirely on the purpose of the study whether an earlier or a later text is preferred.

There is an English official translation of the Soviet Criminal Code, with amendments up to 1932, published by the Foreign Office in 1934. It forms a useful standard of reference, although it is not always clear whether the Soviet lawyers would approve of all nuances of the translation. The best translation of the 1936 Constitution is that by A. STRONG, reprinted as an appendix to S. and B. WEBB's *Soviet Communism, a New Civilisation?* ed. of 1942.

A complete collection of the 1922–6 codification of Soviet Law is given in French by LAMBERT-PATROUILLET, *Les Codes de la Russie Soviétique*, with Introduction by E. LAMBERT, Paris, 1925 ff. For the foreign student who does not know Russian, or who has not all the original texts of the Soviet codes available, it is by far the most reliable source of information on 1926 Law, though not, of course, on present Soviet Law.

In German there are the collections by H. FREUND, *The Civil Law of Soviet Russia*, Berlin, 1924, and *Criminal Code and Law on the Constitution of the Courts*, published by Osteuropa Institute, Breslau, 1925.

Some of the more important recent decrees and laws have been published, in English since 1931, in periodical surveys in the *Slavonic Review*, London.

Russian collections and Commentaries dealing with special fields of Law, used in the present study, are:

E. N. DANILOVA, *The Present Labour Legislation of the U.S.S.R. and of the Union Republics*, 2 volumes, Moscow, 1927, and

A. KANTOROVICH, *Private Trade and Industrial Enterprise, according to the Existing Legislation*, Leningrad, 1925.

The standard sources for official political theory are the collected works of

LENIN (quotations without further notice refer to the English edition *Selected Works*, whilst when " Russian " is added, the 3rd complete Russian ed. is meant); and

STALIN, published under the title *Leninism*. There is a 2-volume English edition of 1928–33, and another of 1940. I always quote the edition used, as some of the older articles are not to be found in the most recent one. So both editions must be used together in order to get a complete picture of the development of Stalin's thought.

An official party-document, published under Stalin's personal editorship, is the *History of the C.P. of the U.S.S.R.*, English ed., Moscow, 1939.

The most important periodicals dealing with the problems discussed in this book are *Sovietskoye Gossudarstvo i Pravo* (" Soviet State and Law "), at present organ of the Law Institute of the Academy of Science, formerly of the Communist Academy, abbreviated *S.G.*, and *Sovietskaja Justicija* (" Soviet Justice "), Organ for the People's Commissariat for Justice (mainly destined for the information and education of the Judiciary), abbreviated *S.J.*

## *B. Books and Articles by Soviet Authors relevant for our Subject (generally in Russian)*

G. AMFITEATROV, " On the Conception of Soviet Civil Law ", in *S.G.*, 1940, No. 11.

G. AMFITEATROV and L. GINSBERG, "The Direction of Economics and Economic Law under the Proletarian Dictatorship", in *15 Years of Soviet Construction,* ed. E. Pashukanis, Moscow, 1932.

K. ANTONOV, "On the Problem of International Law", in *S.G.*, 1938/4.

S. BRATUSZ, "On the State of the Theoretical Work on Soviet Civil Law", in *S.G.*, 1937, Nos. 1–2.

—— "On the Subject-matter of Soviet Civil Law", in *S.G.*, 1940, No. 1.

M. CHELCOV, "The Soviet Bar and the Juridical Character of Soviet Advocacy", in *S.G.*, 1940, No. 4.

D-OV, "On the Revision of the Penal Codes of the Union Republics", in *Sovietskoe Stroitelstvo,* 1929, No. 7.

M. DOCENKO, "The Socialist Soviet Law", in *S.G.*, 1936, No. 3.

N. DURMANOV, "The All-Union Criminal Legislation and the Legislation of the Individual Union Republics", in *S.G.*, 1940, No. 11.

P. ELKIND, "Barrister's Ethics", in *S.J.*, 1940, Nos. 3–4.

A. GODES, "Subject and System of Soviet Civil Law", in *S.J.*, 1939, No. 1.

GOLYAKOV (President of the Supreme Court), "Problems of Socialist Law", in *S.J.*, 1939, No. 1.

SH. GREENGAUS, "The Law-creating Mass-initiative in the Years 1917 and 1918", in *S.G.*, 1940, No. 3.

—— "Soviet Criminal Law during the October Revolution", Ibid., No. 4.

N. KAZANCEV, "Subject and System of the Science of Kollkhos Law", in *S.G.*, 1940, No. 3.

J. KHAVIN, "The Credit Reform and Economic Accountancy", in *Problemy Economiky,* 1931, Nos. 4–5.

KOZHEVNIKOV, "On Concepts of International Law", in *S.G.*, 1940, No. 2.

E. KOROVIN, *The International Law of the Transitional Period,* Moscow, 1924 (there is also a German ed.).

—— "The Soviet Republic and International Law" (in French), in *Revue Générale du Droit International Public,* 1925.

—— "The Soviet Treaties and International Law", in *American Journal of International Law,* 1928.

G. KOZLOV, "The Rebirth of Credit", in *Problemy Economiky,* 1930, No. 2.

KRIVITZKY, "On the Stages of our Economic Development", Ibid., No. 3.

N. KRYLENKO, *Speeches in Court,* 1922–30, Moscow, 1931.

—— *Rights and Duties of the Soviet Citizen* (published also in French and German), Moskau, 1936.

D. J. KURSKY, *Soviet Justice,* Moscow, 1919.

A. LAPTEV, "The Conception of Guilt in Soviet Criminal Law", in *S.J.*, 1938, No. 12.

LIPECKER and SHKUNDIN, "Problems of Civil Law after the XVIIIth Party Conference", in *S.G.*, 1941, No. 4.

M. LITVINOV, Speech at the occasion of the admission of the U.S.S.R. to the League of Nations, reprinted in *Documents on International Affairs,* 1934.

T. MALKEVICH, "On the History of the First Soviet Decrees on the Courts", in *S.G.*, 1940, Nos. 7 and 8–9.

J. MIKOLENKO, "System and Fundamental Principles of the Project of the Civil Code of the U.S.S.R.", in *S.J.*, 1939, No. 7.

J. MIKOLENKO and S. BRATUSZ, "Subject and System of Soviet Civil Law", in *S.J.*, 1938, No. 16.

V. N. MOSHEYNO and Z. T. SHKUNDIN, *Arbitration in Soviet Economics,* 3rd ed., Mcscow, 1941.

P. ORLOVSKY, "The Right of the Citizen's Private Property", in *S.G.*, 1938, No. 6.

E. B. PASHUKANIS, *The General Theory of Law and Marxism,* Moscow, 1925 (there is also a German ed. in the "Marxist Library").

E. B. PASHUKANIS, "The Situation on the Theoretical Front", in *S.G.*, 1930, Nos. 11–12.
—— *Outlines of International Law*, Moscow, 1935.
—— "State and Law in Socialism", in *S.G.*, 1936, No. 3.
A. PIONTKOVSKY, *The Criminal Law of the R.S.F.S.R.* (General Part), Moscow, 1924.
—— *Criminal Law and Marxism*, Moscow, 1927.
K. POLAK, "The Theory of the Essence of Crime in Bourgeois Criminalist Literature", in *S.G.*, 1940, No. 12.
M. RAPPAPORT, "Against Wrecking Theories of International Law", in *S.G.*, 1937, Nos. 1–2.
—— "The Essence of Present International Law", in *S.G.*, 1940, Nos. 5–6.
RAZUMOVSKY, *Problems of Marxist Theory of Law.*
REISSNER, *Law*, Moscow, 1925.
Z. T. SHKUNDIN, "On the Arbitration Process", in *S.G.*, 1936, No. 3.
—— "Plans, Tasks, Contracts and Obligations", Ibid., 1940, No. 4.
P. J. STUCHKA, *The Revolutionary Rôle of Law and State*, Moscow, 1924.
—— *Thirteen Years of Struggle for the Revolutionary Theory of Law*, Moscow, 1931.
—— *Course of Soviet Civil Law*, General Part, 2nd ed., Moscow, 1931 (this book is always referred to by "Stuchka, op. cit., 1931").
M. STROGOVICH, "The Results of the Plenum of the Supreme Court of the U.S.S.R.", in *S.G.*, 1939, No. 1.
V. TADEVOSJAN, "The Struggle against Juvenile Delinquency", in *S.G.*, 1940, No. 4.
*Textbook of Civil Law*, for juridical universities, Moscow, 1938 (chief editor, J. MIKOLENKO).
A. URALSKY, "The Forms of Kollkhoses in the Different Stages of Development", in *Na Agrarnom Frontem*, 1934, No. 4.
A. VENEDIKTOV, "The Organs of Administration of the Socialist State Property", in *S.G.*, Nos. 5–6 (quotations, "Venediktov, op. cit.", refer always to this article).
—— "State Organisations as Legal Entities in the U.S.S.R.", in *S.G.*, 1940, No. 10.
M. VETOSHKIN, "On the Codification of All-Union Law", in *Sovietskoe Stroitelstvo*, 1929, No. 7.
A. J. VISHINSKY, *Revolutionary Legality on the Present Stage*, Moscow, 1933.
—— "The Fundamental Tasks of the Science of Soviet Law", in *S.G.*, 1938, No. 4.
—— (editor) *Soviet Constitutional Law*, Moscow, 1938 (an English translation, by Prof. H. W. Babb, with an Introduction by Prof. John N. Hazard, has been published, in 1949, by the MacMillan Co., New York).
—— "The XVIIIth Congress of the C.P. of the U.S.S.R. and the Tasks of the Theory of Socialist Law", in *S.G.*, 1939, No. 3.
Z. ZAROV, *For Revolutionary Legality*, in *Sovietskoe Stroitelstvo*, 1930, No. 9.

* * *

M. M. AGARKOV, "Basic Principles of Soviet Civil Law", in *S.G.*, 1947, No. 11.
N. G. ALEXANDROV, "The System of the Origin of Labour Relations in Soviet Law", in *Bulletin of the Academy of Sciences*, Section of Law and Economics, 1945, No. 5.
N. G. ALEXANDROV and D. M. GENKIN (editors), *Soviet Labour Law*, Moscow (Yurizdat), 1946.
B. A. ARSENYEV and M. G. SHIFMAN, two articles "On the History of Public Prosecution in the Soviet Courts", in *S.G.*, 1947, No. 5.

S. N. Bratusz, " On the Development of the Legal Personality of Soviet State Enterprises ", in *Problems of Soviet Civil Law*, Academy of Sciences of the U.S.S.R., 1945.

—— " Some Problems of the Civil Law of the U.S.S.R.", in *S.G.*, 1948, No. 12.

N. D. Durmanov, " The First Soviet Penal Code " (1921–2), in *S.G.*, 1947, No. 9.

N. D. Kazancev, " Land Reform in the Baltic Soviet Republics ", in *S.G.*, 1946, No. 2.

—— " The Land Reforms in the People's Democracies ", in *S.G.*, 1949, No. 6.

S. F. Kechekian, " On the System of Socialist Soviet Law ", in *S.G.*, 1946, No. 2.

E. A. Korovin, " The Soviet Contribution to International Law ", in *S.G.*, 1947, No. 11.

M. V. Kozhevnikov, *History of the Soviet Court*, Moscow, Yurizdat, 1948.

B. S. Mankovsky, " The Class Character of the People's Democracies ", in *S.G.*, 1949, No. 6.

V. N. Mozheyko, " On the Legal Character of Soviet State Arbitration ", in *S.G.*, 1947, No. 6.

V. N. Mozheyko and Z. I. Shkundin, *Arbitration in Soviet Economics*, A Collection of the Most Important Enactments and Decisions, with an Introductory Article, Moscow, Yurizdat, 1941.

A. E. Pasherstnik, " Collective Agreements in the U.S.S.R.", in *S.G.*, 1948, No. 4.

J. N. Polyanskaya, " Property Relations in the Kollkhoz *Dvor* ", in *S.G.*, 1947, No. 7.

S. I. Shkundin, " The Influence of the Plan on Obligations ", in *S.G.*, 1947, No. 2.

*Soviet Law in the Period of the Great Patriotic War*, 2 vols., ed. Y. T. Golyakov, Moscow, Yurizdat, 1948.

M. S. Strogovich, *The Law of Criminal Procedure*, Textbook, Moscow, Yurizdat, 1946 (reported, with the subsequent discussion, in *Soviet Studies*, vol. I, No. 3).

I. P. Trainin, " The Problem of the Relations between State and Law ", in *Bulletin of the Academy of Sciences*, Section of Economics and Law, 1945, No. 5.

—— " On Democracy ", in *S.G.*, 1946, No. 1.

—— " The Democracy of a New Type " (People's Democracy), in *S.G.*, 1947, Nos. 1 and 3.

—— " Basic Principles of Soviet Criminal Law ", in *S.G.*, 1947, No. 11.

A. V. Venediktov, " The Right of Socialist State Ownership ", in *Problems of Soviet Civil Law*, Academy of Sciences of the U.S.S.R., 1945.

—— *Socialist State Ownership*, Institute of Law of the Academy of Sciences, Moscow, 1948.

A. J. Vishinsky, *The Theory of Court Evidence in Soviet Law*, 2nd ed., Moscow, Yurizdat, 1946 (reviewed in *Soviet Studies*, vol. I, No. 1).

—— " International Law and International Organisation ", in *S.G.*, 1948, No. 1.

—— " Some Problems of the Theory of State and Law ", in *S.G.*, 1948, No. 6.

Textbooks for universities, prepared by the Juridical Institute of the Academy of Sciences, are frequently re-published on *Civil Law*, *The Law of Civil Procedure*, *Criminal Law*, *The Law of Criminal Procedure*, *Kollkhoz Law*, *Labour Law*, *Constitutional Law* (last editions in our hands are of 1948). Comparison of the different editions, recently produced, is an important help in assessing the trends of development.

## C. *Non-Soviet Studies on Soviet Conceptions of Law, etc.*

E. BURNS, *Russia's Productive System*, London, 1930.

M. DOBB, *Russia's Economic Development*, London, 1929.

S. DOBRIN, " Soviet Jurisprudence and Socialism ", in *Law Quarterly Review*, 1936.

J. N. HAZARD, " Soviet Law: An Introduction ", *Columbia Law Review*, vol. 36, 1936, " Cleaning Soviet International Law of anti-Marxist Theories ", in *The American Journal of International Law*, 1938.

G. W. KEETON, *The Problem of the Moscow Trial*, London, 1933.

H. LASKI, *Law and Justice in Soviet Russia*, London, 1935.

—— A critical discussion of this book, by S. Dobrin, has been published in *Law Times*, 1935, Nos. 277, 295, and 373.

MAKAROV, " The Science of International Law in Soviet Russia " (in German), in *Zeitschrift für ausländisches oeffentliches Recht und Voelkerrecht*, vol. 1936.

MAURACH, *System of Russian Criminal Law* (in German), Studies of the Osteuropa Institute, Breslau, 1928.

—— Ibid., 1933.

B. MIRKINE-GUETZEVITCH, " The Soviet Theory of International Law " (in French), in *Revue Générale du Droit International Public*, 1925 (answer to Korovin, op. cit., 1925, see above).

D. N. PRITT, " The Russian Legal System ", in *Twelve Studies on Soviet Russia*, ed. M. J. Cole, London, 1933.

R. SCHLESINGER, " Recent Soviet Sociological Literature : Law " (in German), *Zeitschrift fuer Sozialforschung*, 1938, No. 3.

—— " Recent Developments in Soviet Legal Theory ", in *Modern Law Review*, December, 1942.

T. A. TARACOUCZIO, *The Soviet Union and International Law*, New York, 1935.

—— A criticism of this book from the Soviet viewpoint by E. A. Korovin, has been published in *Harvard Law Review*, vol. 49 (1936).

TIMASHEV, *Soviet Constitutional Law* (in German), in Studies of the Osteuropa Institute, Breslau.

S. and B. WEBB, *Soviet Communism, a New Civilisation?* (last ed., 1942).

G. WILLISH, *The Importance of the Concessions in U.S.S.R.* (in German), Osteuropa Institute, Breslau, 1932.

J. ZELITCH, *Soviet Administration of Criminal Law*, Philadelphia and Oxford University Press, 1931.

* * *

A. BAYKOV, *Development of the Soviet Economic System*, Cambridge University Press, 1946.

H. J. BERMANN, " Principles of Soviet Criminal Law ", in *Yale Law Journal*, 1947, No. 5.

M. DOBB, *Soviet Economic Development since 1917*, London, 1948.

V. GSOVSKI, *Soviet Civil Law*, 2 vols., University of Michigan Law School, 1948–9.

JOHN N. HAZARD, " The Trend of Law in the U.S.S.R.", in *Wisconsin Law Review*, 1947.

—— " Drafting New Soviet Codes of Law ", in *The American Slavic and East European Review*, vol. VII.

—— *Materials on Soviet Law* (Roneod material, amply reviewed by R. Schlesinger, in *The Law Quarterly Review*, October, 1949, and by A. B. Elkin, in *Soviet Studies*, vol. I, No. 3).

—— " International Law and the U.S.S.R.", in *Soviet Studies*, vol. I, No. 3.

R. SCHLESINGER, *Changing Attitudes in Soviet Russia*, vol. I, " The Family ", in this Library, 1949.

* * *

An extensive bibliography of Materials on Soviet Law, mainly dealing with Western publications on concrete Soviet legislation, has been published by JOHN N. HAZARD and WILLIAM B. STERN in *Proceedings of the American Foreign Law Association*, No. 27, 1945.

* * *

Abbreviations used in this book (for denoting current terms of Soviet political terminology) are:

C.P. of the U.S.S.R.—Communist Party of the U.S.S.R.

N.E.P.—New Economic Policy.

R.S.F.S.R.—Russian Socialist Federative Soviet Republic (the Russian-dominated member-state of the U.S.S.R.).

V.C.I.K.—Vserossiysky (since 1924 Vsesoyusny) Centralny Ispolinitelnly Comitet (All-Russian, respectively All-union, Central Executive Committee, the supreme permanent State organ prior to the 1936 Constitution).

# INDEX